Praise for

ON SETTLER COLONIALISM IN CANADA: RELATIONS & RESISTANCES *and* ON SETTLER COLONIALISM IN CANADA: LANDS & PEOPLES

"This book is like Alka-Seltzer in the still water of settler colonial complacency. The gift of polychoral perspectives provide a roadmap to, as the Cherokee scholar Daniel Heath Justice would say, imagine otherwise. It is a work of great scholarship, investigation, interrogation, and heartship. Reading *On Settler Colonialism in Canada: Relations & Resistances* is like attending the most stimulating conference, but it's a conference you get to hold in your hands. I'm grateful I could attend and will go back again and again."
—SHELAGH ROGERS on *On Settler Colonialism in Canada: Relations & Resistances*

"Remarkable... likely to become a landmark reference work for scholars and interested individuals alike."
—LORENZO VERACINI, author of *Colonialism: A Global History*, on *On Settler Colonialism in Canada: Lands & Peoples*

"*On Settler Colonialism in Canada* disrupts the Euro-settler/Indigenous reconciliation narrative to include racialized un/settlers. The book's polyphony of voices, styles, and experiences stitches patches of critical truth to samples of non-colonial difference to swatches of practical uplift. This diverse collection, this unsettling quilt, this dis-comforter, is not a display item but a sturdy necessity designed for everyday use."
—DAVID GARNEAU on *On Settler Colonialism in Canada: Relations & Resistances*

"A thoughtful, indispensable multi-perspective contribution to the work of decolonizing settler-Indigenous relations and depowering settler colonialism in Canada through truth, self-reflection, and resurgence."
—ALAN HANNA, Associate Professor, University of Victoria, on *On Settler Colonialism in Canada: Relations & Resistances*

"Offers fresh insights into the conceptual and practical challenges of decolonizing settler colonial societies on political and personal levels. With candour and courage, Indigenous and settler authors share how they grapple with critical questions of identity, positionality, unequal power relations, responsibility, and relational accountability in their work. This book is a must-read for all those seeking to forge ethical relationships of solidarity, resistance, and Indigenous resurgence across the colonial divide towards truth, justice, and reconciliation."
—PAULETTE REGAN, author of *Unsettling the Settler Within* and former Director of Research for the Truth and Reconciliation Commission of Canada, on *On Settler Colonialism in Canada: Relations & Resistances*

"Groundbreaking in the depth and scope of its engagement with all aspects of the structuring principle of settler colonialism, this volume is essential reading for Canadians. A major contribution to the literature."
—ROBERTA RICE, Professor and Department Head of Political Science, University of Calgary, and series editor of *Global Indigenous Issues*, on *On Settler Colonialism in Canada: Lands & Peoples*

"This book holds many complicated truths about the inequality of the colonial experience, about implicit and explicit violence, and unceasing pragmatic resistances. The authors bring together multiple perspectives and stories, and they explore hard-edged questions for Indigenous, Black, Chinese, French Canadian, settler, and of course, mixed peoples. Some of the issues are the lethal Starlight Tours, Indigenous women's challenges, denialism, TRC strategies, and most importantly, they ask: Where do we go from here?"
—VAL NAPOLEON, Professor and Law Foundation Chair of Indigenous Justice and Governance, University of Victoria, on *On Settler Colonialism in Canada: Lands & Peoples*

On Settler Colonialism in Canada

Relations & Resistances

EDITED BY

Emily Grafton &
David B. A. MacDonald

Afterword by Gina Starblanket

University of Regina Press

Printed and bound in Canada. The text of this book is printed on 100% post-consumer recycled paper with earth-friendly vegetable-based inks.

Cover art: David Garneau, "Civilized Stone," acrylic on panel, 46 x 61 cm, 2021.
Cover design: Evan Marnoch
Page design and layout: John van der Woude, JVDW Designs
Copyeditor: Rachel Ironstone
Indexer: Patricia Furdek

Library and Archives Canada Cataloguing in Publication

Title: On settler colonialism in Canada : relations & resistances / edited by Emily Grafton & David B.A. MacDonald ; afterword by Jeremy Patzer.
Names: Grafton, Emily (Emily Katherine), editor. | MacDonald, David Bruce, editor
Description: Includes bibliographical references and index.
Identifiers: Canadiana (print) 20250279673 | Canadiana (ebook) 20250279711 | ISBN 9781779400697 (hardcover) | ISBN 9781779400680 (softcover) | ISBN 9781779400710 (PDF) | ISBN 9781779400703 (EPUB)
Subjects: LCSH: Settler colonialism—Canada. | LCSH: Reconciliation—Canada. | LCSH: Indigenous peoples—Canada. | LCSH: Minorities—Canada. | LCSH: Canada—Ethnic relations.
Classification: LCC FC104 .O565 2026 | DDC 971.004—dc23

10 9 8 7 6 5 4 3 2 1

University of Regina Press, University of Regina
Regina, Saskatchewan, Canada, S4S 0A2
TEL: (306) 585-4758 FAX: (306) 585-4699
WEB: www.uofrpress.ca

We acknowledge the support of the Canada Council for the Arts for our publishing program. We acknowledge the financial support of the Government of Canada. / Nous reconnaissons l'appui financier du gouvernement du Canada. This publication was made possible with support from Creative Saskatchewan's Book Publishing Production Grant Program. Support to make "Honouring Treaty Responsibilities in Rural Saskatchewan: The Treaty Land Sharing Network" by Naomi Beingessner, Emily Eaton, and Martha Jane Robbins Open Access was provided by the University of Regina Arts Publication Fund and the President's Publication Fund.

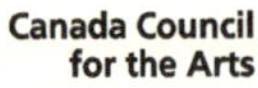

Contents

PART TWO

Prospects for Reconciliation and Relational Decolonization

PART THREE

Settler Colonial Relationalities, Identities, and Belonging

Acknowledgements

We have been working on this book for several years and are grateful for the help, advice, and support of many people. This book project was supported by a Social Sciences and Humanities Research Council of Canada (SSHRC) Connection Grant in Fall 2022, which helped bring numerous contributors to the University of Regina, First Nations University of Canada, and to the mâmawêyatitân centre, Regina, Saskatchewan, for *Settler Colonialism in Canada: Perspectives, Comparisons, and Cases.* These in-person and virtual gatherings culminated in the book project *On Settler Colonialism in Canada: Lands and People* (University of Regina Press, 2025) and this manuscript.

Specifically, we would like to thank kēhtē-ayak Alma Poitras, a chapter contributor, for thoughtfully opening and closing the 2022 gatherings in a good way. Thank you to Desmond McAllister, a chapter contributor to our other book, for your passionate and inspirational steel pan performance. A very special thank you to Dr. Jérôme Melançon, co-applicant to the SSHRC grant and a chapter contributor to our other book, who provided valuable support for the planning and facilitation of these gatherings. We also extend our gratitude to Solomon Ratt for allowing us to reprint some of his excellent and compelling poetry.

Our thanks to Karen Clark, Elsa Johnston, and Rachel Stapleton at University of Regina Press, to their production team, and to our anonymous reviewers. Everyone helped make this book stronger and more focused.

We also express deep gratitude to the research assistants who helped us stay on track over these years, navigating the Covid-19 pandemic (and its many viral waves), meeting funding and reporting deadlines, communicating with contributors, planning and facilitating our 2022 gatherings, and staying on top of chapter collection and organization: Ibukun Fasunhan, Alyssa Parker, and Hannah Tait (University of Regina), and Clare McKendry and Lauren Fillier (University of Guelph).

• • •

Emily Grafton: I thank my parents, Wayne and Jonine, for my early childhood in Winnipeg's inner city, an experience that made me curious and passionate about the politics of Canada. I am especially indebted to my father's stories of our Métis ancestors, the Lafrenières, and this expansive family. I married into the Smith family, my invitation to Treaty 4, where I now reside. This move brought the ever-evolving and expanding gift of family, and I am most grateful to my husband, Matt, and children, Sebastian and Elliotte. Above all, I dedicate this book to my children in my ever-optimistic hopes for the Canada they will grow up in.

David B. A. MacDonald: My work is funded by two SSHRC Insight Grants, 430413 and 430855, and I thank the University of Guelph for their support. Also, much of this was written while I was a visiting fellow at the Auckland Law School, hosted by Te Puna Rangahau o te Wai Ariki / Aotearoa Centre for Indigenous Peoples and the Law in New Zealand, and later as an honorary academic in Politics and International Relations, Faculty of Arts, University of Auckland. I would like to thank my wife, Dana, and son, Gulliver, for their love and support—thanks, family! I was raised in Regina, and when coming back to my hometown, I stayed with my parents and sister, who have always taken an interest in this work: thank you, Mom (Olive), Dad (Bruce), and Rachel. My mom travelled from Barrackpore, Trinidad, to Regina in 1964. She was descended from Indian indentured labourers and spent her childhood in the rural south of Trinidad before studying at Luther College in Regina, where she obtained her BA degree. Mom was always interested in Indigenous Peoples and issues, took a keen interest in the work of the Truth and Reconciliation Commission, and really enjoyed coming to our conference dinner in 2022 and meeting many of the contributors. I dedicate my work on this book to her, commemorating her passing in June 2023.

Contributor Biographies

Adam J. Barker is a settler Canadian originally from the overlapping territories of the Haudenosaunee and Anishinaabe, near Hamilton, Ontario. His work focuses on the production of settler colonial space and identity, processes of social change, and contemporary decolonization activism. Adam holds a PhD in Human Geography from the University of Leicester (UK) and an MA in Indigenous Governance from the University of Victoria (Canada). He is the author of *Making and Breaking Settler Space* (UBC Press, 2021) and co-author with Emma Battell Lowman of the book *Settler: Identity and Colonialism* 2nd ed. (Fernwood Press, 2025).

Leo Baskatawang is an Anishinaabe scholar from Lac des Mille Lacs First Nation in Treaty 3 territory. He is an assistant professor in the Faculty of Law at the University of Manitoba and the author of *Reclaiming Anishinaabe Law: Kinamaadiwin Inaakonigewin and the Treaty Right to Education.* Leo's research interests include Indigenous education and law, treaties, UNDRIP, and the processes of reconciliation and decolonization.

Emma Battell Lowman is a settler Canadian originally from the overlapping territories of the Haudenosaunee and Anishinaabe, near Niagara Falls, Ontario. Her work focuses on Indigenous-settler histories in British Columbia, settler colonialism, Indigenous resurgence, and decolonization in North America. Emma is also a dedicated trade unionist and activist and consults for government, community, and service organizations on reconciliation and team building. Emma holds a PhD in Sociology from the University of Warwick (UK) and an MA in History from the University of Victoria (Canada). She is the co-author with Adam J. Barker of the 2025 book *Settler: Identity and Colonialism* 2nd ed. (Fernwood Press, 2025).

Naomi Beingessner grew up with activist parents on a small mixed farm in Saskatchewan, Treaty 4 territory: the territory of the nêhiyawak, Anihšināpēk, Dakota, Lakota, and Nakoda peoples, and the homeland of the Métis Nation. She was a member of the Treaty Land Sharing Network Coordinating Committee for several years. She has a PhD in Environment and Geography from the University of Manitoba, Canada, and works as a social researcher at the James Hutton Institute in Scotland. Naomi's research focuses on land tenure and property regimes, multi-stakeholder decision-making, and community engagement.

Kurtis Boyer (Michif/Métis) is originally from Southern Saskatchewan, is a citizen of the Métis Nation–Saskatchewan, and is a political scientist working in the areas of Indigenous governance and political psychology. He is currently the Johnson-Shoyama Graduate School Research Chair in Métis Governance and Policy at the University of Saskatchewan, where he is also an assistant professor. In 2024, Dr. Boyer was appointed the first Alphonsine Lafond–Tom Molloy Memorial Fellow on Leadership and Innovation in Indigenous Governance, awarded by the Institute for Research on Public Policy. His work covers issues related to Indigenous politics, self-governance, law, and political behaviour.

Elaine Coburn is the former director of the Centre for Feminist Research and associate professor of international studies at York University. Her writing is concerned with unjust inequalities and how to challenge them. Her work appears in the scholarly journals *International Feminist Journal of Politics*, *International Sociology*, *Philosophy Today*, and *Political Studies*, among others. She writes for the *Literary Review of Canada*, and she has contributed to *Canadian Notes & Queries*, *Herizons*, the *LSE Review of Books*, and *Philosophy Now*, among other writings for the general public.

Jeffrey S. Denis is a settler Canadian of European ancestry and an associate professor of sociology at McMaster University in Hamilton, Ontario (Haudenosaunee, Mississauga, and Attawandaron territory). His research investigates the social psychology of racism and colonialism and the strategies, alliances, policies, and practices that can bring about more just and sustainable societies. He is the author of *Canada at a Crossroads: Boundaries, Bridges, and Laissez-Faire Racism in Indigenous-Settler Relations* (University of Toronto Press, 2020). Jeff is currently completing two major research projects: a community-driven study of reconciliation initiatives and barriers in Kenora, Ontario; and a collaborative study of long-term Indigenous-settler alliances, with a focus on the Shoal Lake 40 First Nation's Freedom Road campaign.

Rita Kaur Dhamoon is grateful to the Songhees Nation of the Lək̓ʷəŋən People, whose land she lives on and benefits from. She is on a journey to return to Sikh ancestral knowledge and practices. She is also an aspiring artist and *dolhki* (two-headed hand drum) player. With over thirty years of activism and community work, Rita hopes to do more to support practices of freedom for communities of colour, Black communities, and Indigenous communities, especially those that promote decolonial, abolitionist, feminist, anti-state, collectivist, caste-free, accessible relations as well as material care for the earth and cosmos. She holds a position as associate professor in the Department of Political Science, University of Victoria (British Columbia). She researches and teaches in the areas of race and gender politics in Canada, troubling inclusion politics, disrupting settler colonialism, post-colonialism and anti-colonialism, feminist theory and practice, solidarity, and critiques of the nation-state.

Enakshi Dua is a full professor in the School of Gender, Sexuality and Women's Studies at York University. She has published extensively on theorizing racism and anti-racism, racism in Canadian universities, equity policies and anti-racism policies, the racialized and gendered histories of immigration processes, and the racialization of masculinity and femininity. Her notable publications include *Decolonizing Antiracism*; *Theorizing Anti-Racism: Linkages in Marxism and Critical Race Theories*; *The Equity Myth: Race, Racialization and Indigeneity at Canadian Universities*; "Our Canadian Culture Has Been Squeamish About Gathering Race-Based Statistics"; "'When You Hear or See Something Wrong It's Up to Everyone to Let People Know': Homonationalism and the Reconstitution of 'White' Heteronormative Masculinity"; "When Home and Harem Collide: The 'Hindu Women's Question' as a Mass Spectacle of the Canadian Nation, Family and Modernity"; *Scratching the Surface: Canadian Anti-Racist Feminist Thought*; *The Hindu Woman's Question*; and *From Subjects To Aliens: Indian Migrants and the Racialisation of Canadian Citizenship.*

She has more than thirty years of experience in feminist, anti-racist, and equity work. She has held a number of administrative positions, including director of the Centre for Feminist Research; chair of the Equity Committee, Canadian Association of University Teachers; the York University Faculty Association's equity officer; co-chair of the Joint Committee on Employment Equity and Inclusion at York University; a member of York's President's Advisory Council on Equity, Diversity and Inclusion and its steering committee; and chair of a sub-committee on developing an EDI strategy that is relevant to faculty. In these positions, she has spearheaded a number of equity initiatives—including participating in the development of a university-wide DEDI framework, a critical analysis of the use of workshops in EDID, targeted equity hires, readiness policies, and development of equity thresholds for employment equity policies.

Emily Eaton is a white settler doing community-based research, teaching, and service devoted to addressing the climate and inequality crises at local and national scales. Central to this work is understanding the power and influence of the fossil fuel industries and mapping pathways to climate action that prioritize the needs of marginalized communities and address the unjust colonial relationship that Canada has with Indigenous Peoples. Her books include *Unjust Transition: The Future for Fossil Fuel Workers*; *The End of This World: Climate Justice in So-Called Canada*; *Fault Lines: Life and Landscape in Saskatchewan's Oil Economy*; and *Growing Resistance: Canadian Farmers and the Politics of Genetically Modified Wheat*.

Vanda Fleury (Michif) is of Red River Métis and German descent and is a citizen of the Manitoba Métis Federation. She was born and raised on the west-central prairies of Manitoba and is currently based in Winnipeg. Her sense of place and love for family and photography have cultivated her connection to landscape narratives. Vanda is a graduate student in Political Science at the University of Northern British Columbia, and her research interests focus on Indigenous feminist interventions on health and wellness. Her work engages with intersectional theory and praxis, Indigenous feminism, photovoice methodology, and decolonization. Vanda is also a film-poetry artist, and her short film *In Good Hands*, a companion piece to her chapter in this volume, screened at the imagineNATIVE Film + Media Arts Festival in Toronto (2022). Vanda's children and the stories of her ancestors are enduring sources of creative motivation.

Emily Grafton has a PhD in Native Studies from the University of Manitoba (Winnipeg). She worked for several years in different orders of government, including the Manitoba Legislative Assembly, Assembly of Manitoba Chiefs (Winnipeg), and City of Regina (Saskatchewan). In addition, Emily has held leadership roles related to Indigenous Peoples and decolonial movements, including as the research-curator of Indigenous content at the Canadian Museum for Human Rights in Winnipeg; executive lead, Indigenization; and the Indigenous research lead at University of Regina. As a descendant of a Métis family who received a Halfbreed land allotment in St. François Xavier, Manitoba, the politics of settler-based dispossession have influenced both her family life and scholarship. She is currently an associate professor of Politics and International Studies at the University of Regina, where her work concerns settler colonialism, reconciliation, Indigenous research practices, and feminist theories. Emily is a faculty advisor for the Saskatchewan Electoral Parity Project (SEPP) and board member for the Canadian Political Science Association (CPSA), and she is the author of *Divided Power: How Federalism Undermines Reconciliation* (2026) with Fernwood Publishing.

Ayumi Goto and **Peter Morin** are best friends and performance artists. They sing together. They laugh together. They cry together. They debate ideas and plan for the destruction of the european colonization of canada. Morin and Goto have exhibited throughout canada and internationally. They also like to jump.

Joyce Green is professor emerita of Political Science at the University of Regina. She is the editor of *Making Space for Indigenous Feminism* (2007 and 2017) and of *Indivisible: Indigenous Human Rights* (2014), both through Fernwood Publishing. She currently lives in ʔa·kiskaqłiʔit—"where two trails meet on the prairie" (known in English as Cranbrook, BC), in ʔamakʔis Ktunaxa—the unceded and stolen territory of the Ktunaxa Nation. She is a citizen of the Ktunaxa Nation and a member of Yaq̓it ʔa·kiskaqłiʔit (Tobacco Plains Indian Band). Dr. Green is of English, Ktunaxa, and Cree-Scots Métis ancestry.

Huma Haider is an independent consultant and international lawyer, with over eighteen years of experience working with international development advisors, conducting policy-relevant research on a range of issues related to conflict, peace-building, justice, governance, human rights, and social development. She is a mixed-race Pakistani and Chinese settler who has lived in various parts of the world and currently lives with her family in Treaty 13 territory. She holds a Master of Laws in International Human Rights from the London School of Economics and a Master of Business Administration from the University of Toronto. Her research areas and publications centre on transitional justice, coexistence, and reconciliation in divided societies; conflict sensitivity; international humanitarian law; and the role of diasporic, refugee, and displaced communities in transitional justice and peace-building. She is a former research fellow at the International Development Department, University of Birmingham, and has worked as a lawyer in the War Crimes Chamber of the Prosecutor's Office of Bosnia and Herzegovina.

David B. A. MacDonald is an Indo-Trinidadian and Scottish settler-academic from Treaty 4 territory, Saskatchewan, and is descended from girmitiyas (indentured labourers). He is professor of Political Science at the University of Guelph and an honorary academic at the University of Auckland. He was previously a faculty member at the University of Otago and École Supérieure de Commerce de Paris. He shares a SSHRC Insight Grant on Indigenous self-determination with co-researcher Sheryl Lightfoot. He has authored numerous books, academic articles, and book chapters on Indigenous-settler relations, comparative genocide studies, and comparative foreign policy in CANZUS states. His publications include *The Sleeping Giant Awakens: Genocide, Indian Residential Schools, and the Challenge of Conciliation* (University of Toronto Press, 2019) and the co-edited *Populism and World Politics: Exploring Inter- and Transnational Dimensions* (Palgrave, 2019). He has a PhD in International Relations from the London School of Economics.

Heena B. Mistry is a historian, writer, and educator. She is a South Asian settler whose family worked as carpenters and contractors in Kenya and Uganda. Her research focuses on South Asian diasporas in British colonies and their relationship with anti-colonial activism in those colonies and in South Asia. She is also the director of equity, diversity and inclusion at Wilfrid Laurier University, where she has developed training and programming to support scholars in applying an anti-oppression lens to their research process and in the classroom.

Rosemary Nagy is a settler Canadian who works in the areas of human rights, transitional justice, settler colonialism, and gender-based violence. Rosemary is professor in the Department of Gender Equality and Social Justice at Nipissing University, which is based in the traditional territory of Nipissing First Nation, under the protection of the Robinson-Huron Treaty of 1850.

Evelyn Poitras, PhD, askitako piasew iskwew, is assistant professor and chair of the Indigenous Business and Economic Development (IBED) initiative, founded by the Ptarmigan Charitable Foundation, in the Faculty of Business, Communication Studies & Aviation at Mount Royal University's Bissett School of Business in Calgary, Alberta. She is Cree and Saulteaux from Peepeekisis Cree Nation in Treaty 4 territory in what is now known as Southern Saskatchewan. Evelyn completed her PhD in Indigenous Studies at Trent University with her thesis, "nikāwiy to ôtānisa Narratives—nehiyaw (Cree) Mother to Daughter Stories for Inherent Role of nehiyaw-iskwewak (Cree Women) in Governance and Numbered Indian Treaty Enforcement, Treaty Four and Treaty Six." Evelyn's mother, Marie Alma Poitras (née Quinney), is originally from Onion Lake Cree Nation in Treaty 6. Evelyn's research interests include the Numbered Treaties; sovereignty issues, including Indigenous governance; nêhiyaw iskwew (Cree woman) governance and leadership; and Indigenous community development. Evelyn has completed the documentaries *To Colonize a People: The File Hills Indian Farm Colony*, on the history of her band, *Peepeekisis*, and *Buffalo: A Memorial*, a personal family story told within the context of the Indian residential school experience.

Marie Alma Poitras is Nēhiyaw-iskwēw (woman of the people who believe in the four spirits of each living organism), whose Nēyhiyawīkāsowin (natural name) is Osāwastim-Otâhkohp-iskwēw (Blanket of the Brown Horse-Woman). Alma is a descendent of a Signatory Chief to Treaty 6 from Onion Lake whose name was Osāwaskwân (Yellow-Cloud). Her grandfather was an interpreter for settler people from Fort Pitt, Saskatchewan. His name was Kāhmāwâcihat (He Who Gathers Them Together) or Joe Quinney. Her parents were Charlie Quinney and Mary Cecile Quinney. Alma holds a teaching certificate from the Ministry of Education (Government of Saskatchewan) and was an elementary school teacher. She also holds a Bachelor of Education (Indian Education) from the Saskatchewan Indian Federated College (University of Regina) and a Bachelor of Education—Elementary (Indian Education) and Master's of Education in Curriculum and Instruction from the University of Regina. Alma is a Knowledge Keeper, Language Keeper, and Kēhtē-aya. She is blessed with many grandchildren and great-grandchildren, whom she is confident will survive the intergenerational trauma of the residential school era and break the cycle of injustice by carrying on the beliefs of their descendants and past generations of human kindness and belief in the eternal and sacred cycle of life of the four legged, the flyers, the swimmers, and the crawlers.

Solomon Ratt was born to parents who were hunters and fishers. At the age of six, Solomon was abducted from his home and taken to the residential school where he began his education. After the residential school, he attended Riverside Collegiate High School. He attended the University of Regina, earning two BAs and an MA. He is a recipient of the Saskatchewan Order of Merit (2021) and the Queen's Platinum Medallion (2022), and he was appointed as a Member of the Order of Canada (2024). He taught Cree at the First Nations University, beginning as a sectional instructor in 1984 before becoming a full-time faculty member in 1986, and ultimately retiring in 2022. Solomon's publications include *nīhithaw ācimowina / Woods Cree Stories* (2014), *mâci-nêhiyawêwin / Beginning Cree* (2016), and *âhkami-nêhiyawêtân / Let's Keep Speaking Cree* (2022), published by the University of Regina Press. Another book through URP, published in January 2023, *kâ-pî-isi-kiskisiyân / ᑳᐯᐃᓯᑭᐢᑭᓯᔮᐣ / The Way I Remember*, won two Saskatchewan Book Awards (2024).

Martha Jane Robbins has been one of the coordinators of the Treaty Land Sharing Network since its inception in 2018. She grew up on a mixed organic farm in Treaty 6 territory, at Laura, Saskatchewan, and has a background in farm politics and social movements through her work with the National Farmers Union. She is currently working on a PhD in International Development (Political Ecology) from the International Institute of Social Studies in The Hague, the Netherlands. She lives in Saskatoon with her partner and two children.

Gina Starblanket is an associate professor in the School of Indigenous Governance at the University of Victoria. She is Cree/Saulteaux and a member of the Star Blanket Cree Nation in Treaty 4. Professor Starblanket studies Indigenous-settler political relations with a specific focus on Indigenous politics in the Prairies, the politics of treaty implementation, and Indigenous movements towards social and political transformation. Professor Starblanket is co-editor of *NAIS: Journal of the Native American and Indigenous Studies Association* and is the author of important sole- and co-authored interventions theorizing relational responsibilities to one another and to the land, including the third edition of *Making Space for Indigenous Feminism* (Fernwood Publishing, 2024), *Storying Violence: Unravelling Colonial Narratives in the Stanley Trial* (Arbeiter Ring Publishing, 2020), and the fifth and sixth editions of *Visions of the Heart: Issues Involving Indigenous Peoples in Canada* (Oxford University Press, 2019 and 2025).

INTRODUCTION

The Importance of Relations and Resistances in Understanding Settler Colonialism in Canada

Emily Grafton and David B. A. MacDonald

WELCOME TO OUR COLLECTION ON RELATIONS AND resistances in settler colonial Canada. Our focus is to explore, from a range of relational perspectives, how contemporary Canadian society grapples with the challenges inherent to settler colonialism. Both editors are political scientists: one is Métis (Emily), and the other, Indo-Trinidadian and Scottish mixed race (David). Our expertise, as well as our own life journeys and perspectives, inform how we have structured and presented this book. Coinciding with the thirtieth anniversary of the *Report of the Royal Commission on Aboriginal Peoples* (1996), this book develops analysis of settler Canada. Our related collection, *On Settler Colonialism in Canada: Lands and Peoples* (2025), offers a critical basis for understanding many aspects of settler state and society. In the present volume, we focus on relational responses and resistances, including reconciliation, decolonialism, and resurgence. We do so to identify potential approaches to addressing, reducing, or overcoming colonial inequities. While our two books are stand-alone collections, they complement each other, and we encourage you to read them together.

This book is focused on Canada as a settler state. Social scientists describe such states as comprising a majority of the population descended from those who colonized and settled territories originally inhabited and controlled by Indigenous Peoples. Processes of settlement were often violent, with European colonizers primarily focused on asserting control of territory.[1] Lands, waters, and indeed anything that could be commodified as "natural resources" were claimed by the state, and today the vast majority of the lands and waters of Canada are subject to Crown ownership and control.[2] Patrick Wolfe has referred to a "logic of elimination" as a key aspect of settler colonialism, where attempts are made to dismantle Indigenous societies and replace them by "new colonial societ[ies] on the expropriated land base."[3] New settler societies are designed to undermine Indigenous Peoples' relationships with, access to, and control over their lands and waters, providing benefit to settler populations.

Identifying who benefits from, and who is disadvantaged by, settler colonial structures and systems is central to settler colonial theory. For instance, in the wake of the current Russian war on Ukraine, it is common to hear folks discuss how Ukrainian refugees have come to Canada since 2022 in search of a safe and peaceful life. Situations where newcomers are welcomed by Canada (as a haven from persecution) contrast sharply with the experiences of Indigenous Peoples under settler colonialism, who continue to seek recognition of rights, restitution of lands, and justice. Canada has historically functioned as a sanctuary to some while exacting harsh discrimination and racialized violence against others. To better understand the social complexities faced by Indigenous Peoples, Black and other racialized folks, and white settlers, we ask: What does meaningful change look like amid ongoing settlerism and resulting inequalities and violence?

To address this question, it is important to understand contemporary settler colonial Canada. The current global order has been shaped and reshaped by centuries of colonial rule, where primarily European countries attempted to replace Indigenous governments with colonizing forms of political and economic order.[4] In what became Canada, the arrival of European powers led to the spread of imperial corporations (like the Hudson's Bay Company) and the Christian churches, respectively, through the fur trade and missionary activities, which over time resulted in the development of settler political structures and society. Today, the settler state and its societies operate through complex relationships among Indigenous Peoples and settler populations. These relationships are shaped by "structural, eliminatory, and land based"[5] institutional regulations, which are further reinforced by settler society. The settler state seeks to exert control over Indigenous Peoples through assimilative policies, the disenfranchisement of Indigenous political and legal systems, and the imposition of oppressive settler social systems and values. These actions are tied to the goals of exclusive land acquisition, such as the French and British taking of Indigenous traditional lands, the reserve system, and Indian residential schools.[6] Control was also manifested through treaty-making processes that enabled the settler state to acquire Indigenous Peoples' lands for European settlement.[7] Importantly, settler colonialism is a structural and permanent[8] feature of the Canadian state, which utilizes political, economic, and legal structures to privilege settler society to the detriment of Indigenous Peoples.

The permanency of settlerism (as an active force in continually reinforcing settler colonialism) has led to resistance movements focused on decolonization and reconciliation. While these are distinct political resistance movements, they are interconnected responses to the historical colonial occupation, and address its ongoing legacies (including continued land dispossession) in contemporary Canada. In Canada, several national bodies have recognized these colonial legacies and resistance efforts, including the Royal Commission on Aboriginal Peoples (RCAP) circa 1996, the Truth and Reconciliation Commission of Canada (TRC) circa 2015, the National Inquiry into Missing and Murdered Indigenous Women and Girls (NIMMIWG) circa 2019, and, more recently, the Office of the Independent Special Interlocutor (OSI) for Missing Children and Unmarked Graves and Burial Sites associated with Indian Residential Schools (2024).

Today, Canadian settler colonial society can be understood as a triad[9] of groups: white settler peoples (of mainly European origin), Black and other racialized groups, and Indigenous Peoples (First Nations, Inuit, and Métis peoples). As Lorenzo Veracini puts it, "Settlers are founders of political orders and carry their sovereignty with them (on the contrary, migrants can be seen as appellants facing a political order that is already constituted)."[10] As such, settlers establish new political and social systems that replace the pre-existing systems of Indigenous Peoples, while more recent immigrants do not necessarily have any input in the creation of these systems, into which they are normally obliged to integrate.[11]

Some argue that settler colonial structures, established through land theft and ongoing dispossession, benefit settlers of European origin and can also provide important benefits to racialized newcomers. Lawrence and Dua note, for example, that racialized settlers also maintain "colonial relationships with Aboriginal peoples."[12] This does not suggest that all groups have an equal position vis-à-vis Indigenous Peoples. Rather, racialized peoples, like European settlers, "live on land that is appropriated and contested, where Aboriginal peoples are denied nationhood and access to their own lands."[13] Conversely, some argue that those newcomers who are racialized minorities do not benefit significantly from Indigenous dispossession but instead face racism, religious and economic exclusion, or other kinds of discrimination.[14]

Indigenous Peoples, too, have differing access to benefits, regulated by the state. For example, the *Indian Act* designates status to some First Nations while denying it to others, who are commonly referred to as Non-Status First Nations. Those without status cannot access the benefits of being a party to a treaty. The Inuit and Métis nations are understood as Indian through the *British North America Act, 1867*, via the court cases *Reference Re Eskimos, 1939*, and *Daniels v. Canada* (2016), respectively, resulting in differences in status and benefits in the eyes of the state. Identity is also influenced by the assimilatory pressures of access or denial to cultural or Traditional Knowledge systems. Historically, these systems were banned in Canada through legislation, or marginalized through social discrimination. Today, the impact of assimilation might vary based on geographical residence; living on reserve or in a predominantly Indigenous community may enhance cultural access compared to living in a large urban setting. The assimilatory pressures that Indigenous Peoples experience can also relate to how racialized newcomers are treated, as some may share similar lived experiences of discrimination from their countries of origin. The settler colonial triad complicates the dynamics of and solutions to colonial inequities, requiring exploration through relational resistances through reconciliation, decolonization, and solidarities.

Social Engagements and Boundaries in Settler Colonial Canada

The settler state has been founded on the legal instruments of *terra nullius* (Latin for vacant, unused, or unowned lands) and the Doctrine of Discovery. These international legal concepts originated in Catholic papal bulls, first developed in the fifth century, and were then later refined during the fifteen century through Spanish exploration and exploitation of parts of Africa and later what became known as the "Americas." They spread through European imperialism and were applied in the regions that became Canada through imperial contact, trade, and diplomacy in the seventeenth century. They continue to be used to deny Indigenous ownership, presence, and nationhood, undermining Indigenous-centred ways of being. According to the TRC, these "legal fictions" formed a key underlying logic of European domination.[15] Contemporary movements for reconciliation and decolonization in Canada are informed by individual and collective opposition, and through the work of the RCAP, TRC, NIMMIWG, and the OSI. These efforts seek to address these historical foundations that contribute to ongoing injustices that Indigenous Peoples face as a result of settler colonialism.

These movements are often framed by the fact that treaties have not been honoured by the Canadian government, provincial and territorial governments, nor by settler society. Instead, settler actors have illegitimately taken lands for settler benefit. Patricia Monture-Angus, a legal scholar from the Mohawk Nation, emphasizes that the Canadian state does not represent Indigenous laws, histories, and cultures, nor did Indigenous Peoples take part in the formation of Canada's institutions. She observes, "We, as individuals, did not participate in the process whereby the legal system was formed. We did not participate in the process of agreeing to the assumptions and values reflected in that system. Further, we have been excluded as Peoples in participating in the formation of that system."[16] Yet, Indigenous nations cannot be reduced to a homogenous population. Instead, this term refers in general to First Nations, Inuit, and Métis nations, and more specifically to the many communities and nations that exist across Indian country. Building on Monture's argument, none of the political systems and relational networks based on this Indigenous difference have been supplanted by the state, even in situations where colonial erosion has occurred.

Critiques of Canada's decolonial and reconciliatory frameworks outline problems in their application.[17] Settler colonialism is insidious, often difficult to detect and dismantle.[18] Moreover, decolonization threatens the survival of the settler colonial enterprise: both state-sanctioned and societal obstacles exist to oppose such change and maintain a status quo of settler benefit. For those striving to overcome settler colonial injustices, successful decolonization efforts require addressing the oppressive forces faced by non-Indigenous racialized minority groups as well.[19] Any attempts that exclude these communities may render reconciliatory and decolonial efforts ineffective. Together, racialized minorities and Indigenous Peoples have the potential to use the decolonial and reconciliatory suggestions our contributors outline to challenge the structures, practices, and attitudes of settler colonialism.[20]

Decolonization is certainly not an easy process. Patrick Wolfe rightly observed that settler colonialism has been "impervious to regime change."[21] Glen Coulthard (Yellowknives Dene) argues that Canada employs the "politics of recognition" in a way that lacks the transformative potential needed to address the ongoing dispossession of Indigenous Peoples' lands and rights.[22] Here, the settler state "recognizes" Indigenous cultural and legal distinctiveness, "via the accommodation of Indigenous identity claims in some form of renewed legal and political relationship with the Canadian state." However, as Coulthard has noted, "instead of ushering in an era of peaceful coexistence grounded on the ideal of reciprocity or mutual recognition, the politics of recognition in its contemporary liberal form promises to reproduce the very configurations of colonialist, racist, patriarchal state power that Indigenous peoples' demands for recognition have historically sought to transcend." These liberal politics of recognition and reconciliation are common political barriers in Canada to decolonization.[23] It is crucial to understand the political mechanics of Canada's liberal democracy to overcome these barriers to decolonial change.

As Himani Bannerji has argued, multiculturalism, rather than enabling diversity and reducing white supremacy, can instead act as a further instrument of settler colonialism, legitimating a pan-Canadian identity that excludes and, thus, marginalizes any identity that differs from a white European–settler norm.[24] Arguably, the introduction of multiculturalism into a settler colonial environment has had some negative repercussions for Indigenous Peoples as rights holders, leading to their being lumped together in a manner similar to racialized groups. They are thus expected to "integrate" as yet another minority group into the European settler colonial mainstream through educational, linguistic, and other forms of standardization. However, multiculturalism, with its promise of "tolerance" and formal equality within settler colonial institutions, insufficiently recognizes the *sui generis*[25] rights of Indigenous Peoples, which existed before colonization and continue still. Newcomers, refugees, and immigrants, through processes of multicultural integration, can unwittingly become part of a larger settler colonial project that disciplines and controls Indigeneity, while perpetuating a narrative of multicultural tolerance and respect for diversity. Multiculturalism, by promoting the normalness of dominant European-derived cultures and institutions, inhibits the problematization of colonial inequality:[26] it is designed to enhance the legitimacy of the state.

The term *reconciliation* in the settler context is contested, often critiqued on the basis that there never was an original golden era of conciliation between Indigenous Peoples and settlers, except perhaps some examples of early trading relationships and intermarriage. Métis artist and scholar David Garneau argues that, in this way, reconciliation terminology is misleading as it suggests a *return* to good relations. Instead, he suggests that *conciliation* may suitably capture the processes of building equitable and fair relations.[27] Some might argue that the idea of reconciliation is impossible to achieve, while others criticize it as merely performative.[28] Claims that "reconciliation is dead" became common several years ago,[29] while some scholars and activists speak of "reconciliation lite," indicating a failure of this concept to adequately address structural oppression and the persistence of existing inequalities.[30]

Some scholars and advocates are committed to achieving authentic reconciliation through decolonization practices. They argue that reconciliation, if fully realized, can lead to genuine transformative change that benefits the whole of Canadian society.[31] For instance, Paulette Regan and Aimée Craft (Anishinaabe-Métis) write, "If the TRC's vision of reconciliation is fully implemented, Indigenous cultural knowledge, governance systems, and laws will be regenerated, and Indigenous nations will be restored to their rightful place as self-determining equal partners in Confederation."[32] The TRC has also emphasized, "To the Commission, reconciliation is about establishing and maintaining a mutually respectful relationship between Aboriginal and non-Aboriginal peoples in this country."[33] These discussions underscore the importance of mutual recognition and respect and the integral role of Indigenous self-determination. Many view reconciliation as a process that can enhance Indigenous autonomy from settler colonial domination, often through reconstituted partnership or treaty.[34]

Reconciliation is certainly problematic when viewed only as a matter of relationships *between* the colonized and the colonizers. As Anishinabe/

Ojibway legal scholar John Borrows aptly puts it, "Reconciliation sounds nice when discussed in the abstract. But reconciliation, practiced in context, requires that Indigenous peoples reconcile themselves to colonialism. This is hardly a cause for celebration."[35] Reconciliation must be concerned with achieving structural change exercised through the establishment of a renewed relationship or these practices risk becoming a tool to legitimate the settler state.

Efforts to challenge settler colonialism can be identified in the growing Indigenous resurgence of Traditional Knowledge, which emphasizes a return to Indigenous laws, practices, and ways of knowing and being.[36] This movement represents an act of Indigenous resistance to settler colonialism. According to the NIMMIWG's *Interim Report*, Indigenous resistance encompasses "a broad range of strategies and activities that promote decolonization" as well as "'everyday acts of resistance' that embody individuals and communities living by their traditional teachings despite overwhelming pressure from the dominant society not to."[37]

Resurgence movements are inherently connected to the distinct Indigenous nations that exist across what is now Canada. Indigenous Peoples have developed unique knowledge systems built upon the ecological and spiritual connections to specific lands that support specific human and other-than-human relationships.[38] These specifics will shape the unique conceptualizations of resurgence movements.[39] For example, the Plains Cree (Nêhiyaw-Askiy), Inuit, and Mi'kmaq nations, among so many others, have different languages, land bases, laws, and cultural expressions that foster distinct political orientations and, thus, differing resurgences against colonialism. As Jeff Corntassel (Cherokee Nation) explains, resurgence is about reclaiming and regenerating the "relational, place-based existence by challenging the ongoing, destructive forces of colonization."[40] It can be undertaken through the revitalization of languages, cultural practices, traditional or country food systems, depleted resources and animal populations, political systems, kinship and relational practices, or any other Indigenous knowledge networks centred in colonial dispossession.

Indigenous resurgence movements are supported through the transfer of intergenerational knowledge and kinship relations, along with specific place-based Indigenous knowledge systems. Michi Saagiig Nishnaabeg scholar and activist Leanne Betasamosake Simpson emphasizes the crucial role of community: "Resurgence cannot happen in isolation."[41] Indeed, Indigenous-centred resurgences must be cultivated, nurtured, and supported by Indigenous communities and their specific knowledge systems. Resurgence can manifest in micro-refusals, such as focusing on everyday actions that embody Indigenous nationhood.[42] It can also include nationwide movements, such as that discussed by scholar Audra Simpson (Kahnawà:ke Mohawk Nation), who documents "Mohawk Life" as the refusal to "disappear" as enacted through consistent acts of claiming and exercising Indigenous existence, with mutual recognition of membership being a key aspect to resurgence.[43] In their work NIMMIWG has explored decolonization processes like "rollback," which involves re-establishing "traditional values, philosophies, and knowledge systems" that Indigenous Peoples use to resist the subjugation or exploitation of themselves and their lands.[44] The contributors in this collection examine a range of responses grounded in solidarity and the refusal to accept Canada's settler colonial context.

Overview of Chapters

This book comprises seventeen chapters that explore the complexities and inequities of settler colonialism in Canada. Part 1, "Decolonizing Education Processes," focuses on a central aspect of settler colonial dominance: education systems. As the late Honourable Murray Sinclair reflected on colonial inequity through assimilative and genocidal actions, laws, and policy practices, "Education got us into this mess and education will get us out of it." This section starts with Anishinaabe scholar Leo Baskatawang's contribution, "On Codifying the Traditional Laws of Indigenous Nations in Canada." In this chapter, Leo argues that Indigenous Peoples must document their laws as an important way to resist the Canadian settler state, which disregards Indigenous laws and ways of being. Leo, a citizen of Lac des Mille Lacs First Nation in Treaty 3 territory, describes the Anishinaabe Nation's efforts to have their education law recognized and affirmed as an act of reconciliation.

The second chapter, "Reflections on Anti-Asian Racism and Settler Colonialism in Canadian Universities," by Heena Mistry, articulates ways by which universities can engage in decolonizing efforts. This chapter calls for settlers to take responsibilities towards dismantling colonial injustices by fostering alliances between racialized peoples (particularly South Asian peoples and diasporic communities) and Indigenous Peoples to create and enable solidarities.

Next, Métis scholar Kurtis Boyer's "Education as a Policy Tool for Reconciliation: Understanding the Need for a Relational View of Mind" examines Indigenous knowledge systems and the assimilative pressures of Western rational thought, which are key drivers in colonial projects. Kurtis argues that efforts to bridge education gaps for Indigenous Peoples are structurally inadequate when framed by colonial mechanisms of Western rational thought. Instead, Indigenous relational knowledge systems should be integrated into policy frameworks to better influence reconciliatory education policies.

This section concludes with Rosemary Nagy's "Settler Researchers: From a Place of Not Knowing." Rosemary argues that settler researchers cannot genuinely understand Indigenous knowledge systems and should not depend on Indigenous Peoples for these teachings. Acknowledging this reality will empower settlers to participate in reconciliation practices in more meaningful ways that produce tangible decolonial change.

Part 2, "Prospects for Reconciliation and Relational Decolonization," offers relational approaches to these processes. It begins with Enakshi Dua and Elaine Coburn's chapter, "Land Acknowledgements in an Era of Reconciliation." This chapter looks at the contemporary practice of land acknowledgements, which are often understood to be rooted in long-standing Indigenous protocols of recognizing relationships with lands. However, within a settler colonial context, various conflicting politics intercede to prevent land acknowledgements from fostering respectful relations. Enakshi and Elaine explore Indigenous perspectives on the inherent relationships and responsibilities with lands to debunk settler-based myths and affirm Indigenous nationhood.

The next chapter, "Honouring Treaty Responsibilities in Rural Saskatchewan: The Treaty Land Sharing Network," is co-authored by Naomi Beingessner, Emily Eaton, and Martha Jane Robbins. Through a discussion of the Treaty Land Sharing Network, this chapter examines how settlers, particularly white farmers, can honour treaty responsibilities in rural Saskatchewan, even when this can involve the reduction of some white privilege. This network serves as an example of reconciliatory land sharing and solidarity in practice.

In his chapter, "Treaty Relations as a Foundation for Reconciliation: Indigenous and Settler Perspectives in Treaty 3 Territory," Jeff Denis explores varied and complex Indigenous perspectives on treaties as a foundation for reconciliation. He asks: Can treaty be an instrument of reconciliation in

Canada? In response, Jeff maps Indigenous Peoples' hesitancy, skepticism, and hopeful regard for treaty, while arguing that reconciliation necessitates settler peoples to develop and engage in meaningful relationships with Indigenous Peoples, grounded in the treaty concept of coexistence.

This section concludes with Métis scholar Vanda Fleury's "She Helped Herself: Rendering Empowerment Through Birth Sovereignty." By documenting her experiences with childbirth, Vanda demonstrates how modern settler-dominated health care is a site of colonial oppression while serving as a location for Indigenous-centred resistance. Ultimately, she establishes birth sovereignty through the use of traditional Indigenous medicines and the revival of ancestral relationships of kinship.

Part 3, "Settler Colonial Relationalities, Identities, and Belonging," builds on the previous section's relational decolonization of and reconciliation with institutions, turning towards personal journeys. Rita Dhamoon leads the section with "Sikh Responsibilities and Dreams: Disrupting Settler Colonialism, Bigger than Settler Colonialism." Here, she explains how Sikhi (the religion and philosophy of Sikhism) can be practised to foster settler alliances with Indigenous Peoples, forging the basis for improved relations. For Rita, Sikhism is inherently decolonial, as it challenges state-centric notions of sovereignty and prioritizes coexisting with Indigenous Peoples in ways that do not rely on settler colonialism.

Peter Morin (Tahltan Nation) and Japanese Canadian settler Ayumi Goto's work, "On the Merits of Being an Asshole," explores relations between Indigenous and racialized peoples in settler colonial spaces. As performance artists, they present a unique dialogue that employs a narrative of refusal, engaging in a generative and emancipatory conversation on the broader goal of decolonizing settler colonialism.

The third chapter in this section is Emma Battell Lowman and Adam J. Barker's "Who Are We Here? Settler Colonialism, Mobility, and Relationships Across Distance." Based in the United Kingdom for many years, but coming from Canada, the authors demonstrate that the term *settler* and its accompanying settler privilege exist in relation to the settler state, society, and beyond. They examine their own settler identities concerning living, at length, in an imperial colonial society in order to question the boundaries of settler identity and interrogate how settler identities are reinforced beyond Canada's borders.

The final chapter in part 3 is Huma Haider's reflective piece, "A Settler Twice Over in a Changing Canadian Landscape: The Importance of Knowledge, Acknowledgement, and Respect to Indigenous-Settler Reconciliation." As a transitional justice legal expert, Huma documents changes in Canadian settler memory and reflects on settler responsibilities to learn Canada's colonial histories. As a mixed-race settler and scholar, she emphasizes the importance of acting on this knowledge to effect reconciliatory change.

The last section of our book, "Indigenous Relational Knowledges in Settler Contexts," focuses on Indigenous authors and their perspectives on settler colonial Canada. We close this book with Indigenous voices who strongly articulate reconciliation and decolonization and Indigenous futurities. Here, we begin with Evelyn and kēhtē-ayak (Elder in the nēhiyawēwin language) Alma Poitras's moving analysis of concepts of Indigenous ancestral knowledges that exist despite the settler context of oppression. In "nikāwiy to ôtānisa Narratives—Cree Mother to Daughter Stories: Calendar of Life, miyo-pimātisiwin (Good Life)," the authors use these knowledge systems to discuss their nēhiyawak (Cree) understandings of Indigenous laws and treaties within and external to the settler state. Here, Indigenous ways of being and doing can help resist the settler colonial order.

Next, Solomon Ratt's poems "tâpwîwin ikwa wâkôwîcihiwîwin—Truth and Reconciliation" and "Where Is the Love?" reflect his personal lived experiences with Indian residential schools and the truth and reconciliation movement in Canada. Solomon is from āmaciwīspimowinihk (Stanley Mission, Saskatchewan), and the poems are each told in Cree (th-dialect), Cree syllabics, and English. This multilingual approach demonstrates that Canada is a settler colonial nation that sought to erase all Indigenous difference, illuminating the ongoing uneasy coexistence of these colonial structures with Indigenous Peoples' ancestral knowledge systems.

The next chapter is by scholar Joyce Green, a citizen of the Ktunaxa Nation and a member of Yaq̓it ʔa·kiskaqǂiʔit (Tobacco Plains Indian Band), and of English and Cree–Scots Métis ancestry. In "Rights and Responsibilities: Indigenous Realities, Indigenous Priorities," Joyce considers Indigenous Peoples' perspectives of rights in the settler Canadian context that is based on imperial colonial rule and settler colonial myth-making. Importantly, this resurgence work is deeply tied to relationality. The stories Indigenous Peoples tell and the values we celebrate are resurgence, resistance, our histories, relationships, and territorial sovereignty.

The final section concludes with Métis scholar Emily Grafton's "Indigenous Women, Settler Colonial State–Sanctioned Gendered Violence, and Reconciliation in Canada." This chapter discusses various ways Indigenous women are subjected to systems of racial, gender, and colonial oppression, which are foundational to settler Canada. Emily highlights how Indigenous women experience—or, more precisely, are ignored by—the contemporary reconciliation movements of settler colonialism.

This collection concludes with an afterword by Cree and Saulteaux scholar Gina Starblanket. Here, Gina interconnects the central themes related to relationality and resurgences evident throughout the chapters. While the authors approach the "colonial condition" from varied standpoints and perspectives, Gina unifies these pieces by emphasizing the "renewal of relational paradigms." She stresses the importance of seeking solutions outside the state to avoid empty gestures or dismissing ideas that may seem too challenging. Gina balances the "enduring impacts" of colonialism with the record of change, stating, "we also require honest accounts of our losses, for they have not been minimal nor are they immaterial for many Indigenous people today."

On Settler Colonialism in Canada: Relations and Resistances is a collection of conversations that aims to provide a deeper conceptual understanding of decolonial efforts and reconciliatory processes in settler colonial Canada. The authors, situated across Canada, look to solidarities and resistances as the means to shift colonial inequities. Although there is no blueprint to Canada's future, through relational solidarities tangible steps towards decolonization, reconciliation, and Indigenous resurgences can occur.

Notes

1 Veracini, "Colonialism, Frontiers, Genocide."
2 Glenn, "Settler Colonialism as Structure."
3 Wolfe, "Settler Colonialism and the Elimination of the Native."
4 Walia, *Border and Rule*.
5 Elkins and Pedersen, *Settler Colonialism in the 20th Century*, quoted in Englert, "Settlers, Workers," 1647.
6 Truth and Reconciliation Commission of Canada (TRC), *Honouring the Truth, Reconciling for the Future*.
7 Daschuk, *Clearing the Plains*.
8 Wolfe, "Settler Colonialism and the Elimination of the Native."
9 Garba and Sorentino, "Slavery Is a Metaphor"; Razack, Smith, and Thobani, eds., *States of Race*; Veracini, *The Settler Colonial Present*.
10 Veracini, *Settler Colonialism*, 3.
11 Veracini, *The Settler Colonial Present*, 41.
12 Lawrence and Dua, "Decolonizing Antiracism," 134.

13 Lawrence and Dua, "Decolonizing Antiracism."
14 Kelley, "The Rest of Us"; Garba and Sorentino, "Slavery Is a Metaphor."
15 TRC, *Honouring the Truth, Reconciling for the Future.*
16 Quoted in Thobani, *Exalted Subjects*, 48.
17 Robinson and Martin, eds., *Arts of Engagement*; Asch, Borrows, and Tully, eds., *Resurgence and Reconciliation.*
18 Lowman and Barker, *Settler.*
19 Veracini, *Settler Colonialism*; Garba and Sorentino, "Slavery Is a Metaphor."
20 Anderson and Samudzi, *As Black as Resistance.*
21 Wolfe, "Settler Colonialism and the Elimination of the Native," 402.
22 Coulthard, *Red Skin, White Masks.*
23 Coulthard, *Red Skin, White Masks*, 3–4; Kulchyski, *Aboriginal Rights Are Not Human Rights.*
24 Bannerji, *The Dark Side of the Nation*, 9–10.
25 The legal term *sui generis* borrows from the Latin meaning of *unique* and refers to Indigenous Peoples rights that are founded not on Canadian laws but on Indigenous legal systems predating colonial contact and domination. Henderson, "Sui Generis and Treaty Citizenship."
26 Dhamoon, *Identity/Difference Politics*, x–xi.
27 Garneau, "Imaginary Spaces of Conciliation."
28 Simpson, "Whither Settler colonialism?," 438–45 and 439. See also: Gaertner, "'Aboriginal Principles of Witnessing'"; James, "A Carnival of Truth?"
29 Yesno, "Is Reconciliation Dead?," as quoted in Regan, "Canada's TRC," 60.
30 Midzain-Gobin and Smith, "Not in the Past."
31 Wilson-Raybould, *True Reconciliation*, 315.
32 Craft and Regan, *Pathways of Reconciliation*, xiii.
33 TRC, *Honouring the Truth, Reconciling for the Future*, 6.
34 Veracini, "Colonialism, Frontiers, Genocide," 5.
35 Borrows, "Canada's Colonial Constitution," 33.
36 Starblanket and Stark, "Towards a Relational Paradigm"; Simpson, "The Sovereignty of Critique"; Simpson, *As We Have Always Done.*
37 National Inquiry into Missing and Murdered Indigenous Women and Girls (NIMMIWG), *Our Women and Girls Are Sacred*, 85.
38 Battiste and Henderson, *Protecting Indigenous Knowledge*, 67.
39 Doerfler, Sinclair, and Stark, eds., *Centering Anishinaabeg Studies*, xvii.
40 Corntassel, "Re-Envisioning Resurgence," 89.
41 Simpson, *Dancing On Our Turtle's Back*, 69.
42 Corntassel et al., eds. *Everyday Acts of Resurgence*, 17.
43 Simpson, *Mohawk Interruptus*, 22–23.
44 NIMMIWG, *Our Women and Girls are Sacred*, 83.

Sources

Anderson, William C., and Zoé Samudzi. *As Black as Resistance: Finding the Conditions for Liberation.* AK Press, 2018.

Asch, Michael, John Borrows, and James Tully, eds. *Resurgence and Reconciliation: Indigenous-Settler Relations and Earth Teachings*. University of Toronto Press, 2018.

Bannerji, Himani. *The Dark Side of the Nation: Essays on Multiculturalism, Nationalism and Gender*. Canadian Scholars Press, 2000.

Battiste, Marie A., and James Youngblood Henderson. *Protecting Indigenous Knowledge and Heritage: A Global Challenge*. Purich Publishing, 2000.

Borrows, John. "Canada's Colonial Constitution." In *The Right Relationship: Reimagining the Implementation of Historical Treaties*, edited by John Borrows and Michael Coyle. University of Toronto Press, 2017.

Corntassel, Jeff. "Re-Envisioning Resurgence: Indigenous Pathways to Decolonization and Sustainable Self-Determination." *Decolonization: Indigeneity, Education & Society* 1, no. 1 (2012): 86–101.

Corntassel, Jeff, Taiaiake Alfred, Noelani Goodyear-Kaʻōpua, Noenoe K. Silva, Hokulani Aikau, and Devi Mucina, eds. *Everyday Acts of Resurgence: People, Places, Practices*. Daykeeper Press, 2018.

Coulthard, Glen S. *Red Skin, White Masks: Rejecting the Colonial Politics of Recognition*. University of Minnesota Press, 2014.

Craft, Aimée, and Paulette Regan, eds. *Pathways of Reconciliation: Indigenous and Settler Approaches to Implementing the TRC's Calls to Action*. University of Manitoba Press, 2020.

Daschuk, James. *Clearing the Plains: Disease, Politics of Starvation, and the Loss of Indigenous Life*. University of Regina Press, 2013.

Dhamoon, Rita. *Identity/Difference Politics: How Difference Is Produced, and Why It Matters*. UBC Press, 2010.

Doerfler, Jill, Niigaanwewidam James Sinclair, and Heidi Kiiwetinepinesiik Stark, eds. *Centering Anishinaabeg Studies: Understanding the World Through Stories*. University of Manitoba Press, 2013.

Elkins, Caroline, and Susan Pedersen. *Settler Colonialism in the 20th Century: Projects, Practices, Legacies*. Routledge, 2005.

Englert, Sai. "Settlers, Workers, and the Logic of Accumulation by Dispossession." *Antipode* 52, no. 6 (2020): 1647–66. https://doi.org/10.1111/anti.12659.

Gaertner, David. "'Aboriginal Principles of Witnessing' and the Truth and Reconciliation Commission of Canada." In *Arts of Engagement: Taking Aesthetic Action In and Beyond the Truth and Reconciliation Commission of Canada*, edited by Dylan Robertson and Keavy Martin. Wilfrid Laurier University Press, 2016.

Garba, Tapji, and Sara-Maria Sorentino. "Slavery Is a Metaphor: A Critical Commentary on Eve Tuck and K. Wayne Yang's 'Decolonization Is Not a Metaphor.'" *Antipode* 52, no. 3 (2020): 764–82. https://doi.org/10.1111/anti.12615.

Garneau, David. "Imaginary Spaces of Conciliation and Reconciliation: Art, Curation, and Healing." In *Arts of Engagement: Taking Aesthetic Action In and Beyond the Truth and Reconciliation Commission of Canada*, edited by Dylan Robertson and Keavy Martin. Wilfrid Laurier University Press, 2016.

Glenn, Evelyn Nakano. "Settler Colonialism as Structure: A Framework for Comparative Studies of US Race and Gender Formation." *Sociology of Race and Ethnicity* 1, no. 1 (2015): 54–74. https://doi.org/10.1177/2332649214560440.

Henderson, James (Sákéj) Youngblood. "Sui Generis and Treaty Citizenship." *Citizenship Studies* 6, no. 4 (2002): 415–40. https://doi.org/10.1080/1362102022000041259.

James, Matt. "A Carnival of Truth? Knowledge, Ignorance and the Canadian Truth and Reconciliation Commission." *International Journal of Transitional Justice* 6, no. 2 (2012): 182–204. https://doi.org/10.1093/ijtj/ijs010.

Kelley, Robyn D.G. "The Rest of Us: Rethinking Settler and Native." *American Quarterly* 69, no. 2 (2017): 267–76. http://www.jstor.org/stable/26360846.

Kulchyski, Peter. *Aboriginal Rights Are Not Human Rights: In Defence of Indigenous Struggles*. Arbeiter Ring Publishing, 2013.

Lawrence, Bonita, and Enakshi Dua. "Decolonizing Antiracism." *Social Justice* 32, no. 4 (2005): 120–43. https://go.gale.com/ps/i.do?p=CIC&u=ureginalib&id=GALE%7CA147523565&v=2.1&it=r&sid=bookmark-CIC&asid=011ba7ce

Lowman, Emma Battell, and Adam J. Barker. *Settler: Identity and Colonialism in 21st Century Canada*. Fernwood Publishing, 2015.

Midzain-Gobin, Liam, and Heather Smith. "Not in the Past: Colonialism Is Rooted in the Present." *The Conversation*, March 28, 2021. https://theconversation.com/not-in-the-past-colonialism-is-rooted-in-the-present-157395.

National Inquiry into Missing and Murdered Indigenous Women and Girls (NIMMIWG). *Our Women and Girls Are Sacred: Interim Report*. National Inquiry into Missing and Murdered Indigenous Women and Girls, 2017. https://publications.gc.ca/site/eng/9.843833/publication.html.

Razack, Sherene, Malinda Smith, and Sunera Thobani, eds. *States of Race: Critical Race Feminism for the 21st Century*. Between the Lines, 2010.

Regan, Paulette. "Canada's TRC: An 'Unsettling' Indigenous-Centred Relational Justice and Reconciliation Model." In *Trading Justice for Peace? Reframing Reconciliation in TRC Processes in South Africa, Canada and Nordic Countries*, edited by Sigríður Guðmarsdóttir, Paulette Regan, and Demaine Solomons. AOSIS Publishing, 2022.

Robinson, Dylan, and Keavy Martin, eds. *Arts of Engagement: Taking Aesthetic Action In and Beyond the Truth and Reconciliation Commission of Canada*. Wilfrid Laurier University Press, 2016.

Simpson, Audra. *Mohawk Interruptus: Political Life Across the Borders of Settler States*. Duke University Press, 2014.

Simpson, Audra. "The Sovereignty of Critique." *South Atlantic Quarterly* 119, no. 4 (2020): 685–99. https://doi.org/10.1215/00382876-8663591.

Simpson, Audra. "Whither Settler Colonialism?" *Settler Colonial Studies* 6, no. 4 (2016): 438–45. https://doi.org/10.1080/2201473X.2015.1124427.

Simpson, Leanne Betasamosake. *As We Have Always Done: Indigenous Freedom Through Radical Resistance*. University of Minnesota Press, 2017.

Simpson, Leanne Betasamosake. *Dancing On Our Turtle's Back: Stories of Nishnaabeg Re-Creation, Resurgence and a New Emergence*. Arbeiter Ring Publishing, 2011.

Starblanket, Gina, and Heidi Kiiwetinepinesiik Stark. "Towards a Relational Paradigm—Four Points for Consideration: Knowledge, Gender, Land, and Modernity." In *Resurgence and Reconciliation: Indigenous-Settler Relations and Earth Teachings*, edited by Michael Asch, John Borrows, and James Tully. University of Toronto Press, 2018.

Thobani, Sunera. *Exalted Subjects: Studies in the Making of Race and Nation in Canada*. University of Toronto Press, 2007.

Truth and Reconciliation Commission of Canada (TRC). *Honouring the Truth, Reconciling for the Future: Summary of the Final Report of the Truth and Reconciliation Commission of Canada*. Truth and Reconciliation Commission of Canada, 2015. https://ehprnh2mwo3.exactdn.com/wp-content/uploads/2021/01/Executive_Summary_English_Web.pdf.

Veracini, Lorenzo. "Colonialism, Frontiers, Genocide: Civilian-Driven Violence in Settler Colonial Situations." In *Civilian-Driven Violence and the Genocide of Indigenous Peoples in Settler Societies*, edited by Mohamed Adhikari. Routledge, 2021.

Veracini, Lorenzo. *Settler Colonialism: A Theoretical Overview*. Palgrave Macmillan, 2010.

Veracini, Lorenzo. *The Settler Colonial Present*. Palgrave Macmillan, 2015.

Walia, Harsha. *Border and Rule: Global Migration, Capitalism, and the Rise of Racist Nationalism*. Fernwood Publishing, 2021.

Wilson-Raybould, Jody. *True Reconciliation: How to Be a Force for Change*. McClelland & Stewart, 2022.

Wolfe, Patrick. "Settler Colonialism and the Elimination of the Native." *Journal of Genocide Research* 8, no. 4 (2006): 387–409. https://doi.org/10.1080/14623520601056240.

Yesno, Riley. "Is Reconciliation Dead? Maybe Only Government Reconciliation Is." *Toronto Star*, February 19, 2020. https://www.thestar.com/opinion/contributors/is-reconciliation-dead-maybe-only-government-reconciliation-is/article_6220f19a-2417-53b3-81f2-5d39f7224c57.html.

PART ONE

Decolonizing Education Processes

On Codifying the Traditional Laws of Indigenous Nations in Canada

Leo Baskatawang

LONG BEFORE COLONIZATION, INDIGENOUS NATIONS IN Canada and around the world lived in organized societies governed by their own laws. In fact, when French merchants and settlers first encountered Indigenous Peoples on Turtle Island, or what is now referred to as North America, about five hundred years ago, they conducted themselves in accordance with local customs and laws. Soon after, the Atlantic coast became a hotbed of international diplomacy, as several treaties were negotiated between different Indigenous and European nations. Of these treaties, the Kaswentha—which was originally negotiated between the Haudenosaunee and the Dutch—is the most significant since it was formally recognized by other Indigenous and European nations as a binding agreement, as well as being a template for establishing peaceful relations with the *other*.[1] Following Britain's victory in the Seven Years' War, however, colonial governors on Turtle Island were spurred on by their regent, King George III, to "make, constitute, and ordain Laws... as near as may be agreeable to the Laws of England" on their respective settlements and jurisdictions.[2]

As European laws took root, Indigenous laws and perspectives were displaced. Then, in the nineteenth century, after many Indigenous nations had already been hit hard by famine and disease, it became public policy to assimilate the "Vanishing Indian."[3] In Canada, this can be most clearly observed through the passing of the *Indian Act*, which imposed severe restrictions on Indigenous communities and governance practices, as well as mandated the Indian residential school system. The impact these policies have had on Indigenous nations and peoples has been devastating, but throughout those dark times, Indigenous Peoples have held fast to their traditional practices and laws for brighter days ahead. Indeed, as Canada now attempts to reconcile its racist history, there is an opportunity to do that by recognizing and affirming the traditional laws of Indigenous nations. This chapter will briefly examine Audre Lorde's "master's tools" construct, as well as provide a historical overview of the relationship between Indigenous nations and Canada, and then discuss efforts being undertaken by the Anishinaabe Nation in Treaty 3 to have their education law recognized and affirmed by the federal government as an act of reconciliation.

When Audre Lorde, who is a self-described Black lesbian, mother, warrior, and poet, famously declared in 1979 that "the master's tools will never dismantle the master's house," she iterated a new form of an old debate that rippled across several academic disciplines.[4] The debate was one that asked how marginalized groups of people—whether they are people of colour, disabled, sexually diverse, or gender nonconforming—can effectively address systemic injustice. From an Indigenous perspective, Lorde's metaphor provided a discursive framework with which to posit our ideas on how to best decolonize our communities. Indeed, many Indigenous scholars, particularly those engaged with cultural resurgence literature such as Leanne Simpson, Glen Coulthard, and Taiaiake Alfred, seem to agree with Lorde that the best way to decolonize our communities is to *use or develop our own tools* to dismantle the "master's house."[5]

Their argument is based on the fact that colonial and state authorities have effectively refused to address the myriad problems that exist within Indigenous communities as a result of the imposition of laws and policies that only serve to benefit the state and its most wealthy citizens. On the other hand, some scholars have also argued that the "master's house" can be infiltrated and dismantled from the inside, using the same tools that have been wielded against us, by occupying positions of authority: we can actively engage in changing the laws and policies that affect our communities. Being that neither position is inherently wrong, I question whether dismantling the "master's house" is in fact the task at hand, or if perhaps the house in which we all find ourselves—Canada, that is—just requires some redecorating to better reflect the values of *everyone* who lives here.

The first point to consider in this reformulation of Lorde's thesis is that the idea of dismantling anybody's house flies in the face of the Indigenous epistemologies that espouse the belief that "we are all related," which is predicated on the notion of striving towards a peaceful coexistence with other nations.[6] Secondly, even if the desire to dismantle another nation's house was there, is it even possible? In Canada, it seems obvious that the state and its institutions, for better or worse, are here to stay. That said, one of the primary issues Indigenous nations have been confronted with over the years is that our systems of law and governance have not been recognized by colonial institutions since our laws and systems of governance primarily stem from the oral tradition. In that regard, the lack of recognizable writing makes it nearly impossible for any outsider to understand that any Indigenous laws actually exist. Thus, it is from that perspective that I would suggest that all Indigenous nations in Canada consider undertaking a process of codifying at least some of their laws, particularly those that relate to education, so that they can be recognized and affirmed by the federal, provincial, and municipal governments of Canada. This does not mean that Indigenous nations have to abandon their traditional practices, but it does require us to be open to use whatever tools are available so that we, as Canadians, can all sit in the same house comfortably, with each *other*.[7]

The Consciousness of Colonization

In order to better understand how and why things are the way they are, in terms of the Crown-Indigenous relationship, it would be instructive to locate the roots of Western political philosophy, which forms the foundation of nearly all laws, regulations, and policies within all modern social institutions (whether that might be education, health care, justice, or social services, to name a few). To begin, Lorde's metaphor of the "master's house" has at least some connection to Georg W.F. Hegel's "master-slave" dialectic, properly translated as "Lordship and Bondage," in *Phenomenology of Spirit*, which theorizes an abstract notion of the development of human self-consciousness.[8] According to Hegel, when an individual "consciousness"—which might also represent a national consciousness—meets an "other consciousness," an inevitable "struggle to the death" will ensue at some point over the course of time in order to establish social order.[9] Thus, when one so-called consciousness vanquishes the other, one becomes the "master," the other a "slave." While influential in its own right, Hegel's idea of human consciousness seems to build off the work of his forebears, namely Thomas Hobbes and Jean-Jacques Rousseau, the latter of whom argued that all people require a ruler to make the rules for all people to live by.[10]

As for Hobbes, he is the author of *Leviathan*, published in 1651. In that work, Hobbes famously contended that in the "natural state of man," there was "no Knowledge of the face of the Earth; no account of Time; no Arts; no Letters; no Society; and which is worst of all, continuall feare, and danger of violent death; And the life of man, solitary, poore, nasty, brutish, and short."[11] Hobbes goes on to state, "For the savage people in many places of *America*, except the government of small Families, that concord whereof dependeth on naturall lust, have no government at all; and live at this day in that brutish manner, as I said before."[12] While it could be argued that Hobbes and his writings are a product of his time, it must also be acknowledged that his ill-informed ideas continue to hold force today. As one example, in 1991, Judge Allan McEachern declared in his *Delgamuukw v. British Columbia* decision that, because Indigenous Peoples "had no written language, no horses or wheeled vehicles, slavery and starvation was not uncommon, wars with neighbouring peoples were common, and there is no doubt, to quote Hobbs, that aboriginal life in the territory was, at best, 'nasty, brutish and short.'"[13] From this, we can see that Hobbes's writings, as well as other writings from that era, continue to reinforce the erroneous notion that Indigenous Peoples are savages who beckon to be ruled, which was ultimately accepted as truth by colonial authorities and used as justification—via the Doctrine of Discovery and *terra nullius*—to appropriate Indigenous lands for the expansion of the colonial empire.[14]

To this point, I have only briefly outlined a couple of texts that have given form to the "master-slave" dialectic at the forefront of imperial discourse since the middle of the seventeenth century. This timeline is interesting since prior to 1651, and the publication of *Leviathan*, there were no governing documents that related to European laws in the territory now known as Canada. Up to that point, colonial settlers and merchants conducted their business interests in accordance with the prevailing customary laws and practices of the Indigenous Peoples with whom they interacted. One of the definitive elements of Indigenous law from precontact until now has been the application of a pipe ceremony. Indeed, the pipe ceremony has been and continues to be used by many Indigenous nations to sanctify all formal socio-political interactions and economic transactions. As Arthur Ray, Jim Miller, and Frank Tough note in *Bounty and Benevolence*, "ceremonial pipestems and the smoking of tobacco were extremely powerful symbols and acts for many First Nations.... By taking part in this sacred ceremony, the participants committed themselves to telling the truth during the course of diplomatic negotiations."[15]

For many Indigenous nations, then, the smoking of tobacco in a pipe ceremony is a spiritual event symbolizing a sworn oath, a contract or exchange, or what might otherwise be considered a proper act of law. That sentiment appears to be corroborated by Jacques Derrida, who states, "Tobacco is a symbol of... the agreement [*engagement*], of the sworn faith, or the alliance that commits the two parties when they share the two fragments of a *symbolon*, when they must give, exchange, and obligate themselves one to the other."[16] Therefore, being that the pipe ceremony is a highly revered and recognized symbol of honour and justice, when one participates in the smoking of tobacco at such a ceremony, one is obligated to not only speak the truth, but also keep their end of the agreement. And as Derrida dutifully reminds us, "one should accredit, guarantee, and legitimate the discourse... otherwise, one pays with words... by which one understands the words in this case are simulacra, money without value—devalued or counterfeit."[17] In other words, one who breaks their word also breaks their honour.

At the time Hobbes wrote *Leviathan*, colonial settlers and merchants had already been engaging with and practising Indigenous legal protocols for over a century.[18] This is significant because if the newcomers had decided to ignore or otherwise violate Indigenous law, it is likely they would have been stranded and left to their own devices on a forbidding land they knew nothing about. If the violation had been egregious enough, there may have even been hostile conflict that would have precluded any future trade negotiations. That said, over the century that the newcomers were being acclimated to the land as well as to Indigenous trade practices, the negotiations were most often conducted honourably and were mutually beneficial.[19] But as more trading posts were established and more boats crossed the ocean, the balance of trade eventually tipped in favour of the newcomers. There is little doubt that the shift in balance enabled colonial settlers to establish permanent settlements and introduce their systems of governance and law. To that point, the first piece of legislation was a Royal Charter issued by King Charles II in 1670, which notably was written only a few years after the publication of Hobbes's *Leviathan*.

The Royal Charter of 1670 was designed to incorporate the Hudson's Bay Company (HBC) and provide the company with monopoly trading rights over a vast tract of land, commonly referred to as Rupert's Land. Although the monopoly trading privilege ultimately proved to be unenforceable, the true significance of the Royal Charter is the British Crown's illegitimate granting of title and benefit of Indigenous lands to the HBC.[20] In effect, the Royal Charter of 1670 granted the HBC the authority to operate as a de facto government of Rupert's Land, a right that was enjoyed for nearly two hundred years, before the company was forced to relinquish its authority according to *Rupert's Land Act, 1869*. The transfer in authority was triangulated, such that the HBC first surrendered its Royal Charter to the British Crown, who then admitted the vast territory of Rupert's Land to Canada under section 146 of the *Constitution Act, 1867*, on the condition that the Canadian government would negotiate treaties with the various Indigenous nations whose land the Royal Charter occupied. Canada then compensated the HBC with £300,000 while also allowing the company to retain a fraction of its rights and privileges.

In describing the circumstances surrounding the Royal Charter of 1670, I have tried to show how the British Crown, and later the Canadian government, had literally written over Indigenous laws, as well Indigenous rights and title to the land, with their own system of law. This process continued with the signing of the Numbered Treaties, which served to validate Canada's claim to all rights and title to the land. It is interesting to note, however, that despite challenging circumstances around treaty negotiations, Indigenous nations still managed to drive a hard bargain. This is evidenced by the fact that Wemyss Simpson, who served as the commissioner for the negtiation of Treaties 1 and 2, tried to negotiate a treaty with the Anishinaabe at the Northwest Angle of the Lake of the Woods in 1871 but was unable to reach an agreement. As a result, Simpson was forced to go back to Winnipeg empty-handed, but he ultimately found success negotiating Treaty 1 with the Anishinaabe and Swampy Cree at Lower Fort Garry later in 1871. The following year, Simpson negotiated Treaty 2 with another band of Anishinaabe at Manitoba Post, which was an HBC trading post on the southwest side of Lake Manitoba.[21]

Although these treaty negotiations, as well as the others that followed, were conducted in accordance with Indigenous legal protocols, such as the invocation of kinship relations, as well as having a pipe ceremony, the treaties have ultimately become distinguished by their written text. While the written text was undoubtedly intended to be a more precise account of the agreement, it has proven to be a woefully insufficient representation of truth, especially as a sole representation of truth, as it is more or less regarded today. Over the years, many Indigenous leaders and scholars have criticized the government's reliance on the written word, arguing that what was *said* at the negotiations is just as important as what was written down.[22] However, it is worth noting that Alexander Morris—who was the successor of Wemyss Simpson and commissioner for Treaties 3 through 6—made detailed notes of what was said at the negotiations and published the transcripts in his book *The Treaties of Canada*, precisely to have a documented record to look back on in case there arose any disagreement about the treaties, so that they may be fulfilled in good faith.[23]

According to Morris, the principle features of the treaty from the government's perspective were "the relinquishment to Her Majesty of the Indian title; the reserving of tracts of land for the Indians, sufficient to furnish 160 acres of land to each family of five; providing for the maintenance of schools, and prohibition of the sale of intoxicating liquors on the reserves, a present of three dollars per head to the Indians and the payment to them of an annuity of three dollars per head."[24] While that may be true, on the other hand, it is also true that Indigenous leadership understood that the value of the land was so great that it could not possibly be bought with cash. Indeed, during the Treaty 3 negotiations, Chief Mawedopenais of Rainy River, Ontario, said to Morris, "The sound of the rustling of the gold is under my feet where I stand; we have a rich country; it is the Great Spirit who gave us this; where we stand upon is the Indians' property, and belongs to them."[25] Beyond its poetic symbolism, Mawedopenais's statement signifies his understanding not only of the land's economic value but also of the concept of property ownership. As such, there is enough reason to suggest that Indigenous leadership actually approached the treaty negotiations with an aim of securing rights—such as the right to education—that would enable them to carry on their traditional ways of life or to participate in the practices of Western society if they so wished.

Renewing and Revitalizing the Treaty Relationship

Being that disastrous education policy has come to define the wretched socio-economic conditions of so many Indigenous communities in Canada, it is worth investigating what the education clause has done for the Indigenous nations who negotiated the Numbered Treaties versus what *could* have been done. To begin, the education clause in the Numbered Treaties is a nondescript line that states, "And further, Her Majesty agrees to maintain schools for instruction in such reserves hereby made as to Her Government of Her Dominion of Canada may seem advisable whenever the Indians of the reserve shall desire it."[26] Of the two key elements to consider, one is the notion that schools will be maintained by the federal government; the other is that the schools will be built whenever the "Indians ... shall desire it." Many Indigenous Elders and scholars have long argued that the Treaty Right to education was not only meant to ensure that all education, including post-secondary education, would be paid and provided for by the Canadian government, but that the form and content of such education would also be determined by Indigenous nations themselves.[27] On that note, the Supreme Court of Canada (SCC) has developed a compendium of treaty interpretation principles that state,

> Treaties should be liberally construed and ambiguities or doubtful expressions should be resolved in favour of the aboriginal signatories; The goal of treaty interpretation is to choose from among the various possible interpretations of common intention the one which best reconciles the interests of both parties at the time the treaty was signed; In searching for the common intention of the parties, the integrity and honour of the Crown is presumed; In determining the signatories' respective understanding and intentions, the court must be sensitive to the unique cultural and linguistic differences between the parties; The words of the treaty must be given the sense which they would naturally have held for the parties at the time; A technical or contractual interpretation of treaty wording should be avoided; Treaty rights of aboriginal peoples must not be interpreted in a static or rigid way. They are not frozen at the date of signature. The interpreting court must update treaty rights to provide for their modern exercise. This involves determining what modern practices are reasonably incidental to the core treaty right in its modern context.[28]

While it is clear from these principles that the SCC thinks that an Indigenous perspective should be included in the interpretation of any Treaty Right, the Government of Canada has been unwilling to observe the opinion of its highest courts on this issue. Indeed, from the state's perspective, the education clause in the Numbered Treaties was taken to mean that schools would only be built on reserves if it seemed "advisable" to the state. While it is difficult to imagine a situation where it is inadvisable to build a school in any community, Indigenous leaders have long contended that the education clause was meant to ensure that their people would receive an education whenever they desire it, and that the state would pay for it, regardless of the advisability of that undertaking. Nevertheless, it has been demonstrated that many of today's socio-economic and political problems within Indigenous communities can be traced back to the state's narrow view of treaty interpretation.[29]

Around the same time that the Government of Canada was negotiating Treaty 6, they had also tabled and passed a new piece of legislation in 1876 called the *Indian Act*, which consolidated previous pieces of legislation. The *Indian Act* was designed to grant the Canadian government exclusive authority over "Indians and Lands Reserved for Indians" under section 91(24) of the *Constitution Act, 1867*. This piece of legislation was unilaterally imposed, without any consultation from the "Indians" it was intended to concern. As such, since its inception, the *Indian Act* has been terribly harmful to Indigenous identity and traditional practices. In addition to restricting who can claim "Indian status," the *Indian Act* has also been used to ban traditional ceremonies such as the Potlatch and the Sundance, as well as force Indigenous Peoples to obtain a "pass" permit to leave their reserves, and, perhaps most importantly, it was used to impose compulsory attendance of Indigenous children at residential schools. While most of these provisions have since been amended, the *Indian Act* continues to dictate who is eligible for registration of so-called Indian status. With regard to the provision of compulsory attendance at residential schools, the Government of Canada ironically excused this decision in a 2008 apology given by former Prime Minister Stephen Harper, stating that residential schools were intended to "meet [the state's] obligations to educate aboriginal children."[30] Although Stephen Harper did not explicitly say as much, it seems that the obligations he spoke of referred to the education clause in the Numbered Treaties. From that perspective, it seems that the residential school system was the Government of Canada's way of fulfilling the Treaty Right to education.

The residential school system stands as one of the most heinous policies ever perpetrated against a human population. The legacy of the residential school system has been extensively researched and studied, so I will keep my discussion of it brief.[31] The system was designed to give the state the authority to forcefully remove Indigenous children from their homes, strip them of their cultural identity, and assimilate them to the norms and values of settler colonial society. In addition to that, many children were raped and murdered by the very people who were tasked to teach and protect them. Indeed, the conditions were so terrible that often children were compelled to run away in the middle of winter, sometimes freezing to death trying to get back home.[32] Suffice it to say, the residential school system was far from anything Indigenous nations had imagined when they secured a Treaty Right to education; nor did they have any choice in the matter. In short, it was a unilateral policy financed by the federal government, carried out by law enforcement, such as the RCMP, and administered by Christian churches, with the singular goal to eliminate "Indians" and their Treaty Rights from the legislative ledgers.

As a result of the harms and abuses that were suffered in the residential school system, the Government of Canada reached a settlement agreement in 2006. At over five billion dollars, the Indian Residential Schools Settlement Agreement is one of the largest class action settlements in Canadian history. The settlement has five components: the Common Experience Payment; Independent Assessment Process; the Truth and Reconciliation Commission (TRC); Commemoration; and Health and Healing Services. With regard to the TRC, after travelling to many parts of Canada in which they hosted seven national events, alongside dozens of other local events, and listening to approximately 6,500 witnesses over a six-year period, the commissioners published a *Final Report* in 2015. In addition to exhaustively documenting the truth of the residential school system from survivors, family members, communities, as well as residential school staff and administrators, the *Final Report* included ninety-four Calls to Action. The Calls to Action were met with great fanfare across the country, including from former Prime Minister Justin Trudeau, who actively campaigned on answering those calls. Unfortunately, the Government of Canada's approach to dealing with the Calls to Action has been to itemize each one, as if it were a list of goods that can be bought at the supermarket and checked off as done.[33] The fact is, the Calls to Action are very much intertwined and interrelated, which signifies that the process of reconciliation itself requires constant participation and renewal if the overarching goal of social justice is to be achieved.

Beyond the work of the TRC, another important development in the mission to reconcile Crown and Indigenous relations in Canada has been the passage of Bill C-15: *An Act Respecting the United Nations Declaration on the Rights of Indigenous Peoples* in the House of Commons. This is significant because the United Nations Declaration on the Rights of Indigenous Peoples (UNDRIP) recognizes Indigenous Peoples' inherent right to self-determination. Article 4, for example, states that Indigenous Peoples "have the right to autonomy or self-government in matters relating to their internal and local affairs, as well as ways and means for financing their autonomous functions."[34] The UNDRIP also recognizes that "Indigenous peoples have the right to maintain and strengthen their distinct political, legal, economic, social and cultural institutions, while retaining their right to participate fully, if they so choose, in the political, economic, social and cultural life of the State."[35] Given that Indigenous nations understand the treaty relationship in accordance with their own principles and systems of law, these articles provide a foundation to enact and enforce those laws in matters relating to the treaty. Article 37 states that Indigenous nations have the right "to the recognition, observance, and enforcement of treaties" and that states must "honour and respect such treaties, agreements, and other constructive arrangements."[36] Moreover, article 18 of the UNDRIP further provides that "Indigenous peoples have the right to participate in decision-making in matters which would affect their rights, through representatives chosen by themselves in accordance with their own procedures, as well as to maintain and develop their own indigenous decision-making institutions."[37]

With regard to education, the UNDRIP states that "Indigenous peoples have the right to establish and control their educational systems and institutions providing education in their own languages, in a manner appropriate to their cultural methods of teaching and learning."[38] Given that the Government of Canada has failed to develop an education policy that respects the cultures of Indigenous Peoples, the time has come, and the impetus is here, to provide Indigenous nations the opportunity to establish their own education systems, in accordance with their own laws and principles, in a way that is enshrined in Canadian law. Indeed, if the

Government of Canada acts in good faith with the principles set out in the related UNDRIP legislation as it has publicly committed to do, it will provide a strong foundation with which to properly implement Treaty Rights as well as fulfill the TRC's ninety-four Calls to Action.

The Government of Canada's commitment to reconciliation with Indigenous Peoples and nations is an important step in the healing process of this longstanding relationship. In making that commitment, it seems that the Canadian government might finally recognize the severity of the harms done to Indigenous Peoples and that there is a genuine political interest to atone for the government's negligence and gross misconduct. If that is true, then this could be an unprecedented opportunity for Indigenous nations in Canada to reclaim control over the governance of their communities in a way that has not been enjoyed since the introduction of the *Indian Act*, especially when it comes to education. In order for that to happen, however, Indigenous nations should accept that they have a responsibility to present their laws in a way that can be recognized and understood by Canadian governments, which is to say that at least some of those laws ought to be written down. That said, education has to be one of those laws that is recognized and understood, particularly *because* of how harmful Canadian education policies have been to Indigenous Peoples in the past. It should be understood, however, that there is a prevailing sentiment among some Indigenous Peoples that they owe the Canadian government nothing and that there is no good reason to trust the government. However, from my perspective, I do not see how we, as Canadians, can coexist as a society in a spirit of peace and goodwill, as stated in the treaties, if we do not learn to effectively communicate with each other.

I submit here that we, as Indigenous Peoples, would do much better to look towards the future, and to the well-being of our children, and our children's children, as opposed to giving in to the hurt and angry feelings from our past. In my home territory, my nation, the Anishinaabe Nation in Treaty 3, has begun the process of codifying its education law, Kinamaadiwin Inaakonigewin. The hope within our nation is that our written education law will not only articulate how we understand our Treaty Right to education and how we wish to administer our own education system, but it will also become officially recognized and affirmed by Canadian governments in the spirit of reconciliation.

I have written more extensively on the Treaty #3 Education Law in my book *Reclaiming Anishinaabe Law*, but for the purpose of this particular contribution, I will just say that the law, as presently constituted, is quite detailed in terms of articulating where the authority of the law comes from, what Treaty 3 education standards and local curriculum will be, and how the education system will be financed.[39] In terms of authority, the Treaty #3 Education Law states that education is a matter of sacred law, where the legislative, executive, and administrative jurisdiction of education is vested in the membership of the Anishinaabe Nation in Treaty 3, who are the rights holders and are represented through the leadership of the Grand Chief of the Grand Council Treaty #3. Beyond that, the law also states that our right to education was recognized and affirmed by the signatories of Treaty 3, and that corresponding case laws and international declarations such as UNDRIP further recognize our right to administer our own education system.

The Treaty #3 Education Law also has a section dedicated to our language, stating that Anishinaabemowin will be the official language of work, and that all staff and administrators will use the language to the greatest extent possible, including using it as the language of classroom instruction.[40] This objective will undoubtedly be difficult to implement, considering the deleterious effects that the residential school system has had on our population, but it is one that is integral to the revitalization of our language. Similarly, the education law also states that traditional ceremonies and practices will be taught in our education system. This process includes the teaching of our oral tradition and local history, as well as land-based practices such as fishing and hunting, which includes teachings about living sustainably off the land. Finally, the Treaty #3 Education Law also provides that our education standards will either meet or exceed provincial standards, and that our expectation is that the funding for the education system will comply with those standards.[41]

From our perspective, that would be in accordance with the spirit and intent of the treaty our ancestors signed, as well as in view of the Canadian government's public commitment to reconciliation. As a nation, we understand that there will likely be many challenges ahead. As such, we can only hope that the Liberal minority government of Mark Carney will work to honour the promises former Prime Minister Justin Trudeau made when he said, "A respectful, cooperative partnership is not only possible, it is a sacred responsibility inherited to us from past generations and entrusted to us by future ones. I promise you that I will be your partner in the years to come and hope that you will be mine. We have much work to do together."[42] It is essential that the prime minister and future Canadian governments are taken to task on that commitment. In more ways than one, the peace and goodwill of the house we all live in depends on it.[43]

All Indigenous nations have an inherent right to education. It is a right that is recognized and affirmed by Canada's Constitution and further acknowledged by the UNDRIP. Moreover, it is a right that bestows the authority upon Indigenous nations to ensure that the education provided to their people is culturally relevant and right. Although systems of writing have displaced oral laws, those laws have not been forgotten. What was once there is still there, even if as palimpsest. That said, many Indigenous nations are now picking up the weapon of their oppressor, the pen, and writing back, seeking justice and restitution for harms done. Canada has publicly committed to the process of reconciliation, and the world is watching. Will it answer calls to action the right way, or will it risk having its house dismantled?

Notes

1 Simpson, *Mohawk Interruptus*, 32.

2 *Royal Proclamation of 1763*, reprinted in R.S.C. 1985, App. II, No. 1.

3 LaRocque, *When the Other Is Me*, 125–27.

4 Lorde, *Sister Outsider*, 107.

5 See Simpson, *As We Have Always Done*; Coulthard, *Red Skin, White Masks*; Alfred, *Peace, Power, Righteousness*.

6 Mills, "What Is a Treaty?," 244. See also Wilson, *Research Is Ceremony*.

7 The concept of "othering" is most commonly understood in post-colonial discourse as a means "of establishing the binary separation of the colonizer and colonized and asserting the naturalness and primacy of the colonizing culture and world view." See Ashcroft, Griffiths, and Tiffin, *Postcolonial Studies*, 186. See also LaRocque, *When the Other Is Me*.

8 See Hegel, "Lordship and Bondage."

9 I would caution here that Hegel's conception of struggle and conflict, such that there is an inevitable death or power imbalance between two parties, stands in contrast to many Indigenous nations' ways of dealing with conflict, to the extent that consultation and compromise are core principles of conflict resolution—precisely in order to preserve harmony and balance in social order. See Johnston, *Ojibway Heritage*, 19.

10 See Rousseau, *The Social Contract*.

11 See Hobbes, *Leviathan*, 104. Original spelling retained in quotations.

12 See Hobbes, *Leviathan*, 105. Italics in original.

13 See *Delgamuukw v. British Columbia*, 1991 CanLII 2372 (BC SC). The misspelling of "Hobbes" is true to the original.

14 For more on this history, especially as it relates to the Doctrine of Discovery, see Newcomb, *Pagans in the Promised Land.*
15 Ray, Miller, and Tough, *Bounty and Benevolence*, 92.
16 Derrida, *Given Time*, 111–12.
17 Derrida, *Given Time*, 61.
18 See Parsons, "Natives, Newcomers, and *Nicotiana*."
19 Ray, *Indians in the Fur Trade*, 65–68.
20 See Ray, Miller, and Tough, *Bounty and Benevolence*, 46.
21 For more on this history, see Craft, *Breathing Life into the Stone Fort Treaty*.
22 Rotman, "Taking Aim at the Canons of Treaty Interpretation."
23 Morris, *The Treaties of Canada*.
24 Morris, *The Treaties of Canada*, 31.
25 Morris, *The Treaties of Canada*, 62.
26 Morris, *The Treaties of Canada*, 323.
27 See Cardinal, *The Rebirth of Canada's Indians*, 35; Stonechild, *The New Buffalo*, 115; Henderson, "Treaties and Indian Education," 249.
28 *R. v. Marshall*, [1999] 3 S.C.R. 456 (*Marshall I*).
29 See Coyle, "As Long as the Sun Shines," 41.
30 Government of Canada, "Indian Residential Schools Statement of Apology."
31 For a comprehensive account of the residential school system in Canada, see TRC, *Honouring the Truth, Reconciling for the Future*; see also Milloy, *A National Crime*; Miller, *Shingwauk's Vision*; Regan, *Unsettling the Settler Within*.
32 For a graphic representation of one student's journey home, see Downie, *Secret Path*.
33 To see the Government of Canada's progress on the TRC's Calls to Action, visit Indigenous Watchdog's status updates online at https://www.indigenouswatchdog.org/2022/04/05/trc-calls-to-action-status-may-13-2022/.
34 United Nations, "United Nations Declaration on the Rights of Indigenous Peoples" (UNDRIP), Article 4.
35 United Nations, UNDRIP, Article 5; Article 27.
36 United Nations, UNDRIP, Article 37 (1).
37 United Nations, UNDRIP, Article 18.
38 United Nations, UNDRIP, Article 14 (1).
39 Although a draft version of the Treaty #3 Education Law has been composed and submitted to Grand Council Treaty #3—the traditional government of the Anishinaabe Nation in Treaty 3—it has yet to be approved and ratified. For more information on the Treaty #3 Education Law, see Baskatawang, *Reclaiming Anishinaabe Law*.
40 Baskatawang, *Reclaiming Anishinaabe Law*, 163.
41 Baskatawang, *Reclaiming Anishinaabe Law*, 165.
42 Assembly of First Nations (AFN) Special Chiefs Assembly, December 8, 2015.
43 Borrows, *Freedom and Indigenous Constitutionalism*, 51.

Sources

Alfred, Taiaiake, *Peace, Power, Righteousness: An Indigenous Manifesto*. Oxford University Press, 1999.

Ashcroft, Bill, Gareth Griffiths, and Helen Tiffin. *Postcolonial Studies: The Key Concepts*. Routledge, 2013.

Baskatawang, Leo. *Reclaiming Anishinaabe Law: Kinamaadiwin Inaakonigewin and the Treaty Right to Education*. University of Manitoba Press, 2023.

Borrows, John. *Freedom and Indigenous Constitutionalism*. University of Toronto Press, 2016.

Cardinal, Harold. *The Rebirth of Canada's Indians*. Hurtig Publishers, 1977.

Coulthard, Glen S. *Red Skin, White Masks: Rejecting the Colonial Politics of Recognition*. University of Minnesota Press, 2014.

Coyle, Michael. "As Long as the Sun Shines: Recognizing That Treaties Were Intended to Last." In *The Right Relationship: Reimagining the Implementation of Historical Treaties*, edited by John Borrows and Michael Coyle. University of Toronto Press, 2017.

Craft, Aimée. *Breathing Life into the Stone Fort Treaty: An Anishinabe Understanding of Treaty One*. Purich Publishing, 2013.

Delgamuukw v. British Columbia, 1991 CanLII 2372 (BC SC).

Derrida, Jacques. *Given Time: I. Counterfeit Money*. Translated by Peggy Kamuf. University of Chicago Press, 1992.

Downie, Gord. *Secret Path*. Simon & Schuster, 2016.

Government of Canada. "Indian Residential Schools Statement of Apology—Prime Minister Stephen Harper." 2008. https://www.rcaanc-cirnac.gc.ca/eng/1100100015677/1571589339246.

Hegel, Georg Wilhelm. "Lordship and Bondage." In *The Phenomenology of Mind*. Dover Publications, 2003 / 1807.

Henderson, James Youngblood. "Treaties and Indian Education." In *First Nations Education in Canada: The Circle Unfolds*, edited by Marie Battiste and Jean Barman. UBC Press, 1995.

Hobbes, Thomas. *Leviathan*. Dutton, 1950 / 1651.

Johnston, Basil. *Ojibway Heritage*. McClelland & Stewart, 1987.

LaRocque, Emma. *When the Other Is Me: Native Resistance Discourse 1850–1990*. University of Manitoba Press, 2010.

Lorde, Audre. *Sister Outsider: Essays and Speeches*. Crossing Press, 1984.

Miller, J.R. *Shingwauk's Vision: A History of Native Residential Schools*. University of Toronto Press, 1996.

Milloy, John. *A National Crime: The Canadian Government and the Residential School System, 1879 to 1986*. University of Manitoba Press, 1999.

Mills, Aaron. "What Is a Treaty? On Contract and Mutual Aid." In *The Right Relationship: Reimagining the Implementation of Historical Treaties*, edited by John Borrows and Michael Coyle. University of Toronto Press, 2017.

Morris, Alexander. *The Treaties of Canada with the Indians of Manitoba and the North-West Territories: Including the Negotiations on which They Were Based, and Other Information Relating Thereto*. Belfords, Clarke & Company, 1880.

Newcomb, Steven. *Pagans in the Promised Land*. Fulcrum Publishing, 2008.
Parsons, Christopher. "Natives, Newcomers, and Nicotiana: Tobacco in the History of the Great Lakes Region." In *French and Indians in the Heart of North America, 1630–1815*, edited by Robert Englebert and Guillaume Teasdale. Michigan State University Press, 2013.
R. v. Marshall, [1999] 3 S.C.R. 456 (Marshall 1).
Ray, Arthur J. *Indians in the Fur Trade: Their Roles as Trappers, Hunters, and Middlemen in the Lands Southwest of Hudson Bay, 1660–1870*. University of Toronto Press, 1998 / 1974.
Ray, Arthur J., Jim Miller, and Frank Tough. *Bounty and Benevolence: A History of Saskatchewan Treaties*. McGill-Queen's University Press, 2000.
Regan, Paulette. *Unsettling the Settler Within: Indian Residential Schools, Truth Telling, and Reconciliation in Canada*. UBC Press, 2010.
Rotman, Leonard. "Taking Aim at the Canons of Treaty Interpretation in Canadian Aboriginal Rights Jurisprudence." *University of New Brunswick Law Journal* 46 (1997): 11–50
Rousseau, Jean-Jacques. *The Social Contract*. Hafner, 1951 / 1762.
Royal Proclamation of 1763, reprinted in R.S.C. 1985, App. 11, No. 1.
Simpson, Audra. *Mohawk Interruptus: Political Life Across the Borders of Settler States*. Duke University Press, 2014.
Simpson, Leanne Betasamosake. *As We Have Always Done: Indigenous Freedom Through Radical Resistance*. University of Minnesota Press, 2017.
Stonechild, Blair. *The New Buffalo: The Struggle for Aboriginal Post-Secondary Education in Canada*. University of Manitoba Press, 2006.
Truth and Reconciliation Commission of Canada (TRC). *Honouring the Truth, Reconciling for the Future: Summary of the Final Report of the Truth and Reconciliation Commission of Canada*. Truth and Reconciliation Commission of Canada, 2015. https://ehprnh2mwo3.exactdn.com/wp-content/uploads/2021/01/Executive_Summary_English_Web.pdf.
United Nations. "United Nations Declaration on the Rights of Indigenous Peoples." September 13, 2007. https://www.un.org/esa/socdev/unpfii/documents/DRIPS_en.pdf.
Wilson, Shawn. *Research Is Ceremony: Indigenous Research Methods*. Fernwood Publishing, 2008.

Reflections on Anti-Asian Racism and Settler Colonialism in Canadian Universities

Heena B. Mistry

THIS CHAPTER EXPLORES HOW, FOR RACIALIZED SETTLERS, locating one's unique position within local and global histories of colonialism should lie at the root of efforts to address systemic racism and settler colonialism in the Canadian higher education landscape. This means understanding the historical context by which racialized settlers arrived in Canada / Turtle Island. It involves centring one's unique location as a guiding principle in addressing the ways in which one both benefits from and is marginalized within the Canadian settler colonial context. I will discuss the importance of mobilizing scholarship concerning South Asian diasporas to inform policy conversations led by post-secondary institutions that address both anti-Asian racism and settler colonialism as interconnected violences. Responding to both, in the Canadian context, requires conversations about how white supremacy mobilizes anti-Asian racism in service of Indigenous dispossession. The work of scholars such as Sunera Thobani, Renisa Mawani, Harsha Walia, and Nishant Upadhyay provide frameworks for understanding the Canadian university's relationship with the Indigenous communities on whose land it is situated, and the ways in which racialized researchers have participated in Indigenous dispossession. In this chapter, I call on racialized settlers to embed understandings of how anti-Asian racism in Canada is shaped by settler colonialism within scholarship and institutional policy.

Introduction

While many scholars of South Asian descent have critically reflected on their positionality within the settler state of Canada, conversations about anti-Asian racism at Canadian post-secondary institutions have, at times, struggled with understanding their interconnectedness with settler colonialism as a foundational principle of these institutions. This chapter reflects on the responsibilities of South Asians in dismantling settler colonialism in Canada. I turn to historiographical reflections and recent initiatives on Canadian university campuses that interrogate Asian and South Asian positionality to understand how gaps in substantive engagement with settler colonialism in Asian diaspora studies impact anti-racism efforts. The author is a racialized woman of South Asian descent who lives on the territory of the Neutral, Huron-Wendat, Haudenosaunee, and Anishinaabeg, including the Mississaugas of the Credit, within Treaties 3 ¾ (1795), 14, and 19. My family and I have been racialized settlers in different parts of the world for three generations. This history is intertwined with implication in Kenyan, South African, and Canadian colonial projects and displacements, resulting from British colonialism in South Asia. My paternal grandparents, my maternal grandfather, my father, and all his siblings were Gujarati settlers in Kenya and Uganda between the 1930s and 1967.

Critically engaging with question of the South Asian diasporas' positionality within settler colonies and their obligations to the Indigenous communities they lived alongside was a central feature in South Asian diaspora politics in the twentieth century. Frequently, and perhaps overwhelmingly, British Indians argued for their inclusion within the civil and political rights extended to white settlers in states like Canada, Kenya, Tanzania, Australia, South Africa, and New Zealand. At other times, such as in the decade immediately following India's independence in 1947, Prime Minister Jawaharlal Nehru directed Indians overseas to align with local anti-colonial projects on the African continent and elsewhere.[1] Iterations of Nehru's argument would appear periodically among the speeches of other Indian anti-colonial nationalists in the years leading up to 1947 as the global Indian diaspora and freedom fighters within India tried to conceptualize what their relationship to one another would be if India were to decolonize. While on a tour of South Africa in 1924, Indian poet and freedom fighter Sarojini Naidu explicitly called for Indians overseas to form alliances with Black communities in South Africa and in British East African colonies.[2] Both Nehru's and Naidu's calls for Indian alliances with Indigenous Peoples positioned Indian diasporas as "co-inheritors" of these colonies, as a racialized population that had contributed to bringing these areas into colonial modernity through their labour on plantations and colonial infrastructure projects, such as railways.

As a historian of South Asian diaspora and as a university administrator who grapples with the practical applications of this history in my everyday work, I argue for the importance of engaging with the question of South Asian diaspora positionality and obligations to dismantling settler colonialism in both scholarship and practice in the post-secondary education sector. There are several key learnings from this history that inform my practice. One is that we must understand empire as a global process that depended on resource extraction and the management of colonized peoples' labour in multiple sites. Another is how empires mobilized "divide and rule" as a strategy to disrupt solidarity between racialized migrants and Indigenous communities to maintain systems of power that facilitated extraction. A key learning from South Asian diaspora history specifically is the harmful pattern of South Asian diasporic nationalisms mobilizing proximity to whiteness to gain access to settler citizenship rights. When surveying conversations about both racism and settler colonialism hosted at Canadian universities, I notice that discussions about anti-Asian racism rarely engage substantively with Asian diaspora positionality within settler colonialism. This gap persists in administrative structures, strategic planning, and in national dialogues about anti-Asian racism. I argue that considering anti-Asian racism and settler colonialism as interconnected processes is essential if we are to realize aspirations of decolonizing Canadian universities.

The first section of this chapter discusses how siloes that persist in the archives of South Asian diaspora in settler colonies echo challenges in addressing antiracism in the post-secondary sector in Canada. I draw on Lisa Lowe's concept of "archival divide and rule" to theorize and elaborate on this observation. I also draw on important moments in Asian diaspora scholarship in Canada to formulate directions for how to address the intertwined challenges of anti-Asian racism and settler colonialism. The second section reviews three national dialogues about anti-Asian racism and internationalization in the Canadian post-secondary education sector. My goal is to understand how the positionality of Asian diasporas in Canada and their obligations towards dismantling settler colonialism appear in these conversations. My review of these national dialogues will show how challenges persist in engaging Asian Canadian diasporas in the project of dismantling settler colonialism. Finally, I highlight areas of possibility and solidarity.

Thinking Across Archival and Institutional Divide and Rule

One of the main barriers to thinking about antiracism, decolonization, and Indigenization together is that "divide and rule" logic permeates institutions with colonial roots or those that remain embedded within settler colonialism. Lisa Lowe's observations on archival divide and rule (as a reflection of divide and rule administrative logic) can help with theorizing this process as it takes shape in post-secondary institutions located in settler colonial states. In *The Intimacies of Four Continents*, Lowe argues that the imperatives of colonial archives reflect the divide and rule administrative logic that prioritizes the sanitary separation of different facets of global imperialism over convergence and connection. These divisions result in separate and discrete bodies of scholarship about single societies, regions, and peoples. This is despite the fact that, in the example of her study, histories of the Americas, Europe, Asia, and Africa were intimately connected, through shared, ocean-crossing, and mobile histories of people, resources, and power relationships.[3] The archives of British imperialism that are situated in the British Library's India Office Records in central London and the records of the Colonial Office in Kew neatly compartmentalize and divide the history of empire by geography and administrative function.

The divisions of British colonial archives neatly compartmentalize and subdivide colonial paper trails by colony and administrative function, ultimately framing them as separate sets of deeply entangled local and global histories of empire. Examples of these neat compartmentalizations within the National Archives of the United Kingdom at Kew Gardens include the records of the Foreign Office, which administered foreign governments in Britain's informal empire, such as Shanghai and Egypt;

the administration of enslaved peoples in different plantation colonies; West African settlements that facilitated the Middle Passage; the War and Colonial Department, which centrally administered the defence of colonies and the acquisition of new territories through war; and the records of the Treaty and Royal Letter Department, whose function was initially the preparation of formal documents of diplomatic representation and treaty negotiation.[4] Lowe argues that these divisions present and reinforce as separate the European histories and the histories of settler colonialism in the Caribbean and North America, British imperialism and indentured labour migrations in Asia, and transatlantic slavery and colonization on the African continent. Rather than treating the colonial archive as a "stable, transparent collection of facts," she treats these compartmentalized records as "hous[ing] the historically specific technologies of colonial governance for knowing and administering colonized populations."[5] Lowe notes how these compartmentalizations of liberal empire lay at the root of racial taxonomies that colonial officials deployed in denying colonized peoples "readiness" for self-government and liberty, in justifying their elimination or assimilation, and in appropriating their lands, labour, and resources. Furthermore, Lowe notes that those who resisted empire built solidarities and intimacies that worked across groups that were compartmentalized separately in colonial archives. To fully understand the genealogy of modern liberalism, which she argues is a genealogy of colonial divisions and hierarchizing of humanity, scholars must read against the archival grain to find relationships between these compartmentalized histories.[6] This call to action is especially relevant to both a historian and someone working within contemporary colonial institutions that replicate and reinforce these very divisions and hierarchies. The divisions present in colonial archives are, to some extent, present in the modern university's own administrative structures, in which the offices that support or work with students, staff, and faculty from communities who have long been marginalized within or excluded from the university are often separate and made to compete with each other for scarce resources. This includes, but is not limited to, offices and units that lead Indigenization; international student supports; disability justice and antiracism initiatives; equity, diversity, and inclusion; human rights; and sexual and gendered violence prevention and support.

A brief overview of how settler colonialism is discussed in Canadian migration historiography illustrates the persistence of divide and rule archival logics in how we understand the history of Asian diasporas in the Canadian settler state and within institutions like universities, which have colonial foundations. Within historiographies of settler states, "divide and rule" archival logics result in the siloing of historiographies of racialized diaspora, Indigenous Peoples, and white settler society. Because of this, in order to understand the full complexity of racialized settler positionality, scholars must read histories that are often organized into separate narratives alongside each other. Several historians of racialized diaspora have called for this very practice. Historian Laura Madokoro's review of Canadian immigration historiography notes how earlier literature generally "[ignored] the possibility that racialized communities might be settlers in their own right." These works instead emphasized "the contributions of various groups to the development of the Canadian nation."[7] After Bonita Lawrence and Enakshi Dua's 2005 intervention, "Decolonizing Anti-Racism," scholars of settler colonial studies sought to better understand the positionality of non-white immigrants in Canada.[8] Despite these developments, Madokoro notes that studies of migration in Canada still don't extensively question the place of migration in perpetuating settler colonial structures.[9] Some recent efforts to rectify this include the Landscapes of Injustice project, which sought to uncover what happened to Japanese Canadian property after questions arose about the need to consider that unceded Indigenous territory comprised the bulk of the real estate that was formerly owned by many interned Japanese Canadians before the Canadian state confiscated it during their internment.[10] In the introduction of the book that developed from this project, editor Jordan Stanger-Ross notes that "the land that Japanese Canadians owned and occupied in coastal British Columbia was overrun in the 'Great Land Rush' that... transformed vast Indigenous territories and geographies into colonial property," while Japanese Canadians "made their lives within the property regimes of the Canadian state that would betray them" at the moment of their internment during the Second World War.[11]

South Asian scholars have sat with questions about the exploitation of South Asians in settler colonial projects of extraction and settlement for some time, with some recent important contributions. Some of the themes that arise in recent works addressing the relationship between South Asians and settler colonialism in Canada include: 1) South Asian involvement in and resistance to processes of land dispossession, resource extraction, appropriation of knowledge, and genocide;[12]

2) shared experiences between South Asian settlers and Indigenous Peoples of colonialism and racialization; and 3) sites of solidarity and locations where solidarities have and continue to destabilize the settler project. Colonies were sites that brought colonized peoples and colonizers into contact. Scholars such as historian Renisa Mawani, critical ethnic studies scholar Nishant Upadhyay, legal scholar Harsha Walia, and sociologist Sunera Thobani have focused on these interactions.

Before moving ahead, I want to point out that the "South Asian diaspora" is not a unified or homogeneous community. There are vast differences in how these various groups experience the settler colonial state. Relationships with Canadian settler colonialism differ for an upper caste Hindu who arrives as an international student at a U15 university, a Sri Lankan Tamil refugee displaced by war, the descendant of indentured Indo-Guyanese plantation workers, a Kashmiri who was displaced by settler colonial projects located within South Asia, a South Asian Muslim who is the victim of Islamophobia, or a Sikh Canadian whose ancestors were displaced by the Sikh genocide in the 1980s. These communities are variously racialized as threats or model minorities to white settler society.[13] Their diverse experiences offer potential sites of solidarity and understanding in the process of dismantling settler colonialism in Canada. Many of these communities, their ancestors, and their families lived through formal decolonization processes in other parts of the world, sometimes many times over.

Renisa Mawani's work responds to archival divide and rule logics in the Canadian context by detailing how colonial officials in British Columbia worried that encounters, friendships, intimacies, and political alliances between Chinese migrants, Indigenous Peoples, Europeans, and mixed-race populations in BC would subvert plans to build the region into a permanent white settlement colony.[14] Mawani's more recent work on the *Komagata Maru* illustrates how white Canadians used their denial of mobility rights to Indigenous Peoples in Canada to justify the denial of mobility rights to British Indians aboard the *Komagata Maru* through refusing them entry into British Columbia. The *Komagata Maru* incident refers to a chartered ship carrying British Indian passengers that was detained at the Port of Vancouver in 1914 for two months before being turned away. Canadian authorities refused to let the passengers ashore. When the case was taken to the British Columbia Court of Appeal, it proceeded quickly, with the court ruling that the British Indian passengers had no right of entry under either Canadian or British law.[15] At the same time, when middle class Indians became aware of and began closely following the *Komagata Maru* ordeal from across the ocean, they denounced the Canadian government's decision by claiming a caste-rooted racial superiority over Adivasi (South Asian Indigenous) communities in India and Black South Africans. In Mawani's words, while "an anticolonial vernacular of indigeneity connected the Indian and Pacific Oceans, gaining traction in its rebuke of Dominion legalities and imperial policies, ... its circulations did not disrupt racial regimes of power and often worked against the legal and political interests of Indigenous communities." Overall, Mawani's work reveals how whites deployed Indigeneity to exclude Indians from the settler state while Indians deployed Indigeneity to argue for their inclusion in the settler polity.[16]

More recently, scholars have critiqued the assumption that proximity and intimacy between non-European migrants and Indigenous Peoples in Canada necessarily produced solidarity, allyship, or even a shared anticolonial stance. Upadhyay reviews and problematizes South Asians working in extractive industries in Canada, including such industries as canning, logging, and mining. Like Mawani, Upadhyay argues that South Asians in Canada are complicit in the ongoing colonization of Indigenous nations and acknowledges that the settler state "requires the labour of racialized peoples to pursue its colonial-capitalist quests."[17] Unlike Mawani, however, Upadhyay argues that "the Canadian settler economy requires the labour of racialized immigrants to pursue its racial colonial capitalist quests," and that while "race, gender, and class may structurally marginalize the labour of diasporic Indians in these different industries, their labour becomes complicit in settler-colonial processes."[18] Upadhyay's later work clarifies that dominant caste Indian diasporic communities on Turtle Island are complicit in ongoing processes of settler colonialism by breaking down the particularities of how dominant caste South Asians benefit from and often obfuscate their responsibilities to dismantling both caste oppression in South Asia and settler colonialism in North America.[19] Upadhyay echoes Nehru's calls to action in the 1950s, imploring South Asians in Canada to "invest themselves in the formation of Indigenous decolonized nations" and to "unsettle their complicities."[20] However, what this specifically means in practice is unclear.

Harsha Walia's theorization of border imperialism takes a globe-spanning perspective. She notes the hierarchical organization of borders, which are "permeable for white expats, a handpicked immigrant diaspora, and a rich investor class," but which also shut out, immobilize, or expel racialized migrants and refugees.[21] Walia's work captures the complexities through which states enact global border imperialisms by solidifying racialized nationalist identities that illegalize populations deemed "undesirable"; permeating border enforcement through restricting access to social services and education; commodifying migrants or temporary workers with deliberately deflated labour power to guarantee capital accumulation for the wealthy within the state's borders; and discursively characterizing deserving and undeserving migrants and refugees.[22]

The issues to which Mawani, Lowe, Upadhyay, and Walia speak are twofold. First, when one reviews the archives of government administrations, public record offices, private papers, and other records of global South Asian diasporas, the instances of solidarity between South Asian diasporic and Indigenous Peoples are few. There is overwhelmingly more evidence of South Asians arguing for inclusion within the white settler project or colonial projects than of solidarity with Indigenous Peoples. Even anti-colonial projects within South Asia often elevated South Asians above colonized Black and Indigenous Peoples within global racial hierarchies. Historiographies of South Asian diaspora history in the Canadian context demonstrate silences pertaining to the positionality of South Asians in relation to Black and Indigenous liberation, often focusing exclusively on South Asians and sometimes on white settlers.[23] Historically, Black and Indigenous liberation frequently lay firmly outside of the project of South Asian liberation in British colonies.[24]

At the same time, the structural toxicities of colonial rule obstructed solidarity between South Asian migrants and Indigenous communities, and even incentivized division. I argue that while Upadhyay delivers an important call to action to South Asians in Canada to revisit and refuse complicity in the settler colonial project, their work undermines and overlooks the centrality of "divide and rule" as a strategy that the colonial state and colonial capitalism deliberately deployed to drive a wedge between communities and prevent solidarities between racialized diasporic and Indigenous Peoples. This was a deliberate strategy in many other British colonies as well. Historian Amitava Chowdhury's work on the development of Indian diasporic identity in the Caribbean notes the deliberate impact that "the colonial cauldron and imperial governmentality played in creating, guiding, shaping, and limiting expressions of identity."

Specifically, imperial administrators and planters in the Caribbean sought to quickly eliminate hints of solidarity between differently racialized labourers by freely circulating and deploying derogatory stereotypes of the "lazy African" and "hardworking coolie."[25]

Renisa Mawani's examination of sites of racially hetereogeneous contact in British Columbia reveal similar instances of imperial officials deploying and configuring racial difference to eliminate solidarity between Chinese and Indigenous workers. Mawani's study illustrates how the labour demands of global capitalism meant that British Columbia became increasingly racially heterogeneous from the 1860s onward, through the growing presence of Chinese, Japanese, and later South Asian migrants and their proximities to Indigenous Peoples, which posed an ongoing source of anxiety to white settlers.[26] Mawani's examination of BC salmon canneries reveals how, at the work sites of colonial extraction in Canada, "racial distinctions were not pre-existent but were refined and reified through the social constellations of cannery spaces themselves."[27] Cannery owners deliberately exploited racial tensions between workers. White, Indigenous, and Chinese workers were differentiated in where they could work, the wages they were paid, and their living quarters and conditions. Mawani ultimately argues that the production and profitability of British Columbia's salmon canneries was made possible through the dual process of the displacement of Indigenous Peoples and the importation of "an abundant racial workforce that was temporary and exploitable."[28]

Nishant Upadhyay's work makes an important contribution to our understanding of South Asians' positionality as racialized settlers in Canada. However, the main limitation of Upadhyay's examination of Punjabi women who worked at these same canneries mere decades after the Chinese workers in Mawani's study is its refusal to acknowledge how racial taxonomies of divide and rule facilitated both resource extraction and dispossession.[29] After examining how the Punjabi women cannery workers Upadhyay interviewed attempted to position themselves as more reliable and dependable than their Indigenous co-workers, and how in doing so they were complicit in the displacement of Indigenous Peoples, Upadhyay maintains that racialized labouring bodies are "complicit in reproducing the settler state."[30] While we must critically reflect on the positionality and complicity of racialized labour in settler colonial contexts, I argue that it is imperative that scholars aim critique at those who primarily control and profit from land dispossession and resource extraction in the Canadian state. Upadhyay's later work addresses this complexity, and demonstrates "how working class jobs enabled quotidian proximities to the Native Other in a more complex, messy, and relational way of knowing the latter. This proximity produced a distinctive sense of belonging to the Canadian state as many knew more intimately that they were on Native Lands."[31] They explore how Sikh communities in BC have positioned themselves as "'steady workers' in the extractive settler economy, yet forged some intimacies with Indigenous communities" as compared with more privileged and "high skilled" Indians working in the Alberta tar sands, whose interviews they discuss earlier in the book.[32] Although it is not specific to the Canadian context, Madhavi Kale's research on the reallocation of labour in service of empire through the recruitment and dispersion of Indian indentured labour reveals the indispensability of Asian labour migration to the maintenance of sites of colonial resource extraction, particularly through plantations and mines, that primarily benefited planters and factory owners in London.[33] Kale's work further complicates the claims that Upadhyay makes about the indifference between complicities and complexities of South Asian positionality in the Canadian context, as it shows that the managed migration of colonized peoples in service of imperial capital must also be considered when thinking through the positionality of South Asian diasporas whose histories are intertwined with these very processes. While Upadhyay's monumental work reflects critically on South Asian complicity in the Canadian context, it lacks any concrete call to action for South Asian settlers once they do carry out this self-reflection.

Decolonizing Anti-Asian Racism on Campus

The critical historical scholarship discussed in the first section of this chapter must be mobilized in practice within post-secondary institutions, as sites that are deeply rooted in land dispossession, extraction, racial classification, and genocide. How we go about decolonizing Canadian universities must also take into consideration how these institutions and the racialized and Indigenous students, staff, faculty, and community members gaining more access to them fit within global constellations of imperial history and contemporaneity. To do this, this section reviews three national dialogues about anti-Asian racism and internationalization in the post-secondary education sector in Canada to understand how the positionality of Asian diaspora in Canada appears in these conversations and what is said about their obligations towards dismantling settler colonialism. I conclude this section with some areas of possibility, action, and solidarity in tackling the distinct but intertwined violences of anti-Asian racism and settler colonialism.

One of the most monumental contributions to discussions about anti-Asian racism on Canadian campuses was an edited collection organized by R.J. Gilmour, Davina Bhandar, Jeet Heer, and Michael C.K. Ma in 2012 in response to the publication of *Maclean's* magazine's 2010 article "Too Asian: Some Frosh Don't Want to Study at an Asian University."[34] The article stereotyped Asian students at Canadian universities as insular, high-achieving workaholics, lumping diverse groups of students of Asian descent with different experiences of and access to post-secondary education and mobilizing the model minority myth against the myth of meritocracy within academia to argue for limits on their admission.[35] The book-length response to "Too Asian" outlined the longer trajectory of Canadian media that framed Asian students as unfairly competing with white settler students as stretching back to the 1980s and echoing the violent rhetoric of the anti-Asian riots of 1907 in Vancouver, when Asian workers in BC were framed as being unfair competition that undercut white workers by accepting lower wages.[36]

The collection contains two wonderful contributions that place into conversation the histories of Indigenous students and Asian students on Canadian campuses and Asian migration and Indigenous histories in Canadian textbooks. The inclusion of these chapters in *"Too Asian?"* highlights the relationship between the systematic devaluing of Indigenous perspectives and experiences of colonization both in scholarship and in the Canadian university in understanding anti-Asian racism in these spaces. Mary Jane Logan McCallum's chapter argues that the gradual inclusion of Indigenous history and histories of racialized communities within Canadian history textbooks, the overall structure and narrative of the textbooks, continues to centre a narrative of white Euro-Canadian linear progress and expansion over time. Further, in promoting narratives of benevolent multiculturalism, Indigenous Peoples are relegated to introductory chapters or introductory sections of chapters, thereby normalizing white privilege in the university. McCallum argues that this narrative fails to take seriously the presence of, continued occupation by, and sovereignty of Indigenous Peoples. It evades critiques of colonialism that Indigenous scholarship has made, as well as Indigenous thinking about history itself.[37] Adele Perry's chapter reflects on photos of Indigenous and Asian graduates from the University of Manitoba to argue that stories of race at Canadian universities, particularly the presence and experiences of Indigenous and Asian students at Canadian universities, have "no clear upward trajectory" and "no easy upward narrative of ever-greater equality and inclusion." She argues that the photos indicate that people of colour have always been part of Canadian campuses, and that their histories are reflective of histories of colonization, immigration policies, and racial politics.[38]

More recent sector-wide conversations about anti-Asian racism in Canadian post-secondary institutions occurred in the aftermath of a series of shootings that took place in Atlanta, Georgia, on March 16, 2021, in which twenty-one-year-old Robert Aaron Long murdered eight people, six of whom were women of Asian descent. Journalist Michelle Chen argues that the shooting symbolized a pattern of violence that emerged with the onset of the Covid-19 pandemic.[39] During this time, anti-Asian racism on Canadian campuses made headlines, most prominently with a Covid-themed undergraduate party at Queen's University, which was criticized by the editorial board of the *Queen's Journal*, a newspaper run by Queen's students, for its insensitivity towards students and their families who were impacted by the spread of the virus in China.[40] The University of British Columbia (UBC) held a forum online in June 2021, and Toronto Metropolitan University held one in November 2021.[41]

The First National Forum, hosted by UBC and the Canadian Race Relations Foundation, was convened in response to a surge in anti-Asian racism and violence during the Covid-19 pandemic. The opening of this forum featured remarks by Elder Larry Grant, whose father migrated to Canada from Guangdong province in China and whose mother is from the Musqueam Indian Band in Metro Vancouver. Grant's remarks pointed to the shared history of Chinese and Indigenous peoples as "the industrial slaves of Western society." He highlighted the harmfulness of narratives that frame Canada as a champion of democracy and freedom when the benefits of Canadian citizenship are accrued "because of a crime against humanity, that assimilation and denial of citizenship" primarily experienced by Indigenous, Asian, and Black people within Canada.[42]

The report that followed the forum provided important direction for universities and other organizations in addressing anti-Asian racism in ways that took account of its deep connection to settler colonialism in Canada as well as colonialism's global history. The seventh of the forum report's nine major themes noted the intersecting impacts of settler colonialism, systemic racism, and white supremacy in all sectors covered in the forum's different panels. Panelists called for racism and white supremacy to be named and confronted, "not just for the benefit of Asian Canadian communities but in solidarity with other racialized communities and equity-deserving groups."[43] When speaking about grassroots organizing and coalition building, panelists emphasized the importance of "proactively demonstrating solidarity and aiding Indigenous, Black and other racially marginalized groups."[44] One of the main considerations put forward for guiding future direction was the acknowledgement of Canada's reality as a settler colonial state founded on white supremacy, violence, displacement, and exclusion as key roots of anti-Asian racism.[45]

Later in 2021, Toronto Metropolitan University (TMU) held a second national forum that built on discussions that had taken place at UBC. One key panel from that conversation provided important direction in addressing anti-Asian racism that accounted for settler colonialism in the Canadian context and focused on coalition building. An important point that all panelists from this conversation emphasized was the need to avoid the minority myth and the "race to the bottom" as divide and rule tactics that white supremacy within settler states deploys to pit racialized groups against each other. All panelists spoke to the importance of encouraging, supporting, and providing space for Asian, Black, and Indigenous communities on campus to regularly build relationality in consistent ways between each other.[46]

This section builds on historical and historiographical reflections on the overlapping histories of settler colonialism and anti-Asian racism in Canada by considering how both violences are discussed at Canadian universities. In doing so, I hope to illustrate how histories can inform educator and administrator practices. I propose that these conversations offer two main directions for practice. First, efforts to address anti-Asian racism on Canadian post-secondary campuses must build literacy in histories of anti-Asian racism as a component of settler colonialism. Efforts to build literacy about anti-Asian racism must emphasize the model minority myth and other ways that racialized labour is often mobilized in service of colonial extraction. This chapter specifically calls on Asian students, staff, and faculty to recognize and disrupt sites at which we are complicit in the extraction and appropriation of knowledge and resources within the university. Second, efforts to address anti-Asian racism on campus must be in collaboration and solidarity with efforts to decolonize and Indigenize the campus. It is imperative that Asian students, staff, and faculty work with Indigenous students, staff, faculty, and external community members to disrupt processes of extraction to research and learn in just and ethical ways. Doing so ensures that the work of decolonizing the university transforms it into a site of knowledge generation that serves the needs of Indigenous, Black, and racialized communities rather than working to include and assimilate them into an existing institution that was built to extract and appropriate knowledge from those very communities.

Conclusion

In this chapter, I surveyed challenges and gaps in engagement with settler colonialism, focusing on intellectual and practical conversations about Asian settlers and the Canadian settler colonial state. I began by exploring the positionality of Asian diasporas in settler colonies; how resistance to settler colonialism has informed liberation projects in other colonies; the archival siloes that led to silences on Asian settler relationships, solidarities, and frictions with Indigenous communities they lived alongside; the dependence of settler colonialism on racialized migrants to maintain extraction and dispossession; and the importance of a global perspective to understanding past and contemporary ways that colonial violence is deployed against Indigenous Peoples and racialized migrants. I discuss how this historical context helps us critically reflect on recent national forums that worked to understand and dismantle anti-Asian racism at Canadian post-secondary institutions. The scholarly works and national conversations discussed in this chapter demonstrate how racialized settlers can critically reflect on moments when they might be implicated in extraction and land dispossession. On campus, Asian students, scholars, and staff can help ensure that research and learning centres the needs of and is led by Indigenous students, staff, and communities. These calls to action form the practical work of decolonizing a university.

In recent years, these conversations have increasingly advocated for and modelled the importance of engaging with Indigenous scholars and leaders whose critiques of settler colonialism work towards resisting both intellectual and economic extraction from Indigenous nations and Asian diasporas within Canada and build transnational and intercommunity anti-colonial solidarity. Colonialism is a global project, and resistance to it requires that Asian settlers in Canada be in dialogue with First Nations, Métis, and Inuit to imagine a sustainable way forward.

Notes

1 "A Foreign Policy for India," September 13, 1927, in *Selected Works of Jawaharlal Nehru*, vol. 2. In 1927, Nehru published a pamphlet titled "A Foreign Policy for India," which insisted that Indians settled in European colonies build solidarity with Indigenous Peoples in a collaborative effort of anti-colonial resistance as opposed to obstructing decolonization or relegating the Indian diasporic political project to pushing for Indian diasporas' equal rights to white settlers.

2 Vahed, "Race, Empire, and Citizenship." See also South African newspaper *The Cape Argus* for the date March 24, 1924, in Nehru Memorial Museum and Library Manuscripts: Sarojini Naidu Papers. Subject File No. 1. This collection was presented to Naidu by the Indian staff of *The Natal Witness*, printed in Pietermaritzburg.

3 Lowe, *The Intimacies of Four Continents*, 1–5.

4 Banton, *Administering the Empire*, 5–7. For more information, see "Records of the Treaty and Royal Letter Department."

5 Lowe, *The Intimacies of Four Continents*, 4.

6 Lowe, *The Intimacies of Four Continents*, 7.

7 Madokoro, "Peril and Possibility," 1–8. Madokoro notes one SSHRC-funded project that sought to uncover what happened to Japanese Canadian property after Japanese internment during the Second World War and how that project discussed the need to consider that unceded Indigenous territory comprised the real estate owned by many interned Japanese Canadians that was confiscated by the Canadian state.

8 Lawrence and Dua, "Decolonizing Anti-Racism."

9 Madokoro, "Peril and Possibility," 1–8.

10 Madokoro, "On Future Research Directions." See "Landscapes of Injustice" online. See also Stanger-Ross, ed., *Landscapes of Injustice*.

11 Stanger-Ross, ed., *Landscapes of Injustice*, 11–17.

12 For settler colonialism as land dispossession and resource extraction, see Wolfe, "Settler Colonialism and the Elimination of the Native." For settler colonialism as the appropriation of knowledge, see Moody, "Trade-Related Aspects of Traditional Knowledge Protection." Moody defines the term *biopiracy* as "the misappropriation, misuse, and unauthorized utilization and acquisition of the traditional knowledge and/or genetic resources which Indigenous peoples have used, maintained, and developed over generations."

13 Thobani, *Exalted Subjects*.

14 Mawani, *Colonial Proximities*, 4.

15 For more on the *Komagata Maru*, see Mawani, *Across Oceans of Law*; Johnston, *The Voyage of the Komagata Maru*; Kazimi, *Undesirables*.
16 Mawani, "Anticolonial Vernaculars of Indigeneity," 154; Mawani, "Specters of Indigeneity in British Indian Migration, 1914."
17 Upadhyay, "'We'll Sail Like Columbus,'" 11.
18 Upadhyay, *Indians on Indian Lands*, 56.
19 Upadhyay, *Indians on Indian Lands*.
20 Upadhyay, "'We'll Sail Like Columbus,'" 297–99.
21 Walia, *Border and Rule*, 5.
22 Walia, *Border and Rule*, 79–85.
23 Walker, "Forty Years in the Wilderness"; Mongia, *Indian Migration and Empire*; Kazimi, *Undesirables*; Twaddle, *Expulsion of a Minority*; Johnston, *The Voyage of the Komagata Maru*.
24 Vahed and Desai, *The South African Gandhi*; Bose, "New Settler Colonial Histories"; Jackson, *Creole Indigeneity*; Aiyar, "From the America of the Hindu to White Man's Country"; Mistry, "Reconfiguring Empire Gently."
25 Chowdhury, "Exploring an 'Old Verbal Ambiguity,'" 209–12.
26 Mawani, *Colonial Proximities*, 37.
27 Mawani, *Colonial Proximities*, 45.
28 Mawani, *Colonial Proximities*, 40–45.
29 Upadhyay, "'We'll Sail like Columbus,'" 279–80.
30 Upadhyay, "'We'll Sail like Columbus,'" 235.
31 Upadhyay, *Indians on Indian Lands*, 73.
32 Upadhyay, *Indians on Indian Lands*, 73.
33 Kale, *Fragments of Empire*. For more on the relationship between global imperialism, capitalism, and labour migration, see Manjapra, "Plantation Dispossessions," 361–87.
34 Gilmour et al., eds., *"Too Asian?"*; Guo, "The Real Reasons."
35 Findlay and Kohler, "The Enrollment Controversy." This article was originally titled "Too Asian: Some Frosh Don't Want to Study at an Asian University."
36 Ng, "Foreword;" Ghabrial, "Pink Panics, Yellow Perils."
37 McCallum, "Condemned to Repeat?," 75–77.
38 Perry, "Graduating Photos," 55–66.
39 Chen, "'She Could Have Been Your Mother.'"
40 Journal Editorial Board, "Coronavirus Party."
41 National Forum on Anti-Asian Racism, "Final Report." See also Toronto Metropolitan University, "National Forum on Anti-Asian Racism."
42 Elder Grant, "National Forum on Anti-Asian Racism."
43 National Forum on Anti-Asian Racism, "Final Report," 23.
44 National Forum on Anti-Asian Racism, "Final Report," 62.
45 National Forum on Anti-Asian Racism, "Final Report," 69.
46 National Forum on Anti-Asian Racism, "Coalition Building," featuring Sanjay Ruparelia, Jasmeet Bahia, Anny Chen, Dr. Delia Douglas, Pamela Palmater, and Vinita Srivastava.

Sources

Aiyar, Sana. "From the America of the Hindu to White Man's Country." In *Indians in Kenya: The Politics of Diaspora*. Harvard University Press, 2015.

Banton, Mandy. *Administering the Empire, 1801–1968: A Guide to the Records of the Colonial Office in the National Archives of the UK*. Institute of Historical Research and the National Archives of the UK, 2008.

Bose, Neilesh. "New Settler Colonial Histories at the Edges of Empire: 'Asiatics,' Settlers, and Law in Colonial South Africa." *Journal of Colonialism and Colonial History* 15, no. 1 (2014). https://doi.org/10.1353/cch.2014.0017.

Chen, Michelle. "'She Could Have Been Your Mother': Anti-Asian Racism a Year After Atlanta Spa Shootings." *The Guardian*, March 16, 2022. https://www.theguardian.com/us-news/2022/mar/16/anti-asian-racism-atlanta-spa-shootings-anniversary.

Chowdhury, Amitava. "Exploring an 'Old Verbal Ambiguity': East Indian Ethnicity and Identity in Trinidad and the British Caribbean." *Canadian Journal of Latin American and Caribbean Studies* 37, no. 73 (2012): 209–20. https://doi.org/10.1080/08263663.2012.10817033.

Findlay, Stephanie, and Nicholas Kohler. "The Enrollment Controversy." *Maclean's*, November 10, 2010. https://www.macleans.ca/news/canada/too-asian.

Ghabrial, Sarah. "Pink Panics, Yellow Perils, and the Mythology of Meritocracy." In *"Too Asian?": Racism, Privilege, and Post-Secondary Education*, edited by Richard J. Gilmour, Davina Bhandar, Jeet Heer, and Michael C.K. Ma. Between the Lines, 2012.

Gilmour, Richard J., Davina Bhandar, Jeet Heer, and Michael C.K. Ma, eds. *"Too Asian?": Racism, Privilege, and Post-Secondary Education*. Between the Lines, 2012.

Grant, Elder Larry. "National Forum on Anti-Asian Racism: Welcome and Opening Remarks." Forum held June 10, 2021. Posted June 17, 2021, by the University of British Columbia, YouTube, 32:37. https://www.youtube.com/watch?v=ch-UCYhUvXQ.

Guo, Jeff. "The Real Reasons the US Became Less Racist Toward Asian Americans: Washington Post Analysis." *The Oregonian*, December 1, 2026. https://www.oregonlive.com/opinion/2016/12/the_real_reasons_the_us_became.html.

Jackson, Shona. *Creole Indigeneity: Between Myth and Nation in the Caribbean*. University of Minnesota Press, 2012.

Johnston, Hugh J.M. *The Voyage of the Komagata Maru: The Sikh Challenge to Canada's Colour Bar*. Expanded and Fully Revised Edition. UBC Press, 2014.

Journal Editorial Board. "Coronavirus Party Shows Queen's Hasn't Learned from Its Past." *Queen's Journal*, February 7, 2020. https://www.queensjournal.ca/story/2020-02-07/editorials/coronavirus-party-shows-queens-hasnt-learned-from-its-past.

Kale, Madhavi. *Fragments of Empire: Capital, Slavery, and Indian Indentured Labor Migration to the British Caribbean*. University of Pennsylvania Press, 1998.

Kazimi, Ali. *Undesirables: White Canada and the Komagata Maru—an Illustrated History*. Douglas & McIntyre, 2012.
"Landscapes of Injustice, a History All Canadians Should Know." *Landscapes of Injustice*, 2017, accessed March 9, 2023. https://www.landscapesofinjustice.com.
Lawrence, Bonita, and Enakshi Dua. "Decolonizing Anti-Racism." *Social Justice* 32, no. 4 (2005): 120–43.
Lowe, Lisa. *The Intimacies of Four Continents*. Duke University Press, 2015.
Madokoro, Laura. "On Future Research Directions: Temporality and Permanency in the Study of Migration and Settler Colonialism in Canada." *History Compass* 17, no. 1 (2019): 1–6.
Madokoro, Laura. "Peril and Possibility: A Contemplation of the Current State of Migration History and Settler Colonial Studies in Canada." *History Compass* 17, no. 1 (2019): 1–8. https://doi.org/10.1111/hic3.12516.
Manjapra, Kris. "Plantation Dispossessions: The Global Travel of Agricultural Racial Capitalism." In *American Capitalism: New Histories*, edited by Sven Beckert and Christine Desan. Columbia University Press, 2018.
Mawani, Renisa. *Across Oceans of Law: The Komagata Maru and Jurisdiction in the Time of Empire*. Duke University Press, 2018.
Mawani, Renisa. "Anticolonial Vernaculars of Indigeneity." In *Across Oceans of Law: The Komagata Maru and Jurisdiction in the Time of Empire*. Duke University Press, 2018.
Mawani, Renisa. *Colonial Proximities: Crossracial Encounters and Juridical Truths in British Columbia, 1871–1921*. UBC Press, 2010.
Mawani, Renisa. "Specters of Indigeneity in British Indian Migration, 1914." *Law & Society Review* 46, no. 2 (2012): 369–403. https://doi.org/10.1111/j.1540-5893.2012.00492.x.
McCallum, Mary Jane Logan. "Condemned to Repeat? Settler Colonialism, Racism, and Canadian History Textbooks." In *"Too Asian?": Racism, Privilege, and Post-Secondary Education*, edited by Richard J. Gilmour, Davina Bhandar, Jeet Heer, and Michael C.K. Ma. Between the Lines, 2012.
Mistry, Heena. "Reconfiguring Empire Gently: Indians and Imperial Reform, 1917–1947." PhD diss., Queen's University, 2019.
Mongia, Radhika. *Indian Migration and Empire: A Colonial Genealogy of the Modern State*. Duke University Press, 2018.
Moody, Oluwatobiloba. "Trade-Related Aspects of Traditional Knowledge Protection." In *Indigenous Peoples and International Trade: Building Equitable and Inclusive International Trade and Investment Agreements*, edited by John Borrows and Risa Schwartz. Cambridge University Press, 2020.
National Forum on Anti-Asian Racism. "Coalition Building: Dismantling Systems of Oppression to Build Solidarity (Plenary Panel #4)." Posted December 1, 2021, by Faculty of Arts—Toronto Metropolitan University, YouTube, 1:19:11. https://www.youtube.com/watch?v=ufI5M1Tb2XM.
National Forum on Anti-Asian Racism. "National Forum on Anti-Asian Racism Final Report." UBC Faculty Research and Publications, October 31, 2021. http://dx.doi.org/10.14288/1.0421710.

Nehru, Jawaharlal. *Selected Works of Jawaharlal Nehru*, vol. 2. Edited by S. Gopal. B.R. Publishing Corporation, 1974.

Ng, Winnie. "Foreword." In *"Too Asian?": Racism, Privilege, and Post-Secondary Education*, edited by Richard J. Gilmour, Davina Bhandar, Jeet Heer, and Michael C.K. Ma. Between the Lines, 2012.

Perry, Adele "Graduating Photos: Race, Colonization, and the University of Manitoba." In *"Too Asian?": Racism, Privilege, and Post-Secondary Education*, edited by Richard J. Gilmour, Davina Bhandar, Jeet Heer, and Michael C.K. Ma. Between the Lines, 2012.

"Records of the Treaty and Royal Letter Department." Catalogue Description. The National Archives, United Kingdom. Accessed March 9, 2023. https://discovery.nationalarchives.gov.uk/details/r/C637.

Stanger-Ross, Jordan, ed. *Landscapes of Injustice: A New Perspective on the Internment and Dispossession of Japanese Canadians*. McGill-Queen's University Press, 2020.

Thobani, Sunera. *Exalted Subjects: Studies in the Making of Race and Nation in Canada*. University of Toronto Press, 2007.

Toronto Metropolitan University. "National Forum on Anti-Asian Racism." Faculty of Arts, 2021. https://www.torontomu.ca/national-forum-on-anti-asian-racism/.

Twaddle, Michael. *Expulsion of a Minority: Essays on Ugandan Asians*. Athlone Press, 1975.

Upadhyay, Nishant. *Indians on Indian Lands. Intersections of Race, Caste, and Indigeneity*. University of Illinois Press, 2024.

Upadhyay, Nishant. "'We'll Sail Like Columbus': Race, Indigeneity, Settler Colonialism, and the Making of South Asian Diasporas in Canada." PhD diss., York University, 2016.

Vahed, Goolam. "Race, Empire, and Citizenship: Sarojini Naidu's 1924 Visit to South Africa." *South African Historical Journal* 64, no. 2 (2012): 319–42. https://doi.org/10.1080/02582473.2012.671353.

Vahed, Goolam, and Ashwin Desai. *The South African Gandhi: Stretcher-Bearer of Empire*. Stanford University Press, 2015.

Walker, James. "Forty Years in the Wilderness: The Indian Diaspora and Canadian Citizenship." *Directions: Research from the Canadian Race Relations Foundation* 4, no. 2 (2008): 64–69.

Wolfe, Patrick. "Settler Colonialism and the Elimination of the Native." *Journal of Genocide Research* 8, no. 4 (2006): 387–409. https://doi.org/10.1080/14623520601056240.

Education as a Policy Tool for Reconciliation

Understanding the Need for a Relational View of Mind

Kurtis Boyer

***Author's Note:** A few sentences in this chapter are adapted from my earlier essay "Where Does Agency Come From?: Exploring Indigenous Models of Mind" (in Sullivan-Clarke 2023). All reused material is reprinted with permission of Broadview Press.*[1]

Introduction

THE SETTLER COLONIAL PROJECT DEPENDS LARGELY ON a particular perspective on cognition. This viewpoint holds that the laws that govern human cognition are distinct from those that govern the natural or instinctual world. This depiction of humans as distinct from the natural world laid the groundwork for a Western cultural legacy characterized by a double dualism: the dichotomy between rationality and irrationality and, by extension, between the human or civilized and the subhuman or uncivilized. When we engage in education for reconciliation, we aim to address the many psychological and structural consequences of settler colonialism. The Truth and Reconciliation Commission's Calls to Action advocate for integrating Indigenous perspectives into education, as represented in Calls to Action 7, 10, and 16.[2] Nevertheless, our approach to education frequently adheres to the same

European model of the mind, which views the learner as separate from natural and irrational forces.

As a Métis scholar I have been lucky to have been influenced by both Métis and Lakota traditions. While recognizing and centring my Métis identity, I have come to see that many concepts now emerging in Western neuroscience, behavioural economics, and policy studies (from embodied cognition to nudge theory) echo principles that have long been present across diverse Indigenous traditions (including those I have been fortunate to engage with).

The claim that the human thought process is fully autonomous, or isolated from the natural world, ignores the reality that the human ability to learn is situated and relationally constituted. A relational approach rooted in both current scientific understandings of the mind, as well as Indigenous thought, is much more suitable for how our ability to learn depends on our interactions with the environment and others, and this, consequently, has profound implications for how we should design and implement educational policies aimed at reconciliation.

An Isolated Mind

Defining what it is to be human has, for much of recent Western thought, depended on a story we have consistently told ourselves. At its core, this is a story of separation. We have separated human from nature, man from woman, civilized from uncivilized, and so on. However, at the core of all of these claims is a more foundational Western philosophical claim: that the knowing mind comes from a consciousness that is anatomically separated from the "outside" world.

To be human was to have reason. René Descartes's proclamation "je pense, donc je suis" (I think, therefore I am) resulted from a project that separated that which determines our thoughts from that which determines the outside material world. In this separation, our thinking mind became able to know the material or non-rational from a position of separation. This idea of a cognition that is separate from the laws of the natural/instinctual world is a prerequisite for what has become the conventional way of defining human autonomy as we know it today. That is, "the capacity to be one's own person, to live one's life according to reasons and motives that are taken as one's own and not the product of manipulative or distorting external forces."[3]

It is widely recognized, albeit with respect to the extensive diversity inherent among Indigenous cultures, that many Indigenous societies do not share in a view that humans are anatomically separate from the "outside" world, but instead acknowledge the central role of community, land, ancestors, and spiritual beings in shaping individual growth and moral conduct. In fact, even Europeans living in what we now call the Middle Ages had a very different way of thinking of one's moral agency and development. For example, most thought that a person's developmental path was at least partly determined by the divine/supernatural.[4] It was not until the advent of "modernity," and in particular humanism, that this story was revised: the sources of development are housed in the self, not the divine, making each individual person the master of her or his destiny.

To some extent, the definition of the human demands that there are instances of a negative case. In that sense—knowing what we are, a self, and a thinking mind, depends in part on maintaining the story that those we considered to be "subhuman" do not have the same capacity to know what they know, to know what their motivations are, to be able to relate to them from a place of independent origination. The value dualism is described by Marie Battiste (Mi'kmaw) in her discussion on cognitive imperialism and Eurocentric diffusionism:

> The distinction between these peoples lies in the superior quality of the European mind or spirit, which contains a certain intellectual or spiritual factor that leads to creativity, imagination, invention, innovation, rationality, and a sense of honor or ethics. The reason for the perceived non-Europe's non-progress is the lack of the perceived intellectual or spiritual factor that is inherent in the "European mind," "European spirit," or "Western man."[5]

"Civilized folk" are such because they are reasonable. Those who are uncivilized lack the full capacity for self-direction and engage in base instinctual reactions to the outside world. Those who are not fully human are not truly free because, in lacking an independent source to mediate primal urges, their consciousness as well as their actions will be determined by the biological function of those primal urges. Because this story says that reason and emotion are separate, one can cultivate reason over one's "urges." This view—that we can cultivate reason—creates philosophical opportunities that enable certain actions and policies to emerge.

One of the foremost policies in settler colonial Canada is the Indian residential school system, which aimed to assimilate Indigenous Peoples into Euro-Canadian society. The objective was to eliminate Indigenous cultures, languages, and identities, figuratively "killing the Indian" in the child.[6] This was done under the guise of "civilizing" Indigenous children, a notion anchored in the value dualism of "civilized" and "uncivilized." The separation of the "child" and the "Indian" in this phrase reflects the colonial belief that Indigenous identity and the perceived "rationality" of Euro-Canadian society could not coexist. Those promoting the settler colonial system believed that by "killing" the Indian, or forcibly suppressing Indigenous identity and culture, it was cultivating reason and civilizing the child. The more fundamental belief underlying this was that there was such thing as a "civilized mind"—characterized as a source of reasoning separate from emotion and other base urges.

The liberal tradition, which underlines much of settler Canadian society today, is a political and philosophical ideology that emphasizes individual freedom, equality under the law, and the protection of civil liberties. It advocates for a society where citizens have the right to express their thoughts, make choices, and pursue their life goals without undue interference from the government or other societal structures. Much of this tradition assumes that the mind exists anatomically separate from the outside world. In describing what sort of qualities this lived experience entails, Ward notes, "persons can build upon their experiences, forming an experience unique in shape and pattern, contributing distinctive personal actions to the world which manifest their nature and what they have made of it by their relatively free decisions."[7] These claims not only underpin the liberal ideals that fuel societal notions of personal freedom; they also shape our assumptions about education and self-improvement, asserting that self-awareness and self-knowledge are fundamental to personal growth and the pursuit of a fulfilling life.

Education for Change

Governments have a variety of tools at their disposal when implementing policies. Implementation and, in particular, pursuing compliance from the public can either be pursued via "hard" measures (e.g., laws that prohibit or mandate action) or "soft" ones (e.g., educational campaigns). Some policy goals require the whole society to change behaviour. The way governments respond to pandemics, for example, may require citizens to alter even the most basic social conventions, such how they greet each other. Similarly, lowering the emission of greenhouse gases may require getting people to increase their use of public transit, adopt a plant-based diet, and other actions. As a policy tool, education plays a central role in the way policy objectives related to reconciliation are pursued by government and publicly funded institutions, like universities. Indeed, Murray Sinclair has said that "education is the key to reconciliation—at all levels."[8]

Across Canada, some school systems and universities have introduced compulsory Indigenous learning requirements to support change at the individual level. For example, in response to the findings of the Truth and Reconciliation Commission, the province of Alberta integrated mandatory Indigenous content for all students in the province, from kindergarten through grade 12.[9] The University of Saskatchewan and the University of Winnipeg have created policies that have likewise integrated Indigenous course requirements into their curricula.[10] Policy interventions like these use education as the means to create behavioural change. Like similar policy goals, achieving this level of behavioural change greatly depends on whether the target population succeeds at learning and internalizing the rationale, the science, or the socialization necessary for making these changes. While an important and commendable first step, policy interventions like Indigenous learning requirements operate from an assumption: that by simply increasing the opportunity for education, people will naturally be drawn towards increasing their sensitivity to reconciliation.

As illustrated in the following section, there should be doubts about the efficacy of an approach based solely on expanding learning opportunities or mandating learning to increase public awareness of reconciliation-related issues. Problematically, this approach remains rooted in a view of the mind as rational, isolated, and independent from "non-rational" factors. It disregards the significant role that environmental factors and other "non-rational" influences play in the learning process.

The Mind as Relationally Constituted

From the denial of climate change to the rise of social extremism, there has been a growing awareness of the need to account for the role of "non-rational" forces in moulding behaviour.[11] Some fields, like behavioural economics or policy studies, have begun to respond to this need by acknowledging how the external environment, or choice architecture, "nudges" our cognitive and emotional process in directions that are sometimes misaligned with our core values.

While some diversity courses do have a positive effect on students' beliefs,[12] some studies show that anti-Indigenous prejudice can grow if the course is not properly designed or facilitated.[13] This is because while a person's ability to learn about topics related to reconciliation is partly a function of their individual cognitive processes (like inductive reasoning, memory, or attention), it is also influenced by a number of other factors, including their emotional responses, unconscious biases, and social environment. The avoidance of challenging information is well understood in behavioural economics and includes an unconscious use of physical avoidance, inattention, biased interpretations, and even some forms of forgetting.[14] In courses aimed at increasing sensitivity around race, diversity, and privilege, Kernahan and Davis found an association between feelings, such as resentment, and limitations of student engagement. This was because the course content triggered increased feelings of guilt and responsibility.[15] In another study, Hogan and Mallott found that due to the association of defensive and emotional reactions to course content that is common among students—even when there is an increased awareness regarding historical and contemporary social justice issues—the awareness does not often correlate with a reduction in antagonism.[16]

Over a decade ago, Verna St. Denis (Métis/Beardy's and Okemasis Cree Nation), a long-time advocate for educational reform, warned that "offering cultural awareness workshops can also provide another opportunity for non-Aboriginals to resent and resist Aboriginal people."[17] These defensive reactions come most often when "white, middle-class students' own privilege and place in society are directly challenged."[18] A result of students experiencing a challenge to their privilege is a perception that Indigenous instructors are more aggressive, or that the course is not "objective" because it seemingly presents dominant settler peoples and cultures in negative ways.[19] This perception, in turn, leads to classroom disruption—often illustrated in gender studies—as students begin to seek a sense of "false objectivity" as demonstrated in comments like "violence happens to men too—we just never hear about it." Beyond these explicit forms of resistance, perhaps the more common and more insidious forms take shape as white/non-Indigenous students become reluctant to engage in course work or participate in class discussions.[20]

To advance policy objectives related to reconciliation, a comprehensive shift in the views and behaviour of most people is required. Marion Buller (Mistawasis Nêhiyawak), commissioner of the National Inquiry into Missing and Murdered Indigenous Women and Girls (NIMMIWG), has called for a "paradigm shift" to occur across Canada.[21] However, simply providing an opportunity to learn may not be enough to ensure the lesson's effectiveness. Simply integrating reconciliation-related content into curriculum without deliberate, thoughtful pedagogical strategies can have minimal impact or even lead to counterproductive results.[22] Unconscious reactions, environmental circumstances, and other "external" effects all have an impact on learning, yet the dominant educational model does not adequately address these issues.

The shortcomings of this model highlight the need for more effective teaching methods. Such methods should take into account the unconscious and emotional components of learning to promote a deeper comprehension and engagement with complex problems like reconciliation. Without acknowledging the considerable interaction between internal cognition and outside factors, these problems cannot be fully understood. Advances from within cognitive neuroscience have begun to reveal the extent to which our thoughts are formed by unconscious and embodied reactions to the environment.[23] Yet, while this idea that a person's thoughts are relationally constituted may be new to Western science, this notion has long been reflected in the relational metaphysics, ethical systems, and cultural protocols that still pervade many Indigenous cultures today. For example, relaying the views of nêhiyaw Elder Louis Sunchild, Kathy Walker (Okanese First Nation) states that "internally, one domain of the self (e.g. cognitive) not only has an effect or resonance in another domain (e.g. physical)—it 'exists' in that other domain as well and a similar extrinsic connection exists among all living entities with the capacity for resonance."[24]

For generations and generations, our experience, Indigenous thought has reminded us, comes from the integration of our "parts." More recently, Western science has begun to increasingly support a view of our experience as relationally determined. For example, in 1954, electroencephalogram (EEG) studies began showing that our conscious experience unfolds due to an integrated process. These studies found that the parts of our brain that are active when we perform certain bodily motions also become active when we simply see another doing the same action.[25] So not only are our experiences relationally constituted through the integration of the physical to mental and so on, but our internal faculties are expressed through their integration with the "outside" world.[26]

Further findings from neuroscience support the idea that "we are the whole" or that our experience depends on how our bodies are integrated with those "outside" of our bodies in the natural environment. For example, unique kinds of vision motor neurons called "mirror neurons" are now believed to be activated both when we perform specific goal-directed hand (and mouth) movements and when we observe or hear about the same actions: doing an action and observing or imagining an action activate the same brain neurons.[27] Since mirror neurons respond to both conditions, it has been argued that the mirror system functions as a kind of action representation because it links action and action-perception. When it comes to being emotionally moved by another, the innateness of this process has been corroborated through a sub-field of neuroscience that links neural processes to social behaviour.[28] The non-conscious, automatic process of "mirroring" is what many claim provides a theory of the brain's ability to manifest representations of sensations experienced by other people.[29]

Simply put, there is rising evidence to support the idea that everything around us influences our experiences. Mirror neurons are activated both when we conduct specific actions as well as when we observe or even imagine someone else performing those actions. This shows that whether we are performing the action or simply watching it, our brain perceives actions and emotions in the same way. As a result, we actively contribute to comprehending and empathizing with the feelings of others rather than acting as detached observers. Like that relayed by Walker, this theory gives us a profound indication of how interconnected we are. Modern scientific studies are clearly supporting the nêhiyaw tâpisinowin, or a Plains Cree, world view that relays an understanding that "there is no clear separation between the realities of self, society, environment, or the cosmos."[30]

Conclusion

At its core, much of the settler colonial project in Canada depended on a particular view of cognition, where the rules governing how humans think are separate from the laws of the irrational/natural/instinctual world. European political, economic, and social modes framed imperial colonial expansion and settler colonial development, and this was exercised through conceptualization of cognition. In this view, the human mind is defined by a state of isolation. Yet, we know that there are "non-rational" factors at play that ultimately determine a person's behaviour.

Developing a national commitment to healing and forging a new relationship between Indigenous and non-Indigenous peoples has made reconciliation one of Canada's most important social policy goals. Education plays a central role in the way many policy objectives related to reconciliation are pursued by government and publicly funded institutions, like universities.

Yet, the way we often employ education for reconciliation begins with a European model of mind—one that views the development of the learner as something separate from external forces. To truly achieve reconciliation, education must centre Indigenous ways of knowing, reflecting the diversity of Indigenous thought and practices, and offering relational approaches that foster deeper understanding and learning.

The story of the human thought process as rational, fully autonomous, or isolated from the natural world does not provide a means to address the reality that the ability to learn is situated and relationally constituted. A relational understanding of mind is more reflective of Indigenous thought. Because it better equips us to grasp how dependent our conscious experience, and consequently our ability to learn, is on how we are related to the "external" and "irrational" world, this area of Indigenous thought is also a more suitable starting point for considering how education can be used for reconciliation.

Notes

1 Kurtis Boyer, "Where Does Agency Come From?: Exploring Indigenous Models of Mind," in *Ways of Being in the World: An Introduction to Indigenous Philosophies of Turtle Island*, ed. Anne Sullivan-Clarke (Broadview Press, 2023).

2 Truth and Reconciliation Commission of Canada (TRC), *Calls to Action*.

3 Christman, "Autonomy in Moral and Political Philosophy."

4 McClusky, "Medieval Theories of Free Will."

5 Battiste, "Cognitive Imperialism."

6 The expression "to kill the Indian in the child" is commonly, but incorrectly, attributed to Duncan Campbell Scott, deputy superintendent of the Department of Indian Affairs from 1913 to 1932. It was said by Richard Pratt, an American military officer and founder of the Carlisle Indian Industrial School in Pennsylvania. Despite the misattribution, the sentiment

expressed in this phrase provides a disturbing glimpse into the philosophy underpinning Canada's residential school system and the larger colonial enterprise. See Pratt, "'Kill the Indian in Him.'"

7 Ward, "Persons, Kinds and Capacities," 83.

8 Murray Sinclair, quoted in Stoicheff, "Education the Key to Reconciliation."

9 Government of Alberta, "Education for Reconciliation."

10 See University of Saskatchewan, "Indigenous Learning Requirement"; University of Winnipeg, "Indigenous Course Requirement."

11 See Salmela and von Scheve, "Emotional Roots of Right-Wing Political Populism"; Leiserowitz, "Climate Change Risk Perception."

12 Palmer, "The Impact of Diversity Courses."

13 Case, "Raising White Privilege Awareness"; Nelson, "Assessing the Impact of Diversity Courses."

14 Golman, Hagmann, and Loewenstein, "Information Avoidance."

15 Kernahan and Davis, "Changing Perspective."

16 Hogan and Mallott, "Changing Racial Prejudice through Diversity Education."

17 St. Denis, "Aboriginal Education and Anti-Racist Education."

18 Bowman, "Disequilibrium and Resolution."

19 Phillips, "Resisting Contradictions."

20 Palmer, "The Impact of Diversity Courses."

21 Scherer, "Canadian Inquiry Calls Deaths of Indigenous Women 'Genocide.'"

22 McGregor, "Effectiveness of Role Playing"; Stephan, Renfro, and Stephan, "The Evaluation of Multicultural Education Programs," 227–42; Pfeifer, Brown, and Juvonen, "Prejudice Reduction in Schools."

23 Glenberg, "Few Believe the World Is Flat"; Masson, "Toward a Deeper Understanding of Embodiment"; Lakoff, "Explaining Embodied Cognition Results."

24 Lightning, "Compassionate Mind."

25 Gastaut, "On the Significance of 'Wicket Rhythmus,'" 687; Gastaut and Bert, "EEG Changes During Cinematographic Presentation."

26 Ahenakew, quoted in Walker, "Okâwîmâwaskiy," 108.

27 Gallese, "Embodied Simulation"; Gallese and Goldman, "Mirror Neurons and the Simulation Theory of Mind-Reading"; Rizzolatti and Fadiga, "From Mirror Neurons to Imitation."

28 Decety and Norman, "Empathy: A Social Neuroscience Perspective," 541–48; Jackson, Meltzoff, and Decety, "How Do We Perceive the Pain of Others?"

29 Iacoboni, *Mirroring People*; Iacoboni, "Imitation, Empathy, and Mirror Neurons."

30 Walker, "Okâwîmâwaskiy," 108.

Sources

Battiste, Marie. "Cognitive Imperialism." In *Encyclopedia of Educational Philosophy and Theory*, edited by Michael A. Peters. Springer Singapore, 2017. http://doi.org/10.1007/978-981-287-588-4_501.

Bowman, Nicholas A. "Disequilibrium and Resolution: The Nonlinear Effects of Diversity Courses on Well-Being and Orientations Toward Diversity." *Review of Higher Education* 33, no. 4 (2010): 543–68. https://doi.org/10.1353/rhe.0.0172.

Case, Kim. "Raising White Privilege Awareness and Reducing Racial Prejudice: Assessing Diversity Course Effectiveness." *Teaching of Psychology* 34, no. 4 (2007): 231–35. https://doi.org/10.1080/00986280701700250.

Christman, John. "Autonomy in Moral and Political Philosophy." *The Stanford Encyclopedia of Philosophy* (Fall 2020 Edition), edited by Edward N. Zalta. https://plato.stanford.edu/archives/fall2020/entries/autonomy-moral/.

Decety, Jean, and Greg J. Norman. "Empathy: A Social Neuroscience Perspective." In *The International Encyclopedia of the Social & Behavioral Sciences*. Elsevier, 2015.

Gallese, Vittorio. "Embodied Simulation: From Neurons to Phenomenal Experience." *Phenomenology and the Cognitive Sciences* 4, no. 1 (March 2005): 23–48. https://doi.org/10.1007/s11097-005-4737-z.

Gallese, Vittorio, and Alvin Goldman. "Mirror Neurons and the Simulation Theory of Mind-Reading." *Trends in Cognitive Sciences* 2, no. 12 (1998): 493–501. https://doi.org/10.1016/S1364-6613(98)01262-5.

Gastaut, Henri. "On the Significance of 'Wicket Rhythmus' in Psychosomatic Medicine." *Electroencephalography Clinical Neurophysiology* 6 (1954).

Gastaut, Henri J., and Jacques Bert. "EEG Changes During Cinematographic Presentation (Moving Picture Activation of the EEG)." *Electroencephalography and Clinical Neurophysiology* 6 (1954): 433–44.

Glenberg, Arthur M. "Few Believe the World Is Flat: How Embodiment Is Changing the Scientific Understanding of Cognition." *Canadian Journal of Experimental Psychology / Revue Canadienne de psychologie expérimentale* 69, no. 2 (2015): 165–71. http://dx.doi.org/10.1037/cep0000056.

Golman, Russell, David Hagmann, and George Loewenstein. "Information Avoidance." *Journal of Economic Literature* 55, no. 1 (2017): 96–135. https://doi.org/10.1257/jel.20151245.

Government of Alberta. "Education for Reconciliation." 2022. https://www.alberta.ca/education-for-reconciliation.aspx.

Hogan, David E., and Michael Mallott. "Changing Racial Prejudice Through Diversity Education." *Journal of College Student Development* 46, no. 2 (2005): 115–25. http://dx.doi.org/10.1353/csd.2005.0015.

Iacoboni, Marco. "Imitation, Empathy, and Mirror Neurons." *Annual Review of Psychology* 60, no. 1 (2009): 653–70. https://doi.org/10.1146/annurev.psych.60.110707.163604.

Iacoboni, Marco. *Mirroring People: The New Science of How We Connect with Others*. Farrar, Straus and Giroux, 2009.

Jackson, Philip L., Andrew N. Meltzoff, and Jean Decety. "How Do We Perceive the Pain of Others? A Window into the Neural Processes Involved in Empathy." *NeuroImage* 24, no. 3 (2005): 771–79. https://doi.org/10.1016/j.neuroimage.2004.09.006.

Kernahan, Cyndi, and Tricia Davis. "Changing Perspective: How Learning About Racism Influences Student Awareness and Emotion." *Teaching of Psychology* 34, no. 1 (2007): 49–52. https://doi.org/10.1080/00986280709336651.

Lakoff, George. "Explaining Embodied Cognition Results." *Topics in Cognitive Science* 4 , no. 4 (2012): 773–85. http://dx.doi.org/10.1111/j.1756-8765.2012.01222.x.

Leiserowitz, Anthony. "Climate Change Risk Perception and Policy Preferences: The Role of Affect, Imagery, and Values." *Climatic Change* 77 (2006): 45–72. https://doi.org/10.1007/s10584-006-9059-9.

Lightning, Walter. "Compassionate Mind: Implications of a Text Written by Elder Louis Sunchild." Master's thesis, University of Alberta, 1997.

Masson, M.E.J. "Toward a Deeper Understanding of Embodiment." *Canadian Journal of Experimental Psychology / Revue Canadienne de psychologie expérimentale* 69, no. 2 (2015): 159–64. https://doi.org/10.1037/cep0000055.

McClusky, Colleen. "Medieval Theories of Free Will." *Internet Encyclopedia of Philosophy*. 2017. https://iep.utm.edu/freewi-m/.

McGregor, Josette. "Effectiveness of Role Playing and Antiracist Teaching in Reducing Student Prejudice." *Journal of Educational Research* 86, no. 4 (1993): 215–26. https://doi.org/10.1080/00220671.1993.9941833.

Nelson, Matthew. "Assessing the Impact of Diversity Courses on Students' Values, Attitudes and Beliefs." PhD diss., University of Southern California, 2010. https://www.proquest.com/openview/dd2990ec6f93639228 2a7826295370fe/1?pq-origsite=gscholar&cbl=18750.

Palmer, Betsy. "The Impact of Diversity Courses: Research from Pennsylvania State University." *DiversityWeb*. 2000. https://web.archive.org/web/20050412023630/http://www.diversityweb.org/Digest/W00/research.html.

Pfeifer, Jennifer H., Christia Spears Brown, and Jaana Juvonen. "Prejudice Reduction in Schools: Teaching Tolerance in Schools—Lessons Learned Since Brown v. Board of Education About the Development and Reduction of Children's Prejudice." *Social Policy Report* 21, no.2 (2007). https://eric.ed.gov/?id=ED521699.

Phillips, Jean. "Resisting Contradictions: Non-Indigenous Pre-Service Teacher Responses to Critical Indigenous Studies." PhD diss., Queensland University of Technology, 2011. https://eprints.qut.edu.au/46071/.

Pratt, R.H. "'Kill the Indian in Him, and Save the Man': R.H. Pratt on the Education of Native Americans." Carlisle Indian School Digital Resource Center. Accessed September 28, 2024. https://carlisleindian.dickinson.edu/teach/kill-indian-him-and-save-man-r-h-pratt-education-native-americans.

Rizzolatti, G., and L. Fadiga. "From Mirror Neurons to Imitation: Facts and Speculations." In *The Imitative Mind: Development, Evolution and Brain Bases*, edited by Andrew N. Meltzoff and Wolfgang Prinz. Cambridge University Press, 2002.

Salmela, Mikko, and Christian von Scheve. "Emotional Roots of Right-Wing Political Populism." *Social Science Information* 56, no. 4 (2017): 567–95. https://doi.org/10.1177/0539018417734419.
Scherer, Steve. "Canadian Inquiry Calls Deaths of Indigenous Women 'Genocide.'" Reuters, June 3, 2019. https://www.reuters.com/article/world/canadian-inquiry-calls-deaths-of-indigenous-women-genocide-idUSKCN1T41WT/.
St. Denis, Verna. "Aboriginal Education and Anti-Racist Education: Building Alliances Across Cultural and Racial Identity." *Canadian Journal of Education / Revue Canadienne de l'éducation* 30, no. 4 (2007): 1068–92. https://doi.org/10.2307/20466679.
Stephan, Cookie, Lausanne Renfro, and W.G. Stephan. "The Evaluation of Multicultural Education Programs: Techniques and a Meta-Analysis." In *Education Programs for Improving Intergroup Relations: Theory, Practice, and Research*, edited by Walter G. Stephan and W. Paul Vogt. Teachers College Press, 2004.
Stoicheff, Peter. "Education the Key to Reconciliation: Making Good on the Truth and Reconciliation Commission's (TRC) 94 Calls to Action." *Saskatoon StarPhoenix*, November 22, 2017.
Truth and Reconciliation Commission of Canada. *Calls to Action*. Truth and Reconciliation Commission of Canada, 2015. https://ehprnh2mwo3.exactdn.com/wp-content/uploads/2021/01/Calls_to_Action_English2.pdf.
University of Saskatchewan. "Indigenous Learning Requirement." Academic Policies—College of Arts & Science, University Catalogue 2025–26. Accessed August 7, 2025. https://programs.usask.ca/arts-and-science/policies.php#IndigenousLearningRequirement.
University of Winnipeg. "Indigenous Course Requirement." Accessed June 22, 2023. https://www.uwinnipeg.ca/indigenous/indigenous-course-requirement/index.html.
Walker, Katherine. "Okâwîmâwaskiy: Regenerating a Wholistic Ethics." PhD diss., University of British Columbia, 2021. https://open.library.ubc.ca/soa/cIRcle/collections/ubctheses/24/items/1.0398723.
Ward, Keith. "Persons, Kinds and Capacities." In *Rights and Wrongs in Medicine: King's College Studies 1985–6*, edited by Peter Byrne. King Edward's Hospital Fund for London, 1986.

Settler Researchers

From a Place of Not Knowing

Rosemary Nagy

WHEN MAURICE SWITZER OF THE MISSISSAUGAS OF Alderville First Nation spoke to my gender studies class on the rights of Indigenous Peoples in early 2022, he asked us, "Who in this room has Treaty Rights?" All the Indigenous students raised their hands, and all the settlers, including myself, kept their hands down. But, no! "We all have Treaty Rights," he explained, "because we are all parties to the treaty." As one of my Indigenous students noted in our debriefing afterwards, "really, it seems like settlers have all the rights!" This is because Indigenous Peoples must prove their rights through the settler court system, while the legal status quo ensures that settler rights to land and resources are the default position. While we settlers in the room did not raise our hands in part because we were thinking about our treaty responsibilities, Maurice's simple exercise completely unsettled our presumptions. For me, it revealed my unconscious sense of entitlement, and it challenged me to rethink the meaning of a treaty relationship as I realized that even my idea of treaty responsibility was probably underlaid with a sense of conferral from on high.[1]

I felt more than a little foolish when Maurice—who asks to be referred to as an *Oshkaabewis* ("helper" in Anishinaabemowin)—kindly corrected us. After all, I had been working in the area of settler colonialism for twelve years, having engaged in projects on residential schools, the Truth and Reconciliation Commission, and MMIWG2S, with a focus on sex work and human trafficking. How could I have gotten the answer so wrong? But then, as I reflected further on Maurice's teaching, this had been but one of many moments of abrupt revelation in my learning journey over the last decade. The meta-lesson, I concluded, is that I will never know everything I ought to know. Of course, this applies to any topic I might "profess" to teach or research. But, in the context of being a white settler,[2] it is especially important to embrace that place of not knowing.

To be clear, I am not saying we should embrace settler denial. Rather, I mean exactly the opposite: we should always be in a place of readiness to learn. Or, as Anishinaabe scholar Tricia McGuire-Adams puts it, we should be ready for a "process of continual unlearning and relearning that challenges one's identity on stolen Indigenous territories while committing to Indigenous-led decolonial and resurgence practices."[3] However, I believe there is also a limit to what non-Indigenous people can know, especially those who are white and otherwise privileged, because of the limits—indeed problems with—attempting to put ourselves in the "shoes of the other." Arguably, privilege comes with a degree of insularity and subsequently a risk of projecting fantasies or biases onto the other.[4] Thus, I propose that radical ignorance is a fundamental starting point for how settlers might conduct research *with* or *for* Indigenous Peoples or engage in research *on* the Indigenous-settler relationship.

On the Limits of Settler Knowledge

Firstly, we can never truly know the lived experience of being Indigenous in a fundamentally racist, colonial society in which we as settlers are structurally complicit. As settlers, we are all historically and systemically located in relation to land dispossession, cultural genocide, and gendered and racialized violence, whether or not this was by choice.[5] In terms of *not knowing*, I am not talking about intellectual knowledge, which can be gleaned through listening, reading, and watching. I am talking about the kind of knowledge that lies in our guts and our hearts, a knowledge grounded in mind, body, spirit, and emotions. Even if we share affinities of experience that arouse feelings of empathy or solidarity, it is nonetheless important to recognize that kindred experiences of discrimination or violence are "incommensurable," as Eve Tuck and Kevin Yang put it.[6] This is because we as white settlers do not live the collective history of land dispossession and genocide in the same way as Indigenous Peoples. I think this point is fairly evident in the split in my class's gut responses to Maurice's question.

Secondly, I also am not sure how much we, as cultural outsiders, can come to know and actualize Indigenous ways of knowing and being, which seems to be part of the push towards the Indigenization of universities. One facet of this concern is that settler endeavours of Indigenization, particularly in institutional contexts such as a university, may amount to what Cash Ahenakew describes as an assimilative "grafting" of Indigenous knowledges onto Western epistemological frameworks.[7] While grafting could be a "generative process" of hybridity, the current context is such that "we are operating with severely uneven environments shaped by historical circumstances."[8] Consequently, grafting is rarely, if ever, a mutual exercise, but one of subtly continued domination and assimilation. Ahenakew writes,

> Indigenous knowledges and methodologies can be either incorporated as a colourful (but insignificant) alternative to what is considered "normal," which confirms the benevolence of the proponent of inclusion, or perceived as something that is already integral to the dominant logic and therefore also insignificant, given that it offers nothing new.[9]

Examples of superficial inclusion might be perfunctory and performative land acknowledgements or the gifting of tobacco to Elders without really understanding what that means. Academic legitimacy (i.e., peer review, funding, and criteria for tenure and promotion) still centres on cognition and writing rather than orality, the senses, and metaphorical land engagement. Moreover, something is lost when Indigenous knowledges are "translated" or "shoe-horned" into Western frameworks. In particular, argues Saami scholar Rauna Kuokkanen, Indigenous logics of reciprocity and relationality are lost in the face of rationalism, detachment, objectivity, anthropocentrism, and individualism.[10]

It is worth noting that transformative research paradigms rooted in feminisms, queer theory, critical race, critical disability, and postcolonialism challenge the production of "objective" and "common sense" knowledge as being deeply biased in terms of gender, race, ability, and so forth. These anti-oppressive approaches question and decline the "scientific" standards listed above by emphasizing contextualization, intersubjectivity, plurality, relationality, experientialism, and marginalized knowledges.[11] Transformative or anti-oppressive research is inherently political, with specific values and social justice objectives embedded in the research process itself.[12] These approaches align with Indigenous methodologies insofar as they share emphases on relationality, reciprocity, inclusivity, empowerment, and social transformation.[13]

Yet, with the exceptions of post-colonial and Global South feminisms, these anti-oppressive approaches still largely operate within Eurocentric ways of knowing and being. Wright and colleagues argue that despite positive alignments, Western researchers "continue to struggle to fully grasp relational ontologies and epistemologies to the extent emphasized by Indigenous worldviews." This is because in Western understandings of reality, the world is viewed as something external or "out there." They explain this difference using Shawn Wilson's example in language: "in English, a 'pen' is described using a single word, while the word in Cree translates to 'something that you write with.'"[14] The pen in Cree is not an object external to the self but part of a relationship.

Indigenous relationality to ancestors, the land and water, animals and plants, and even pens, is something I struggle to grasp. While I may be cognitively conversant in things such as "holistic worldviews" and various medicine wheel metaphors, this is not for me an intuitive or embodied knowledge. How do we move beyond our own cultural referents in order to deeply appreciate the idea that animals, plants, and landscapes are "active teachers"?[15] The short answer, of course, is to keep listening, reading, watching, and doing: that is, keep learning. However, there is arguably an inherent and necessary limit to how much we settlers can come to know.

One the one hand, many Indigenous Peoples speak of learning the culture and language that was stolen from them, and so perhaps this learning is also possible for non-Indigenous people who are welcomed and guided by Indigenous teachers and communities. In particular, learning an Indigenous language is likely key to cultural immersion. On the other hand, we cannot ignore the unequal structural and historical environment in which settlers learn. There are risks of cultural appropriation and "moves to innocence" that "attempt to relieve the settler of feelings of guilt or responsibility without giving up land or power or privilege, without having to change much at all."[16] Furthermore, as Iris Marion Young has argued, it would be a mistake to assume that we can simply take on the perspective of "the other."

Young argues that it "is neither possible nor morally desirable for persons engaged in moral interaction to adopt one another's standpoint."[17] To act as though our positions were reversable, as though we could imagine life through the eyes of "the other" on the basis of some commonality, is to obscure difference. "The perspective of the other can too easily be represented as the self's other represented to itself—its fantasies, desires, and fears."[18] Moreover, who we are is constituted in part through our relations with other people. Consequently, Young writes, "it is hard to see how any of us could suspend our perspective mediated by our relations to others, in order to adopt their perspectives mediated by their relation to us."[19]

Young helpfully proposes the idea of *asymmetrical reciprocity* as the basis for moral respect, egalitarian mutuality, and democratic dialogue between groups. Asymmetrical reciprocity entails recognition that our positions are irreducible and irreversible. She argues that understanding across difference is "both possible and necessary," but it is a mode of "*being with* rather than being in one another's place."[20] We must meet the other with openness and moral humility; acknowledge the limits of *knowing the other* that is a result of our irreversible social and historical positions; and consider the world that lies *between us* as a way of enlarging our thinking in terms of *plurality* and not just commonality. This idea of "enlarged thinking," which comes from Hannah Arendt, is about viewing the world through a plurality of perspectives rather than aggregating or merging viewpoints.[21] At a superficial level, this is not dissimilar to the Mi'kmaw concept of *Etuaptmumk*, which means "the gift of multiple perspectives" and is usually translated into English as "Two-Eyed Seeing."[22] Before explaining Two-Eyed Seeing in the final section of the chapter, I will first dive a little deeper into asymmetrical reciprocity and the idea that bringing together knowledges and perspectives is a gift.

Knowledge as Gift, Gratitude, and Response-Ability

Young draws on a theory of *gift-giving* to further explain asymmetrical reciprocity and writes, "The ethical relation is also asymmetrical in the sense that opening onto the other person is always a *gift*, the trust to communicate cannot await the other person's promise to reciprocate, or the conversation will never begin."[23] A gift, by definition, she argues, must be freely given with no expectation of being owed anything back. Otherwise, it is not a gift but a mechanistic exchange. Of course, we might later give a gift in return to someone who has gifted something to us, but this is "a new offering, with its own asymmetry."[24] An answer to a question, for example, is a gift because the speaker could choose to withhold explanation for reasons of her own. The appropriate response, Young suggests, is to accept the answer with openness and "being able to see one's own position, assumptions, perspective as strange." Young explains this as "wonder." Wonder is not exoticization of the other or "dominative desire to know and master the other person." Rather it is a stance "of openness across, awaiting new insight about their needs, interests, perceptions, or values."[25]

Young's point on openly accepting the gift of an answer is important given how often Indigenous Peoples are disbelieved or questioned when they speak of their experiences. In the context of research, it is also worth noting that the word *data* itself originates from the Latin word *dare*, meaning *to give*. But I worry that Young's formulation insufficiently addresses the responsibilities incumbent on the receiver, thereby placing too much risk on the marginalized person or group to take the leap and "trust to communicate." Furthermore, within Indigenous world views, gift-giving is always imbued with a responsibility to give back. Thus, I suggest, while the ethical relationship between settler knowers and Indigenous knowers is asymmetrical in Young's sense of irreducibility and irreversibility, reciprocity for the gift of knowledge and communication entails gratitude rather than wonder.

Kuokkanen explains that the "logic of the gift" within Indigenous world views is grounded in relationships with the human and non-human world. Reciprocity and responsibility are embedded in "a close interaction of sustaining and renewing the balance of the world by means of gifts." The logic manifests in "give-back" ceremonies, such as the Potlatch, whereby "gifts cannot be given unless the receipt of countergifts is guaranteed." This is not a transactional exchange of gift being given for a counter-gift; rather, it is to "actively acknowledge the relationships and coexistence with the world without which survival would not be possible."[26] Similarly, Robin Wall Kimmerer explains that "gifts from the earth or from each other establish a particular relationship, an obligation of sorts to give, to receive, and to reciprocate."[27] For Kimmerer, like Young, a gift is by definition "something for nothing." But a gift also "creates an ongoing relationship" and "certain obligations are attached."[28] These obligations include expressions and acts of gratitude. Kimmerer further suggests that gratitude itself is a gift that "incite[s] a cycle of reciprocity."[29]

As Leanne Betasamosake Simpson explains, Indigenous diplomacy is imbued with gift-giving alongside other spiritual practices such as storytelling, oral tradition, ceremonies, and feasting. These practices are "designed to bond people together toward a common understanding" in an ongoing relationship based on principles of "reconciliation, restitution, mediation, negotiation, and maintaining sacred and political alliances between peoples."[30] Treaties are one such ongoing relationship. There is much evidence to show that the Crown negotiated the Numbered Treaties using duress and duplicity.[31] Indigenous resurgence movements point to Indigenous diplomacy and legal traditions as a way forward, as a way of returning to original understandings of respect and reciprocity in a nation-to-nation relationship. Karine Duhamel writes that for Indigenous Peoples, treaties are informed "by a strong sense of giftedness and responsibility related to law, culture, language, history and way of life."[32] Given that we are all treaty people, we settlers should embrace this sense of giftedness, rights, and responsibilities in our research and daily lives.

This depth of relationality and responsibility seems to be missing from Young's account insofar as she separates each act of gift-giving as something new, rather than seeing gift-giving as an interdependent cycle. Young's account of asymmetry and the irreversibility of viewpoints is highly important because it captures the sociohistorical, epistemological, and ontological limits of knowing the other. But we need to supplement her reliance on gift-giving to include the cycle of reciprocity, or what Kuokkanen explains as the gift's implied "response-ability." With response-ability, obligation rests in the "ability to respond, to remain attuned to the world beyond self and be willing to recognize its existence through gift giving."[33] Our recognition of the relational duties attached in accepting the gift, she argues, is what "makes the gift possible."[34] Gratitude, rather than wonder (which Young herself admits is a dangerous concept), is a more appropriate posture of acceptance because, Kimmerer explains, it "self-perpetuates cycles of giving and receiving."[35]

Kelly Oliver, in her work on witnessing, similarly writes about response-ability on the part of the listener. For Oliver, we can only respond ethically to one another as subjects, not as objects. Subjectivity refers to how we perceive ourselves and how we accordingly act in the world.[36] Importantly, when we respond to one another as subjects, we respect one another's agency. Response-ability requires that we "open up rather than close off the possibility of response by others."[37] I take this to mean that there is a reciprocal cycle of nurture and respect for the agency and self-determination of the other.[38] Oliver writes that the "turn toward otherness" requires critical self-reflection as we interrogate our roles in structures of domination and seek to transform our society. This "response ethics," argues Oliver, shifts us "beyond recognition," that is, (in our context) beyond assimilative forms of accommodation or acknowledgement that serve to reinforce the colonial status quo.[39] In the university setting, argues Kuokannen,

> The recognition of the gift of indigenous epistemes amounts to a more respectful and responsible scholarship as the academy is *compelled to accept responsibility for its own ignorance and act upon it.* It enables a vision of a discursive space where indigenous people can be encountered in their own terms.[40]

The academy's response-ability to the gift is "to be taught, to learn, to learn to listen" while critically interrogating biases, beliefs, and institutional inequities.[41] Kuokkanen calls for "unconditional" acceptance of Indigenous knowledges without attempts at "bridging" or "translating."[42] Responding to Indigenous knowledges as a gift, as opposed to a harvesting of information, entails a lived relationship with one another where we aim to nurture and respect agency and self-determination. Reciprocity founded on gratitude is both egalitarian *and* asymmetrical. Reciprocity is egalitarian because gratitude for the gift of Indigenous knowledges is neither superficial nor assimilative but based on an openness beyond self. It is asymmetrical, however, because openness beyond self is simply that: openness. Openness is not appropriation or reversibility. It is a reaching beyond ourselves with gratitude, acceptance, and a responsibility to respect and make space for Indigenous self-determination.

Settler Research from a Place of Not Knowing

This final section offers some concrete suggestions about what it means to conduct research from a place of not knowing. I unpack the framework of Two-Eyed Seeing, or the "gift of multiple perspectives," and further recommend participatory action research as two approaches that fit well with the limits of settler knowledge. To start, however, I first note the abundance of information on settler allyship. Allyship is a practice, not an identity that we can self-proclaim; as the Anti-Oppression Network puts it, "our work and our efforts must be recognized by the people we seek to ally ourselves with."[43] The allyship literature emphasizes the importance of humility, listening, critical self-reflection, relational accountability, and a commitment to dismantling colonial structures and attitudes.[44] These principles and practices are foundational to doing research *with* or *for*[45] Indigenous Peoples or *on* the Indigenous-settler relationship. If you cannot answer, at the very least to yourself, the question of "who are you and why do you care,"[46] then you probably should not be starting research in this area. Métis scholar Natalie Clark, in a compelling essay, teaches that we need to explain who we are and why we care in order "to situate ourselves in our writing, to start from our intentions."[47] Making clear our purposes and working with spirit and intentionality is a form of relational accountability.[48]

Importantly, however, we further need to interrogate the desire to "help" Indigenous Peoples if that is our explanation as to why we care. Over the years, I have often heard white settler students express their desire to help, and it is no doubt heartfelt. The problem, however, is that the desire to "help" may be rooted—and will most likely *appear* to be rooted—in the colonial history of "civilizing" and "saving" Indigenous Peoples. While a settler directly helping an Indigenous person may well be appropriate in specific situations, the concept of helping too often takes an individualized focus that ignores broader systemic structures. Rather than simply "helping" Indigenous Peoples, it is important to reverse the gaze and instead work to fix what Paulette Regan has called "the settler problem."[49] When we write up our research, for example, we might think in terms of writing for fellow settler Canadians or engaging in some reflection on our positionality. Statements of positionality should not be confessional or guilt-laden but rather an acknowledgement of who we are, why we care, and what are our responsibilities.

Furthermore, as Shawn Wilson puts it, "to care is not enough, to be compassionate is not enough, to know the truth is not enough. We must use this awareness to guide our actions—as researchers and as human beings."[50] Wilson's emphasis on our role as human beings is important: we enter into this kind of research not simply as someone who needs a term paper or a publication—although we should be up front in acknowledging that this is part of our interest in doing the research. Even if we do not engage directly with Indigenous Peoples during our research, we should understand our research as being in relationship, for example, between settler Canadians, Indigenous Peoples, and the land on which we live. As noted earlier, because we are all treaty people, honouring the spirit and intent of treaty requires enacting the gift-giving nature of the treaty relationship and its attendant responsibilities. Thus, we need to ensure that our research is relevant and respectful to Indigenous perspectives and cultures. Furthermore, as Wilson states, "living a lifestyle that is congruent with what you are trying to achieve through your research is crucial, as is incorporating what you learn from your research back into your lifestyle afterward."[51]

Some settler researchers will have the opportunity to engage in a direct relationship with Indigenous Peoples who may act as research participants, co-researchers, or advisors to a project. The framework of Two-Eyed Seeing, first advanced by Mi'kmaq Elders Albert and Murdena Marshall in the context of an Integrative Science program at Cape Breton University, may be a helpful guide to this kind of collaborative work. Elder Albert Marshall (Moose Clan Mi'kmaw Nation) explains Two-Eyed Seeing as the "weaving together" of Indigenous and mainstream knowledges, where we draw on the strengths of each knowledge system "for the benefit of all."[52] Given the difficulty settlers have in grasping the depth of Indigenous relationality, Wright and colleagues note, "Two-Eyed Seeing can assist in bridging this gap of understanding through bringing together both Indigenous and Western worldviews in a collaborative and equitable approach to research."[53]

While I cannot do justice here to the richness of Two-Eyed Seeing, or how different researchers have variously taken it up, I want to emphasize that it is not intended to be a blending or merging of the two knowledge systems or the subsumption of Indigenous knowledges into Western frameworks.[54] Rather, it is a moving back and forth between the two, a process of "co-learning" and problem-solving that is grounded in authentic relationships and a commitment to redress the power imbalance between Indigenous and Western knowledges. A Two-Eyed Seeing approach might incorporate Indigenous ways of knowing and being, as well as specific Indigenous methods such as storytelling, oral history, conversation, or land-based activities. But the fullness of Two-Eyed Seeing goes beyond academia. To quote Elder Albert Marshall, "it is about life: what you do, what kind of responsibilities you have, how you should live while on Earth...i.e., a guiding principle that covers all aspects of our lives: social, economic, environmental, etc."[55]

Some of the literature stresses the complementarity of knowledges, even viewing Two-Eyed Seeing as a form of reconciliation.[56] However, Broadhead and Howard pointedly note that one eye "is essentially healthy, while the other is partly diseased."[57] Thus, they emphasize, we should only allow "*resonant* areas of Western [knowledge] to *enter into relationship*."[58] In other words, it is not a simple fifty-fifty split between Indigenous and Western ways of knowing and being. Rather, it is asymmetrical. Consequently, settler researchers must be willing to simply accept Indigenous perspectives, "take a back seat,"[59] and persist in the discomfort of not knowing.[60] For settler researchers, a Two-Eyed Seeing approach depends on the ongoing involvement and support of at least one person with Indigenous knowledges and perspectives: a co-researcher, a Knowledge Keeper, an Elder, or community member.[61] Additionally, with participatory action research (PAR) design, Indigenous participants can be directly involved in the research process.

I have chosen to highlight PAR design not only because it is compatible with Two-Eyed Seeing, but also because it allows for the limits of settler knowledge. Thinking back to Wilson's point that caring requires outcomes and action, PAR is typically associated with social justice goals and is oriented towards personal and social change in both its process and outcomes. PAR treats research participants, especially marginalized groups, as experts in their own lives and as agents exercising self-determination. Participants are seen as co-generators of knowledge, meaning they are actively involved in all or some stages of the research process, including setting the research objectives and research questions.[62] Indigenous and allied researchers note how PAR aligns with the "Four Rs" of Indigenous methodologies as articulated by Kirkness and Barnhardt: relevance, respect, reciprocity, and responsibility.[63] As laid out in the following diagram, the Four Rs map onto the four PAR stages of *diagnosis* (identifying the problem); *planning* (developing a research strategy to address the issue); *action* (implementing the research strategy and working for social change); and *reflection* (analysis, evaluation, and sharing).

In terms of the limits of settler knowledge, the PAR idea and practice of co-generating knowledge is especially conducive to asymmetrical reciprocity. This is because the university researcher is not "the expert" so much as a facilitator who brings her skills and resources to bear in the process of together making meaning and deciding how to shape the outcomes and outputs of the research.

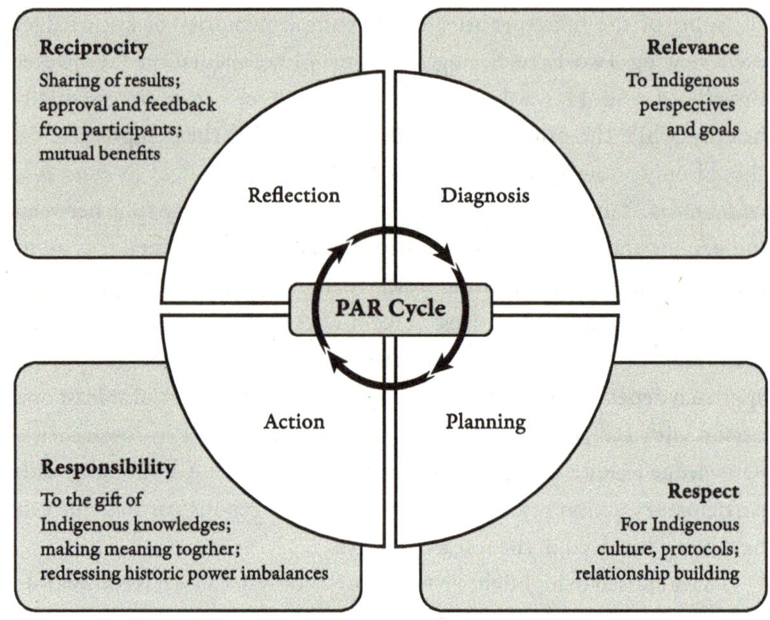

The above diagram is drawn from my own work with the Northeastern Ontario Research Alliance on Human Trafficking (NORAHT).[64] NORAHT was a research partnership between Nipissing University, the Union of Ontario Indians: Anishinabek Nation, Victim Services of Nipissing District, and Centered Fire Counselling and Consulting.[65] Over seven years, we worked to identify gaps and barriers to regional services for women, especially Indigenous women, experiencing violence, exploitation, and abuse in the sex industry. We hosted eight PAR workshops across the region with service providers and people with lived experience (both Indigenous and non-Indigenous). In these workshops, our participants identified action steps, which the NORAHT team then undertook through further research. We also held three follow-up conferences to meet our participants' request for further education, including one conference that we co-organized with the PACT Grandmothers and Missanabie Cree First Nation. The NORAHT team operated by consensus, and we understood ourselves to be working for our participants, who rarely had either the time or the resources to develop service provider toolkits and other outputs. That said, we were able to work closely with four women with lived experience in the sex industry, two of whom are Indigenous, in order to educate service providers and conduct analysis of anti-trafficking discourse in Canada. Importantly, we were able to pay these four women for their time and knowledge, as was also the case for our project Elder and any person who attended our workshops on their own behalf (i.e., rather than as an employee of a service organization).

Certainly, not everyone will be able to conduct PAR projects, due to lack of time, a shortage of willing participants, or limited access to resources such as honoraria for the extensive involvement of participants. Even so, settler researchers can still work with Indigenous communities or organizations from the start to ensure that they are fulfilling the Four Rs of research, following traditional protocols, and abiding by ethical principles of ownership, control, access, and possession (OCAP) of Indigenous knowledges.[66] Getting feedback and approval from research participants (and maybe also the sponsoring Indigenous organization) prior to the publication of any findings is important, as is sharing the final publications or outputs with participants and the broader community. Researchers should also consider providing oral and visual materials or poetry and other metaphorical writings as part of the research outputs.[67] If you do not have Indigenous communities or persons supporting your project that is *with* or *for* them, then it may be best to focus your energies on researching the Indigenous-settler relationship and redressing the settler problem. Whatever one's research focus, hopefully it is underpinned by a decolonial commitment to the return of Indigenous life and land—a commitment that we act upon in our daily lives.

Conclusion

In this chapter, I have proposed that settler researchers start from a place of radical *not* knowing as a way of trying to do research in an authentic, accountable, and open-minded way. By accepting Indigenous knowledges as a gift, both in developing a research approach and in gathering "data," we are building reciprocity and responsibility into our relationships with Indigenous individuals and communities. I want to conclude by saying that this is going to be difficult, and you will most likely make mistakes. That may sound negative, but it is meant to be supportive. Through my own learning journey with NORAHT and other research projects, I have most certainly made mistakes, experiencing both humility and, once or twice, inner humiliation. This is uncomfortable but also part of the learning process. Obviously, we should always strive to avoid harming anyone, and the care required includes making sure we are not taking up Indigenous space when talking, are avoiding making assumptions, and are learning to sit in silence. Furthermore, as Aaron Mills writes in his article about learning his people's Anishinaabe ways, "I came in with the wrong kind of humility. I knew I had everything to learn. I didn't know that I didn't know what learning is. I had to learn how to learn."[68] This is a profoundly important lesson. In learning to learn, we must always engage with the sense of response-ability, as Oliver and Kuokkanen both put it, to the gift of Indigenous knowledges. Gratitude for the gift involves responsibility and reciprocity, but we must always be mindful that it is an asymmetrical reciprocity due to the irreversibility and irreducibility of Indigenous and settler positions and experiences. Thus, it is not necessarily *knowing* so much as it is *acceptance* with gratitude.

Notes

1 See: Kulchyski, "Aboriginal Rights Are Not Human Rights," 51. Kulchyski argues that Aboriginal rights are "asserted in the practice of Aboriginal culture. They will not be handed down from on high as a gift from the King or the United Nations. . . . They are won in blockades, in occupations, in marches and walks, through patience and practices, through petitions, through determination and the strength of indigenous nations and their allies."

2 This chapter is largely directed towards white settlers. I want to acknowledge the complexities of how racialized groups are differentially located within settler colonialism vis-à-vis white supremacy—e.g., through the transatlantic slave trade, the "White Canada" policy that formally existed until 1970, ongoing anti-Asian and anti-Black racism, Islamophobia, and so on. Additional intersections of gender, class, ability, and so forth are beyond my scope. See: Dhamoon, "Relational Othering"; Morgensen, "White Settlers and Indigenous Solidarity"; Thomas, "Who Is a Settler."

3 Steadman, quoted in McGuire-Adams, "Settler Allies Are Made," 763.

4 Ahmed, "The Politics of Bad Feeling"; Boler, "The Risks of Empathy."

5 Snelgrove, Dhamoon, and Corntassel, "Unsettling Settler Colonialism," 19.

6 Tuck and Yang, "Decolonization Is Not a Metaphor."

7 Ahenakew, "Grafting Indigenous."

8 Ahenakew, "Grafting Indigenous," 327.

9 Ahenakew, "Grafting Indigenous," 336.

10 Kuokkanen, "What Is Hospitality in the Academy?"

11 See Held, "Decolonizing Research Paradigms," 4–5.

12 Potts and Brown, "Becoming an Anti-Oppressive Researcher."

13 For a detailed discussion, see Snooks et al., "Blending Feminist, Indigenous, and Participatory Action Research Methodologies."

14 Wright et al., "Using Two-Eyed Seeing," 2; Wilson, *Research Is Ceremony*.
15 Marker (2004), quoted in Ahenakew, "Grafting Indigenous Ways of Knowing onto Non-Indigenous Ways of Being," 327.
16 Tuck and Yang, "Decolonization Is Not a Metaphor," 10.
17 Young, "Asymmetrical Reciprocity," 39.
18 Young, "Asymmetrical Reciprocity," 45.
19 Young, "Asymmetrical Reciprocity," 47.
20 Young, "Asymmetrical Reciprocity," 50. Emphasis added.
21 Arendt, *The Human Condition*.
22 Roher et al., "How Is *Etuaptmumk*/Two-Eyed Seeing Characterized," 1.
23 Young, "Asymmetrical Reciprocity," 50. Young draws on three French philosophers, Emmanuel Levinas, Luce Irigaray, and Jacques Derrida, to make this argument.
24 Young, "Asymmetrical Reciprocity," 54.
25 Young, "Asymmetrical Reciprocity," 56.
26 Kuokkanen, "What Is Hospitality in the Academy?," 65.
27 Kimmerer, *Braiding Sweetgrass*, 25.
28 Kimmerer, *Braiding Sweetgrass*, 25–27.
29 Kimmerer, *Braiding Sweetgrass*, 115.
30 Simpson, "Politics Based on Justice."
31 Simpson, "Politics Based on Justice"; Long, *Treaty No. 9*, 12; Duhamel, "Treaty 1 in Context."
32 Duhamel, "Treaty 1 in Context," 38.
33 Kuokkanen, "What Is Hospitality in the Academy?," 66.
34 Kuokkanen, "What Is Hospitality in the Academy?," 70.
35 Kimmerer, *Braiding Sweetgrass*, 165.
36 Although Oliver does not engage Indigenous philosophies, her emphasis on embodied and ecological relationality is an interesting point of connection. See Oliver, "Witnessing, Recognition, and Response Ethics."
37 Oliver, *Witnessing*, 15.
38 I explore Oliver's work in the context of witnessing in Nagy, "Settler Witnessing."
39 See Coulthard, *Red Skin, White Masks*; Simpson, *Mohawk Interruptus*.
40 Kuokkanen, "What Is Hospitality in the Academy?," 77.
41 Kuokkanen, "What Is Hospitality in the Academy?," 76.
42 Kuokkanen, "What Is Hospitality in the Academy?," 77–78.
43 Anti-Oppression Network, "Allyship."
44 See Gehl, "Ally Bill of Responsibilities"; Unsettling America, "Allyship and Solidarity Guidelines"; Morris, "Decolonizing Solidarity"; McGuire-Adams, "Settler Allies Are Made, Not Self-Proclaimed"; Regan, *Unsettling the Settler Within*; Snelgrove, Dhamoon, and Corntassel, "Unsettling Settler Colonialism."
45 To be clear, research *for* Indigenous Peoples means research that is engaged with or requested and guided by Indigenous Peoples. I distinguish "research *for*" from the Eurocentric history of "research *on*" Indigenous Peoples.
46 Clark, "Red Intersectionality," 48.

47 Clark, "Red Intersectionality," 48.
48 See also Wilson and Hughes, "Why Research Is Reconciliation."
49 Regan, *Unsettling the Settler Within*, 34.
50 Wilson and Hughes, "Why Research Is Reconciliation," 6.
51 Wilson and Hughes, "Why Research Is Reconciliation," 9.
52 Bartlett, Marshall, and Marshall, "Two-Eyed Seeing," 335.
53 Wright et al., "Using Two-Eyed Seeing," 2.
54 Roher et al., "How Is *Etuaptmumk*/Two-Eyed Seeing Characterized?," 13.
55 Quoted in Roher et al., "How Is *Etuaptmumk*/Two-Eyed Seeing Characterized?," 7.
56 Kapyrka and Dockstator (2012), noted in Wright et al., "Using Two-Eyed Seeing."
57 Broadhead and Howard, "Confronting the Contradictions," 112.
58 Broadhead and Howard, "Confronting the Contradictions," 118.
59 Wright et al., "Using Two-Eyed Seeing," 16.
60 Wilson and Hughes, "Why Research Is Reconciliation," 10.
61 Wright et al., "Using Two-Eyed Seeing," 15.
62 MacDonald, "Understanding Participatory Action Research."
63 Kirkness and Barnhardt, "First Nations and Higher Education." See also Stanton, "Crossing Methodological Borders."
64 Snooks et al., "Blending Feminist, Indigenous, and Participatory Action Research Methodologies." For further information on our project, see Northeastern Ontario Research Alliance on Human Trafficking (NORAHT), http://noraht.nipissingu.ca.
65 Founding partners included the Amelia Rising Sexual Violence Support Centre of Nipissing and the AIDS Committee of North Bay & Area. As individual members of the NORAHT switched jobs, so, too, did organization partnerships. I acknowledge my fellow team members, Brenda Quenneville (co-director with me), Gina Snooks, Rebecca Timms, Elder Donna Debassige, Kathleen Jodouin, and Lanyen Chen. Megan Bellefeuille, Jylelle Carpenter-Boesch, and Sydnee Wiggins were part of the team as undergraduate research assistants.
66 FNIGC, *Ownership, Control, Access and Possession (OCAP™)*.
67 Ahenakew, "Grafting Indigenous Ways of Knowing onto Non-Indigenous Ways of Being."
68 Mills, "Driving the Gift Home," 169.

Sources

Ahenakew, Cash. "Grafting Indigenous Ways of Knowing onto Non-Indigenous Ways of Being: The (Underestimated) Challenges of a Decolonial Imagination." *International Review of Qualitative Research* 9, no. 3 (2016): 323–40. https://doi.org/10.1525/irqr.2016.9.3.323.

Ahmed, Sara. "The Politics of Bad Feeling." *Australian Critical Race and Whiteness Studies Association Journal* 1 (2005): 72–85.

Anti-Oppression Network. "Allyship." Accessed December 12, 2022. https://theantioppressionnetwork.com/allyship/.

Arendt, Hannah. *The Human Condition*. University of Chicago Press, 1958.

Bartlett, Cheryl, Murdena Marshall, and Albert Marshall. "Two-Eyed Seeing and Other Lessons Learned Within a Co-Learning Journey of Bringing Together Indigenous and Mainstream Knowledges and Ways of Knowing." *Journal of Environmental Studies and Sciences* 2, no. 4 (2012): 331–40. https://doi.org/10.1007/s13412-012-0086-8.

Boler, Megan. "The Risks of Empathy: Interrogating Multiculturalism's Gaze." *Cultural Studies* 11, no. 2 (1997): 253–73. https://doi.org/10.1080/09502389700490141.

Broadhead, Lee-Anne, and Sean Howard. "Confronting the Contradictions Between Western and Indigenous Science: A Critical Perspective on Two-Eyed Seeing." *AlterNative: An International Journal of Indigenous Peoples* 17, no. 1 (2021): 111–19. https://doi.org/10.1177/11771801211996326.

Clark, Natalie. "Red Intersectionality and Violence-Informed Witnessing Praxis with Indigenous Girls." *Girlhood Studies* 9, no. 2 (2016): 46–64. https://doi.org/10.3167/ghs.2016.090205.

Coulthard, Glen S. *Red Skin, White Masks: Rejecting the Colonial Politics of Recognition*. University of Minnesota Press, 2014.

Dhamoon, Rita Kaur. "Relational Othering: Critiquing Dominance, Critiquing the Margins." *Politics, Groups & Identities* 9, no. 5 (2021): 873–92.

Duhamel, Karine, "Treaty 1 in Context: Understanding Spirit and Intent." *Canadian Issues* (Spring/Summer 2021): 38–43.

FNIGC. *Ownership, Control, Access and Possession (OCAP™): The Path to First Nations Information Governance*. First Nations Information Governance Centre, Ottawa, 2014. https://achh.ca/wp-content/uploads/2018/07/OCAP_FNIGC.pdf.

Gehl, Lynn. "Ally Bill of Responsibilities." LynnGehl.com, 2012. https://www.lynngehl.com/ally-bill-of-responsibilities.html.

Held, Mirjam B.E. "Decolonizing Research Paradigms in the Context of Settler Colonialism: An Unsettling, Mutual, and Collaborative Effort." *International Journal of Qualitative Methods* 18 (2019). https://doi.org/10.1177/1609406918821574.

Kimmerer, Robin Wall. *Braiding Sweetgrass: Indigenous Wisdom, Scientific Knowledge, and the Teachings of Plants*. Milkweed Editions, 2020.

Kirkness, Verna J., and Ray Barnhardt. "First Nations and Higher Education: The Four Rs—Respect, Relevance, Reciprocity, Responsibility." In *Knowledge Across Cultures: A Contribution to Dialogue Among Civilizations*, edited by Ruth Hayhoe and Julia Pan. Comparative Education Research Centre, University of Hong Kong, 2001.

Kulchyski, Peter. "Aboriginal Rights Are Not Human Rights." *Prairie Forum* 36 (2011): 33–53.

Kuokkanen, Rauna. "What Is Hospitality in the Academy? Epistemic Ignorance and the (Im)Possible Gift." *Review of Education, Pedagogy, & Cultural Studies* 30, no. 1 (2008): 30–82. https://doi.org/10.1080/10714410701821297.

Long, John S. *Treaty No. 9: Making the Agreement to Share the Land in Far Northern Ontario in 1905*. McGill-Queen's University Press, 2010.

MacDonald, Cathy. "Understanding Participatory Action Research: A Qualitative Research Methodology Option." *Canadian Journal of Action Research* 13, no. 2 (2012). https://doi.org/10.33524/cjar.v13i2.37.

McGuire-Adams, Tricia. "Settler Allies Are Made, Not Self-Proclaimed: Unsettling Conversations for Non-Indigenous Researchers and Educators Involved in Indigenous Health." *Health Education Journal* 80, no. 7 (2021): 761–72. https://doi.org/10.1177/00178969211009269.

Mills, Aaron. "Driving the Gift Home." *Windsor Yearbook of Access to Justice* 33, no. 1 (2016): 167–86. https://doi.org/10.22329/wyaj.v33i1.4816.

Morgensen, Scott L. "White Settlers and Indigenous Solidarity: Confronting White Supremacy, Answering Decolonial Alliances." *Decolonization, Indigeneity, Education and Society* (blog), May 26, 2014. https://decolonization.wordpress.com/2014/05/26/white-settlers-and-indigenous-solidarity-confronting-white-supremacy-answering-decolonial-alliances/.

Morris, Katie Boudreau. "Decolonizing Solidarity: Cultivating Relationships of Discomfort." *Settler Colonial Studies* 7, no. 4 (2016): 1–18. http://dx.doi.org/10.1080/2201473X.2016.1241210.

Nagy, Rosemary. "Settler Witnessing at the Truth and Reconciliation Commission of Canada." *Human Rights Review* 21, no. 3 (2020): 219–41. https://doi.org/10.1007/s12142-020-00595-w.

Oliver, Kelly. *Witnessing: Beyond Recognition*. University of Minnesota Press, 2001.

Oliver, Kelly. "Witnessing, Recognition, and Response Ethics." *Philosophy & Rhetoric* 48, no. 4 (2015): 473–93. https://doi.org/10.5325/philrhet.48.4.0473.

Potts, Karen L., and Leslie Brown. "Becoming an Anti-Oppressive Researcher." In *Research as Resistance: Revisiting Critical, Indigenous, and Anti-Oppressive Approaches*, edited by Susan Strega and Leslie Brown. Canadian Scholars' Press/Women's Press, 2015.

Regan, Paulette. *Unsettling the Settler Within: Indian Residential Schools, Truth Telling, and Reconciliation in Canada*. UBC Press, 2010.

Roher, Sophie I.G., Ziwa Yu, Debbie H. Martin, and Anita C. Benoit. "How Is Etuaptmumk/Two-Eyed Seeing Characterized in Indigenous Health Research? A Scoping Review." *PLOS One* 16, no. 7 (2021). https://doi.org/10.1371/journal.pone.0254612.

Simpson, Audra. *Mohawk Interruptus: Political Life Across the Borders of Settler States*. Duke University Press, 2014.

Simpson, Leanne Betasamosake. "Politics Based on Justice, Diplomacy Based on Love: What Indigenous Diplomatic Traditions Can Teach Us." *Briarpatch* 42, no. 3 (2013). https://briarpatchmagazine.com/articles/view/politics-based-on-justice-diplomacy-based-on-love.

Snelgrove, Corey, Rita Dhamoon, and Jeff Corntassel. "Unsettling Settler Colonialism: The Discourse and Politics of Settlers, and Solidarity with Indigenous Nations." *Decolonization: Indigeneity, Education & Society* 3, no. 2 (2014): 1–32.

Snooks, Gina, Rosemary Nagy, Rebecca Timms, Donna Debassige, Kathleen Jodouin, Brenda Quenneville, and Lanyan Chen. "Blending Feminist, Indigenous, and Participatory Action Research Methodologies: Critical Reflections from the Northeastern Ontario Research Alliance on Human Trafficking." *Feminist Formations* 33, no. 2 (2021): 160–84. https://doi.org/10.1353/ff.2021.0030.

Stanton, Christine Rogers. "Crossing Methodological Borders: Decolonizing Community-Based Participatory Research." *Qualitative Inquiry* 20, no. 5 (2014). https://doi.org/10.1177/1077800413505541.

Thomas, Ashleigh-Rae. "Who Is a Settler, According to Indigenous and Black Scholars." *Vice*, February 15, 2019. https://www.vice.com/en_ca/article/gyajj4/who-is-a-settler-according-to-indigenous-and-black-scholars.

Tuck, Eve, and K. Wayne Yang. "Decolonization Is Not a Metaphor." *Decolonization: Indigeneity, Education & Society* 1, no. 1 (2012): 1–40.

Unsettling America. "Allyship and Solidarity Guidelines." Unsettling America: Decolonization in Theory & Practice. https://unsettlingamerica.wordpress.com/allyship.

Wilson, Shawn. *Research Is Ceremony: Indigenous Research Methods*. Fernwood Publishing, 2008.

Wilson, Shawn, and Margaret Hughes. "Why Research Is Reconciliation." In *Research and Reconciliation: Unsettling Ways of Knowing through Indigenous Relationships*, edited by Shawn Wilson, Andrea V. Breen, and Lindsay DuPré. Canadian Scholars, 2019.

Wright, A.L., C. Gabel, M. Ballantyne, S.M. Jack, and O. Wahoush. "Using Two-Eyed Seeing in Research with Indigenous People: An Integrative Review." *International Journal of Qualitative Methods* 18 (2019). https://doi.org/10.1177/1609406919869695.

Young, Iris Marion. "Asymmetrical Reciprocity: On Moral Respect, Wonder and Enlarged Thought." In *Intersecting Voices: Dilemmas of Gender, Political Philosophy, and Policy*. Princeton University Press, 1997.

PART TWO

Prospects for Reconciliation and Relational Decolonization

Land Acknowledgements in an Era of Reconciliation

Enakshi Dua and Elaine Coburn

> "Queen's university is situated on the territory of the Haudenosaunee and Anishinaabek."[1]

> "This is not a land acknowledgment. / What is there to acknowledge / What once was ours to care for is now yours to benefit from"[2]

SINCE 2015, LAND ACKNOWLEDGEMENTS (LAS) ARE SPOKEN at the beginning of school events, the start of sporting and corporate meetings, film and theatre performances, academic and public conferences. They are ubiquitous in written and sometimes video form on websites and official materials by governments, corporations, and non-governmental organizations. Typically, a few minutes or a few sentences long, they recognize historical and ongoing Indigenous presence on lands now known as Canada.[3] Drawing on longstanding Indigenous protocols, some refer to specific treaties, covenants, and other formalized relationships among Indigenous Peoples with the land. They recall responsibilities to diverse Indigenous Peoples and the lands that Indigenous Peoples have inhabited since time immemorial, where meaningful reconciliation demands a taking up of those responsibilities.

Yet, land acknowledgements are ambiguous. Gina Starblanket from the Star Blanket First Nation, Treaty 4, suggests that there is a "politics of incoherency"[4] between Indigenous and colonial understandings about land acknowledgements. These reflect longstanding, fundamental disjunctures between Indigenous and colonial world views that inform divergent interpretations of land acknowledgements, their deployment, and political meanings. Thus, land acknowledgements recall responsibilities to Indigenous Peoples and their lands, but in practice, government and re-settler[5] actors often take up LAs in self-serving ways. State policies of reconciliation seek to constrain the legal import of land acknowledgements and reposition them within what Yellow Knives Dene political theorist Glen Coulthard has described as a colonial politics of recognition. If reconciliation is configured as official government policy, it is also an ideology mobilized by many re-settlers to legitimate their presence through (mis)interpretations of LAs. Rather than act as a spur to new, reciprocal relationships with Indigenous Peoples and the lands that sustain all life, state "reconciliation" as policy and as re-settler ideology repositions land acknowledgements so as to reaffirm the ongoing occupation of Indigenous lands.[6]

In this chapter, we explore the incoherent politics of land acknowledgements in an era of contested reconciliation. We open by bringing together Starblanket's concept of the politics of incoherency with Coulthard's work critiquing colonial state recognition in an era of state-defined reconciliation. We then explore divergent Indigenous and colonial state deployments of land acknowledgements and struggles over their meanings by tracing the genealogy of LAs, originally from Indigenous protocols, through their uptake in re-settler space. We next show how the Government of Canada deploys a recognition framework of performative "reconciliation," suggesting continuities between this politics and the state's efforts to contain, constrain, and interpret Indigenous world views in ways congruent with its own interests—and offer ways that LAs can be read within this framework. In our discussion, we argue that land acknowledgements must be linked with Land Back, for a transformed relationship that restores state and re-settler responsibilities to Indigenous Peoples and the land, a struggle now ongoing for more than half a millennium.

This chapter is intended primarily for non-Indigenous speakers of LAs, inviting them to reflect on LAs in their complications, their divergent and co-opted and contested meanings. Our arguments are drawn from our own understandings of how land acknowledgements operate, from our perspectives as re-settlers. But this contribution is developed in conversation with a robust field of Indigenous social and political thought, so we hope it is useful to Indigenous studies scholars as well.

The Politics of Incoherency in a "Reconciled" Canada[7]

The concept of the politics of incoherency developed when Starblanket sought to analyze divergent Indigenous and colonial interpretations of treaties. She argues that for Indigenous Peoples, treaties represent "diplomatic processes for negotiating relations of non-violent and generative co-existence between living beings in shared geographies."[8] The diplomatic practice of treaty-making unfolds within an ontological framework where, whatever differences there are among diverse Indigenous Peoples, it is a widely shared understanding that "land is not a property that can be transferred or sold."[9]

In contrast to this *relational* approach, which emphasizes the importance of developing respectful reciprocal relationships with unalienable land, the colonial government represents treaties in *transactional* terms, conceiving land as transferrable property, under the authority of the Crown. Starblanket explains:

> The treaties are depicted in Canadian political institutions as historical events in which Indigenous peoples are said to have consensually ceded and surrendered title to the land, and relinquished our existing political authority to the Crown, in exchange for a fixed spectrum of rights and entitlements.[10]

In this way, the colonial state takes up treaties on its own terms: selectively, partially, and in ways that contain Indigenous political authority, so as to legitimate and reproduce its own sovereign authority and interpretations of land-as-property. Treaties become historical, depoliticized symbols of racialized "identity and culture"[11] or transactions confirming land transfer to the colonial state rather than expansive political and legal practices that make strong, ongoing demands upon all those on Indigenous lands, especially treaty partners.

The fundamental disjuncture between Indigenous and colonial world views that inform divergent relational and transactional interpretations of treaties shape sharply contrasting understandings of land acknowledgements. Today, Indigenous Peoples draw on longstanding protocols within their nations to write contemporary LAs, while mobilizing them in new ways, both to counter self-serving colonial mythologies that legitimate the Canadian state and to reaffirm the ongoing relevance of their own relational political practices. Against this approach, the colonial state seeks to limit, constrain, and reinterpret land acknowledgements in transactional ways that are congruent with the state's ongoing authority over Indigenous Peoples. To understand the state's role in shaping interpretations of LAs, we turn to Coulthard's critique of recognition politics.

Like Starblanket, Coulthard emphasizes that Indigenous Peoples, whatever their differences, generally understand "the land as a mode of reciprocal *relationship*."[12] Fulfilling relational responsibilities to the land is thus a fundamental commitment for self-determining Indigenous nations, and one way of understanding substantive reconciliation. Yet, the colonial state cannot respect these commitments, Coulthard maintains, because they fundamentally undermine the legitimacy of the colonial state. Therefore, the state engages with a politics of recognition that purports to respect Indigenous relationship with the lands, only to undermine such acknowledgements by "rendering consistent Indigenous assertions of nationhood with the state's unilateral assertion of sovereignty over Native peoples' lands and populations."[13] Indigenous Peoples are recognized only in depoliticized expressions of racialized identity and culture that allow and, in fact, newly legitimate the state's ongoing occupation of Indigenous land.

We argue that land acknowledgements are a colonial politics of recognition where, in a spirit of "reconciliation," the state purports to recognize Indigenous Peoples, but only to reassert colonial authority over Indigenous lands on a newly legitimated basis. In the unequal context of colonialism, the incoherent politics of land acknowledgements are interpreted in ways congenial to the colonial status quo, even as Indigenous Peoples continue their own political practices and land acknowledgement protocols on their own terms.

Indigenous Political Practices of Land Acknowledgments

Despite the diversity of Indigenous Peoples, there is broad agreement that recognizing the land is a longstanding practice among original peoples in Canada and worldwide:

> Indigenous communities globally have sustained practices and protocols of recognizing, acknowledging, announcing, welcoming, and inviting each other as well as non-Indigenous people since time immemorial. Cree scholar Karyn Recollet reminds us, "When we talk about the newness of territorial acknowledgments, these aren't new. Acknowledging relationships to space and place is an ancient Indigenous practice that flows into the future."[14]

Similarly, Anishinaabe scholar Joe Wark observes that land acknowledgements, as practices of territorial recognition, have long histories prior to the arrival of the colonizers. Contemporary protocols, he maintains, are variants on these longstanding practices:

> Indigenous peoples of Turtle Island (North America) have always engaged in practices of recognizing each other in terms of language, nation, territory, clan, and lineage.... While pre-colonial territorial borders may have been fluid and overlapping, there was always an awareness of the demarcation of territory... and all nations had protocols about how to behave in someone else's territory.[15]

These traditional, still-living protocols respect the specific relationships of particular Indigenous nations with given lands, while developing diplomatic ties that support land-sharing with other nations, within an ontological and spiritual paradigm where land is understood to be inalienable.

Recalling the origins of land acknowledgements, Mohawk scholar Janice Hill writes about her own community practices: "It was historically customary that when someone was approaching our settlement, they would light a fire to indicate they wished to enter."[16] In Hill's experience, the practice no longer includes lighting a fire, but does include relationship-building protocols through "formal words, food and at times, gifting."[17] Such protocols matter, she argues, because they recognize the importance of "Land, Language and Kinship" to Indigenous Peoples and their stewardship of the land, from time immemorial.[18]

This is a political practice, since, as Anishinaabe writer and scholar Armand Garnet Ruffo observes, land acknowledgements and associated protocols participate in managing "intrusions" by building relationships with "visitors," and so this diplomacy is "fundamentally tied to people and nationhood."[19] Their use today, despite genocidal colonial violence that has sought to extinguish Indigenous Peoples and peoplehood,[20] speaks to the persistence of diverse Indigenous Peoples and their commitments to renewing their own political practices of relationship-building across their lands and territories, on their own terms.[21]

Contemporary Land Acknowledgements in Re-Settler Spaces

Now enacted largely for and often by non-Indigenous persons, contemporary land acknowledgements take on new functions. Many trace their introduction in re-settler spaces to the 2015 *Final Report* of the Truth and Reconciliation Commission (TRC), which investigated the genocidal violence of the residential school systems, schools that were mandatory for Status Indian children for over a century.[22] The United Way in Halifax recalls, for instance, starting land acknowledgements following the TRC's Calls to Action.[23] Similarly, the University of Waterloo explains that its land acknowledgement is part of the university's "response projects" to calls for truth and reconciliation, following the TRC.[24] For some, LAs were a response to the TRC's call for the "relearning" of histories on lands known as Canada,[25] thus linking land acknowledgement with broader practices of reconciliation.

Four years after the TRC *Final Report*, the demand for land acknowledgements was made explicit in the report from the National Inquiry into Missing and Murdered Indigenous Women and Girls (NIMMIWG), which asks Canadians to

> decolonize by learning the true history of Canada and Indigenous history in your local area. Learn about and celebrate Indigenous Peoples' history, cultures, pride, and diversity, acknowledging the land you live on and its importance to local Indigenous communities, both historically and today.[26]

Importantly, and oft forgotten, the call for LAs was tied to other actions to decolonize Canada, since the National Inquiry's final report, *Reclaiming Power and Place*, included 231 Calls for Justice. Thus, LAs in re-settler contexts are meant to participate in broader relationship-building with Indigenous Peoples and with place, inviting re-settlers to *learn the true history* of these lands, not alone but in concert with a host of other initiatives.

In recalling the "true history" of these lands, LAs take up what Anishinaabe/Métis scholar Aimée Craft and re-settler writer Paulette Regan[27] argue is part of the work of meaningful or substantive reconciliation, which demands (among other actions)

> the rejection of colonial legal assumptions, such as the Doctrine of Discovery and terra nullius, that have systematically dispossessed, marginalized, and impoverished Indigenous peoples within their own territories.[28]

We suggest, following and enlarging on Craft and Regan, that land acknowledgements have three reconciliation purposes: first, to debunk the Doctrine of Discovery and *terra nullius*; second, to counter the persistent colonial myth of the Vanishing Indian; and third, to recall the ongoing salience of diverse Indigenous political practices. Deconstructive elements to land acknowledgements seek to undo harmful colonial myths, while there is a reconstructive dynamic, affirming the ongoing political practices of Indigenous Peoples as critical guides to contemporary and future relationships among Indigenous Peoples, the land, and with other peoples.

Three Functions of Land Acknowledgements

As even a cursory survey of LAs shows, they, first and foremost, challenge the longstanding colonial myths of the Doctrine of Discovery and *terra nullius*. These are the closely connected ideas that the colonizers "discovered" what is now North America, arriving on "empty" land, because Indigenous Peoples' supposed religious, racial, or civilizational inferiority meant their presence did not count ontologically, legally, or politically.[29]

Characteristically, the provincially funded ArtsNB in New Brunswick counters *terra nullius* by recognizing that "it carries out its work on the traditional unceded territory of the Wolastoqiyik, Mi'kmaq and Peskotomuhkati peoples."[30] The City of New Westminster in British Columbia makes clear its efforts to challenge *terra nullius*:

> We recognize and respect that New Westminster is on the unceded and unsurrendered land of the Halkomelem speaking Peoples. We acknowledge that colonialism has made invisible their histories and

> connections to the land. As a city, we are learning and building relationships with the people whose lands we are on.[31]

Against settler practices of overwriting Indigenous names with European designations for cities and lands, such acknowledgements insist on historical Indigenous presence and recall specific Indigenous Peoples' relationships with the land "since time immemorial." This helps to re-establish the true histories of these lands, countering the tenacious colonial myths of the Doctrine of Discovery and *terra nullius*.

Second, many land acknowledgements emphasize contemporary Indigenous relations with the land, so challenging the persistent trope of the Vanishing Indian. In this centuries-old narrative, Indigenous Peoples are consigned to prehistory either because they are racially doomed within a white supremacist evolutionary story or because they are civilizationally doomed within a narrative of European cultural superiority, so leaving Indigenous lands open for settler futurities.[32] The Vanishing Indian may be lamented, because Indigenous Peoples are noble savages and their loss associated with the end of national innocence, or celebrated, because they are barbarians whose disappearance announces the triumph of a more advanced, modern Western civilization.[33] Against this narrative, which secures settler futurities and denies them to Indigenous Peoples, many LAs have language that emphasizes contemporary Indigenous presence and inherent rights.

The land acknowledgement of the Royal British Columbia Museum in Victoria recognizes prior and contemporary Indigenous presence:

> Long before colonial settlers arrived in what later became known as British Columbia, the land on which the museum and archives now stand was the traditional territory of the Lekwungen peoples, *today* represented by the Songhee and Xwsepsum (Esquimalt) Nations.[34]

Given persistent ideas about Indigenous Peoples as "a vanishing race that is regrettably inferior, passive, part of the past,"[35] many land acknowledgements provide a counternarrative that refuses their erasure as contemporaries.

Third, land acknowledgements do not only answer back to colonial myths; they reaffirm the contemporary salience of Indigenous political practices. Many LAs insist upon ongoing obligations under treaties and covenants. In Winnipeg, the local Canadian football team observes, for instance, that "the Winnipeg Blue Bombers are proud to be the first CFL team in history to implement an acknowledgement statement before every game, recognizing that Investors Group Field is located on traditional Treaty One Territory."[36] Similarly, the Villains Theatre, a small company in Halifax, Nova Scotia, emphasizes contemporary treaties and explicitly rejects interpretations that such treaties meant that Indigenous Peoples "surrendered" their lands:

> This territory is covered by the "Treaties of Peace and Friendship" which Mi'kmaq and Wolastoqiyik (Maliseet) people first signed with the British Crown in 1725. These treaties did not deal with the surrender of lands and resources but in fact recognized Mi'kmaq and Wolastoqiyik (Maliseet) title and established the rules for what was to be an ongoing relationship between nations.[37]

Referring to treaties, covenants, and unceded territorial relationships articulates the inherent rights of Indigenous Peoples, especially rights to relationships with the land as part of the inherent right to self-government. LAs emphasize continuity with past Indigenous political practices and their contemporary salience to generative, "ongoing relationships" between Indigenous nations and the land.

The Nightmarish Question: Whose Lands Are We On?

Today, about a decade after LAs became more widespread in re-settler settings and routines, it is easy to forget the impact that land acknowledgements once had. Yet, the fact of asserting Indigenous presence against the colonial erasure of their histories and contemporary presence was originally a radical statement in re-settler contexts. As Métis scholar Chelsea Vowel recalls, "When territorial acknowledgments first began, they were fairly powerful statements of presence, somewhat shocking, perhaps even unwelcome in settler spaces. They provoked discomfort and centered Indigenous priority on these lands."[38]

For Anishinaabe writer Armand Garnet Ruffo, land acknowledgements make clear that, "no, the land was not vacant when [re-settlers'] ancestors arrived, and it was not theirs for the taking."[39] Similarly, in 2017, Alison Norman, a research advisor at the Ontario Ministry of Indigenous Relations and Reconciliation, suggested that LAs "recognize that we, as settlers and as people who are not part of First Nations or Indigenous groups, are here on *their* land."[40] As Stephan Marche explains, for re-settlers, LAs "ask a basic, nightmarish question: 'Whose land are we on?'"[41] In so unsettling the taken-for-granted colonial occupation of Indigenous lands, "a speech act of land acknowledgement *can* be part of a reckoning with colonialism."[42] LAs help re-establish the true histories of Canada while recognizing ongoing Indigenous presence and the contemporary power of Indigenous political practices for fostering generative relationships with the land.

Land Acknowledgements and State Reconciliation[43]

The construction of colonialism and re-settler occupation as innocent has long roots but is continually reinvented, both by the colonial state and in associated, popular ideologies. Today, the Government of Canada propagates official narratives to claim that Canada and re-settlers legitimately occupy these lands. Here and in the next section, we explore how Indigenous demands for reconciliation are reconfigured in state policy, for the state's own purposes, while operating in related but distinct ways as popular ideology, in ways comforting to re-settler interests. Following Coulthard, we explore the Government of Canada's politics of recognition as a pathway to "reconciliation" with Indigenous Peoples and so to a newly legitimated state and re-settler occupation. In the Canadian state's understanding of a "reconciled" nation, we argue, land acknowledgements can be—and are—interpreted by states and by re-settlers in ways that claim congruency between Indigenous self-determination and colonial sovereign authority.

In 2021, in a late response to the United Nations Declaration on the Rights of Indigenous Peoples (UNDRIP) and its recent passage into Canadian law,[44] the Government of Canada published a document entitled "Principles Respecting the Government of Canada's Relationship with Indigenous Peoples" (hereafter Principles). The opening sentence employs apparently unambiguous nation-to-nation language that has been hard-fought by Indigenous Peoples:

> The Government of Canada is committed to achieving reconciliation with Indigenous peoples through a renewed, nation-to-nation, government-to-government, and Inuit–Crown relationship based

> on recognition of rights, respect, co-operation, and partnership as the foundation for transformative change.[45]

Besides this promise for "reconciliation" through a "renewed" relationship based on "recognition" that demonstrates commitment to "transformative change," the Government of Canada explicitly describes this as a process that demands "decolonization."[46]

There is no pretense that the foundation of Canada and subsequent relations with Indigenous Peoples have, historically, been a relationship of peaceful coexistence. Rather, the Principles emphasize a desire to end "troubled" practices of the past and to forge a new relationship between the Government of Canada and Indigenous Peoples, to

> seek to turn the page in an often troubled relationship by advancing fundamental change whereby Indigenous peoples increasingly live in strong and healthy communities with thriving cultures. To achieve this change, it is recognized that Indigenous nations are self-determining, self-governing, increasingly self-sufficient, and rightfully aspire to no longer be marginalized, regulated, and administered under the *Indian Act* and similar instruments.

Moreover, the Government of Canada makes strong commitments to recognizing the "inherent rights" of Indigenous Peoples, notably including

> the rights that derive from their political, economic, and social structures and from their cultures, spiritual traditions, histories, laws, and philosophies, especially their rights to their lands, territories and resources.

The government explicitly sets aside its own traditions, laws, and philosophies as sources of Indigenous rights, emphasizing that Indigenous rights are inherent, arising from Indigenous Peoples' own practices and relationships with their lands and territories.

The Principles contains a fundamental contradiction, however, since if Indigenous self-determining rights are inherent to diverse Indigenous Peoples, then they do not depend upon the "recognition" that the Government of Canada offers. In fact, the Principles affirms, retroactively, that the *Constitution Act, 1982*—which states that "the existing aboriginal and treaty rights of the aboriginal peoples of Canada are hereby recognized and affirmed" (section 35, (i))—has "reconciliation" as its "fundamental purpose." Reconciliation and the "recognition" of Indigenous rights are so resituated under the auspices and authority of the colonial state's Constitution. Subsequently, the document makes explicit the claim that Indigenous rights are subsumed under the Canadian state: "Indigenous self-government is *part of* Canada's evolving system of cooperative federalism and distinct orders of government" (emphasis added).

The Government of Canada thus seeks to "turn the page" from its "troublesome" history with Indigenous Peoples, in a transformed or "reconciled" Canada that recognizes Indigenous Peoples' inherent right to self-determination. Yet this is immediately contradicted, since Indigenous self-government is then declared to be assured *within* the Canadian Constitution, as "part of" the state's "cooperative federality" and "distinct orders of government." In a self-serving colonial narrative, the incoherent politics of Indigenous self-determination and colonial authority over Indigenous Peoples are "reconciled" within the Canadian federal state.

Within a colonial politics of recognition, former Prime Minister Justin Trudeau and other representatives of the Government of Canada therefore read land acknowledgements, like this one, when in Ottawa, confident that they pose no threat to the Canadian state:

> Before I begin, I'd like to recognize the Algonquin Nation, on whose traditional territory we are gathering. We acknowledge them as the past, present, and future caretakers of this land.[47]

Yet if the LA affirms past Algonquin presence, so rejecting *terra nullius* claims, and emphasizes the Algonquin as the present and future caretakers of the land, so rejecting the Vanishing Indian trope and affirming Indigenous futurities, the incoherent politics of Algonquin nationhood and Canadian colonialism can be read "as if" they are congruent. Interpreted through the colonial state's "reconciliation" lens, the Canadian state's occupation is legitimated through the LA rather than unsettled by that reading, given the presumption of the Crown as the guarantor of the Algonquin Nation's "inherent" rights to self-determination—however contradictory it is to assert inherent Indigenous rights as granted by the colonial state.

Educating Re-Settlers into State-Led Reconciliation

Such Government of Canada policies may inform re-settler readings of land acknowledgements in ways that legitimate re-settler occupation. Cree scholar Michelle Daigle explains that "Indigenous stories" are reinterpreted or mediated through "colonial power" in ways that enable "settler colonial business" to continue uninterrupted. She observes:

> In an era of reconciliation and healing... Indigenous stories simultaneously become mediated by colonial power to make our lives calculable and manageable and are mobilized, alongside performances of recognition and remorse, to allow settler colonial business to resume as usual.[48]

Land acknowledgements are part of this "spectacle of reconciliation," Daigle emphasizes:

> Specifically, in an era of reconciliation, white settlers' spectacular performances of apologies, land acknowledgments, and multicultural celebrations of Indigenous culture and art become crucial in reifying geographies of nation purity on a large scale.[49]

Everyday Canadians can take up land acknowledgements in ways that reflect their own interests, so reconciling Indigenous self-determining presence with their legitimated re-settlement of Indigenous lands.

Even a re-settler who has not read the Government of Canada's understanding of recognition and reconciliation under the Crown's authority can read land acknowledgements in that spirit, comforting their own presence on Indigenous lands. The Law Society of Alberta's "basic" land acknowledgement, for instance, reads as follows:

> We would like to take this opportunity to acknowledge the traditional territories of the Indigenous peoples of the Treaty 6 region and the Métis Settlements and Métis Nation of Alberta, Regions 2, 3 and 4. We respect the histories, languages, and cultures of First Nations, Metis, Inuit, and all First Peoples of Canada, whose presence continues to enrich our community.[50]

The recognition of "traditional" territories counters *terra nullius* but decouples that fact from the political and legal implications of historical Indigenous presence, which becomes mere historical fact. Likewise, the affirmation of "respect" for the "histories, language, and cultures" of Indigenous Peoples becomes a gesture of "recognition" that acknowledges how Indigenous cultures "continue to enrich" re-settler cultures, so recognizing ongoing Indigenous presence on these lands—but without unsettling colonial futurities now "reconciled" in a richly multicultural Canada that includes Indigenous Peoples.

Such self-serving interpretations are possible for virtually every element of land acknowledgements. Rather than being read as commitments to relational responsibilities to Indigenous Peoples and their lands, land acknowledgements referring to treaties and covenants, like the Dish with One Spoon, can be read as coexisting unproblematically with the authority of the Crown or as "transactional," so authorizing re-settler occupation of Indigenous lands. The City of Toronto's "guide" to land acknowledgements, for instance, baldly asserts the transactional interpretation, maintaining that "treaties are the legal basis for acquiring land by settlers and they allowed for the settlement of Canada."[51] All three aims of LAs—challenging *terra nullius* and the Vanishing Indian and insisting on the contemporary relevance of Indigenous political practices and imaginaries—can be undone by interpretations broadly similar to the Government of Canada's reconciliation politics, legitimating the state and, by extension, re-settler occupation on Indigenous lands.

Critiques of LAs: From Indigenous Protocols to Re-Settler Innocence

Given such interpretations, many Indigenous actors point to the contradictions and limits of LAs. Land acknowledgements have changed not only in terms of their original Indigenous context but also in their meaning and purpose. Rather than participating in the generative practice of relationship-building that supports the ongoing renewal of Indigenous connections and responsibilities to the land or encouraging re-settlers to ask the "nightmarish" question of whose land we are on, they participate in the rearticulation of the legitimacy of the colonial state and re-settler occupation. In the context of the ongoing colonial dispossession and exploitation, LAs are interpreted in ways deeply embedded in the Canadian state's rhetoric of reconciliation and re-settler claims to innocence.

In this vein, Ruffo suggests that LAs today have little to do with traditional Indigenous protocols and now work mainly to erase re-settler guilt.[52] Thus they are "about settler Canadians talking to themselves to assuage their guilt."[53] Responsibilities to transform political, economic, and social relations with Indigenous Peoples are replaced by the simple articulation of a land acknowledgement. In so doing, LAs allow re-settlers to position themselves as legitimate inhabitants of the land and innocent in that occupation, since as "good" settlers they have recognized Indigenous presence.

In a 2019 interview, Beausoleil First Nation scholar Hayden King regretted his participation in writing land acknowledgements for his university. He points out that territorial acknowledgements and their articulations offer re-settlers a substitute for learning about Indigenous Peoples and their political practices. A scripted land acknowledgement, especially one written by an Indigenous person like himself,

> effectively excuses them [non-Indigenous speakers] and offers them an alibi for [not] doing the hard work of learning about their neighbours and learning about the treaties of the territory and learning about those nations that should have jurisdiction.[54]

Institutions that offer acknowledgements, especially in privileged places like government organizations and universities, use LAs to legitimize their presence on Indigenous lands. "There is a danger of the acknowledgement just becoming that excuse, through which these institutions provide themselves permission to be on that territory," King laments.[55] LAs now serve as an alibi to re-settler complacency about their occupation, giving "permission" for re-settlement.

Expressing similar frustrations, Wark writes that land acknowledgements are no longer about Indigenous Peoples but instead re-establish re-settler "benevolence and innocence":

> Land acknowledgements are rhetorical devices that reference a mythical fabrication of Indigenousness that is consistent with settler dreams of benevolence and innocence. By erasing genuine Indigenous presence, these acknowledgements seek to solve the "Indian problem" by unilaterally and prematurely declaring colonization to be over and settlers to be the legitimate inhabitants of the land.[56]

Finally, Daigle, a member of Constance Lake First Nation in Treaty 9, suggests that land acknowledgements can be "respectful and meaningful"[57] when taken up in ways that activate "the relational accountability that is embedded in this legal and political practice, by calling up one's kinship relations."[58] In practice, LAs are more often part of a "spectacle of reconciliation" that serves only to assuage "white guilt."[59] LAs are enacted in "hollow gestures of lip service as routine-like territorial acknowledgments are quickly forgotten and brushed aside to resume business as usual, according to well-established colonial and racialized power asymmetries."[60] They can, moreover, be mobilized to support a reconciliation narrative that normalizes and legitimates an unjust colonial status quo that is "void of any real political and legal change in structural relations between Indigenous hosts, faculty, students, and staff, and educational institutions and settlers working at such institutions." Indeed, she argues, "such performances further propagate the myth that Canadians are reconciling their relationship and that everything is okay."[61] The co-optation of LAs into narratives of colonial state legitimacy and re-settler innocence creates a distinction between the "good" settler, who performs the land acknowledgement, and the "bad" settler, who fails to carry one out.

Struggles continue over meaningful ways to recognize Indigenous relationships with the land, however, where LAs are one site for those struggles. If Indigenous actors renew their world views, including in part through LAs, the colonial state and many re-settlers actively seek to limit and contain their import, incorporating them into new narratives of colonial and re-settler innocence in a reconciled Canada.

From Land Acknowledgments to Land Back

How should LAs be understood? What work do they do, and for whom, and what questions do they elide? Writing before land acknowledgements became commonplace in re-settler contexts, LaRocque observes different meanings of land and home. She recognizes the affective charge of land, for both Indigenous and re-settler peoples, but brings the question back to the hard material interests:

> Of course, people love land (or home) in myriad ways. But "love" is not just about attitudes and sentiments, it is about who ends up with the actual land mass with its enormous resources.[62]

There are material stakes behind the struggles over LAs and their meanings. The politics of incoherency is about the disjuncture between Indigenous world views and colonial paradigms, but the differences are not only discursive. They are struggles about the relationships between Indigenous and re-settler peoples and the ongoing dispossession of Indigenous Peoples of their own lands.

At their best, LAs draw on traditional practices to insist on the ongoing salience of diverse Indigenous political imaginaries and practices, the fact of Indigenous contemporary and future presence on their own lands, and the importance of re-settler responsibilities to Indigenous Peoples on their territories. This reflects Indigenous Peoples' enduring presence and their renewal of their own political practices and imaginaries, despite more than five hundred years since the invasion of European peoples and the genocide they carried out.

Too often, colonial actors read land acknowledgements for their own purposes, taking them up as affective statements that are sufficient, in and of themselves, to assert a new era of "reconciled" Indigenous and re-settler coexistence on Indigenous lands. Historical Indigenous presence is read as nothing more than a fact, rather than as challenging the colonial state's legitimacy given Indigenous Peoples' inherent rights to the lands from time immemorial. Such (mis)readings are widespread, and a host of Indigenous scholars have critiqued land acknowledgements as rote, tokenistic, and serving to legitimize settler occupation. These critics point to the move to innocence, the performative production of the "good" government and the "good" re-settler, who, by enunciating land acknowledgements, breaks with the "bad" colonial state re-settler of the past. The nightmarish question of whose lands re-settlers are on is transmuted into a complacent assertion of pacified coexistence in a new era of reconciliation, the land acknowledgement acting as an end point rather than an entry into the long, difficult journey of working towards right relationships between re-settlers and Indigenous Peoples.

Ultimately, if Indigenous Peoples' political authority is to be respected, land acknowledgements must be articulated with the material politics of land, as LaRocque reminds us. In short, we must move from land acknowledgements to Land Back, raising questions about compensation and resources. This demands a dramatic shift from understanding Indigenous Peoples as cultural remnants within a reconciled Canada to respect for self-determining political authorities with distinctive philosophical orders, rooted in their relationships with the land from time immemorial. Yet there is little motive for colonial states to take up Indigenous political practices and imaginaries, because the consequences are transformative and, indeed, revolutionary. They threaten not just the authority but the very existence of what Métis scholar Joyce Green, a citizen of the Ktunaxa Nation, has called "Project Canada,"[63] a country conjured ideologically and materially, at once "imagined into being" in the nineteenth century[64] and whose existence demands the destitution of Indigenous Peoples' "land, resources and political power."[65] The surveillance, criminalization, and attacks on Wet'suwet'en land defenders is one example of the state violence that meets Indigenous Peoples when they seek to assert their self-determining rights to relationships with their own lands against the authority of the Crown and the interests of corporations whose profits depend upon resource extraction.

There is much more that needs to be explored. Daigle refers to the ways that LAs can assuage "white guilt,"[66] a reminder of dynamics of racialization that we have not explored, especially the role of whiteness in LAs and how whiteness is bound up with colonial teleologies of settlement. A more complete analysis would take up the ways that violence against Indigenous Peoples is imbricated in white supremacy in much the same way as is the violence against and the exclusions of racialized peoples, not least through racist immigration policies. The enslavement of Black and Indigenous Peoples on Canadian lands and the exclusions, or the legally precarious inclusion, of racialized peoples further complicates land acknowledgements in ways that demand much fuller treatment than we give here.

We close by observing that, traditionally, land acknowledgements were an opening rather than an end point, marking the beginning of the long journey of creating reciprocal relationships to Indigenous Peoples and to their lands, which sustain all life. The real work remains to be done.

Notes

1 Queen's University, "Land Acknowledgement."

2 George, "This Is Not a Land Acknowledgement," 3.

3 On lands claimed by the Canadian state, Indigenous Peoples are diverse, so this simplifies narratives across distinct peoples for the purposes of the chapter.

4 Starblanket, "The Numbered Treaties and the Politics of Incoherency."

5 LaRocque, *When the Other Is Me*, 7. We follow Métis scholar Emma LaRocque's designation of European settlers as "re-settlers" since, she observes,

"Native peoples were the original settlers, in the sense of being a deeply rooted and settled Indigenous presence on this land we now call Canada."

6 Coulthard, *Red Skin, White Masks*.

7 We use "reconciliation" in quotes to indicate the state's policies of reconciliation and associated ideologies, in contrast with Indigenous uses of reconciliation against histories of colonialism and genocide. This is an example of the incoherent politics between Indigenous and colonial state actors.

8 Starblanket, "The Numbered Treaties and the Politics of Incoherency," 444.

9 Starblanket, "The Numbered Treaties and the Politics of Incoherency," 453.

10 Starblanket, "The Numbered Treaties and the Politics of Incoherency," 445.

11 Starblanket, "The Numbered Treaties and the Politics of Incoherency," 450–56.

12 Coulthard, *Red Skin, White Masks*, 60.

13 Coulthard, *Red Skin, White Masks*, 107.

14 Stewart-Ambo and Yang, "Beyond Land Acknowledgment in Settler Institutions," 21.

15 Wark, "Land Acknowledgements in the Academy," 193.

16 Robinson et al., "Rethinking the Practice and Performance," 23.

17 Robinson et al., "Rethinking the Practice and Performance," 23.

18 Robinson et al., "Rethinking the Practice and Performance," 24.

19 Robinson et al., "Rethinking the Practice and Performance."

20 MacDonald, *The Sleeping Giant Awakens*; Starblanket, "The Numbered Treaties and the Politics of Incoherency," 443–59.

21 See Alfred, *Wasáse*; Coulthard, *Red Skin, White Masks*; Simpson, "Indigenous Resurgence and Co-Resistance."

22 Truth and Reconciliation Commission of Canada (TRC), *Honouring the Truth, Reconciling for the Future*. See also Wilkes et al., "Canadian University Acknowledgment."

23 Johnson, "Understanding Our Land Acknowledgement."

24 University of Waterloo, "About Territorial Acknowledgement."

25 See, for instance, Wilkes et al., "Canadian University Acknowledgment."

26 National Inquiry into Missing and Murdered Indigenous Women and Girls (NIMMIWG), *Reclaiming Power and Place: Executive Summary*.

27 Craft and Reagan, "Introduction," 29–30.

28 Craft and Reagan, "Introduction," 12.

29 See Allard-Tremblay and Coburn, "The Flying Heads of Settler Colonialism."

30 ArtsNB, "Indigenous Land Acknowledgement."

31 McManus, "New West Council Approves."

32 Berry, "The Myth of the Vanishing Indian"; Vine Deloria Jr., "Introduction."

33 See Allard-Tremblay and Coburn, "The Flying Heads of Settler Colonialism."

34 Royal BC Museum, "History of the Territory." Emphasis added.

35 Wark, "Land Acknowledgements in the Academy," 201.

36 Winnipeg Blue Bombers, "Indigenous Community."

37 Villains Theatre, "Land Acknowledgement."
38 Chelsea Vowel, quoted in Stewart-Ambo and Yang, "Beyond Land Acknowledgment in Settler Institutions," 22.
39 Armand Garnet Ruffo in Robinson et al., "Rethinking the Practice and Performance," 27.
40 Shahzad, "What Is the Significance of Acknowledging." Emphasis added.
41 Marche, "Canada's Impossible Acknowledgment."
42 Couture in Robinson et a., "Rethinking the Practice and Performance of Indigenous Land Acknowledgement," 27.
43 Dua is exploring, more fully, the dynamics of settler governmentality and the role of state intervention in land acknowledgement to limit LAS.
44 UNDRIP was adopted at the United Nations in 2007 with 144 votes in favour and 4 against (Australia, Canada, New Zealand, and the United States), as well as 11 abstentions. In 2010, the Government of Canada approved of UNDRIP as an "aspirational" document, but it did not become law until 2021, five years after Cree Member of Parliament Romeo Saganash proposed its adoption in a private member's bill. Government of Canada, "Backgrounder."
45 Government of Canada, "Principles Respecting."
46 "Decolonization" is explicitly used by the Government of Canada but not defined in the document.
47 Government of Canada, "Prime Minister Justin Trudeau's Speech." Trudeau continued to preface speeches with this kind of acknowledgement through the course of his tenure in office.
48 Daigle, "The Spectacle of Reconciliation," 709.
49 Daigle, "The Spectacle of Reconciliation," 707.
50 Law Society of Alberta, *Land Acknowledgement Guide*, 11.
51 City of Toronto, "Land Acknowledgement."
52 Armand Garnet Ruffo in Robinson et al., "Rethinking the Practice and Performance."
53 Robinson et al., "Rethinking the Practice and Performance," 26.
54 CBC Radio, "'I Regret It'"
55 CBC Radio, "'I Regret It.'"
56 Wark, "Land Acknowledgements in the Academy," 193.
57 Daigle, "The Spectacle of Reconciliation," 711.
58 Daigle, "The Spectacle of Reconciliation," 711.
59 Daigle, "The Spectacle of Reconciliation," 705.
60 Daigle, "The Spectacle of Reconciliation," 711.
61 Daigle, "The Spectacle of Reconciliation," 711.
62 LaRocque, *When the Other Is me*, 137.
63 Green, "Canaries in the Mines of Citizenship," 716.
64 Green, "Canaries in the Mines of Citizenship," 721.
65 Green, "Canaries in the Mines of Citizenship," 716.
66 Daigle, "The Spectacle of Reconciliation," 705.

Sources

Alfred, Taiaiake. *Wasáse: Indigenous Pathways of Action and Freedom.* University of Toronto Press, 2005.

Allard-Tremblay, Yann, and Elaine Coburn. "The Flying Heads of Settler Colonialism; or the Ideological Erasures of Indigenous Peoples in Political Theorizing." *Political Studies* 71, no. 2 (2021): 359–78. https://doi.org/10.1177/00323217211018127.

ArtsNB. "Indigenous Land Acknowledgement." https://artsnb.ca/web/about/indigenous-land-acknowledgement/.

Berry, Brewton. "The Myth of the Vanishing Indian." *Phylon* 21, no. 1 (1960): 51–57. https://doi.org/10.2307/273734.

CBC Radio. "'I Regret It': Hayden King on Writing Ryerson University's Territorial Acknowledgement." *CBC News*, January 18, 2019. https://www.cbc.ca/radio/unreserved/redrawing-the-lines-1.4973363/i-regret-it-hayden-king-on-writing-ryerson-university-s-territorial-acknowledgement-1.4973371.

City of Toronto. "Land Acknowledgement." https://www.toronto.ca/city-government/accessibility-human-rights/indigenous-affairs-office/land-acknowledgement/.

Coulthard, Glen S. *Red Skin, White Masks: Rejecting the Colonial Politics of Recognition.* University of Minnesota Press, 2014.

Craft, Aimée, and Paulette Reagan. "Introduction." In *Pathways of Reconciliation: Indigenous and Settler Approaches to Implementing the TRC's Calls to Action*, edited by Aimée Craft and Paulette Reagan. University of Manitoba Press, 2020.

Daigle, Michelle. "The Spectacle of Reconciliation: On (the) Unsettling Responsibilities to Indigenous Peoples in the Academy." *Environment and Planning D: Society and Space* 37, no. 4 (2019): 703–21. https://doi.org/10.1177/0263775818824342.

Deloria, Vine Jr. "Introduction." In Christopher Lyman, *The Vanishing Race and Other Illusions: Photographs of Indians by Edward S. Curtis.* Pantheon Books, 1982.

George, Heather. "This Is Not a Land Acknowledgement." *Collections: A Journal for Museum and Archives Professionals* 18, no. 1 (2022): 3–4. https://doi.org/10.1177/15501906211072910.

Government of Canada. "Backgrounder: United Nations Declaration on the Rights of Indigenous Peoples Act." 2021. https://www.justice.gc.ca/eng/declaration/about-apropos.html.

Government of Canada. "Prime Minister Justin Trudeau's Speech to the Assembly of First Nations Special Chiefs Assembly." December, 6, 2016. https://www.pm.gc.ca/en/news/speeches/2016/12/06/prime-minister-justin-trudeaus-speech-assembly-first-nations-special.

Government of Canada. "Principles Respecting the Government of Canada's Relationship with Indigenous Peoples." Last modified September 1, 2021. https://www.justice.gc.ca/eng/csj-sjc/principles-principes.html.

Green, Joyce. "Canaries in the Mines of Citizenship: Indian Women in Canada." *Canadian Journal of Political Science / Revue canadienne de science politique* 34, no. 4 (2001): 715–38. https://doi.org/10.1017/s0008423901778067.

Johnson, Michelle. "Understanding Our Land Acknowledgement and Recognition Statement." United Way Halifax, June, 22, 2022. https://www.unitedwayhalifax.ca/blog/land-acknowledgement/.

LaRocque, Emma. *When the Other Is Me: Native Resistance Discourse 1850–1990*. University of Manitoba Press, 2010.

MacDonald, David B. *The Sleeping Giant Awakens: Genocide, Indian Residential Schools, and the Challenge of Conciliation*. University of Toronto Press, 2019.

McManus, Theresa. "New West Council Approves Interim Land Acknowledgement for Meetings." *New Westminster Record*, November 1, 2021. https://www.newwestrecord.ca/local-news/new-west-council-approves-interim-land-acknowledgement-for-meetings-4711163.

National Inquiry into Missing and Murdered Indigenous Women and Girls (NIMMIWG). *Reclaiming Power and Place: Executive Summary of the Final Report*. https://www.mmiwg-ffada.ca/wp-content/uploads/2019/06/Executive_Summary.pdf.

Queen's University. "Land Acknowledgement." https://www.queens.ca/indigenous/ways-knowing/land-acknowledgement.

Robinson, Dylan, Kanonhsyonne Janice C. Hill, Armand Garnet Ruffo, Selena Couture, and Lisa Cooke Ravensbergen. "Rethinking the Practice and Performance of Indigenous Land Acknowledgement." *Canadian Theatre Review* 177, no 1 (2019): 20–30. https://doi.org/10.3138/ctr.177.004.

Royal BC Museum. "History of the Territory." https://royalbcmuseum.bc.ca/about/museum-information/history-territory.

Shahzad, Ramna. "What Is the Significance of Acknowledging the Indigenous Land We Stand On." *CBC News*, July 15, 2017. https://www.cbc.ca/news/canada/toronto/territorial-acknowledgements-indigenous-1.4175136.

Simpson, Leanne Betasamosake. "Indigenous Resurgence and Co-Resistance." *Critical Ethnic Studies* 2, no. 2 (2016): 19–34. https://doi.org/10.5749/jcritethnstud.2.2.0019.

Starblanket, Gina. "The Numbered Treaties and the Politics of Incoherency." *Canadian Journal of Political Science / Revue canadienne de science politique* 52, no. 3 (2019): 443–59. https://doi.org/10.1017/S0008423919000027.

Stewart-Ambo, Theresa, and K. Wayne Yang. "Beyond Land Acknowledgment in Settler Institutions." *Social Text* 39, no. 1/146 (2021): 21–46. https://doi.org/10.1215/01642472-8750076.

Truth and Reconciliation Commission of Canada (TRC). *Honouring the Truth, Reconciling for the Future: Summary of the Final Report of the Truth and Reconciliation Commission of Canada*. Truth and Reconciliation Commission of Canada, 2015. https://ehprnh2mwo3.exactdn.com/wp-content/uploads/2021/01/Executive_Summary_English_Web.pdf.

University of Waterloo. "About Territorial Acknowledgement." https://uwaterloo.ca/truth-and-reconciliation-response-projects/about-truth-and-reconciliation-response-projects/about-territorial-acknowledgement.

Villains Theatre. "Land Acknowledgement." https://villainstheatre.com.
Wark, Joe. "Land Acknowledgements in the Academy: Refusing the Settler Myth." *Curriculum Inquiry* 51, no. 2 (2021): 191–209. https://doi.org/10.1080/03626784.2021.1889924.
Wilkes, Rima, Aaron Duong, Linc Kessler, and Howard Ramos. "Canadian University Acknowledgment of Indigenous Lands, Treaties, and Peoples." *Canadian Review of Sociology / Revue canadienne de sociologie* 54, no. 1 (2017): 89–120. https://doi.org/10.1111/cars.12140.
Winnipeg Blue Bombers. "Indigenous Community." https://www.bluebombers.com/indigenous-community.

Honouring Treaty Responsibilities in Rural Saskatchewan

The Treaty Land Sharing Network

Naomi Beingessner, Emily Eaton, and Martha Jane Robbins[1]

Introduction

SINCE THE CONCLUSION OF THE TRUTH AND RECONCILIATION Commission of Canada in 2015, there has been heightened interest by organizations and individuals across Canada in addressing the historic and ongoing injustices of settler colonialism. Yet, in 2016, when Colten Boushie, a Cree man from Red Pheasant First Nation, was killed by Gerald Stanley, a white farmer, in Stanley's farmyard near Biggar, Saskatchewan,[2] the truth of ongoing colonial violence was laid bare in the comment sections of social media. While some commentators expressed disgust about the incident and were horrified by the subsequent acquittal of Gerald Stanley, all too many suggested that the Saskatchewan farmer had a right to protect his property against the Indigenous youth who had entered Stanley's farmyard with a flat tire. These commentators, and Stanley himself when he was on trial, cast Boushie and his friends as dangerous invaders with malicious intent,[3] and some offered that the young Cree man got what he deserved.

Also working against the spirit of reconciliation, during the 2010s, the land base accessible for Indigenous Peoples to practise their Inherent and Treaty Rights steadily shrank through the privatization of Crown lands. Inherent Rights flow from Indigenous Peoples' continued occupation and use of their homelands long before the arrival of European settlers. They are collective rights that Nations understand as given by the Creator that vary across Indigenous societies. They generally include "rights to the land, rights to subsistence resources and activities, the right to self-determination and self-government, and the right to practice one's own culture and customs including language and religion."[4] Treaty Rights, negotiated during treaty-making between Indigenous nations and the Crown, reaffirmed Inherent Rights and added new rights "on top," including the right to continue land-based ways of life "as before" the signing of treaty.[5] By privatizing Crown lands, the Saskatchewan government has reduced the land base available for people to exercise rights such as hunting, trapping, harvesting plants, and practising ceremony.

It was out of the context of deeply harmful public expressions of racism and government actions that undermined Treaty and Inherent Rights, alongside a growing awareness about the need for truth and reconciliation, that the Treaty Land Sharing Network (TLSN) emerged. TLSN is a group of mainly white settler farmers, ranchers, and other landholders who have come together to offer safe land access for Indigenous Peoples to practise their ways of life in Treaty 4 and 6 areas of Saskatchewan and Alberta. Building on the growing awareness of rural landholders about colonial histories and ongoing violence, the network is attempting to work within the spirit of the Numbered Treaties and the broader movements for reconciliation.

As three white settlers and coordinators of TLSN, we write about the origins of our organization and reflect on its successes and contradictions. We begin this chapter by explaining that TLSN was formed in response to the erosion of Indigenous Rights and a rise in public expressions of racism in Saskatchewan. Next, we describe the rootedness of our movement in treaty relationships and treaty implementation, which requires that Indigenous Rights to hunt, trap, fish, gather, practise ceremony, etc. be maintained across the full extent of treaty territories. Finally, we reflect on some of the tensions at the heart of our work. These include the varying interpretations of what *sharing* means among our members, the different levels of comfort around hunting, and how barriers and obstacles to land access can be reduced while at the same time strengthening relationships between Indigenous Peoples and non-Indigenous.

The Origin of the Network

The idea behind the Treaty Land Sharing Network emerged in 2017 during a conversation between Valerie Zink, a white prairie settler from a farming family, and Philip Brass, a Saulteaux and Cree artist, hunter, and land-based educator from the Peepeekisis Cree Nation. The topic of discussion was the difficulty and danger facing Indigenous Peoples wanting to access land to exercise Inherent and Treaty Rights, including harvesting animals and plants and practising ceremony. Reserve lands make up only 1.55 percent of land in Saskatchewan,[6] while "Aboriginal" people made up 16 percent of Saskatchewan's population in 2016.[7] Reserve lands provide an insufficient land base for Indigenous Peoples to maintain their lifeways. As such, Indigenous Peoples have always relied on Crown lands (the land that the Crown promised during treaty-making would be available for Indigenous use) to exercise their Inherent and Treaty Rights. Yet, the Saskatchewan government is rapidly selling off these lands, thereby constraining Indigenous access to land through their policies of privatization. The TLSN was formed, in no small part, in response.

While nearly 90 percent of the landmass of Canada is Crown land (41 percent federal and 48 percent provincial),[8] the situation is radically different in Southern Saskatchewan, where 85 percent of land south of the forest fringe is privately owned or leased under terms that exclude public (including Indigenous) access.[9] Since 2007, the Saskatchewan government, under the conservative Saskatchewan Party premierships of Brad Wall and Scott Moe, has sold more than 1.2 million acres of Crown land,[10] further diminishing the patchwork of lands available to exercise Indigenous Rights. In a 2017 article in *Briarpatch* magazine, Brass argued, "Our right to hunt is recognized in Treaty 4, and within the Canadian Constitution (1982), but most importantly it's an inherent right.... It's an inherent Indigenous right to maintain our lifestyle, to hunt and to gather year-round. If we lose these Crown lands, the province is essentially extinguishing that right."[11]

Indigenous harvesting rights are also being threatened because of the devastation of native prairie ecology. Native prairie is critical habitat for wildlife and plants that are harvested for medicines, ceremonies, and food.

But the native prairie of Southern Saskatchewan has been declining for decades and continues to be eradicated through cultivation for cropland.[12] In fact, the conversion of native grasslands is one of the largest losses of biodiversity in the world. A recent report estimates less than 10 percent of native prairie remains in the province,[13] and old-growth temperate grassland is diminishing in areas of Saskatchewan at a much faster rate than in other provinces and states in the Northern Great Plains.[14]

In response to the loss of Indigenous access to land, the growing interest among rural landholders in reconciliation, and the expressions of racism surrounding rural property in the wake of the Gerald Stanley trial, Valerie Zink invited four women to discuss the possibility of creating a network of rural landholders who would commit to sharing their privately held land with Indigenous Peoples. These initial coordinating committee members, settlers who all grew up on the Prairies, had a variety of experiences in farming, academia, non-profit work, government, social movements, and rural issues. We agreed that as settler partners in treaty, we couldn't wait for the provincial government to reverse its policy trajectory and implement treaties as intended: our responsibility was to act.

We began reaching out to rural landholders in 2018 through personal and organizational connections. In February of 2019, we held our first meeting with prospective members. We agreed that a visible, public indication of the network's goals—such as signs posted in fields—was necessary to counteract the very public racism Indigenous Peoples face. The 2018 acquittal of Gerald Stanley for the killing of Colten Boushie was still fresh in people's minds, and expressions of rural racism were on the rise.[15] The vitriol on social media against Indigenous Peoples, including Boushie's family after his death in 2016, was overwhelming, and Indigenous Peoples were expressing increased concerns about being able to move about the province safely.[16] In this polarized atmosphere, rural landholders who became involved in the network did not want to be lumped together with the vocal supporters of Stanley in the media and online and wanted to take action to support Indigenous Peoples.

The first meeting of landholders ended by gathering input for a mission statement and name for the network, prioritizing the concept of sharing land, as intended by treaty. By the end of the summer of 2019, we agreed on the mission statement:

> The Treaty Land Sharing Network is a group of farmers, ranchers, and other landholders who have come together to begin the crucial work of honouring Treaties. In the spirit of sharing the land, we provide safe places for Indigenous people to access land and exercise their rights. We are committed to implementing the Treaty relationship, engaging in ongoing learning together as we practice being Treaty people, and establishing a different way forward for rural Saskatchewan.[17]

From February 2019 to June 2021, we continued to hold educational events on potential network members' farms to better educate ourselves about treaty obligations and antiracism work. In November 2019, we held a gathering that brought together Indigenous harvesters and interested landholders. Here, Indigenous participants affirmed Elders' accounts of treaties wherein they agreed to share the land with settlers so that settlers could use the land "to the depth of a plough"[18] for agriculture, while Indigenous lifeways would continue on the same lands. Elders spoke of the sacredness of treaty and the importance of relationships to living in a good way. Settlers were also encouraged to build trust with Indigenous Peoples, which would entail taking risks and the possibility of facing ridicule or pressure from other settlers.

The ensuing years built on this foundation of a relational understanding of treaty responsibilities. Milestone events included six gatherings on land held by landholders in the network between 2020 and 2023; obtaining grant funding for TLSN signs and creating and distributing them; forming partnerships with the Office of the Treaty Commissioner (OTC), the Anishinabe Nation Treaty Authority (ANTA), and the Yorkton Tribal Council (YTC); adding Indigenous Peoples and farmers to the coordinating committee; spearheading a letter with thirty-three environmental, Indigenous, faith-based, and labour organization signatories to the provincial government opposing Crown land sales; the creation of a website and online directory of lands within the network; a formal launch of the network with extensive media coverage on July 15, 2021;[19] critiquing the trespassing legislation brought into law in January 2022, that subsequently occasioned public debate;[20] engaging our members and Indigenous harvesters and supporters in the work of the network through new working groups; forming an Indigenous Advisory Circle; and the expansion and launch of the network on the Alberta side of Treaty 6.[21] The number of

Launch of the Treaty Land Sharing Network in July 2021 with Saskatchewan Treaty Commissioner Mary Culbertson, Indigenous Harvester Brad Desjarlais and TLSN members Mary Smillie and Ian McCreary. *Photo credit: Treaty Land Sharing Network*

acres shared in the network has increased from around ten thousand in July 2021[22] to more than forty thousand across fifty-eight locations by mid-2024.

TLSN is composed of members[23] who have land in the network, including private landholders and institutional landholders like Nature Saskatchewan and the Lumsden Beach Camp. We are currently focused on areas of Treaties 4 and 6 within Saskatchewan and Treaty 6 within Alberta, but we make ourselves available to people on the ground in other locations with interest and organizing capacity. TLSN opens its events and advocacy to supporters with the hope that they may eventually become members themselves or recruit other landholders to the network. Indigenous Peoples are generally not members of the network (unless they are also landholders with land in the network) but are active supporters of the network; several sit on the coordinating committee, the Indigenous Advisory Circle, and working groups of the network, and many Indigenous Peoples attend our events and are active on our Facebook page. Indigenous harvesters access lands in the network through the following protocols, published on the network's website: "Land users are asked to contact landholders before their initial visit so that any information vital to everyone's safety can be communicated. Land access is by foot only, and gates and fences must be left as they are found. Open fires are not permitted unless agreed upon in advance." To the network's knowledge, these protocols are well-respected by Indigenous harvesters.

The Foundation of Treaty Relationships

TLSN is rooted in an understanding of the Numbered Treaties as the original agreements that allow for settler existence in these lands. Following Cree and Saulteaux scholar Gina Starblanket,[24] our network is working against Canada's interpretation of treaties as historical, one-time transactions that ceded and surrendered Indigenous lands and title to the Crown. This interpretation, upheld by the provinces, is one that sustains ongoing processes of settler colonialism by denying Indigenous rights, including jurisdiction, over the full extent of First Nations' territories. Instead, we are educating ourselves and our members about Indigenous interpretations of treaties that are rooted in an understanding of coexistence and sharing of the land.

In Cardinal and Hildebrandt's book, which we have studied together as a network, treaty Elders of Saskatchewan present their understandings of the spirit and intent of treaty. Importantly, the Elders agree that "the land and water could never be sold or given away by their Nations."[25] This is a point corroborated in a book-length study by Sheldon Krasowski, which establishes that there were major inconsistencies between what was discussed and witnessed during the negotiation of treaties and the written documents produced by the Crown.[26] At no time, as Krasowski shows, did First Nations surrender or cede their lands.

According to treaty Elders, the treaty relationship between First Nations and the Crown and its subjects was "to consist of mutual ongoing caring and sharing arrangements between the treaty parties, which included a sharing of duties and responsibilities for land, shared for livelihood purposes with the newcomers."[27] As Elder Peter Waskahat offered, "The sacred earth could never be sold or given away, according to the principles of the First Nations, but it could be shared. The First Nations decided that the earth could be shared with newcomers and that it could be shared to the depth of a plough blade. The earth could be shared so that everyone could peacefully co-exist."[28] In this way, settler farming and Indigenous livelihood practices were understood not as mutually exclusive but as coexisting and overlapping with Indigenous Peoples' continued use of the land for harvesting practices, as before. In fact, non-agricultural uses were generally not negotiated during treaty-making, something Aimée Craft (Anishinaabe-Métis) makes clear in her book about Treaty 1, where ownership over, and access to, resources such as minerals and water were not negotiated.[29]

As we understand it, the concept of coexistence included a promise that Indigenous Peoples would be able to live as before, under their own laws, and that the treaties would not interfere with their political sovereignty, which has its origin in their relationship with the Creator. Starblanket has summarized that "treaties are regarded by Indigenous peoples as land-use frameworks, which generally involve the establishment of separate governments and jurisdictions in distinct spaces, and dual governance and jurisdiction in shared spaces and matters of mutual concern."[30]

Inspired by the oral histories and the growing awareness about Indigenous understandings of treaties, our network attempts to practise their true spirit and intent. It seems clear to us that settlers were welcomed to farm on these lands, but that this was an invitation to coexist and enter into good relations with Indigenous Peoples—their land uses, laws, sovereignty, jurisdiction, and their existing relationships with all of Creation.[31]

Of course, Canada never intended to respect Indigenous land uses and sovereignty. In 1876, as the ink was drying on Treaty 6, Canada passed the *Indian Act*, denying Indigenous Peoples what was just agreed to in the treaties. This included Indigenous livelihood practices, freedom of movement, jurisdiction, and sovereignty while also stealing Indigenous lands and confining Indigenous Peoples on reserves.

While settlers may have been welcomed to take up farming in these lands, they were certainly not invited to hold lands for their exclusive use as common law property. Settler land use and jurisdiction was not supposed to abolish Indigenous livelihood and sovereignty in these same lands. What the Crown brought to the treaty relationship was promised to be "on top of"—not taking away from—existing Indigenous life, lands, and livelihoods. With this in mind, TLSN is attempting to understand land held by settlers as compatible with overlapping Indigenous uses, including harvesting and practising ceremony. Network members open their land to Indigenous Peoples in this spirit.

Network Challenges and Contradictions

While land is clearly the basis of TLSN's work, how settlers understand land is one of the key challenges to living the spirit and intent of treaties. The notion of land as private property and the control over specific parcels of land that private ownership entails, first advanced in Britain in the seventeenth century and imposed in Canada with colonization, is firmly ingrained in settlers and has been for generations. Settling in the Prairies came with the promise, from Canada, of free land and the security and prosperity that land ownership would bring. Private property is entrenched in landholders' individual understandings of land ownership and extends to their engagement with existing legal, institutional, and livelihood structures and frameworks. It is the basis upon which settler colonialism was built and continues to exist. The contrast between land perceived and institutionalized as something to be owned versus land as something that people cannot have ownership over, but are rather stewards of, is a defining and enduring tension in TLSN work. Shifting from a system of private land ownership to one of land sharing, as laid out in the Numbered Treaties, is a daunting task, and obviously not one that can be accomplished by a group of individual landholders. Ultimately, implementation of treaties must happen on a nation-to-nation basis with settler landholders participating within a renewed framework that would see wide-sweeping changes to land relations in Canada. While the Crown's will to honour those original agreements is absent, TLSN can only accomplish so much.

The tension between private property and shared land use and governance models also plays out at the farm level. As movements like Land Back gain traction and highlight the need to return land and decision-making to Indigenous Peoples, settlers voice their inhibitions and fears. One TLSN member outlined, "A lot of people are under the assumption that if you let First Nations people in they are going to take all your land away.... On the other hand, the one guy here said he's been at [TLSN] meetings and there'll be somebody on the First Nations side who's a little radical and it can make you take a step back and think, that's the way it is. You're going to have people like that on either side. Everybody has their own thoughts, but to me, if everybody just stays calm you work things out."

Likely, some settler reticence stems from a lack of knowledge or misunderstanding of treaties as well as misconceptions that movements like Land Back might demand that settlers, in turn, lose their lands and livelihoods in Canada. Reticence also likely stems from unexamined racism and from anxieties about landholders' roles and relationships to the land they farm or ranch as they try to live in alignment with their treaty responsibilities. At an initial gathering in February 2019, one landholder expressed concern about how to maintain control while opening up access to Indigenous land users—indicative of seeing land sharing as settlers granting Indigenous Peoples permission to access land that remains firmly *theirs*. In contrast, someone else suggested that settlers should not be assumed to have the right to offer access as this would be antithetical to recognizing rights to land that has never been ceded. Another TLSN member reflected on the complexity for settlers trying to find a positive way forward:

> I think it's tricky because you think about farmers or ranchers and family farms have been working on the land for sometimes 100 years now. Those people's identities and their income and the things that they do are tied to the land too now. It's such a hard concept to think that these people could give their land back. But if, as a country, we are actually serious about reconciliation then we have to find ways to make sure that land is there for Indigenous people to access

> because being Indigenous and being able to live out your culture, you need to have access to the land. They are tied together. You can't have one without the other.

From the initial gathering and other early conversations, it was decided that the main focus of the network would be on increasing safe access to land for the exercise of Inherent and Treaty Rights, and this remains the driving focus of the network. To access lands, Indigenous harvesters must make an initial phone call to the landholder so that any information vital to everyone's safety (electric fences, prickly neighbours, guard dogs, etc.) can be communicated. But the coordinating committee has continued to promote a common understanding among network members that they are not granting permission; rather, their lands are open for access. Language matters, and we are intent on shifting the language away from *giving permission*, a perspective rooted in private property, towards the language of *sharing land as treaty intended*. In our experience, this linguistic shift has often been one of the first steps for settler members to reframe their own thinking.

TLSN also engages members and potential members in joint learning on treaties, decolonization, prairie history, and antiracism in an attempt to bring settlers further along in their understanding of Treaty Rights and responsibilities and not to place the burden of education on Indigenous Peoples. As the work has progressed, the network has also engaged in advocacy on specific issues such as Crown land sales and trespassing legislation. These efforts, in combination with the educational and land sharing events, are attempts to shift the range of possible narratives and broaden policy scenarios in Saskatchewan, making land sharing an accepted and normal practice and moving the needle towards overlapping land uses in shared space.

From the beginning, the TLSN coordinating committee was conscious that land sharing as a reflection of treaty and an acknowledgement of Inherent and Treaty Rights meant minimizing the barriers to access for Indigenous Peoples. With this intent, we set out to build a network that did not require Indigenous Peoples to enter into relationships with settlers in order to access land within the network. At the outset, this was a difficult proposition for many TLSN members and potential members. Given entrenched cultures around private property, some landholders did not feel safe or comfortable with people accessing their land without knowing who they were or why they were there. Some also felt strongly that they would benefit from building relations with Indigenous Peoples. These members and supporters articulated a desire to learn from Indigenous Peoples, to break down barriers between Indigenous and non-Indigenous people, and to work together towards reconciliation, among other things. However, the coordinating committee feels strongly that settlers' desire for relationships and need to surveil their land should be de-centred and Indigenous Peoples' rights to hunt, harvest, and practise their ceremonies must take precedence.

Some Indigenous participants at a November 2019 gathering expressed the need for breaking down barriers through building relationships and getting to know one another, and others spoke of the need to bring more people, both Indigenous and non-Indigenous, to the meetings, to be in conversation with each other. Multiple Indigenous participants spoke about the lack of safety for them when entering privately held land and about the ongoing and overlapping traumas caused by colonization. Subsequently, during a series of land sharing events throughout 2020, the message that Indigenous Peoples wanted contact with landholders in advance of accessing the land in order to feel safe was echoed. These perspectives have helped TLSN to evolve our understanding of relationship-building.

While the network's aim of reducing barriers to land access for Indigenous Peoples as much as possible remains of central importance and is a benchmark used to evaluate new strategies and activities, there also remains a tension between barrier-free access and an acknowledgement that some form of relationship is desired both by Indigenous Peoples and settlers for reasons of safety and trust-building. "I think it's a good thing and that the best way for people to understand each other is to actually be together. Just sitting around talking and stuff like that," offered one TLSN member. As it stands, land can be accessed through the network without engaging in any other network activities, and there is no requirement for Indigenous Peoples accessing the land to have a relationship with the landholder.

TLSN has continued to work to build relationships under the principle that relationships can be and should be built through the network rather than as a requirement of land use. TLSN partnerships with OTC, ANTA, and YTC have provided the network with institutional support, connections to Elders and Knowledge Keepers who have been immeasurably important to the success of land sharing events and overall learning within the network, and good relationships with grassroots Indigenous harvesters living in reserve communities. Our latest collaboration with the Comeback Society, an organization dedicated to urban Indigenous Peoples connecting to culture, promises deeper connections with urban Indigenous Peoples looking for access to land. TLSN has also begun conversations with the Federation of Sovereign Indigenous Nations (FSIN) and is making direct connections with Indigenous leaders on- and off-reserve. Relationships with individuals continue to be fostered through on-the-land events and online events, and outreach to specific Nations in close proximity to TLSN members is underway. Creating spaces for relationship-building has provided a rich experience, and participants, particularly at in-person events, have reflected gratitude, interconnectedness, healing, and appreciating the land in a different way when walking it together.

Another facet of relationship-building key to the success of the network is that of TLSN members with their rural neighbours, primarily as a way to ensure safety for Indigenous land users, but also to counter misconceptions and recruit potential members. Settlers were encouraged by an Indigenous person at the November 2019 gathering to have talks in coffee shops and local meeting places. This participant acknowledged that their white friends are scared of retaliation and being outcast in their communities if they are seen to be supporting Indigenous Peoples and their rights. But the need to take on the risk of uncomfortable interactions with neighbours was reiterated by others at the same event, who noted that Indigenous Peoples bear the brunt of negative stereotypes, racism, and discrimination every day. As one TLSN member stated, "At some point we have to be willing to take a stand and to find some courage somewhere and say, you know what, if it leads to tense relationships or conflict well so be it. It's worthwhile and I feel confident in my position and my goals and my motivations, then that's what happens."

One of the most contentious discussions while formulating the principles and protocols of the network was around hunting. Concerns from settlers included worries about protecting grazing cattle, the potential destruction of crops by hunters with quads or other vehicles, the potential for human harm, and the impact on wildlife conservation. Matthew Braun, who presented on behalf of the Nature Conservancy of Canada at an early meeting of landholders, noted that hunting can be a means of managing natural habitat and is not necessarily in opposition to conservation goals. An Indigenous participant at a 2019 gathering acknowledged the concerns about what might happen to livestock and proposed a guideline of foot access only and a limitation to bow hunting, but was unequivocal that the treaties mean landholders do not have the right to deny access outright. They also cautioned against "recreating an elite" should a network like ours consider imposing any vetting of Indigenous Peoples specifically for the purposes of hunting. Another Indigenous participant at the same meeting spoke of how Canadian laws get in the way of practising their way of life and reinforced how central hunting is to their livelihood and supporting food security, especially for urban Indigenous Peoples.

Taking these perspectives as well as the centrality of hunting as both a Treaty and Inherent Right into account, and after hosting a focus group on the topic with Indigenous harvesters and network members, the network took a firm position that hunting is non-negotiable and that network members cannot cherry-pick which activities can take place on the land when they sign up to the network. While not allowing for a "no-hunting" exception, some network members need to regulate the timing or location of hunting for safety reasons (for example, a children's camp is not safe for hunting when campers are present). Not allowing members to pick and choose land uses has hindered membership in a few cases, but it has also provoked further learning and discussion of what the practice of Treaty and Inherent Rights means and what sharing the land requires. Some network supporters have revised their views on hunting and become members through the process of learning more about hunting as a right. As an Indigenous participant at a 2019 gathering reiterated, Indigenous Peoples understood treaty as a framework for mutual respect and understanding, and settlers posting *no trespassing* or *no hunting* signs would run counter to our relationships as treaty people.

Conclusion

TLSN has and will continue to face structural obstacles such as the entrenchment of private property, inherent tensions such as the need to build relationships while not erecting barriers to land access, and challenges like the discussions around hunting. Yet, as the network has taken shape, it has been rewarding to witness the amount of interest in this outwardly simple but often more complicated idea of rural landholders beginning to honour their treaty responsibilities. The membership of the network has steadily grown. This is partly as a result of media interest in key events and advocacy work, as well as increased public awareness (sometimes via presentations to other organizations or through existing members' personal connections) and the network's efforts to shepherd potential members through their discomfort or hesitancy to a place of greater understanding and willingness to act. We have been intentional in confronting difficult topics and giving both space and additional information as needed to work through obstacles together. Interest has also come from outside Saskatchewan, and with expansion into Alberta and interest elsewhere, the network is exploring what it might mean to take this idea into different contexts (recognizing both the capacity limits of our current structure and the necessity of place-based organizing).

The network has continued to build momentum by holding both large and small gatherings and land sharing events. These have been moments where people can come together to further develop the network, to feel welcome in a rural place, and to strengthen their identity as network members. Land sharing events have provided a place for participants to be buoyed by collective energy, sharing, learning, and, most importantly, to be physically present on the land. Attendees have expressed hope the TLSN is offering a small step in righting relations. Bradley Desjarlais, a hunter from Fishing Lake First Nation, told a reporter that when he came to the TLSN launch, "I had to slap myself because I was sitting with a bunch of white people and they're telling me I can access their land for hunting or picking medicine or berries? In rural Saskatchewan, what I'm used to is having the warden called on me."[32]

However, the Treaty Land Sharing Network still has a long way to go and much work to do. Most obviously, TLSN cannot implement treaties single-handedly on private land. After all, the treaty relationship was established on a nation-to-nation basis, and neither Canada nor the provinces seem willing to entertain the true spirit and intent of treaties, which would require recognizing Indigenous jurisdiction and, therefore, challenge Canada's claim to exclusive jurisdiction and supreme sovereignty in these lands. Normalizing land sharing on privately held land is a small step that we are still very far from attaining on the long road to treaty implementation. Obstacles such as opposition to hunting may only require more education on Inherent and Treaty Rights, more learning on hunting as symbiotic with conservation, and more work bringing landholders into conversation with Indigenous harvesters. However, some tensions are beyond the reach of the network to resolve, such as the system of private property butting up against the basis of treaty as sharing the land. But as network members move towards more land sharing in practice, the network is pushing the narrative and the policy options in Saskatchewan beyond the typical and deeply held notions of private property and towards a more honest understanding of treaty relations. As a network, we are attempting to chart a different future based on honouring Inherent and Treaty Rights, righting the relationship with Indigenous Peoples here, in this place, and confronting policies and mindsets that maintain racist and colonial structures.

Notes

1 A few passages and paragraphs in this chapter are reproduced from Beingessner, "Changing Relations of Agricultural Land Tenure." Direct quotations from network members and supporters in this chapter were collected as part of Beingessner's doctoral project and are presented here without attribution to protect participants' identities.
2 MacDonald, "Settler Silencing."
3 MacDonald, "Settler Silencing," 7, 11–12.
4 First Nations and Indigenous Studies, "Aboriginal Rights."
5 Alook et al., *The End of This World.*
6 Government of Canada, "Indian Lands Registry System (ILRS)."
7 Statistics Canada, "Aboriginal Identity (9), Age (20)."
8 Neimanis, "Crown Land."
9 Government of Saskatchewan, "Hunters and Trappers Guide." Accessed Feb. 10, 2023. This guide has since been updated to a 2025 publication called "Hunters Guide."
10 M. Schaefer, personal communication, July 13, 2021.
11 Zink and Brass, "Land and Reconciliation."
12 Sawatzky and Piwowar, "Changes in Prairie Grassland Extent."
13 Marchand, Fisher, and Donald, *Saskatchewan Native Prairie Habitat Inventory.*
14 World Wildlife Fund, *Plowprint Report*, 3.
15 Edwards, "In Saskatchewan, the Stanley Verdict"; Lindberg, "The Myth of the Wheat King."
16 Dinh, "Social Media Storm."
17 Treaty Land Sharing Network, "About Us."
18 Indigenous accounts of treaty-making affirm that Indigenous Peoples only agreed to share the land with settlers to the depth of a plough. See Cardinal and Hildebrandt, *Treaty Elders of Saskatchewan*, and Krasowski, *No Surrender.*

19 Examples of media coverage include DeKay, "Farmers Embrace Treaty Land Sharing Process," and Tait, "Land-Sharing Network."
20 Brown, "TLSN Group Opposed"; Pearce, "Indigenous Land Users Concerned."
21 Kienlen, "Alta. Farm Joins."
22 Tait, "Land-Sharing Network."
23 Members are those who have land in the network, and supporters are people who have participated in network events but who do not have their land signed up.
24 Starblanket, "Crises of Relationship," 13–33.
25 Cardinal and Hildebrandt, *Treaty Elders of Saskatchewan*, 10.
26 Krasowski, *No Surrender*.
27 Cardinal and Hildebrandt, *Treaty Elders of Saskatchewan*, 15.
28 Elder Waskahat as quoted in Cardinal and Hildebrandt, *Treaty Elders of Saskatchewan*, 31.
29 Craft, *Breathing Life into the Stone Fort Treaty*.
30 Starblanket, "Crises of Relationship," 20.
31 There is ongoing debate about whether Indigenous nations entered into treaties freely or under duress. Some have pointed to Canada's policy of starvation, which came at the same time that the buffalo were being hunted into near extinction as a method of inducing Chiefs to sign treaties; others have suggested that Chiefs were purposefully deceived by the treaty negotiators. The treaty Elders in Cardinal and Hildebrandt's book suggest that treaties were understood as sacred undertakings that Chiefs entered into in good faith and with the hope for good relations of mutual respect and coexistence.
32 Raine, "Network Acknowledges Treaty Land Rights."

Sources

Alook, Angele, Emily Eaton, David Gray-Donald, Joël Laforest, Crystal Lameman, and Bronwen Tucker. *The End of This World: Climate Justice in So-Called Canada*. Between the Lines, 2023.

Beingessner, Naomi. "Changing Relations of Agricultural Land Tenure and Access in the Canadian Prairies." PhD diss., University of Manitoba, 2022. http://hdl.handle.net/1993/37144.

Brown, Angela. "TLSN Group Opposed to Province's New Trespassing Legislation." BattlefordsNOW, January 21, 2022. https://battlefordsnow.com/2022/01/21/tlsn-group-opposed-to-provinces-new-trespassing-legislation/.

Cardinal, Harold, and Walter Hildebrandt. *Treaty Elders of Saskatchewan: Our Dream Is That Our Peoples Will One Day Be Clearly Recognized as Nations*. University of Calgary Press, 2000.

DeKay, William. "Farmers Embrace Treaty Land Sharing Process." *Western Producer*, July 30, 2021. https://www.producer.com/news/farmers-embrace-treaty-land-sharing-process/.

Dinh, Victoria. "Social Media Storm Following Death of Colten Boushie Sparks Fear in First Nations Youth: FSIN." *CBC News*, August 22, 2016. https://www.cbc.ca/news/canada/saskatchewan/social-media-colten-boushie-1.3731676.

Edwards, Kyle. "In Saskatchewan, the Stanley Verdict Has Re-Opened Centuries-Old Wounds." *Maclean's*, March 5, 2018. https://www.macleans.ca/news/canada/saskatchewan-racism-gerald-stanley-colten-boushie/.

First Nations and Indigenous Studies. "Aboriginal Rights." Indigenous Foundations, University of British Columbia, 2009. https://indigenousfoundations.arts.ubc.ca/aboriginal_rights/.

Government of Canada. "Indian Lands Registry System (ILRS)." Last modified August 8, 2023. https://services.aadnc-aandc.gc.ca/ILRS_Public/Home/Home.aspx.

Government of Saskatchewan. "Hunters and Trappers Guide." Ministry of Parks, Culture, Heritage and Sport, 2021. https://publications.saskatchewan.ca/api/v1/products/68827/formats/93283/download (accessed February 10, 2023).

Kienlen, Alexis. "Alta. Farm Joins Treaty Land Sharing Network." *Western Producer*, August 7, 2024. https://www.producer.com/news/alta-farm-joins-treaty-land-sharing-network/.

Krasowski, Sheldon. *No Surrender: The Land Remains Indigenous*. University of Regina Press, 2019.

Lindberg, Darcy. "The Myth of the Wheat King and the Killing of Colten Boushie." *The Conversation*, March 1, 2018. https://theconversation.com/the-myth-of-the-wheat-king-and-the-killing-of-colten-boushie-92398.

MacDonald, David B. "Settler Silencing and the Killing of Colten Boushie: Naturalizing Colonialism in the trial of Gerald Stanley." *Settler Colonial Studies* 11, no. 1 (2021): 1–20. https://doi.org/10.1080/2201473X.2020.1841505.

Marchand, Joanne, Teal Fisher, and Erika Donald. *Saskatchewan Native Prairie Habitat Inventory: A Collaborative Study between Saskatchewan Polytechnic and Environment Canada*. Saskatchewan Polytechnic and Environment Canada, 2020.

Neimanis, V.P. "Crown Land." *Canadian Encyclopedia*, May, 18, 2011. Updated by Lia Le Brun Robles Gil on November 14, 2024. https://www.thecanadianencyclopedia.ca/en/article/crown-land.

Pearce, Nick. "Indigenous Land Users Concerned About New Trespassing Law." *Saskatoon StarPhoenix*, January 20, 2022. https://thestarphoenix.com/news/local-news/indigenous-land-users-concerned-about-new-trespassing-law.

Raine, N.C. "Network Acknowledges Treaty Land Rights, Declares Land Open to Use." *Eagle Feather News*, July 17, 2021. https://archive.eaglefeathernews.com/news/network-acknowledges-treaty-land-rights-declares-land-open-to-use.

Sawatzky, Katie Doke, and Joseph Piwowar. "Changes in Prairie Grassland Extent in Saskatchewan from 1990 to 2015." *Prairie Perspectives: Geographical Essays* 21 (2019): 1–8.

Starblanket, Gina. "Crises of Relationship: The Role of Treaties in Contemporary Indigenous-Settler Relations." In *Visions of the Heart: Issues Involving Indigenous Peoples in Canada*, edited by Olive Patricia Dickason, David Alan Long, and Gina Starblanket. Oxford University Press, 2020.

Statistics Canada. "Aboriginal Identity (9), Age (20), Registered or Treaty Indian Status (3) and Sex (3) for the Population in Private Households of Canada, Provinces and Territories, Census Metropolitan Areas and Census Agglomerations, 2016 Census—25% Sample Data." Government of Canada, October 25, 2017. https://open.canada.ca/data/en/dataset/c37a4986-4e08-490a-9759-808d35010342.

Tait, Carrie. "Land-Sharing Network Building Bridges Between Saskatchewan Farmers, Indigenous Community." *Globe and Mail*, September 8, 2021. https://www.theglobeandmail.com/canada/alberta/article-treaty-land-sharing-network-building-bridges-between-saskatchewan/.

Treaty Land Sharing Network. "About Us." https://treatylandsharingnetwork.ca/about/.

World Wildlife Fund. *Plowprint Report*. World Wildlife Fund, 2017. https://c402277.ssl.cf1.rackcdn.com/publications/1103/files/original/plowprint_AnnualReport_2017_revWEB_FINAL.pdf?1508791901.

Zink, Valerie, and Philip Brass. "Land and Reconciliation." *Briarpatch*, October 19, 2017. https://briarpatchmagazine.com/articles/view/land-and-reconciliation.

Treaty Relations as a Foundation for Reconciliation

Indigenous and Settler Perspectives in Treaty 3 Territory

Jeffrey S. Denis

Introduction: Sacred Covenants, Broken Promises

IN 2023, MANY ANISHINAABE AND SOME SETTLER[1] CANADIans in Northwestern Ontario and Eastern Manitoba celebrated the 150th anniversary of Treaty 3. The occasion was marked by public gatherings across the region, an arts and music festival, a canoe trip to the site of the Treaty 3 signing (Animakee Wa Zhing), public viewing of the original treaty manuscript, and other events and ceremonies. Gary Allen, CEO of the Treaty #3 Investment Group and former Chief of Nigigoonsiminikaaning First Nation, explained:

> I think it's important [to celebrate the anniversary] because we are all Treaty people, no matter where you live in the district. It's about recognition, education, and understanding. We have this partnership [between the region's twenty-eight First Nations and non-Anishinaabe people]. Everything that we do, health, education, economics, we're all tied in together, [and] we want to recognize that special relationship.[2]

Indeed, Indigenous Peoples commonly view nation-to-nation treaties as sacred covenants that involve sharing land and resources and respecting one another's political autonomy.[3] As Cree and Saulteaux scholar Gina Starblanket says, treaties are a mechanism for governing "relationships with and between all elements of creation."[4] They are living agreements whereby "Indigenous and non-Indigenous people have distinct rights and responsibilities."[5] Treaty relations are also ongoing and require "constant renewal."[6]

Some non-Indigenous scholars likewise emphasize the importance of honouring treaties[7] and "decolonizing" treaty consciousness among settlers.[8] Chris Hiller, for example, seeks to identify "forms of reflection and action [that] might foster and support concrete efforts among settlers to bring about a full and just recognition of treaty rights, relationships, and responsibilities."[9] Based on research in Treaty 3 territory, my book *Canada at a Crossroads* concluded that settler Canadians and their governments must fulfill their treaty obligations because treaties are the only basis for Canadian society that does not rely on racist assumptions like the Doctrine of Discovery.[10] As Anishinaabe scholar Aaron Mills argues, "treaty is the only legitimate justification for the constitution of shared political community on Turtle Island."[11]

Yet, implementing treaties is a complex task.[12] The reality is that many settlers express deep-seated ignorance about and opposition towards treaties with Indigenous Peoples.[13] Treaty mythologies—such as the view that treaties represent "static, fixed-term land transactions through which Indigenous peoples ceded and surrendered their rights to the land and to political jurisdiction"[14]—are widespread. Drawing on and promoting these mythologies, settler governments have long sought to use—and continue to use—treaties as instruments of colonialism or tools to expropriate Indigenous lands and resources.[15] As Anishinaabe scholar Hayden King has explained, between 1784 and 1830, his Mississauga "ancestors were defrauded of [their] territory" via a series of "blank treaties," leading them to migrate from the Bay of Quinte to Beausoleil First Nation.[16] Across Canada, hundreds of treaty violations have been documented, leading to numerous lawsuits, settlements, grievances, and, at best, a mixed bag of Supreme Court rulings.[17] In most cases, treaty disputes have arisen not from "cultural misunderstandings" but rather from broken promises and deliberate "mal interpretations" by the Crown.[18]

Given these various perspectives and experiences, it is important to further investigate the contemporary potential and limits of treaties to help generate more just and sustainable relationships between peoples and with the land. In its Call to Action 45, the Truth and Reconciliation Commission (TRC) instructed the Government of Canada to co-develop with Indigenous Peoples a new royal proclamation that would, among other things, "renew or establish Treaty relationships based on principles of mutual recognition, mutual respect, and shared responsibility."[19] But what might this look like on the ground in specific communities? And what does it mean for Indigenous and settler people to be treaty partners today?

Treaty 3 Case Study

Taking Treaty 3 as a case study, this chapter critically examines Indigenous and settler perspectives on treaties as a foundation for reconciliation. It utilizes data from a wider research project that I am conducting in partnership with the non-profit community group Reconciliation Kenora (Ontario). In 2018, Reconciliation Kenora invited me to present on my previous research on Indigenous-settler relations in Fort Frances (the southern part of Treaty 3), where I lived between 2007 and 2009. Although I am a white settler who grew up in Toronto and am now an associate professor of sociology at McMaster University in Hamilton, Ontario (homelands of the Attawandaron, Haudenosaunee, and Mississaugas, and part of the Dish with One Spoon Wampum Agreement),[20] I retain strong connections to Treaty 3 and a sense of responsibility to the region. We applied for a SSHRC grant and received funding for a research project to better understand what reconciliation means to Kenora-area residents,[21] barriers to reconciliation, and actions that have been taken and that should be taken to improve local relationships. Guided by an Elders circle, the research design originally called for in-person sharing circles.[22] However, the Covid-19 pandemic had other plans. The chapter therefore instead draws on forty-two in-depth interviews—mainly conducted online via Zoom—with Anishinaabe, Métis, and settler community leaders, Elders, and Knowledge Keepers who have been engaged in reconciliation activism and/or Indigenous-led change efforts in Treaty 3 territory.

Rather than being a random sample of the Canadian public, the interviewees were all knowledgeable about the topic and committed to improving Indigenous-settler relationships and/or supporting Indigenous resurgence. Yet, even within this select group, participants offered a wide range of responses to questions about not only the meaning of reconciliation but also the relationship between reconciliation and treaties. All participants were asked the following questions (among others):

1. What does the term "reconciliation" mean to you?
2. It is sometimes said that "we are all Treaty people."[23] What does this mean to you and what, if anything, do Treaties have to do with reconciliation?

Responses were analyzed through an inductive, grounded theory approach.[24] Perhaps not surprisingly, participants who expressed more skepticism about reconciliation also tended to be more skeptical about treaties and their potential to foster equitable and sustainable relationships. However, most participants shared deep and nuanced perspectives that highlight the importance of recognizing ongoing treaty relations and upholding core treaty principles (e.g., relational accountability), while also casting a critical lens on the motives and actions of past and present Crown officials, corporations, and settlers.

Caveats

Before outlining the main perspectives shared in interviews, it is important to acknowledge some caveats. First, beyond treaties, the discourse of reconciliation is also fraught terrain. The TRC described reconciliation as "an ongoing individual and collective process" that involves recognizing Indigenous and Treaty Rights, healing relationships, supporting cultural revitalization, and promoting public education and dialogue.[25] Canadian courts, meanwhile, have been more concerned with how to reconcile Indigenous Peoples' pre-existing rights and ongoing presence with the assumption of Crown sovereignty.[26] Given the lack of action to implement TRC Calls to Action,[27] the revelation of unmarked graves at residential school sites across Canada, including in Treaty 3,[28] and the ongoing violence and injustices against Indigenous Peoples, from missing and murdered Indigenous women and girls[29] to resource extraction projects undertaken without the consent of Indigenous Peoples, some Indigenous activists have declared that "reconciliation is dead."[30]

As documented elsewhere,[31] participants in the Reconciliation Kenora project attributed diverse meanings to the term *reconciliation*. Consistent with the TRC, some focused on education, healing, and relationship-building. Settlers were somewhat more likely to take this approach and emphasized reconciliation as an important value or goal. Others preferred the Anishinaabemowin term *Azhe-mino-gahbewewin*, a name gifted to Reconciliation Kenora by the late Elder Clifford Skead, which (he explained) refers to "looking back in order to move forward in a good way." This concept is rooted in local context and avoids some of the political baggage of reconciliation. Still others, especially Indigenous Peoples, rejected reconciliation on the basis that there was never a good relationship between the local First Nations and non-Anishinaabe (and therefore nothing to reconcile) and/or that reconciliation is a misplaced goal and Indigenous Peoples should focus on resurgence first. In short, there was little consensus about what reconciliation means, or whether it should be a priority, even among those engaged in reconciliation activism.

Second, even in this post-TRC era, the wider settler public remains largely oblivious to treaties and their implications, especially as understood by Indigenous Elders. Some settlers reject treaties as "special rights/privileges." Others accept a narrow view of treaties as one-time exchanges that "extinguished" Indigenous Peoples' land rights. Either way, such views reflect and reinforce settlers' sense of group superiority and entitlement to Indigenous lands and resources.[32] This chapter focuses instead on community leaders' and Elders' views regarding whether and how treaty principles may be used to improve Indigenous-settler relations.

Third, the case study is specific to Treaty 3, which was negotiated between Anishinaabe leaders and Canada's treaty commissioners in 1873 and covers 55,000 square miles from west of Thunder Bay to north of Red Lake, along the Minnesota border, and into Eastern Manitoba. Treaty 3 was meant to be the first post-Confederation treaty, but the Crown's previous attempts to negotiate a treaty had failed because the Anishinaabe refused to surrender their lands or allow settlement in their region.[33] The treaty that was eventually reached set a precedent for future numbered treaties in Central and Western Canada, including higher treaty annuities and provisions that had not been included in previous treaties with the Crown. While many of the core ideas discussed in this chapter likely apply to other treaty areas, we must recognize that (1) there are dozens of treaties across Canada, including pre-colonial treaties between Indigenous Peoples[34] and with other-than-human beings,[35] Peace and Friendship Treaties,[36] Numbered Treaties,[37] and so-called modern treaties,[38] each with unique features; and (2) large parts of Canada, including most of

British Columbia, are not covered by treaties. Thus, perspectives on the reconciliation-treaties relationship may be quite different elsewhere.

Perspectives on Reconciliation and Treaties

At the risk of oversimplification, most participants' perspectives on reconciliation and treaties could be categorized into one of three groups: pro-treaty optimists, cautious optimists, and skeptics. Consistent with the TRC,[39] some Indigenous and non-Indigenous people who are working for reconciliation understand treaties as bridges between nations that entail legal and moral obligations, which, if honoured, would help rectify colonial injustices. In their view, honouring treaties could be a path towards reconciliation. Many treaty advocates also acknowledge the complexities of treaty interpretation and implementation, such as the fact that multiple written and oral accounts of Treaty 3 (and other treaties) exist; contrary to the Crown's "official" text, it is highly doubtful that the Anishinaabe ever agreed to "surrender" their land. Still others, mainly Anishinaabe Elders and activists, view most treaties—including Treaty 3—as colonial tools, based on coercion and manipulation, and therefore question the capacity of existing treaties to foster meaningful reconciliation. These participants also tend to critique the concept of reconciliation and challenge its relevance. Nevertheless, a seemingly growing awareness and faith in core treaty principles, as articulated by Anishinaabe Elders, provides a glimmer of hope amid the ongoing violence of settler colonialism.

Pro-Treaty Optimists

About one-quarter of participants—mainly settlers, but some Indigenous—could be considered pro-treaty optimists. They upheld reconciliation as a valuable goal and believed that honouring treaties was a fundamental means of working towards reconciliation.

For example, Elaine Bright, a white settler lawyer who has worked with residential school survivors, said, "Treaties are at the core... of reconciliation because I think... they are the essence of the relationship between Indigenous and non-Indigenous people." She also worried that "among non-Indigenous people there's very little understanding of the fact that it was a nation-to-nation Treaty... and that we [settlers] still have obligations, and they, Indigenous people, have rights." The Canadian education system historically has been assimilationist, even genocidal,[40] and Indigenous participants reported ongoing racism and violence in schools. However, some also noted recent efforts by the public and Catholic school boards to invite Anishinaabe Elders into schools and to celebrate "Treaties Recognition Week."[41] While these initiatives provide a meaningful introduction to the notion of treaty relations, an Anishinaabe teacher stated that the provincial curriculum is still inadequate.

An Anishinaabe activist agreed that honouring treaties is a prerequisite to reconciliation. As a first step, she said, "it's important for people to read the Treaty." She described teaching her children about Treaty 3 and saying to them, "it's important for you to know, as Anishinaabe, what your Treaty Rights are, and if you're not too sure, spend some time reading it." While the efforts to educate her children are laudable, it is crucial to note that the meaning of treaties is not just captured in the Crown's "official" text. As will be discussed below, there are multiple written accounts of the Treaty 3 negotiations, plus Anishinaabe oral histories, which provide a more accurate and complete picture of the treaty.[42]

Rory McMillan, a white settler and former city councillor, agreed that honouring treaties is crucial for reconciliation, but acknowledged that Treaty 3 and other treaties across Canada have been repeatedly violated:

> I think for me when we say "Treaty people," it's that we all signed the Treaties. We all made a commitment...to honour those Treaties, and that has not been done....For me, personally, it's for power and control. We keep breaking the Treaties, we keep taking the land and resources, and we question why trust is an issue. It's pretty clear to me.

For McMillan, fulfilling treaty commitments could be a step towards reconciliation. While in office, he worked hard to raise awareness of this issue and supported a fellow councillor in convincing city council to fly the Treaty 3 flag at Kenora city hall. He also understood that the history of broken treaty promises had fostered mistrust and that, to (re)build respectful relationships, settler governments must listen to Anishinaabe teachings, stop taking land and resources, and start honouring treaties. Like the other participants quoted above, however, he did not (at least in our interview) problematize the treaty itself or what was agreed to.

Cautious Optimists

Approximately half the participants—including both Indigenous and settler—could be considered cautious optimists. Although still pro-treaty as a path towards reconciliation, they emphasized the complexities around treaty interpretation and implementation. They also tended to be ambivalent about the concept of reconciliation, though, overall, many endorsed it as a long-term project that entails implementing the TRC Calls to Action and more.

Lori Nelson, a white settler and former director of the local museum, believed in honouring treaties and recognizing Indigenous nationhood, but raised serious questions about what Treaty 3 actually said. For her, an act of reconciliation would be trying to figure out exactly what was agreed upon, especially from an Anishinaabe perspective, and then living up to that agreement. In her words:

> There's a recognition of the nationhood of the Indigenous people.... There's a lot of talk about honouring Treaties, and the fact that they haven't been honoured, but I think, mixed in with that is, with Treaty 3, for instance, we have a written document that says, "this was the Treaty," and it was signed by the various parties, but is this really what was agreed upon?... Obviously, there's questions about that.... So, even if we're upholding the documented Treaty, are we really upholding the agreement in the spirit in which the agreement was made?... I think examining that further is a step towards reconciliation.

This is a critical point. Indeed, there are at least five different accounts of Treaty 3. Beyond the original Treaty 3 manuscript, these include (1) the "official" account published by Treaty Commissioner and Lieutenant Governor of Manitoba Alexander Morris, in which he gloats about convincing the initially reluctant and "[un]reasonable" Anishinaabe to treat;[43] (2) an account by an anonymous journalist for *The Manitoban* newspaper, which is also included in Morris's publication; (3) the Paypom Treaty, named after the Anishinaabe Elder who kept the notes of Métis translator Charles Nolin, whom the Anishinaabe Chiefs had hired because they did not trust the Crown[44] and wanted their own written record; (4) Anishinaabe oral histories;[45] and (5) an unpublished, unedited transcript in the handwriting of Treaty Commissioner Simon J. Dawson, who, unlike Morris, had longer-term and, apparently, respectful relationships with the Anishinaabe.

As Nelson suggested, there are significant discrepancies between these accounts. Most significantly, as highlighted by white settler historian Sheldon Krasowski,

> although the text of Treaty Three clearly stated that the Indigenous Peoples "cede, surrender, and yield up" their lands, both eyewitness accounts [Dawson and Paypom] and Treaty Three oral histories affirm that this clause was not discussed during the verbal negotiations.[46]

This was not an aberration. Canada's treaty commissioners' negotiating strategy in the late nineteenth and early twentieth centuries was "to discuss only the benefits of a treaty and to ignore its liabilities," acknowledging "there is no evidence that Alexander Morris or his fellow treaty commissioners discussed the surrender clause during any of the treaty negotiations."[47] If anything, the Canadian government had a strategic plan to deceive over the "surrender clause" and land sharing.

The implications are staggering. As Anishinaabe Elder Robert Greene told me in an interview, "under British common law, words or ideas that were not talked about during the negotiations are not part of the Treaty; they're not part of the agreement." Although the Anishinaabe Chiefs agreed to share (half of) their land and resources in exchange for certain benefits (treaty annuities, farming tools, etc.) and agreed to a mutually beneficial partnership with the settlers, they did not surrender their land, their sovereignty, or their inherent right to self-government.[48] Elder Greene also noted that Morris, who had a reputation as a devious lawyer, edited versions of the treaty negotiation minutes to suggest that the Chiefs surrendered lands and resources, when in fact they only agreed to share the land to the depth of a plow. Morris's account and the treaty manuscript therefore must be read with a critical lens and in the context of other accounts, especially those kept by Anishinaabe. The point, moreover, is to honour the spirit and intent with which the Anishinaabe entered the treaty, not the Crown's written text. If that is done, we can be cautiously optimistic about developing more just and sustainable relationships.

Erv Stach, a white settler retired judge, concurred. He said, "At its core, I think reconciliation means trying to restore us to a respectful partnership in the sense that was intended by the First Nations at the time [the treaty was negotiated]." By implication, the Anishinaabe had honourable intentions and believed deeply in the ceremonies that sanctified the treaty, whereas Canada's treaty commissioners, as documented by Krasowski[49] and others, were often underhanded and manipulative. What needs to be honoured therefore is the "respectful partnership... intended by the First Nations," not the Crown's text. Part of the problem, Stach said, echoing Bright above, is that most settlers are poorly educated about treaties. But, in his mind, "being a Treaty person is acknowledging that we live in the territories of the First Nations people and that we should strive to recapture the intent, to become partners, to live together with one another in a sharing way, and to honour and respect one another's traditions."

What might it look like, in practice, to honour the spirit and intent with which the Anishinaabe entered the treaty? There are multiple possible answers. A local Métis leader offered one example:

> Reconciliation to me [is] about understanding what the Treaty's all about... and that we're all Treaty people.... I heard a story [that] I thought was just fitting. Somebody I know went to Eagle Lake and they're in the community and they'd gone to powwows there. And then they went over another time... and they were cleaning up the garbage that was left there... recycling as well. And one of the Elders come up to him and said, "I know you're here. You come every time we have a powwow, and you bring gifts." And he says, "but why are you here cleaning up?" He goes, "I'm here cleaning up because this is our land too." And the Elder said to him, "Now you get it." So that really opened me up to think, "You know what? Just because it's that community doesn't mean we can't get involved in helping clean up [or] helping out where we can. We're all responsible."

It is certainly possible to problematize this story. Eagle Lake is a First Nation. Although part of Treaty 3 territory, it is not really "our [non-Anishinaabe] land too." One may also question whether the emphasis on "helping clean up" suggests a saviour complex. Nonetheless, the broader point is that we—Indigenous and non-Indigenous alike—all have obligations to keep the land, air, and water healthy and clean, and that taking such actions is a way of fulfilling one's responsibilities to one another and the earth and thereby honouring the spirit of treaty. The more we all willingly do this, the closer we get to something like reconciliation.

Skeptics

A third group of participants—about one-quarter—was deeply skeptical of treaties and their potential to foster reconciliation. They also tended to be critical of the term *reconciliation*, even as they worked in various ways to improve relationships between peoples and with the land. These views were more often expressed by Indigenous Peoples, but also by a few settlers.

For example, when asked about the phrase "we are all treaty people," Ogichidaa[50] Daryl Redsky laughed heartily, dismissed it as a buzz phrase, and said,

> Personally, I think Treaties are overrated. They're one-sided. Treaty doesn't really benefit me. It benefits the settler. It benefits the government. So, I don't think too highly of Treaties. It's just another mechanism used on our people by the settlers. [Some] people call it *manidoo mazina'igan* ["the sacred paper"]. But I don't see anything sacred that was written by a non-Indigenous person.... What was the process that made it sacred? There's nothing sacred about it. The thought behind it was to help take the land, take the resources, keep the Indian in a concentration camp, and administer their poverty. To me, that's what the Treaty represents. We're losing parts of our Treaty every day. They're taking rights, right from under our noses.... Treaty was supposed to protect me. Treaty doesn't do that. Treaty's there to benefit the other society, not us. And reconciliation [*pause*]—I don't know if we can put those two together. I have a Treaty medallion here, and when I look at [it], I see my ancestor standing with a non-Indigenous person.... That was the day that everything went awry for us.... The Treaty didn't come from us... It came from the English; it came from the Crown. And when my ancestors were forced to sign it, they probably didn't even know what they were signing because they signed it with an *X*. I got my suspicions. Anybody could forge an *X*.

This powerful quotation questions whether a treaty can be sacred if one party never intended to honour it or if it was later used to impoverish and control another party. Redsky also questions whether his ancestors even signed the treaty, and he is not alone in raising such questions. In fact, multiple accounts of Treaty 3 suggest that most Anishinaabe Chiefs simply "touched the pen of the clerk," who then signed *X*s on their behalf.[51] Elder Greene suggested that touching the pen meant that the Chiefs accepted the spirit of the treaty, as they and the Creator intended, but that they did not necessarily trust the written word. If so, this means it can be simultaneously true that the written treaty text is not sacred, the treaty commissioners and/or the government had bad intentions, the treaty has been disingenuously used to dispossess Indigenous Peoples of their land and to benefit settlers, *and* that the treaty, as understood and intended by the Anishinaabe leaders in 1873, nevertheless contains meaningful principles that are still worth revitalizing, honouring, and applying.

Given the colonial injustices imposed on Anishinaabe people shortly after 1873, including the flooding of reserve lands, gardens, and wild rice fields, the depletion of sturgeon populations, the restrictions on hunting and fishing, the ban on selling agricultural produce to settlers, the extraction of gold and other minerals without consent, the ban on Indigenous spiritual practices, the establishment of the residential school system, the ban on lawyers pursuing land claims, and the forcible relocation and "extinguishment" of First Nations within Treaty 3,[52] it is understandable that some Indigenous Peoples remain cynical of the value of treaties or reconciliation. For some participants, the problem was not so much the treaty itself but the fact that the Crown broke it almost immediately by imposing the *Indian Act* in 1876, which unilaterally defined who was and was not "Indian" and sought to regulate virtually every aspect of First Nations life. For Elder Tommy Keesick, a veteran of the 1974 Anicinabe Park occupation,[53]

> the Treaty was no good because it was meant [by the settler government] to be broken.... You see, when the Treaties came, that's when the Anishinaabe started experiencing homelessness, starvation, no work, no money. [Before the treaty] we had everything. We had our own medicines. We had our own healers.... We didn't need money to buy food or clothing.... Everything was there for us.... And the Treaties reduced the land mass.

Elder Keesick described how the government imposed harvesting limits and how the Anishinaabe Nation was broken into smaller reserve lands where different groups were sometimes mixed together or pitted against one another in a battle for scarce resources.

Geri Kakeeway, an Anishinaabe educator, raised a further concern. Referencing Tuck and Yang's "Decolonization Is Not a Metaphor,"[54] she said that when settlers use the phrase "we are all treaty people," it sometimes sounds like a "move to innocence," as if they are trying to self-Indigenize or make themselves an "innocent non-oppressor." But, in fact, she added,

> let's be real here. There are people who have greatly benefited more so in that Treaty relationship, and it ain't us, despite the fact that a lot of people like to throw it in our faces that we get everything for free, which is a load of crock.

Dynamic Perspectives

Overall, while settlers are more likely to reject treaties as "unfair" to them or to accept a narrow view of treaties consistent with the Crown's text, and while Indigenous Peoples are more likely to endorse a holistic vision of treaties consistent with Indigenous oral histories or to reject treaties as colonial tools for appropriating land, it is important to remember that perspectives on these issues are not static. Over time, and through life experiences, individuals can learn and sometimes change their views on treaties and reconciliation. Many interviewees spoke of an increasing pessimism, especially about reconciliation, given settler governments' failure to implement most of the TRC and NIMMIWG recommendations to date.

Conversely, a grassroots Anishinaabe leader explained why he is now more hopeful than ever about the potential of Treaty 3 to foster just and sustainable relations. When he first heard the phrase "we are all treaty people," he said he was "upset with it" because he thought the Anishinaabe got a raw deal and now settlers were trying to horn in on what few rights his people had. After attending university, and especially after speaking with Elders about the intentions of the Anishinaabe Chiefs who entered the treaty, he developed "a different take on it." In his words, "our vision of the Treaty was to coexist, to share, but we never surrendered our land." Since the treaty commissioners "put in the surrender clause later" or did not discuss it with the Anishinaabe, he and his Elders do not consider it to be part of the treaty. What they did agree to, however, was honourable, and it was sanctified by ceremony and meant to last forever:

> We're all binded by the Treaty, whether you like it or not. You can [have] a redneck attitude, it still will not change that it says there in the Treaty that we have to get along, we have to share.... You have that responsibility. I have that responsibility. We were born with it already, by that Treaty that was [made] in 1873. There's no way you can get past it [as] residents of Canada.... And we can co-exist. We have lots of land. We have lots of resources... This responsibility—truth and reconciliation—lies with every chief, every politician, every individual in Canada.

Conclusion

In working through these diverse perspectives on treaties and reconciliation, it is necessary to consider some critical questions:

- Is an agreement valid if it was signed under duress, coercion, or manipulation? At the 1873 treaty discussions, Morris was accompanied by dozens of armed troops whom he claimed "exercised a moral influence which contributed most materially to the success of the negotiations."[55] He also allegedly met privately with one Chief before the negotiations who ultimately broke ranks with the other Chiefs.

- Is an agreement valid if it was not signed by one or more of the parties? According to multiple accounts, Anishinaabe Chiefs simply "touched the pen" of the clerk, who then signed *X*s on their behalf.

- Is an agreement valid if the terms were unilaterally changed after the fact? There is no evidence that the land surrender was directly discussed. It does not appear in Anishinaabe oral histories, the Paypom Treaty, or even Dawson's notes. If it was included in the written text without the Chiefs' knowledge, what does this mean for the treaty as a whole? For land rights today?

- Is an agreement valid if it has been (repeatedly) broken? Even according to narrow settler interpretations, Canadian courts have confirmed that Treaty 3 has been violated, resulting in multiple settlements. Numerous Treaty Land Entitlement claims and other cases alleging treaty violations are outstanding within Treaty 3 and elsewhere.

- If an agreement is not valid, then what?

Despite these concerns, many Anishinaabe Elders say it is still important to honour the spirit and intent that their ancestors brought to the treaty discussions. The problem is how to live up to the spirit of the treaty, especially at a nation-to-nation level, when there is such widespread ignorance and racism among the settler public, when most Canadians understand so little about treaties and are motivated to protect their power and resources, when even some of those who are engaged in reconciliation work have oversimplified views of treaties, or when, as shared with me by an Anishinaabe expert on Treaty 3, even some First Nations Chiefs do not have a solid grasp of the treaty.

In this context, how can treaties be a vehicle for reconciliation? Are settlers prepared to "live in Indigenous sovereignty," as Carlson-Manathara[56] puts it? Are we prepared to develop meaningful relationships with local Indigenous nations and follow Indigenous law and jurisdiction, rather than settler law and jurisdiction, at least where the two conflict? Are we prepared to be responsible stewards of shared treaty lands, for the benefit of future generations? The Crown has no honour. But perhaps, as many residents hope and pray, a critical mass of Indigenous and non-Indigenous people in Treaty 3 and beyond will find ways to realize the aims of the Anishinaabe who entered treaty in the spirit of "respect, responsibility, and renewal."[57]

Notes

1 I use the term *settler* to refer to Canadian citizens and permanent residents who are not Indigenous to Canada. Following Lowman and Barker, I believe this term highlights the tensions that stem from a settler colonial system. Since this system is intertwined with capitalism, white supremacy, and hetero-patriarchy, I also recognize that relationships with Indigenous Peoples and lands, and levels of colonial privilege and complicity, vary depending on class, race, gender, sexuality, and other structural factors. The term *settler* is also inappropriate for groups such as refugees or enslaved people. When making broad claims that may encompass such groups, I therefore sometimes use the generic term *non-Indigenous*. However, most of

the non-Indigenous people who live in Treaty 3 and who were interviewed for this research are white (of European descent) and are identified as such. For more on these terminological debates, see Lowman and Barker, *Settler*; Thobani, *Exalted Subjects*; Vowel, *Indigenous Writes*.

2 Bradbury, "Treaty 3 Celebration Tour."

3 Cardinal and Hildebrant, *Treaty Elders of Saskatchewan*; Craft, *Breathing Life into the Stone Fort Treaty*; Hill, *The Clay We Are Made Of*.

4 Starblanket, "Crises of Relationship," 5.

5 Starblanket, "Crises of Relationship," 5.

6 Stark, "Respect, Responsibility and Renewal," 155.

7 Asch, *On Being Here to Stay*; Krasowski, *No Surrender*.

8 Sehdev, "People of Colour in Treaty," 273.

9 Hiller, "'No, Do You Know What *Your* Treaty Rights Are?,'" 383.

10 Denis, *Canada at a Crossroads*.

11 Mills, "What Is a Treaty?," 219.

12 Borrows and Coyle, *The Right Relationship*.

13 Angus Reid Institute, "Truths of Reconciliation"; Martino, "'Follow All the Rules.'"

14 Starblanket, "Crises of Relationship," 6.

15 Alfred, "Deconstructing the British Columbia Treaty Process"; Woolford, *Between Justice and Certainty*.

16 Denis et al., "Treaty Relations and Decolonization."

17 McIvor, *Standoff*.

18 Asch, *On Being Here*; Denis et al., "Treaty Relations and Decolonization"; Krasowski, *No Surrender*.

19 TRC, *Calls to Action*.

20 For more on the Dish with One Spoon, see Hill, *The Clay We Are Made Of*; Simpson, "Looking After Gdoo-Naaganinaa."

21 Kenora, Ontario, is the largest city in Treaty 3 territory, with about fifteen thousand year-round residents, 24.6 percent of whom identify as Indigenous. Statistics Canada, "Census Profile."

22 One circle was conducted with eleven Indigenous and settler youth at a local high school.

23 I first heard this phrase in the *Report of the Ipperwash Inquiry*, in 2007, but it was used earlier by the Saskatchewan Office of the Treaty Commissioner. According to Emily Grafton, Treaty 4 Elders say the "Treaty people" are the settlers. Similarly, in Aotearoa/New Zealand, Pakeha/settlers are considered "people of the Treaty," whereas Maori are considered "people of the land." David MacDonald, personal communication, October 2022.

24 Charmaz, *Constructing Grounded Theory*.

25 TRC, *What We Have Learned*, 121.

26 McIvor, *Standoff*.

27 Jewell and Mosby, eds., *Calls to Action Accountability*.

28 APTN National News, "Wauzhushk Onigum Nation Finds 171 Anomalies."

29 NIMMIWG, *Reclaiming Power and Place: The Final Report*.

30 Ballingall, "Reconciliation Is Dead."

31 Denis and Beckman, "Azhe-mino-gahbewewin."
32 Denis, *Canada at a Crossroads*.
33 In 1870, the Boundary Waters Anishinaabe negotiated a right-of-way agreement for Canadian soldiers to pass through their territory on the way to Red River. Subsequent attempts at a comprehensive treaty failed because Anishinaabe leaders said the Crown had not kept its right-of-way treaty promises. See Grand Council Treaty #3, "Our Nation"; Krasowski, *No Surrender*.
34 Simpson, "Looking After Gdoo-Naaganinaa."
35 Stark, "Respect, Responsibility and Renewal."
36 Wicken, *Mi'kmaq Treaties on Trial*.
37 Krasowski, *No Surrender*.
38 Kulchyski, "Trails to Tears."
39 TRC, *What We Have Learned*.
40 TRC, *What We Have Learned*; Tuck and Yang, "Decolonization Is Not a Metaphor."
41 In 2016, Ontario passed legislation declaring the first full week of November to be Treaties Recognition Week.
42 Kraswoski, *No Surrender*; Luby, "'The Department Is Going Back on These Promises.'"
43 Morris, *The Treaties of Canada*.
44 The Crown had already broken promises under the right-of-way agreement of 1870.
45 As Chief Mawedopenais said at the treaty discussions, "our hearts and our brains are like paper; we never forget." Morris, *The Treaties of Canada*, 69.
46 Krasowski, *No Surrender*, 274.
47 Krasowski, *No Surrender*, 272.
48 Anishinaabe oral history suggests that "half of the lands would be shared to the depth of a plow and that the other half would be reserved for the Anishinaabe." Krasowski, *No Surrender*, 116.
49 Krasowski, *No Surrender*.
50 As Redsky explained, Ogichidaa is often translated as *warrior*, but more directly means *person of big heart*, whose responsibility includes protecting the Anishinaabeg. It is a title bestowed in ceremony.
51 Krasowski, *No Surrender*.
52 Denis, *Canada at a Crossroads*; Lovisek, Waisberg, and Holzkamm, "'Deprived of Part of Their Living'"; Waisberg, Lovisek, and Holzkamm, "Ojibwa Reservations."
53 On the significance of Anicinabe Park, see Rutherford, *Canada's Other Red Scare*.
54 Tuck and Yang, "Decolonization Is Not a Metaphor."
55 Morris, *The Treaties of Canada*, 54.
56 Carlson-Manathara with Rowe, *Living in Indigenous Sovereignty*.
57 Stark, "Respect, Responsibility and Renewal," 145.

Sources

Alfred, Taiaiake. "Deconstructing the British Columbia Treaty Process." 2000. https://www.sfu.ca/~palys/Alfred-2000-DeconstructingTheBCTreatyProcess.pdf.

Angus Reid Institute. "Truths of Reconciliation: Canadians Are Deeply Divided on How Best to Address Indigenous Issues." June 16, 2018. https://angusreid.org/wp-content/uploads/2018/06/2018.04.23_indigenous_fullreport.pdf.

APTN National News. "Wauzhushk Onigum Nation Finds 171 Anomalies During Search of St. Mary's School Site." *Aboriginal Peoples Television Network*, January 17, 2023. https://www.aptnnews.ca/national-news/wauzhushk-onigum-nation-finds-171-anomalies-during-search-of-st-marys-school-site/.

Asch, Michael. *On Being Here to Stay: Treaties and Aboriginal Rights in Canada*. University of Toronto Press, 2014.

Ballingall, Alex. "Reconciliation Is Dead and We Will Shut Down Canada, Wet'suwet'en Supporters Say." *Toronto Star*, February 11, 2020.

Borrows, John, and Michael Coyle, eds. *The Right Relationship: Reimagining the Implementation of Historical Treaties*. University of Toronto Press, 2017.

Bradbury, Allan. "Treaty 3 Celebration Tour to Make Southern Stop Tomorrow." *Fort Frances Times*, July 19, 2023. https://fftimes.com/news/local-news/treaty-3-celebration-tour-to-make-southern-stop-tomorrow/.

Cardinal, Harold, and Walter Hildebrandt. *Treaty Elders of Saskatchewan: Our Dream Is That Our Peoples Will One Day Be Clearly Recognized as Nations*. University of Calgary Press, 2000.

Carlson-Manathara, Elizabeth, with Gladys Rowe. *Living in Indigenous Sovereignty*. Fernwood Publishing, 2021.

Charmaz, Kathy. *Constructing Grounded Theory: A Practical Guide through Qualitative Analysis*. Sage Publications, 2006.

Craft, Aimée. *Breathing Life into the Stone Fort Treaty: An Anishinabe Understanding of Treaty One*. Purich Publishing, 2013.

Denis, Jeffrey S. *Canada at a Crossroads: Boundaries, Bridges and Laissez-Faire Racism in Indigenous-Settler Relations*. University of Toronto Press, 2020.

Denis Jeffrey S., and Sarah Beckman. "Azhe-mino-gahbewewin: Returning to a Place of Good Standing in Treaty #3 Territory." In *Reading Sociology: Decolonizing Canada*, 4th ed., edited by Johanne Jean-Pierre Vanessa Watts, Carl E. James, Patrizia Albanese, Xiaobei Chen, and Michael Graydon. Oxford University Press, 2022.

Denis, Jeffrey, et al. "Treaty Relations and Decolonization: Indigenous Community and Academic Perspectives." Congress 2023: Reckonings and Reimaginings. Transcript to be published in *Journal of Canadian Studies*.

Grand Council Treaty #3. "Our Nation." 2023. http://gct3.ca/our-nation/.

Hill, Susan M. *The Clay We Are Made Of: Haudenosaunee Land Tenure on the Grand River*. University of Manitoba Press, 2017.

Hiller, Chris. "'No, Do You Know What Your Treaty Rights Are?' Treaty Consciousness in a Decolonizing Frame." *Review of Education, Pedagogy, and Cultural Studies* 38, no. 4 (2016): 381–408. https://doi.org/10.1080/10714413.2016.1203684.

Jewell, Eva, and Ian Mosby, eds. *Calls to Action Accountability: A 2022 Status Update on Reconciliation*. Yellowhead Institute, 2022. https://yellowheadinstitute.org/wp-content/uploads/2022/12/TRC-Report-12.15.2022-Yellowhead-Institute-min.pdf.

Krasowski, Sheldon. *No Surrender: The Land Remains Indigenous*. University of Regina Press, 2019.

Kulchyski, Peter. "Trails to Tears: Concerning Modern Treaties in Northern Canada." *Canadian Journal of Native Studies* 35, no. 1 (2015): 69–81.

Lovisek, Joan A., Leo G. Waisberg, and Tim E. Holzkamm. "'Deprived of Part of Their Living': Colonialism and Nineteenth-Century Flooding of Ojibwa Lands." In *Papers of the Twenty-Sixth Algonquian Conference*, edited by David H. Pentland. University of Manitoba, 1995.

Lowman, Emma Battell, and Adam J. Barker. *Settler: Identity and Colonialism in 21st Century Canada*. Fernwood Publishing, 2015.

Luby, Brittany. "'The Department Is Going Back on These Promises': An Examination of Anishinaabe and Crown Understandings of Treaty." *Canadian Journal of Native Studies* 30, no. 2 (2010): 203–28.

Martino, Nick. "Follow All the Rules': Hunter and Angler Identity Formation, Group Boundaries, and the Ethno-Racialization of Poaching in Ontario." PhD diss., McMaster University, 2023.

McIvor, Bruce. *Standoff: Why Reconciliation Fails Indigenous Peoples and How to Fix It*. Nightwood Editions, 2021.

Morris, Alexander. *The Treaties of Canada with the Indians of Manitoba and the North-West Territories: Including the Negotiations on Which They Were Based, and Other Information Relating Thereto*. Belfords, Clarke & Company, 1880.

National Inquiry into Missing and Murdered Indigenous Women and Girls (NIMMWG). *Reclaiming Power and Place: The Final Report of the National Inquiry into Missing and Murdered Indigenous Women and Girls*. National Inquiry into Missing and Murdered Indigenous Women and Girls, 2019. https://www.mmiwg-ffada.ca/final-report/.

Rutherford, Scott. *Canada's Other Red Scare: Indigenous Protest and Colonial Encounters During the Global Sixties*. McGill-Queen's University Press, 2020.

Sehdev, Robinder Kaur. "People of Colour in Treaty." In *Cultivating Canada: Reconciliation Through the Lens of Cultural Diversity*, edited by Ashok Mathur, Jonathan Dewar, and Mike DeGagné. Aboriginal Healing Foundation, 2011.

Simpson, Leanne. "Looking After Gdoo-Naaganinaa: Precolonial Nishnaabeg Diplomatic and Treaty Relationships." *Wicazo Sa Review* 23, no. 2 (2008): 29–42. https://doi.org/10.1353/wic.0.0001.

Starblanket, Gina. "Crises of Relationship: The Role of Treaties in Contemporary Indigenous-Settler Relations." In *Visions of the Heart: Issues Involving Indigenous Peoples in Canada*, edited by Olive Patricia Dickason, David Alan Long, and Gina Starblanket. Oxford University Press, 2020.

Stark, Heidi Kiiwetinepinesiik. "Respect, Responsibility and Renewal: The Foundations of Anishinaabe Treaty Making with the United States and

Canada." *American Indian Culture and Research Journal* 34, no. 2 (2010): 145–64. http://dx.doi.org/10.17953/aicr.34.2.j0414503108l8771.

Statistics Canada. "Census Profile, 2021 Census of Population: Kenora, Ontario." Government of Canada, last modified August 2, 2024. https://www12.statcan.gc.ca/census-recensement/2021/dp-pd/prof/details/page.cfm?Lang=E&SearchText=Kenora&DGUIDlist=2021A00053560010&GENDERlist=1,2,3&STATISTIClist=1&HEADERlist=0.

Thobani, Sunera. *Exalted Subjects: Studies in the Making of Race and Nation in Canada*. University of Toronto Press, 2007.

Truth and Reconciliation Commission of Canada (TRC). *Calls to Action*. Truth and Reconciliation Commission of Canada, 2015. https://www.trc.ca/assets/pdf/Calls_to_Action_English2.pdf.

Truth and Reconciliation Commission of Canada (TRC). *What We Have Learned: Principles of Truth and Reconciliation*. Truth and Reconciliation Commission of Canada, 2015. https://publications.gc.ca/collections/collection_2015/trc/IR4-6-2015-eng.pdf.

Tuck, Eve, and K. Wayne Yang. "Decolonization Is Not a Metaphor." *Decolonization: Indigeneity, Education & Society* 1, no. 1 (2012): 1–40.

Vowel, Chelsea. *Indigenous Writes: A Guide to First Nations, Métis & Inuit Issues in Canada*. Highwater Press, 2016.

Waisberg, Leo G., Joan A. Lovisek, and Tim E. Holzkamm. "Ojibwa Reservations as 'An Incubus Upon the Territory': The Indian Removal Policy of Ontario, 1874–1982." In *Papers of the Twenty-Seventh Algonquian Conference*, edited by David H. Pentland. University of Manitoba, 1996.

Wicken, William C. *Mi'kmaq Treaties on Trial: History, Land, and Donald Marshall Junior*. University of Toronto Press, 2002.

Woolford, Andrew. *Between Justice and Certainty: Treaty Making in British Columbia*. UBC Press, 2006.

She Helped Herself

Rendering Empowerment Through Birth Sovereignty

Vanda Fleury

THIS CHAPTER EXPLORES ANTI-INDIGENOUS RACISM AND patient safety through the lens of health justice. Central to this chapter is the harm I experienced as a patient accessing Western health-care services, and as a result, I explore my relationship with birth sovereignty through embodied resiliency as an Indigenous woman and mother. I have engaged in activities inspired by the revival of cultural practices, sought contemporary supports of registered midwives, and planned for holistic, out-of-hospital births. This is a personal account that privileges knowledge about family-centred birthing, historically and in the present, to contribute to dismantling Canada's colonial narratives that typically ignore or devalue Indigenous women's life experiences. Health justice is a decolonial remedy, drawn out by the usefulness of "story medicine"[1] to provide benefit to Indigenous health in settler colonial society. I demonstrate this through "photovoice"[2] methodology, a process that brings together photography and the "structured use of photographs" to speak to "salient issues."[3] Drawing from both sides of my camera lens, photovoice offers a critical and creative expression of my family birth narratives. This process of cataloguing my journey of birth sovereignty through photovoice empowered me to create evocative snapshots that are layered with personal interpretations and meaningful experiences. Ultimately, this work challenges the medicalization of childbirth and reimagines health and wellness in an Indigenous-centred and decolonial present.

Seeking Indigenous Health Justice in Settler Colonial Canada

It is important that, as Indigenous Peoples, we tell our stories and remember our histories. I write from a motivation to help others and from an understanding that our experience is vital to collective knowledge. Many Indigenous Peoples believe that "stories convey knowledge, knowledge does not convey the story."[4] To share knowledge through story gives us opportunities to hear shared experiences and to affirm our cultural understandings. These stories become lifelines, where we can give voice to our individual and personal experiences in the face of colonial injustices. My story is about birth sovereignty and my personal experiences with anti-Indigenous racism that led me to seek a return to family-centred birthing. To tell my story, I rely on health justice. This is based on "story medicine,"[5] a healing approach that prioritizes Indigenous oral histories and the relationships that reconnect us to past generations, where the unearthing of knowledge is strengthened by listening, by reflecting on, by taking inspiration from, and by stitching together gender-affirming narratives to support the reconstruction of health and well-being.[6]

Indigenous reclamation of the past is mandatory in our struggle to control our futures. For me it is strategic, and it is personal. Central to my story medicine is the harm I experienced as a patient accessing Western health-care services at a hospital in Winnipeg, Manitoba, in 2013. I am Métis, and my husband is Anishinaabe from Shoal Lake 40 First Nation, and I feel that being perceived as an Indigenous family directly impacted the quality of care we received prior to the birth of our son. My experience is validated by Dr. Alika Lafontaine, president of the Canadian Medical Association from 2022 to 2023, who is Indigenous, and points out that Métis, First Nations, and Inuit peoples are marginalized by biases, discrimination, and stereotypes in mainstream health care.[7] Consequently, I have come to understand my experiences as part of these larger and ongoing issues.

These issues are those processes of settler colonialism that required racist ideologies to justify colonial domination and that, in turn, frame the settler state. These ideologies selectively draw from history to form a national consciousness,[8] promote frontier mythologies,[9] and treat Métis, First Nations, and Inuit peoples as "Other."[10] Joyce Green's definition of racism is particularly valuable, as it provides the context for "othering" and outlines the process of this colonial domination. Her analysis suggests that

> racism becomes part of the structural base of the state, permeating the cultural life of the dominant society both by its exclusive narrative of dominant experience and mythology, and by its stereotypical rendering of the "Other" as peripheral and unidimensional.[11]

Racism is insidious and it is systemic. Foreign (Western) world views within health-care and other social services continue to oppress us and hurt our families. We—Indigenous Peoples—must examine our experiences in the context of this colonial past because it negatively impacts our roles as mothers and caregivers. According to Indigenous scholar Kim Anderson, "producing life and raising children are understood as the creation of a people, a nation, and a future."[12] This Indigenous framing of motherhood can heal some of the colonial harm we experience through health care.

Anderson's subsequent work, *Life Stages and Native Women: Memory, Teachings, and Story Medicine*, centres story medicine as a healing tonic, whereby our Indigenous roots infuse our identities with character; our lived experiences are validated with context, meaning, and agency.[13] As an Indigenous mother, I have engaged in activities inspired by the revival of cultural practices and made choices to privilege this knowledge. In part, I cultivate my identity by working in the layers of birth knowledge and community narratives in west-central Manitoba, Canada. The connections I have made through story medicine are a source of pride that influenced my process through pregnancy and birth, as well as postpartum health and well-being. If I want my children to claim their birth right, I must claim mine too.

This chapter is anchored by three photovoice images related to my story medicine, related to birth sovereignty. Embracing the camera as a means for self-reflection, storytelling, and community engagement, I have layered each photo with meaningful discussions of my experiences and personal interpretations that challenge the medicalization of childbirth. Part of a structured series of photographs, the three are titled "A Long Shadow," "In Good Hands," and "Earthly Details."[14] Conceived by Wang and Burris in the early 1990s, photovoice methodology is popular with the public, activists, educators, and researchers because the focus rests on "education for critical consciousness," a concept coined by Brazilian educator Paulo Freire.[15] Photovoice empowers individuals to explore their thoughts, experiences, memories, family narratives, and cultural knowledge in connection to social justice issues. As described by Palibroda and colleagues,

"Images captured through photovoice tell stories that identify concerns, depict struggles or show a particular view of a community. Through photographs, marginalized individuals offer insight and teach others about their experiences."[16] Remarkably few studies have been designed to hear first-hand accounts by Indigenous women, and, as such, photovoice draws out the usefulness of story medicines to result in Indigenous health justice.

Anti-Indigenous Racism and Patient Harm

I am grateful for my three children. My oldest child was born at term at the hospital where we planned for his birth. During this event, we were denied proper care, repeatedly, and I feel we were disrespected in our most vulnerable hours. Cross-sectional studies highlight the insidiousness of racism and its association with the harm Indigenous Peoples experience in the health-care system. According to Philips-Beck and colleagues, "Racism is often manifested with more subtlety than violent verbal or physical attacks. It can be implied through actions as well as attitudes and through a lack of consideration to such things as safety and comfort of others deemed undeserving."[17] My waters came at 2 a.m., and by five o'clock my husband, Jesse, and I were at the obstetrical triage desk, where we engaged with a clerk and nurse. Before I was even examined, I heard one of them state, "This is your first birth, and it's going to be a long time before things progress." Her condescending tone was a precursor to the lack of compassion experienced in the hallways and public spaces of that hospital.

It was true that I had never given birth before. Nor had I ever witnessed a birth. However, I came to the hospital with the assumption that I would have meaningful guidance and a degree of privacy for the physical transformations. I went from one centimetre dilated to ten in only four hours. In that time, I complied with the nurse's commands to go outside for a walk. I tested positive for Group B streptococcus, for which I needed an IV antibiotic before the birth to prevent it passing to the baby. I dragged the drip along the waterfront sidewalk, and the pole had a dual purpose as my crutch when my contractions increased in intensity and length. I made my way back to the delivery ward of the hospital with difficulty, but when I described these changes to the nurse, she seemed annoyed. Her response was hostile, and she said, "You'd better get used to it because the contractions will only get worse. Keep walking." I was turned away without any meaningful consultation or physical exam.

It seemed like my labour was a public spectacle, and I felt a powerful need to turn inward. Knowing I needed to ground myself, the only space I could find was a public bathroom adjacent to the local coffee shop. When I recall this memory, I see a vivid image of the trash can overflowing with waste. I remember the panic. It was a critical stage of the active birthing process, and inside the stall my body was already urging me to push. Had I answered the call, both the baby and I could have sustained injuries. What about the health risks posed by the unsanitary conditions of a public restroom? Surrounded by health-care professionals, infrastructure, and everything Western medicine should have had to offer, we were essentially on our own.

Once again, we approached the admitting desk, and though I was not examined right away, they did provide us a curtained space that was adjacent to the patient admitting area. My mental health was deteriorating because I was under the impression that there was a long birthing process still ahead. No one was present to assure us that the progression, transformation, and pain were normal. I was nauseated and felt like I was spiralling in a vortex. Jesse was timing the contractions, and they were sixty seconds apart, frequent, and sometimes overlapping. I was desperate when I told him to get someone and advocate for us. He had to speak aggressively with the nurse and outright demand an assessment.

A visibly irritated nurse begrudgingly attached the cardiotocography belt and finally initiated a physical exam where she confirmed "you are definitely at ten!" I could hear nervous chatter and papers flying as I was officially admitted into the LDRP (labour, delivery, recovery, and postpartum) unit. Within minutes I was whisked away by a different team of nurses who, for the record, treated us with compassion and dignity. I crossed over into a delivery room and my baby was born not more than fifteen minutes later. Moments after he took his first breaths of air, he was placed on my stomach and instinctively did a breast crawl up to my waiting arms. It was a profound moment that is positively imprinted in my memory. It honours the sacred life force and synergy I felt with my newborn.

I never received an apology for the racism and the misdiagnosis of these health-care services. I know I am not insignificant, and neither are my children and my family. The actions of the medical staff with whom we dealt in triage should have been guided by the insight that there is no universal timeline for birthing and that every woman's process is different, whether or not it is their first delivery. There were short-term emotional impacts from the harm I suffered, and long-term effects that I recognize with the passage of time. I would have negative flashbacks to the event, feeling a deep sense of injustice. I felt humiliated and angry too. It transferred into a general avoidance of the Western medical system, combined with feelings of anxiety when I engage with health-care professionals.

My trauma compounded when I became aware of a troubling view around maternal health that was revealed when I shared that the experience was an assault on my dignity. I was met with harsh attitudes by other Indigenous women who suggested "the baby is safe and healthy, that's all that matters. Let it go." I felt not only devalued as an Indigenous woman but also trivialized as a mother voicing her concerns about our negative encounters. Sharing my story and perspective should not be associated with loving my child any less. In fact, I would argue the opposite. Years later, creative outlets like photovoice, film poetry, and other writing projects distill my frustration and anger.

Fleury, "A Long Shadow"

Confronting the Medicalization of Birth

Decolonization is an active dynamic, and it was visceral in my second pregnancy. I did not want a repeat scenario, and there was tremendous relief when I received a call from Ode'imin (formerly known as the Birth

Centre) in Winnipeg. A registered midwife with the College of Midwives of Manitoba welcomed us into their circle of care. To challenge negative memories, I situated myself within a holistic framework that explored birth sovereignty and considered what it could look like for our birth plan as an Indigenous family. I craved a support network where I would be emboldened by culturally appropriate dynamics that are flexible and unique to my family narratives.

Anishinaabe-Dine midwife Melissa Brown is based in Manitoba and offers full-spectrum doula training. In her view, centring spirit, culture, and traditions has transformative effects, and, as she remarked in an interview with Jennifer Cox, from the University of Winnipeg, in this way, "we can heal and strengthen our families and communities."[18] I contemplated my in-hospital experience, wondering how it might have played out had we been in a secure and culturally safe environment. My grandma Gloria, for example, has assisted in over twenty births. What if I had been surrounded by my aunts and other women providing the guidance and support I needed? As that thought came into focus, I actively conceived our multidimensional sacred space.

Indigenous scholars acknowledge that grandmothers play an indispensable role in shaping our minds and are often the foundation of a family. Without a doubt, grandmothers are the greatest teachers and should hold a primary position in understandings of our place in this world as Indigenous women.[19] Exploring these intergenerational relationships, Grace Ouellette maintains that

> their source of wisdom and knowledge can be found in their own experiences and in their grandmother's teachings, which have been passed on for generations through oral tradition. Decolonization and co-existence can be achieved through the recovery of these sources.[20]

My healing work involved working closely with my grandma Gloria to centre story medicine around the collection of stories concerning local Métis midwives.

Our time together involves place-based adventures where we visit local landmarks, gather plants and medicines, and take pictures. We enhance our family narratives by collecting pieces of documentary heritage[21] and sharing stories, like the one we cherish about her mom, Eva, who would "stay out" to dig Seneca root with her extended family. During these camping trips, they worked together to harvest a wide variety of medicines, many of which Aunty Caroline depended on in her role as a midwife. In response to my need for this story medicine, Gloria authored a diary-style book illuminating customs, medicines, and experiences of local birth workers and families, though names and details have been altered as a measure of privacy.

I introduce myself as Gloria's granddaughter when I am home in the Uno Valley on the west-central prairies of Manitoba. She has resided there for over sixty years and is now the lone resident. She connects us to the memories and stories reflected in the landscape and is recognized as a custodian of local knowledge. Uno is a section on the old Alphabet Line of the Grand Trunk Pacific Railroad that follows the flow of the Assiniboine River. Located approximately fifty kilometres north of Virden, Manitoba, it is adjacent to Chan Khaga Dakhóta Oyáte (Birdtail Sioux First Nation); Beulah is to the east, Miniota is to the southeast, and Birtle is to the north. A community that was once in the pocket of Crown land, it was a bustling hamlet of intergenerational Métis families that were wage labourers on the Canadian National Railway. Other sources of livelihood included gardening, hunting, trapping, trading, and sharing resources among families, cousins, and friends made it rich in other ways. For members of my immediate and extended family, these characteristics continue to call us home.

The feelings of place, purpose, and comradery are timeless, and I am confident they are inspired by the community and family relationships at the heart of the historic Métis buffalo hunts. From the rail lines to the waterways near present-day St. Lazare, ancestral homelands extending throughout the Birdtail and Qu'Appelle Valleys also birthed the Hudson's Bay Company trading posts and Forts Ellice I and II. These lands are situated on Treaty 2 territory, at the confluence of the Assiniboine and Qu'Appelle Rivers. It was a popular location for Indigenous Peoples participating in the continental trade network for thousands of years and was rich in resources for shifting populations that included the Métis, Assiniboine, Cree, Dakota, Nakota, and Mandan peoples.[22]

Métis Midwives and the Roots of Story Medicine

The memories of our ancestors are strengthened by the stories we remember and share. Unearthing story medicines about the Métis midwives who historically bonded to my family was transformative for my health and well-being. This research empowered me because it located my family in the continuum of Indigenous kinship, where each of my own birthing stories was a ripple in the water. In 1920, Gloria's father was delivered by midwife Mrs. Boyer, whose ceremony involved cleaning and wrapping the baby, then smudging in all directions with an eagle feather within the first few minutes after birth. Gloria's husband was delivered by Mrs. Biecier on the Welby plains of east-central Saskatchewan in 1928. At the Sainte Madeleine cemetery, the old cross acknowledging her death also celebrates life, and etched on the wood are the words "she was well known as a midwife who brought 400 babies or more into this world."

Ste. Madeleine was a Métis community eventually swallowed up by a pasture program led by the Prairie Farm Rehabilitation Administration. In a recent 2024 government-to-government land transfer between the Province of Manitoba and the Manitoba Métis Federation, one hundred acres of these historic lands were returned to Red River Métis citizens.[23] Sainte Marthe, just southwest, is in close proximity to Rocanville, Saskatchewan. Ste. Marthe, Ste. Madeleine, and St. Lazare formed a triad, and within the pages of the small leather pocketbook that Aunty Caroline carried is a written testament to our kinship connections across these communities. A midwife committed to detail, she recorded the names of the hundreds of babies she delivered, the parents, extended families, locations, and other first-hand knowledge related to the birth.

Aunty Caroline is remembered for never losing a child in all the years she was catching babies and held "authority"[24] as a midwife. She was respected for her knowledge of medicines and was vigilant about cleanliness. She wore her integrity in her custom style, bleached-white and starched aprons made from flour sacks. Aunty Caroline raised my great-grandma Eva, who was her birth helper throughout the twenties and thirties.[25] These lifelines extended to Gloria, too, even though she was born at the Birtle hospital in the 1940s. Coincidentally, when it was time to deliver the baby, the nurses and doctors were not present. But great-grandma Eva knew what to do by reaching back to the birth knowledge she acquired in those formative years shadowing Aunty Caroline, and, in Gloria's words, "she helped herself."[26]

Decolonization is using the roots of story medicine to reclaim the past and to make contemporary connections. As a personal contribution, I framed my daughter's bedroom as an ethnobotany project. Commemorated on the walls are historical photos of Métis midwives who supported the women of our past with prenatal, childbirth, and postpartum care. The canvas also includes unique characteristics of our family birth narratives that are adorned with plants like tobacco, bearberry, cedar, wolf willow, mint, and hyssop, many of which were harvested in Uno. Layered across the ceiling is prairie sage, gathered at Ste. Madeleine, intertwined with twinkling lights. The space crosscuts generations, where our story medicine is accessible through tangible objects and interpretive representations.

I want this room to inspire my children so that they can navigate their place within our family and communities. Symbolically connected to Aunty Caroline's black leather register is a black portfolio that documents my research and shares pictures, old and new, of foundational people and events. It holds the memories of burying my children's placentas in Uno, where one is at the base of an oak tree, on the hill overlooking the valley towards the Assiniboine River, and two others rooted at a silver willow and a maple, gracing the bank of a stream that flows into the Minnewastha Creek (good water). Anderson explains that in the past, "Connections between the baby, family, community the natural world, and the spirit world were ensured,"[27] and in a similar vein, we honour those traditional practices. The portfolio and ethnobotany space are a refreshing way for my children to connect with story medicine and to illuminate the path home. I hope these sources of inspiration build their cultural confidence so that they may be used as a remedy for decolonization.

Fleury, "In Good Hands"

Embodied Resiliency: My Second Delivery

A contraction woke me up at 5:45 a.m., and my waters came shortly after, at 6:30. A calm excitement transformed into an impending sense of urgency, and I have since learned from my body and personal rhythms that I underestimated the timing between the stages of labour. Our plan was for an out-of-hospital water birth at the Birth Centre, and early morning rain made what was usually a thirty-minute drive even longer. It was an epic ride, complete with the type of sensationalized moments seen in Hollywood films! Clocking in at 8:55 a.m. gave us enough time to check vitals and plunge into the warm waters already prepared for us, and six minutes later, at 9:01, our baby was born in the Primrose Room. Suitably, the primrose flower signifies new beginnings, and marks new phases and new life.[28]

Guided by my hands and the midwife's calm voice, I heard "There's a head! When you are ready, you are going to catch your baby." The process of receiving her was energizing, and it is now part of my identity and shared narrative with my daughter. Her dad joined us, and we all spent the first hour floating in the water together. We enjoyed toast and coffee in bed at 10:30 a.m. and were heading home by 3:30 that afternoon, with less urgency, of course. It was so different from the in-hospital birth. The well-being of mother and child was paramount, and the relationship with my midwife was based on mutual respect. I felt validated and redeemed, and it was an incredibly empowering experience.

A Living Canvas: My Third Pregnancy

Birth sovereignty was a return to the meaningful customs and reclaimable sources of Indigenous women's knowledge. This was the fabric of both my second and third pregnancies, and it was never about replicating the past. During the birth of my third child, I was supported by the primary and contemporary services of my midwife, while my spiritual well-being was inspired by my historical birth work. The ethnobotany project's three antique images of the Métis midwives represented ancestral strength, and seeing them brought me comfort and encouragement. At times I felt like I had extended care, and I felt especially close to Aunty Caroline. There was a discernible electricity on the second floor of my home the night leading up to the birth, and I acknowledged these women with a spirit dish before I went to bed.

Past injustice at the in-hospital birth may have fuelled my motivation. But I was now following my intuition and tuning in to the rhythm of my body that suggested my process would be quick. Fear of the unknown had dissipated, and I wanted another water birth that would be in the comfort and safety of my family home. According to the Taproot Collective, a sovereign birth "understands that a woman/person is free to choose her/their birth provider, birth setting, and/or route of birth. As she/they govern her/their own body, she/they can choose a hospital, birth center or home birth."[29] I would not be destabilized by pressure to conform to a system or set of ideals that was not right for us.

I was also on familiar ground with my midwife, who had supported me and my family during my second pregnancy and delivery at the Birth Centre. Though it was not part of the birth plan, she took the time to explain and demonstrate the fundamentals, should the labour progress faster than anticipated. When my waters came at 5:30 a.m., I called the midwife and filled our tub with warm water. In just twenty minutes, I experienced five contractions, each growing more powerful. I settled into the water and shortly thereafter was aware that I was bracing my feet at the foot of the tub. It occurred to me that for a third time I was holding the baby in. Then I heard the familiar voice of my midwife: "Trust your body, it knows what to do." She had prepared me with sufficient knowledge to keep the baby and myself safe.

Furthermore, I had used the years in between to do my own research, and, in that moment, I used it to maintain my composure. I felt a sense of courage from talking birth stories with my grandma Gloria too. Without panic or chaos, I sat upright and called out to my husband, who knelt beside the tub. It was serene when her head emerged. I told him to hold back, not to pull, as the shoulders needed to turn naturally. They did, and moments later the fetal ejection response landed her safely in my grasp, then in her dad's hands for a second catching. Together, we received our baby. I looked down and held the gaze of her intense brown eyes through the water, before she came up. The midwife had dropped off her birth kit a few days earlier, and we had also prepared supplies like a thermometer, blanket, and toque for keeping her warm in the water. I had been well coached to keep her high enough that she could breastfeed but low enough to respect the umbilical cord and placenta.

The thick scent of sage and the smudge danced in the air with our playlist of Indigenous flute music. The first people to join us were our two children, who had been sleeping peacefully downstairs. They peeked their heads around the corner, holding expressions of amazement and delight! I did not want them present for the birth; however, I wanted them nearby. Offers to take them away for a few days, though well-meaning, made me uncomfortable. From my perspective, a home birth granted us the autonomy to acknowledge our children's place within our family structure, normalizing birthing and ensuring they did not feel left behind. Anderson shares the traditional perspective of Mosôm Danny Musqua, a Saulteaux storyteller from Keesekoose First Nation in Saskatchewan, who maintains it is critical that children have a sense of belonging.[30] In a complementary act of inclusion, alongside their father, my children offered tobacco and lit a sacred fire on the grounds of our home the day before the baby arrived. This was to guide her spirit, according to their father's Anishinaabe customs.

Nobody seemed surprised that the birth happened fast, considering the patterns that emerged from my previous births. I delivered the placenta shortly after, and it was like a living canvas of our storylines. The midwife traced her interpretation of its form and composition to environmental and hereditary factors, and my son was so captivated that she invited him to share the experience. He was hands-on and glove-free exploring the texture and feel, and I could see what a powerful experience it was for him. It reminds me that the rigid ideologies around gender roles in childbirth are conditioned, and I hope more Indigenous boys position themselves as birth helpers.

To do this, it is important that, as Indigenous women and mothers, we use story medicine to challenge these "fixed" and often stubborn narratives. To my disappointment, there were those in our circles who reinterpreted our birth story to give the impression that Jesse delivered the baby without the presence of our midwife. Some made quite a fuss! It is a reaction that troubles me because it fixates on a one-dimensional idea that the man would "naturally" take on a power position in relation to the "passive" woman giving birth. But this was not a mainstream hospital delivery room, and I was anything but subordinate and passive in this process. While I acknowledge the support and courage of my partner in what was likely an anxious situation for him, retelling the story of our homebirth through the blurred lens of a gendered power imbalance is contrary to birth sovereignty. I also recognize that for Indigenous family and friends, our paths to decolonization have crossroads that are nuanced and complex. But story medicine is an opportunity to learn and teach, and pointing to this experience allows us to reimagine family-centred birthing and how that can be supported in a variety of situations.

The baby's breastfeeding latch was strong, and we stayed in the warm water for two hours. I remember profound feelings of happiness, pride, and excitement about our return to family-attended birthing. Our gathering that morning had a similar dynamic to the family kitchen parties I grew up with. The midwife was seated by the tub, our birth helper had a chair in the shower, Jesse was making rounds with coffee and cookies, and my children were visiting with everyone. Even our little dog was there! We were empowered as a family, and laughter carried throughout our home. We held meaningful conversations that flowed naturally, from American politics in 2019 to the Indigenous women responsible for crop production in Cahokia almost a thousand years ago.[31] With a touch of humour and irony, I juxtapose the filthy public washroom in the hospital to our home bathroom where I found redemption.

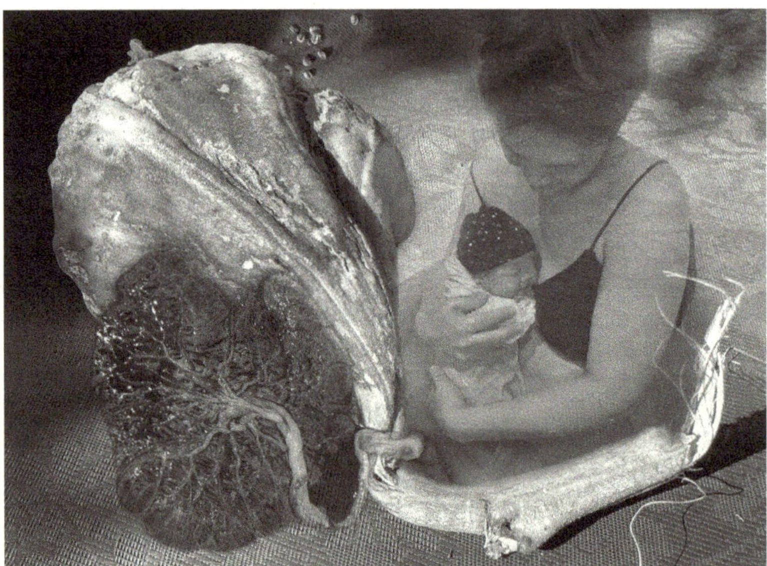

Fleury, "Earthly Details"

Sowing the Seeds of Health Justice

Birth sovereignty suggests our bodies are sacred spaces. Therefore, what we consume is important, and the historical connections to Indigenous food, land, science, art, and world view were vital ingredients in my story medicine. Cahokia (at present-day St. Louis, Illinois) was once a large urban Indigenous centre that existed between 600 and 1400 CE, and it grew exponentially with the success of agriculture and kinship networks. Gayle Fritz's research shows that "farming was the prerogative, the responsibility, the skill set, and the spiritual domain" of the Indigenous women and girls who nurtured and maintained the fields.[32] Cahokia's agricultural footprint included squash, maygrass, sunflower, marsh elder, chenopod, and erect knotweed.[33]

It is a legacy that reflects the depth of Indigenous plant cultivation, and one that widely impacted my birth work and personal expression of the sacred. With a Three Sisters garden as the foundation, I prioritized the preparation and consumption of home-grown food that nourished us in the prenatal stages. As the garden blossomed, it supported us during breastfeeding that lasted eighteen to twenty-four months with each child. In parallel harmony, I am from a family of prolific gardeners and hunters, and our family narratives inspired me to follow their land-based approach to health and wellness.

The sunflower in particular stems from deep-seated traditions in Indigenous North America,[34] and growing a garden strengthened my connection. People are dazzled by the imagery of the open-faced flower, as is evident from popular art and selfies, but my gaze is on the form and contours, where I see a resemblance to the placenta. Moreover, from the earth around Cahokia there was an abundance of red flint clay used to make effigies adorned with sunflower iconography, celebrating Indigenous women. Fritz emphasizes that there is a "symbolic association between sunflowers and Old Woman Who Never Dies, a key mythological personage who is likely to be represented by the female flint-clay statues."[35] To harvest "good medicine" is to draw from these stories and complementary sources of inspiration embedded in our ancestral narratives.

As an Indigenous mother, I share my birth sovereignty journey as a personal act of decolonization. I am committed to taking up space as an Indigenous woman, and photovoice is an expression of my agency, where each angle speaks to my multidimensional experiences. I continue writing our family narratives through story medicine and other ethnobotany projects that support these initiatives. To sow the seeds of birth sovereignty is to render our cultural stories as sources of empowerment, to call out anti-Indigenous racism in health care, to challenge the medicalization of birth. It is reimagining health and wellness in an Indigenous-centred and decolonial present.

Notes

1 See Anderson, *Life Stages and Native Women*, with a foreword by Maria Campbell.
2 Wang and Burris, "Empowerment Through Photo Novella."
3 MacDonald, "What Is a Photo Voice Project?"
4 Waters, ed., *American Indian Thought*, xv–11.
5 See Anderson, *Life Stages and Native Women*.
6 Anderson, *Life Stages and Native Women*, 3–4, 161, 176. Story medicine is akin to the process of "digging up medicines," a popular phrase introduced by oral historian participant Mosôm Danny Musqua and commonly referred to throughout Anderson's book.
7 Lafontaine, "Status Quo."
8 Green, "Towards a Détente," 88.
9 Green, "Towards a Détente," 89.
10 Green, "Towards a Détente," 88. Reprinted with permission by the author.
11 Green, "Towards a Détente," 89.
12 Anderson, *A Recognition of Being*, 170.
13 Anderson, *Life Stages and Native Women*, 4.
14 Vanda Fleury, "A Long Shadow," "In Good Hands," and "Earthly Details," photo-based mixed media, Winnipeg, 2020. These images also appeared in the webinar "Safe and Respectful First Nations, Métis, Inuit and Maternal Care," with presentations by Vanda Fleury, Brenda Epoo, and Dr. Karen Lawford. Hosted by Healthcare Excellence Canada (Ottawa, Ontario), the event acknowledged World Patient Safety Day on September 17, 2021. The images were also included in the public group exhibition *HeART of Healthcare Virtual Art Exhibit Honouring Safe Maternal and Newborn Care*, Healthcare Excellence Canada, Ottawa, Fall 2021.
15 Freire, *Pedagogy of the Oppressed*, quoted in Wang and Burris, "Empowerment Through Photo Novella."
16 Palibroda et al., *A Practical Guide to Photovoice*, 10.
17 Phillips-Beck et al., "Confronting Racism," 3.
18 Cox, "Urban Indigenous Doula Project."
19 See Anderson, *A Recognition of Being*, as well as Ouellette, *The Fourth World*.
20 Ouellette, *The Fourth World*, 38.
21 A plethora of family narratives are documented in R.M. of Ellice Centennial Book Committee, *Ellice 1883–1983*.
22 R.M. of Ellice Centennial Book Committee, *Ellice 1883–1983*, 12.
23 Bettens, "Manitoba Moves to Transfer 100 Acres."
24 Kim Anderson discusses the significance of women holding authority and community dynamics in "Grandmothers and Elders," chapter 6 of her book *Life Stages and Native Women*, 126–59.
25 There are parallel stories in Kim Anderson's "The Life Cycle Begins: From Conception to Walking," in Anderson, *Life Stages and Native Women*, 48, 49.
26 Gloria Fleury, personal correspondence, ongoing oral history project: 2006–22. Uno, Manitoba.

27 Anderson, *Life Stages and Native Women*, 63.
28 Symbolshub Team, "Significance of the Primrose Flower Meaning."
29 Novotny, "Birth Sovereignty."
30 Anderson, *Life Stages and Native Women*, 66.
31 Fritz, *Feeding Cahokia*, 1.
32 Fritz, *Feeding Cahokia*, 46.
33 Fritz, *Feeding Cahokia*, 117–18.
34 Fritz, *Feeding Cahokia*, 21.
35 Fritz affirms that "Old Woman Who Never Dies" was honoured by the farmers for "her role as giver of all plant food, protector of children, bringer of summer, and rejuvenator of living and dying things." Fritz, *Feeding Cahokia*, 101.

Sources

Anderson, Kim. *Life Stages and Native Women: Memory, Teachings, and Story Medicine*. University of Manitoba Press, 2011.

Anderson, Kim. *A Recognition of Being: Reconstructing Native Womanhood*. Sumach Press, 2000.

Bettens, Cierra. "Manitoba Moves to Transfer 100 Acres of Historic Land to Red River Métis." *APTN News*, July 22, 2024. https://www.aptnnews.ca/national-news/manitoba-moves-to-transfer-100-acres-of-historic-land-to-red-river-metis/.

Cox, Jennifer. "Urban Indigenous Doula Project Receives CIHR Funding." *Indigenous News*, University of Winnipeg. December 8, 2020. https://news.uwinnipeg.ca/urban-indigenous-doula-project-receives-cihr-funding/.

Fleury, Vanda. "Earthly Details." Photo-based mixed media. Winnipeg, Manitoba, 2020.

Fleury, Vanda. "In Good Hands." Photo-based mixed media. Winnipeg, Manitoba, 2020.

Fleury, Vanda. "A Long Shadow." Photo-based mixed media. Winnipeg, Manitoba, 2020.

Freire, Paulo. *Pedagogy of the Oppressed*. Translated by Myra Bergman Ramos. The Seabury Press, 1970.

Fritz, Gayle J. *Feeding Cahokia: Early Agriculture in the Northern American Heartland*. University of Alabama Press, 2019.

Green, Joyce A. "Towards a Détente with History: Confronting Canada's Colonial Legacy." *International Journal of Canadian Studies* 12 (1995): 85–105.

Lafontaine, Alika. "Status Quo: How Health System Design Prevents Impactful Transformation of Indigenous Patient Care." National Indigenous Cultural Safety Learning Series, webinar hosted October 7, 2020. http://www.icscollaborative.com/webinars/status-quo-how-health-system-design-prevents-impactful-transformation-of-indigenous-patient-care.

MacDonald, Fiona. "What Is a Photo Voice Project? The Process." Community Through Care. Accessed September 11, 2024. https://www.communitythroughcare.net/what-is-a-photo-voice-project.

Novotny, Kate. "Birth Sovereignty." Taproot Doula Project, October 9, 2018. https://taprootdoula.com/2018/10/09/birth-sovereignty/.

Ouellette, Grace. *The Fourth World: An Indigenous Perspective on Feminism and Aboriginal Women's Activism*. Fernwood Publishing, 2002.

Palibroda, Beverly, with Brigette Krieg, Lisa Murdock, and Joanne Havelock. *A Practical Guide to Photovoice: Sharing pictures, Telling Stories and Changing Communities.* Prairie Women's Health Centre of Excellence (PWHCE), March 2009. https://rpay.link/guide/pdf20.pdf.

Phillips-Beck, Wanda, Rachel Eni, Josée G. Lavoie, Kathy Avery Kinew, Grace Kyoon Achan, and Alan Katz. "Confronting Racism Within the Canadian Healthcare System: Systemic Exclusion of First Nations from Quality and Consistent Care." *International Journal of Environmental Research and Public Health* 17, no. 22 (2020). https://doi.org/10.3390/ijerph17228343.

R.M. of Ellice Centennial Book Committee. *Ellice 1883–1983*. R.M. of Ellice Centennial Book Committee, 1983.

Symbolshub Team. "Significance of the Primrose Flower Meaning." SymbolShub.org, November 23, 2019. https://symbolshub.org/flowers/primrose-flower-meaning/.

Wang, Caroline, and Mary Ann Burris. "Empowerment Through Photo Novella: Portraits of Participation." *Health Education & Behavior* 21, no. 2 (1994): 171–86. https://doi.org/10.1177/109019819402100204.

Waters, Anne, ed. *American Indian Thought: Philosophical Essays*. Black Publishing, 2004.

PART THREE

Settler Colonial Relationalities, Identities, and Belonging

Sikh Responsibilities and Dreams

Disrupting Settler Colonialism, Bigger than Settler Colonialism

Rita Kaur Dhamoon

> ਨਾਨਕ ਲੀਨ ਭਇਓ ਗੋਬਿੰਦ ਸਿਉ ਜਿਉ ਪਾਨੀ ਸੰਗਿ ਪਾਨੀ[1]
> "O Nanak, like water in the water, that person is merged with the Source."
>
> —ਗੁਰੂ ਗ੍ਰੰਥ ਸਾਹਿਬ ਜੀ / *Gurū Granth Sāhib Ji*, Ang 633

THIS CHAPTER IS A CALL TO PEOPLE WITH NON-WESTERN origins living in settler colonial places, and who have access to their ancestral practices and epistemologies, to explore these traditions to rethink our relationships and responsibilities to each other, to Indigenous Peoples and places, and to the more-than-human world. My engagement with non-Western ways of life is rooted in my rediscovery of my ancestral teachings of *Sikhī*, which, in Punjabi, means learner or discipline and represents a process of self-transformation. What might Sikhī offer in terms of struggles *against and beyond settler colonialism*, even as Sikhs and other people with non-Western ancestries settle on unceded, treaty, or settler-corrupted treaty lands and benefit from dispossession? In the first section, I show that Sikhī offers *anti-colonial political directions*, so that conditions of possibility between Indigenous Peoples and those with non-Western ancestry/ancestries are not strangulated by settler colonialism. In the second section, I consider the ways in which Sikhī opens up dreams of living otherwise, because it is a way of being in the world that is *bigger than settler colonialism*. By way of a conclusion, I consider the analytic and methodological implications of turning to non-Western traditions to unbind subjectivities and relations from settler colonialism. Let me begin first by providing some context about Sikhī.

A Brief Overview of Sikhī

Sikhī was founded in the fifteenth century in Punjab (a region now in India and Pakistan) by Guru Nanak Sahib-ji, the first Sikh Guru or Teacher. According to Sikhī, one of his first teachings was "Na Koi Hindu Na Koi Musulman" (There is no Hindu or Muslim) whereby our souls are not defined by attachments to a religion and associated hierarchies—which, in my mind, would now include "There are no Sikhs"—but by connection to Waheguru/God/Creator/the Divine/Primal Being (herein shortened to Waheguru). Nanak Ji offered ordinary people who did not read Brahmin texts (only Brahmins were permitted to read directly from religious scriptures) alternatives to inequities of hierarchal life and Brahmin-led caste divisions. This represented a dramatic change to the status quo. According to the ancient Vedic texts (written between 1500 and 900 BCE) only the highest caste, Brahmins, were deemed eligible to perform Hindu rituals (assumptions based on intellectual and priest superiority); the Kshatriya (nobles or warriors) traditionally held other positions of power; Vaishyas (commoners/merchants) were deemed ordinary people who produced, farmed, and traded; and the Shudras (ordinary workers/peasants such as labourers, artists, etc.) traditionally served the higher castes. Later in ancient India, Shudras, who worked with leather, were rendered untouchable. In the nineteenth century, the Sanskrit word *Dalit* came to be used instead of *untouchable*. The caste system was based on religious Hindu principles of purity and pollution, set at the time of birth and unchangeable (unlike class, in which there can be mobility between ranks), such that Dalits and other caste-oppressed people continue to suffer violence, degradation, and segregation.[2]

Guru Ji emphasized spiritual and societal transformation based on detachment and ego-loss, community gatherings, and democratized language and culture through poetry, song, and colloquialism so that everyone could access spiritual texts. He spoke against femicide and sati (widow immolation), and for women's rights; he foregrounded spirituality and truth through social conduct and responsibility, rather than theology or ideology; and he founded a communal kitchen. Guru Nanak Ji saw Waheguru in nature and the universe, and not just in humans; for him, Waheguru is timeless and without form, and is revealed in various human practices, hues and colours, trees, flora, fauna, singing birds, water, and air. Against the backdrop of Brahmin supremacy and Mughal violence, as well as teachings by Sufi and Hindu and Muslim poets and bards, and Buddhist presence, emerged a radical tradition: Sikhī.

Guru Nanak Ji was followed by nine successive human Gurus (divine messengers), in which ਗੁਰਬਾਣੀ or *Gurbani* (the sacred compositions by Sikh Gurus) was revealed from "God" (and as such is not a syncretic faith). As well as in person, *Gurbani* was shared in written sacred scripture ਗੁਰੂ ਗ੍ਰੰਥ ਸਾਹਿਬ ਜੀ or *Sri Gurū Granth Sāhib Ji* (SGGS) under the direction of the fifth Guru, Arjan Dev Ji. It is composed of shabads (divine messages in the form of hymns and sacred songs) poetically set to ragas (melodies). The SGGS is the guiding force for our spiritual life. The tenth Guru, Guru Gobind Singh Ji, passed Guruship to the Khalsa Granth ("First Book") and Panth (Sikh learners) in 1699, in which there was not a single successor but a collective who live under the teachings of the SGGS, which is the eternal Guru. Today, some thirty million people across the world follow *Gurmat* (the counsel of the Gurus).

While Sikhī is typically seen as an organized religion, I follow Arvind Pal-Mandair's[3] approach to it as a philosophy or a way of life, with institutions intentionally built by Gurus to practise the teachings (e.g., *gurdwaras* or temples, *langar* or community kitchens). Some of the values often cited about Sikhī include a devotional practice, belief in sex equality, living a full life aware of the divine within us, a rejection of caste, and an active commitment to service to humanity and the world, underpinned by spirituality. Like most faiths, however, these values are not always practised, and inequities and discrimination remain. For example, despite the fact the *Gurū Granth Sāhib Ji* includes compositions that are anti-casteist, discrimination and violence against Dalits by Sikhs continues today. This includes by the Shiromani Gurdwara Parbandhak Committee (SGPC), which administers Darbar Sahib (the Golden Temple, the main Sikh temple in India) and manages the gurdwaras in three Indian states. This has led to the rise of separate places of worship for Dalits (Mazhbis and Ramdassias) and other caste-oppressed people. As well, Sikh communities continue to be plagued by caste hierarchies embedded in marriage, religious rituals, spatial arrangements of living and eating, and labour.[4]

But when approached *as a way of life* (rather than a religion), the *Gurū Granth Sāhib Ji* seamlessly teaches about the earthly and spiritual realms and offers a path of freedom, love, mercy, justice, and harmonious detachment. These teachings are why I prefer a de-territorialized approach to Sikhī,[5] one not intrinsically tied to Punjab as the homeland (despite my historical and heart connection to Amritsar in Punjab) or even some socialist claim to "the commons"; this is not only because Indigenous Peoples have been forcibly displaced for thousands of years, since at least the pre-Dravidian period/early Harappa period (circa 3300 BCE–1300 BCE)[6] in what we now know as Punjab, but also because it presumes the right to possess a place, and this, to me, contradicts the Sikhī idea of detachment.

As I find myself rediscovering my ancestral lineage (at the age of fifty-something), Sikhī offers ways of being in the world, seeing the world, and learning by centring the interconnectedness of all things. This process is guided by the first phrase of the Sikh scripture, "Ik Oankar (ੴ)," which is interpreted in various ways but which I take to mean Oneness or what Harinder Singh calls 1Force[7] and Mandair defines as "one that is at the same time many or a many that is simultaneously one"[8]—like water in water, as the epigraph to this chapter states—with the self, each other, and everything in the universe. This Oneness originates in a genderless Waheguru, who/which can be reached via different paths. This Oneness connects the mind with everything in the universe that is infinite and eternal; it is not singular or universalizing, but unique flowing energies that move and reside in everything and connect humans and more-than-humans. It is this interconnectedness that increasingly propels my work, my connection to the many places I have lived, to my nineteenth-century Indian ancestors who died fighting for India's liberation against British colonialism, to the many women and queer, trans, and nonbinary people who did/do revolutionary work that too often gets forgotten, to the oceans that my diasporic family has crossed, to the trees that protected my family from heartbreak, and to this beautiful place of Lekwungen and W̱SÁNEĆ peoples that is still being possessed, gentrified, exploited, extracted, and poisoned by settler actions even as Indigenous Peoples regenerate and rejuvenate their own traditions.

Of course, not everyone has access to their ancestral practices, teachings, and knowledge due to various histories of colonialism, imperialism, wars, forced displacements, casteism, genocide, enslavement, dispossession, border-making, and involuntary detention. And there are good reasons that keep us away from our ancestral knowledge, including safety from patriarchy, homophobia, transphobia, colourism, ableism, and casteism in our "homelands" and in the diaspora. However, for the reasons above, where it is possible and chosen, I propose that non-Western ancestral ways of being can help navigate settler colonialisms. To illustrate the openings that non-Western teachings can bring to *disrupting* and *decentring* settler colonialism, I turn to Sikhī.

Anti-Colonial Sikhī: Diasporic Disruption and Refusal of Colonial Rule and Control

Anti-Statist

First, Gurmat-based (i.e., the counsel of Gurus) interventions into politics situate sovereignty in terms of the 1Force/Creator/Ik Oankar (ੴ), rather than state sovereignty. *Gurbani* does not explicitly address whether the nation-state is necessary for society or not, which is not surprising since nation-states had not yet fully emerged in their modern formation at the time of the Sikh Gurus (1469–1708). But the Gurus were aware of ruling authorities (including the Mughal princes and aristocracy), systems of rule (e.g., subas/provinces), and the land-owning class (zamindars), for they had clear views on how to rule;[9] this is evident in that they founded and helped govern eleven cities to spread Waheguru's teachings, collect offerings, and enshrine Sikhī values. Drawing on this Gurmat-based understanding of power, Harleen Kaur and prabhdeep singh kehal consider the response of Sikhs to the 2020 Movement for Black Lives.[10] They argue that Sikhs are intrinsically sovereign and therefore "do not seek the safety or approval of a nation-state and its mechanisms of power."[11] Indeed, "Sikhs must intentionally consider how our relationships with any state—past and present—enables the exploitation of other communities, especially if these relationships structurally benefit Sikhs.... Uncritical or mechanical allegiance to any nation is contradictory to Sikhī-informed liberation."[12] Kaur and kehal warn against structural ignorance about anti-Black racism and genocide against Indigenous Peoples because this merely reinforces race-craft of the state[13] and disregards Guru Nanak Ji's active rejection of injustices. A "Gurmat-centred framework must take seriously how we as Sikhs, or as Sikh-Americans [and, I would add, Sikhs everywhere], have implicated ourselves to . . . state-sponsored contract and system of exploitation."[14]

Santbir Singh Pannu also argues that allegiance to nation-states is inconsistent with Sikhī. "Sikhī," he says, "has formed and shaped principles like anti-authoritarianism, anti-statism, egalitarianism, consensus-based decision making, local and collective decision-making models, and support for the marginalized."[15] As he notes, Sikhī is based on a ਸਰਬੱਤ ਖਾਲਸਾ or Sarbat Khālsā system of governance that emphasizes freedom of the mind, heart, and body, and that has anarchist impulses (although, during the mid- to late eighteenth century, there were hierarchies within each Indian Misl or sovereign political entity/kingdom). By extension, anti-colonialism rooted in Sikhī entails de-investment in hierarchies and tools of discipline and punishment, including those that are state-led. In the context of the United States, Judge and Brar go further to argue that "to imagine and celebrate American subjectivity and possibility within the epistemic coordinates of capitalist modernity requires the continuous production of black and indigenous death, as well as violence abroad."[16] Such violence also requires false narratives of Sikh (heteronormative, able-bodied, model minority) exceptionalism and fantasies of American redemption. Sikhī, say Judge and Brar, does not need to be bound with the violence of American settler colonialism, enslavement, and imperialism, nor with the American dream, but instead could present a different stage on which to end the game of America.[17]

Interrogating Inclusion

While there are notable examples of Sikhs seeking inclusion in the nation-state through legal fights (such as the right to wear the turban or kirpan in public places) and through multicultural demands for state-based recognition (such as formal apologies for past wrongs), in my view Sikhī is not driven by the desire for inclusion in mainstream society. On the contrary, Sikhī entails the liberative process of detachment, whether from family, clan, community, or nation-state; this is a process of transformation towards non-ego or ego-loss. As such, Sikhī invites critical interrogation of human attachments to political communities and national identities, thus questioning not only the terms of inclusion but the very premise that inclusion is desirable.

To help Sikhs develop a Gurmat-centred political framework, Kaur and kehal emphasize that Sikhs must examine how "we" are, intentionally or unintentionally, always structurally invested in settler colonial genocide and police brutality against Black people. Kaur and kehal challenge Sikh national campaigns for more inclusion since they mean accepting the very social order that surveils, polices, criminalizes, incarcerates, and deports Black people. A Gurmat-based response, Kaur and kehal state, is alternatively rooted in ardaas (ਅਰਦਾਸ), or humble prayer for change; anand (ਅਨੰਦ), or the activity of rejoicing in existential love; Naam (ਨਾਮ), or active contemplation of Creator's timeless and formless virtues; and Ik Oankar (ੴ), or the 1Force. [18]

Instead of normalizing systems of policing and prisons that disproportionality impact Black people's lives, Kaur and kehal propose that Gurmat is oriented to making communities stronger and safer through community-driven (rather than state-driven) quality affordable housing, living-wage employment, accessible public transportation, education, and health care.[19] In other words, their grounding in Gurmat foregrounds human agency to question terms of colonial inclusion because it is rooted in hierarchies of power. Inclusion that is dependent on state criteria maintains colonizing conditions by the very presumption of state/Crown sovereignty in Canada's case, or constitutional sovereignty in the US case; and these systemic conditions, I contend, are fundamentally in tension with Sikhī.

Miri Piri *(Political-Spiritual Realms)*

Gurbani also teaches that Sikhs should adopt balance and integration between participation in governance (ਮੀਰ or mir) and spirituality or communal spirit of living (ਪੀਰ or pir). Perhaps for some practising Sikhs, this entails becoming an elected representative of a legislature, which may explain why there were more Sikhs elected in the 2019 Canadian federal election (eighteen Sikh MPs) than any other ethnic minority group, including the first Sikh national party leader (and one with a turban!), Jagmeet Singh. Sikhs have responsibilities to serve the collective consciousness as well as communities of Sikhs. Indeed, as the leader of the New Democratic Party, Jagmeet Singh has, at times, enacted the role of ਸੰਤ ਸਿਪਾਹੀ or Sant-Sipahi (Warrior-Saint), which for Sikhs means being both a soldier who is able to fight for worthy causes (such as protecting those suffering) and also a wise, knowledgeable, and Dharmic person with understanding of the 1Force. But, whether because of external constraints, such as the party system, or the visceral racism directed towards Jagmeet Singh, the possibilities of living as Sant-Sipahi or following Miri-Piri falls apart when aligned with settler colonial ways, in which liberal democracy and its institutions are naturalized as the norm. If we start from the place that settler colonial ways cannot be redeemed—because they are intrinsically perpetrating violence against Indigenous Peoples and others who are invited/seduced/necessary to build and uphold colonialism, including Sikhs who have been forced to leave India for economic and environmental reasons, or casteism, or the rise of Hinduvta supremacist policies (since the end of the 1980s)—a revolutionary way to proceed is to engage in "diasporic refusal" of hegemonic norms. Drawing from Audra Simpson's (Kahnawà:ke Mohawk Nation) work, Beenash Jafri says diasporic refusal is different from resistance in that resistance tends to reaffirm terms of engagement set by the state.[20] Alternatively, diasporic refusal requires a critical consciousness of complicity in ongoing colonization and recognition and fashioning "new forms of relationality and co-existence.... Underpinning acts of refusal is the promise of other modes of existence."[21]

So long as Indigenous Peoples remain subjected to colonialism and do not consent to settler sovereignty, diasporas should refuse national allegiances and pride in Canada and the United States, which includes elected officials disengaging with Canadian and American expressions of nationalism (such as swearing an oath to the reigning monarch or taking an America-first approach to economic policy). Moreover, regardless of political party ideology, when elected in settler colonial societies, Sikh allegiance is inevitably split between the state and the ਪੰਥ or Panth; in the Canadian case, this is evident in the fact the Sikhs elected to the Parliament of Canada have not always successfully advocated for policy matters and human rights affecting Sikhs in India or elsewhere (such as recent expedited resettlement of Afghan Sikhs who face persecution by Afghan authorities).[22]

The political-spiritual doctrine of Miri-Piri promotes the regality of Guru Ji and is also rooted in the earthly realm (unconstrained by nation-states) and the timeless realm; this is even as the Sikh Panth in India and diaspora have been circumscribed by the nation-state since the early twentieth century.[23] Sikhī is about creating freedom for the whole universe, which cannot happen while Indigenous sovereignties are discounted by Canadian, American, and Indian governments, or when Black people continue to be murdered at the hands of the police, or when Sikhs and Muslims are targeted by Hindutva policies, or when our plants and soils are poisoned by resource extraction, or when the rainforests are being destroyed for profit. In the earthly mortal realm, "Guru Nanak Sahib proclaimed that there was no political authority other than *Akal Purakh* (ਅਕਾਲ ਪੁਰਖ/the Divine). Guru Arjan Sahib [the fifth Sikh Guru] later echoed this by stating that there was no savior Monarch, but only the Immortal Being."[24] There is the Akal Takht Sahib in Amritsar, Punjab, which acts as the seat of earthly political authority and brings together leaders, emissaries, or administrators from outside of Amritsar. While deliberations are sanctified in the divine space of the Akal Takht and therefore not just political,[25] the Akal Takht has been criticized for its stance opposing same-sex marriage and excluding Sikh women and Dalits from performing kirtan at Darbar Sahib. In other words, it does not consistently meet standards of equity and justice.

Miri-Piri is, in my mind at least, a wide-ranging principle that rejects homophobia, sexism, and casteism. It also includes the practice of ਲੰਗਰ or langar, in which a communal kitchen provides free food to feed both the physical body and the spirit, offered to everyone in the same way regardless of caste, status, gender, or class. Started by Guru Nanak Ji, and developed by the second Guru, Angad Ji, and his wife, Mata Khivi, langar is not charity but an active practice of opposing poverty created by ruling classes; it is about "centring people's needs whilst also challenging our conventional modes of production.... Establishing sovereign spaces outside and beyond the state's discipline, fuelled by *Langar* and collective action, represents a departure from the traditional exploitative modes of exchange.... *Langar* becomes a site for 'political-spirituality' [that centres 1Force]."[26] To further promote equity, the second Guru Ji helped standardize a linguistic script (Gurmurkhi) so that the masses could read sacred poetry and sing shabad (the guiding sound of wisdom) for themselves rather than relying on the Brahmin priestly class. Guru Ram Das Ji, the fourth Guru, founded Darbar Sahib in Amritsar with four doors open on all sides as a rejection of Brahmin practices that excluded Dalits. Other Sikh Gurus emphasized physical skills like horse riding and swordsmanship, so as to sharpen discipline and skills when fighting injustice. And another defended those being persecuted and forcibly converted, including Brahmins who faced oppression from Mughal Emperor Aurangzeb even though Brahmins had historically punished Sikhs for breaking from a caste-based system. In the contemporary era, too, Miri-Piri directs Sikhs to participate in political governance and in the communal spirit of living, such that colonialism must be actively rejected, and other kinds of political and spiritual decolonial relationships built.

Care for the More-Than-Human World

The *Gurū Granth Sāhib Ji* further reminds us repeatedly that the natural elements are essential to life, that these elements are sacred and need to be protected and cared for:

> ਪਵਣੁ ਗੁਰੂ ਪਾਣੀ ਪਿਤਾ ਮਾਤਾ ਧਰਤਿ ਮਹਤ ||
> pavan guroo paanee pithaa maathaa dhharath mehath ||
> Air is Guru / penetrates everything everywhere, Water is the Father, and Earth is the Great Mother of all.

And:

> ਪਉਨ ਪਾਨੀ ਧਰਤਿ ਆਕਾਸ ਘਰ ਮੈ (ਨ) ਧਰ ਹਰਿ ਬਨੇ
> Paun paanee dharatee aakaas ghar ma(n) dhar har banee ||
> Air, water, earth and sky—Creator has made these as home and temple.

Gurbani emphasizes the need to be in harmony with Earth and all creations (Oneness), specifically referencing various species of trees, eulogizing species that are necessary for life, celebrating the wonder of all beings, colours, forms, wind, water, fire, wilderness. In doing so, *Gurbani* is not dictating the possession of land, water, or natural resources, but instead advancing an understanding of the sacredness of the earthly world, including its animals, plants, rocks, rivers, and humans.

Aside from resonances with epistemologies and ontologies of Indigenous Peoples in which more-than-human life is kin, *Gurbani* evokes responsibility *to* place, to Earth, water, and air. In other words, human life is intimately tied to caring for the elements of ecological life (and the wider cosmos). This responsibility intrinsically entails diasporic refusal of settler colonial capitalist extraction of natural resources that depletes Earth of its minerals, poisons rivers and waterways, and releases toxins in the air; put differently, Sikhī is aligned with supporting Indigenous Peoples' assertations for Land Back (including in Palestine) and opposing resource extraction for profit (rather than for need). Certainly, in settler colonial contexts, "while our connection to this land might be important, it is not critical to our languages, stories, knowledge systems, and selves" in the same way as it is for Indigenous Peoples of these lands.[27]

Bigger than Settler Colonialism

Thus far, I have explored some ways that Sikhī is oriented to anti-colonial disruption. In this section, I want to signal the ways in which Sikhī is also bigger than critique of colonialism, transcending settler colonizing formations of relationship.

Spiritual Wellness

Settler colonial practices, structures, and processes not only strangulate Indigenous ways of being and Indigenous relations with Black people, people of colour, and other marginalized people in order to serve ruling interests, but they also break spiritual wellness through hetero-patriarchal, casteist, capitalist white supremacy.[28] In other words, these systems of oppression interact in ways that create and uphold rigid hierarchies that determine access to resources, opportunities, and power. Sikhī offers one pathway to spiritually heal. "Sikhī," says Pannu, "is intensely focused on social and political egalitarianism, but more than these materially obvious forms of equality is the underlying assumption of Gurū Nānak Sahib that the most important form of bondage that a human experiences is the imprisonment of their mind."[29] Colonialism is certainly not the only source of imprisoning the mind, but Sikhī can temper colonial mentalities. This is specifically through humility and the practice of falling in love with Guru through ਨਿਸ਼ਕਾਮ ਸੇਵਾ or nishkkam seva (selfless service with no desire for reward/recognition) and ਸ਼ਹੀਦੀ or shahīdi (martyrdom/suffering for a just cause).[30] Seva encourages people to apply their labour and skills to build loving community life, to assist those less fortunate, especially to improve health and well-being, so that they, too, can be more active members of society. ਨਾਮ ਸਿਮਰਨ or naam simran (a spiritual process of constant remembering, contemplating, and habituating Creator's virtues) through reading, singing, and poetry also brings us closer to Waheguru and the state of being in ਚੜਦੀ ਕਲਾ or chardhi kala (the mental state of eternal durability, optimism, joy, high spirits, and self-dignity—an acceptance of life's ebbs and flows without attachment to fear or jealousy). As Sharanjit Kaur Sandhra says of chardhi kala, "it needs to be a collective sangat."[31]

Sikhī Praxes of Sangat, Kirat, Naam, Wvand

When imagining a world beyond settler colonialism, I want to dream in ਸੰਗਤ or sangat (community) about a society that encapsulates the political-spiritual doctrine of Miri-Piri, as Guru Nanak Ji did when he set up Kartarpur Sahib, a city in Pakistan-Punjab, in 1504. He settled here "after undergoing the *udasis* (epical journeys 'to meet Wisdom-oriented' ones), as there did not exist any other city that would abide by these new principles inherent in the Ik Oankar worldview."[32] It was here that he plowed fields and started ਲੰਗਰ or langar (free community kitchens as a place of social and political refuge), and offered Sikhī principles of ਕਿਰਤ ਕਰੋ or Kirat Karo, ਨਾਮ ਜਪੋ or Naam Japo, and ਵੰਡ ਚੱਕੋ or Wvand Chakko. *Kirat Karo* is a call to work "with passion and dedication to earn an honest living while remembering God with every stroke of the brush; laying of every brick and sewing of every stitch on a sick patient. *Kirat kamai* therefore brings to life the world-wide concept of 'Work is Worship.'"[33] Hard work (including running an honest trade, as Bhagat Raidas did in his nonviolent revolt against casteism) helps to provide the means for the most basic needs for survival—food, shelter, and warmth—for everyone. *Naam Japo* is a call to meditate on, remember, and contemplate 1Force. And *Wvand Chakko* requires that we share what we have and consume it together as a community, or in more Marxist terms (well before Marx was alive!) redistribute wealth, food, services, and goods. Indeed, in my understanding, Sikhī is inherently anti-capitalist because capitalism is rooted in exploitation and profit above anything else, and the drive for capital accumulation and profit contravene the principles of Kirat and Wvand, which are about taking responsibility to redistribute resources/gains. This (anti-capitalism) is fundamental to not only disrupting relationships between Sikhs, Indigenous Peoples, Black people, Asians, and others that are embedded in colonial capitalism, but it also explicitly confirms meaningful human connections, limiting what humans take from the natural world to what is needed for subsistence, the importance of redistributive practices, and meaningful (not alienating!) work.

Dreams of Begumpura

Gurbani also contains a utopian vision of a just society, presented by the bhakti radical Bhagat Raidas—often Hinduized by the spelling Ravidas, according to Bharti—through forty poems set to sixteen ragas in the SGGS, as ਬੇਗਮਪੁਰਾ or Begumpura.[34] It is believed that the Raidas family worked as cleaners of cattle carcasses, and Bhagat Raidas was a tanner from the Dalit caste; he saw caste discrimination as a disease at the root of social divisions and revolted against the violence of untouchability. Begumpura articulates a heartfelt desire to create a society where no one faces discrimination on the basis of caste, gender, or social and economic status, and where caste would be abolished; all people would be able to have their basic needs met; people would pay no taxes; they could move freely without regulation by authorities (something particularly freeing for Dalits); no one would own property or wealth; hierarchies would be rejected; and there would be no wrongdoing or sorrow, worry, terror, or torture. This is not only a dream of a society that is socially just and where people live in harmony,[35] but several Gurus created new cities of safe haven to realize this dream and practise Sikhī. In fact, Begumpura is used interchangeably with Guru Arjan Ji's notion of Halemi Raj, which is a modest, just, peaceful regime, in which the ਹੁਕਮਿ/hukam or divine command is followed.

Sant Raidas Ji used language that would be accessible to the voiceless, to those trapped by the gendered caste and class systems. He shared with Guru Nanak Ji the call to abolish caste and to ensure everyone was well fed. He especially praised labour that involved using one's hands and doing hard work, such as colouring leather or shoemaking, tasks Brahminism designated as untouchable work. Underlying the vision of Begumpura is a world without capitalism or poverty because wealth promotes inequity and poverty causes suffering, and neither is desirable (which was contrary to the Brahmin belief that poverty and wealth were the outcomes of previous lives). His poetry calls for both spiritual and social emancipation and offers a method of humble, devotional, and reformist social protest.

The vision for Begumpura signals that *Gurbani* contains within it an impulse for revolutionary relationships. As prabhdeep singh kehal and manmit singh state in their 2022 call for contributions to a new zine called the *Begumpura Collective*,

> Envisioned by the Saint Ravidas Ji, a caste-oppressed renowned figure within Dalit, Sikh, and Ravidassia communities, Begumpura (ਬੇਗਮਪੁਰਾ) was Guru Ravidas's poetic articulation of futures beyond the two millennia–old violences of brahminism. Embodying what we could today describe as projects of abolition (caste, prison, property), decolonization, and self and communal sovereignty,

> Begumpura (ਬੇਗਮਪੁਰਾ) represents a set of physical, emotional, spiritual, temporal, and political relations based in agency, liberation, and kinship. It represents a city outside the confines of current spatial and temporal relations that transcend any and all borders. Begumpura (ਬੇਗਮਪੁਰਾ) represents a collective invitation, partly born out of deep heartbreak and grief from the shifting forms of brahminical violence, while also rooted in desires to feel and build liberatory worlds.

It is the possibility of liberatory worlds that transcend settler colonialism that signals for me relationships beyond systems of private property, state boundaries and state rule, exploitation of the land, hierarchical institutions, and coercive forces of power. Following manmit singh, this includes abolition of gender, or at least the absence of gender, because Sikhī fosters a devotional goal to become one with Ik Oankar or 1Force without ਨਿਰੰਕਾਰ or nirankar (form) and ਨਿਰਗੁਣ or nirgun (attributes). Indeed, manmit singh approaches the SGGS as a gender-abolitionist text, in which it is our hearts, not our embodied gender or gender desires, that matter. The authors of the Sikhri (Sikh Research Institute) report on Sikhī and sexuality emphasize that it is the extreme ends of lust (i.e., abstinence and indulgence) that is warned against in Sikhī because it can consume us and distract from prayer, and that sexual desire, regardless of orientation, is an earthly pleasure.[36] prabhdeep singh kehal also reminds us that the human body is temporary, and Guru Ji refers to the material world "as an illusion because They told us of the *anand* [bliss] that awaits."[37] In short, in my view, Sikhī teaches that liberation is genderless—obtained through complete self-surrender to Waheguru.

What I take from these kinds of readings of Sikhī is that it is possible to foster different kinds of relationship with the original peoples of places now occupied by settler societies, and with others who live there, that are not asphyxiated by settler colonial formations. Begumpura offers an imagined world in which relationships are characterized by kinship, equity, care, shared living arrangements, redistribution of wealth so that everyone is secure, where there is pleasure and joy and love, freedom to move around without burdens or restrictions, mutual aid, the absence of gender or caste or class, and spiritual wholeness where earthly existence is not be renounced but fully lived.

Conclusion: Implications for Studies of Settler Colonialism

By way of a conclusion, I want to punctuate some of the key analytic implications of turning to non-Western ancestral philosophies. First, because Sikhī originated prior to the first major wave of European colonialism (circa 1415), it offers a way of being that is outside of modern colonial time. By this I do not mean that non-Western ancestral onto-epistemologies are unaffected by power or by colonialism; as Mandair shows, Sikhī arose and was articulated within struggles of power, and was transformed from a philosophy to a religion because of Brahminization and British colonial Judeo-Christian assumptions.[38] Rather, my point is that non-Western onto-epistemologies bring pre-colonial and non-modern ways of living that can mitigate against hegemonies of rule and control. In this sense, we need not rely on Western modernity to find ways to be against and transcend settler colonialism.

Second, settler colonial structures and histories of one nation-state are not siloed from settler colonial structures elsewhere. A single-country focus on modern Anglo-American settler colonialism misses the crucial problem of multidirectional local and global regimes of territorialization, finance, militarization, whiteness, cishetero-patriachy, and property ownership that usurp Indigenous Peoples and places at a transnational scale. Accordingly, settler colonialism is better critiqued through the lens of empire rather than just individual nation-states.[39]

Third, settler colonialism is multi-faceted such that attempted genocide against Indigenous Peoples and Indigenous insurgence are entangled with other histories of white supremacy and resistance; Shaista Patel shows that the attempted Indigenous genocide in North America is tied to Europe's Crusades against its Muslim Other, and the theft and enslavement of millions of Africans.[40] These intertwined violent practices are not just a historical concern, for in the contemporary era the construct of the model minority (i.e., economically exceptional minorities who are upwardly mobile and parroting mainstream Western societal values) South Asian, including Sikhs, is deployed by mainstream white societies and weaponized in the war against Indigenous, Black, Muslim, and Arab peoples. Indeed, some of these contemporary dynamics are shaped by Indian histories of violence, including anti-Blackness among South Asians, which is rooted in the trafficking, enslavement, and reproductive control of several hundred thousand Africans in South Asia between the seventh and twentieth centuries. Of these, many thousands have descendants—commonly referred to as Siddis (sometimes spelt Sidi or Seedi)—disproportionately living in poverty in contemporary India.[41] Accordingly, critiques of settler colonialism cannot be siloed from critiques of other structures of violence, including slavery, gendered divisions of labour, and racist hierarchies.

Fourth, when refusing settler colonialism, there are lessons to be learned from the many historical and contemporary global connections across communities of Black, Indigenous, and people of colour. For instance, in the early twentieth century, Dr. B.R. Ambedkar (a Dalit leader and one of the writers of the post-partition Indian Constitution) and American sociologist and pan-Africanist civil rights activist W.E.B. Du Bois exchanged letters of solidarity.[42] In the 1970s, the Dalit Panthers in India were inspired by the Black Panthers in the United States; and Bayard Rustin, an African American civil rights, gay rights, and nonviolence activist who helped lead the 1963 March on Washington, organized a Free India Committee in the United States.[43] In other words, *relationship-building* across communities is an empirical fact and has always been essential to diasporic refusal.

Fifth, non-Western ancestral onto-epistemologies can bring into view aspects of political life that are not usually examined within settler colonial studies. In the case of Sikhs and other South Asians, for instance, caste has historically shaped our forced and voluntary journeys across borders but is typically ignored even in critical settler colonial studies.[44] Yet, caste continues to benefit some in the South Asian diaspora while penalizing others, especially in terms of endogamy, public office opportunities, access to education, and labour.[45] Casteism needs to be annihilated, as Ambedkar argued, wherever it exists.[46] In settler societies, the task is to work towards caste annihilation without eclipsing Indigenous presence or pathologizing Indigenous and Black people as only suffering, sad, dying, or dead. One of the challenges, however, is that ancestral knowledge still comes through the English language and Western scholarly standards rather than the original languages (which in the case of Sikhī includes Punjabi, Hindi, Sanskrit, Sindhi, and Persian), and this can skew ancestral teachings.

Finally, settler colonial structures and processes are operationalized and upheld *directly* by targeting local Indigenous Peoples and nationalizing state sovereignty, and simultaneously *indirectly* by maneuvering Black people and people of colour (some of whom are Indigenous from elsewhere) and nationalizing migration.[47] In the case of Canada, for instance, the presumption of Crown sovereignty over Indigenous lands is demonstrated by agents of the Crown (whether in the early nineteenth century or now) taking control of who is extended and denied entry into the borders of the Canadian nation—whether as temporary foreign workers, refugees, or immigrants.[48] As such, following the lead of Indigenous land defenders, anti-colonialism necessarily entails refusal of Crown sovereignty. In my own case, I want to foreground to other Sikhs that the Westphalian state is a Western historical invention, that our non-Western ancestral teachings of Sikhī are not bound to states but with ਅਕਾਲ ਪੁਰਖ or Akal Purakh (that 1Force around us and within us, which is timeless, formless). Indeed, ਸਰਬੱਤ ਦਾ ਭਲਾ or sarbat da bhalla ("for everyone's benefit" or "kindness to all subjects") is not possible under conditions of settler colonialism. In this sense, Sikhī necessitates abolition of ruling colonial regimes that undermine people's sovereignty and liberation.

Ultimately, if it is possible, a turn to non-Western ancestral traditions (and maybe ancient traditions of those now marked as white Western people) may create openings to have *different kinds of relationships* with Indigenous Peoples and places, with those who have settled on lands long stewarded by Indigenous Peoples, with the more-than-human-world, and with our collective earthly and spiritual journeys. *We do not have to be determined by structures of settler colonialism or other systems of rule and control*, for there is much to be gleaned from ancestral knowledge that pre-dates and transcends the modern age of colonialism.

Acknowledgements

My heartfelt thanks to my mother, Krishna Kaur Dhamoon, as well as manmit singh and Jatinder Singh for everything that they teach me and for the generous gift of feedback on this chapter.

Notes

1 Following Harleen Kaur and prabhdeep singh kehal, I use Gurmurkhi words intentionally to decolonize discussions on Sikhs in a Western context. This usage also fosters connections with the Sikh language in the diaspora. See Kaur and kehal, "Sikhs as Implicated Subjects."

2 See Mani, *Debrahmanising History*.

3 Mandair, *Sikh Philosophy*.

4 Manmit and Manu, "When Will Caste-Oppressed and Queer and Trans Folk Find Liberation."

5 Sian and Dhamoon, "Decolonizing Sikh Studies."

6 Kenoyer, "Trade and Technology of the Indus Valley"; Avari, *India: The Ancient Past.*

7 Singh, "Who Is God to a Sikh?"

8 Mandair, *Sikh Philosophy*, 58.

9 Grewal, *Guru Gobind Singh.*

10 Kaur and kehal, "Sikhs as Implicated."

11 Kaur and kehal, "Sikhs as Implicated," 69.

12 Kaur and kehal, "Sikhs as Implicated," 72.

13 Kaur and kehal, "Sikhs as Implicated," 72.

14 Kaur and kehal, "Sikhs as Implicated," 78.

15 Pannu, "The Divine Light of Anarchy," 137.

16 Judge and Brar, "Guru Nanak Is Not at the White House."

17 Judge and Brar, "Guru Nanak Is Not at the White House," 155, 159.

18 Kaur and kehal, "Sikhs as Implicated," 83.

19 Kaur and kehal, "Sikhs as Implicated," 79.

20 Jafri, "Refusal/Film."

21 Jafri, "Refusal/Film," 113.

22 Singh and Kaur, *Miri-Piri*, 48–53.

23 Singh and Kaur, *Miri-Piri*, 5, 45.

24 Singh and Kaur, *Miri-Piri*, 11.

25 Pannu, "The Divine Light," 85.

26 Sikh Socialists, "Langar in Transition," 99–100; Singh, "Who Is God to a Sikh?"

27 Sehdev, "People of Colour in Treaty," 268.

28 Caste hierarchies are integral to unfree labour and exploitation of labour of Dalits (and Advasis/Indigenous people) and capital accumulation of land and wealth for the ruling classes. While some think of white supremacy as a Anglo-American matter and caste as a matter for South Asia, caste and race are also tied together. For instance, upper-caste South Asian diasporas in the United States have historically mobilized caste to uphold Brahminical and also white supremacy. See Bakrania, "Caste-ing White Supremacy." In India and in the diaspora, racism against those with Nepalese and East Asian origins can overlap with lower-caste designations. As well, darker-skinned Dalits face compounded oppression. See Yengde, "race and Caste."

29 Pannu, "The Divine Light of Anarchy," 138.

30 Pannu, "The Divine Light of Anarchy," 139.

31 Sandhra, "White Feminism or Feminisism Redefined?"

32 Singh and Kaur, *Miri-Piri*, 9.

33 Pardesi, "Social Justice from a Sikh Perspective."

34 Bhagat Raidas (c. 1450–1520) is sometimes claimed by Sikhs as a saint, sometimes a Guru, other times ignored or downplayed by Sikhs who object to the fact that he was a poor Dalit. Those who follow Ravidassia teachings sometimes do so under the frame of Sikhī, or other times outside of Sikhī as

a free-standing Dalit way of life and/or religion that is also informed by the radical anti-casteist thinker B.R. Ambedkar.

35 Bharti, "Raidas Saheb and the Idea of Begumpura."

36 Singh and Kaur, *Sikhi & Sexuality*, 8, 9.

37 Singh and Kaur, *Sikhi & Sexuality*.

38 Mandair, *Sikh Philosophy*.

39 For examples of global anti-imperial approaches to settler colonialism, see Desai, *Indian Migration and Empire*; Getachew, *Worldmaking After Empire*; Henderson, "Federalism and Settler Imperialism."

40 Patel, "The 'Indian Queen' of the Four Continents."

41 Chew, "Africans of India."

42 Equality Labs, "South Asians for Black Lives."

43 Chatterjee, "Beyond Gandhi and King."

44 One good exception is Patel, "Complicating the Take of 'Two Indians.'"

45 Equality Labs, "Caste in the United States."

46 Ambedkar, *Annihilation of Caste*.

47 Macklin, "Historicizing Narratives"; Mongia, *Indian Migration and Empire*.

48 Macklin, "Historicizing Narratives," 57.

Sources

Ambedkar, B.R. *Annihilation of Caste*. Penguin Random House, 2016 (1936).

Avari, Burjor. *India: The Ancient Past—A History of the Indian Sub-Continent from 7000 BC to AD 1200*. Routledge, 2007.

Bakrania, Falu. "Caste-ing White Supremacy: Thind, Cisco, and the Politics of Belonging." *Ethnic Studies Review* 46(1-2): 117–134.

Bharti, Kanwal. "Raidas Saheb and the Idea of Begumpura." *Forward Press*, March 11, 2019. https://www.forwardpress.in/2019/03/raidas-saheb-and-the-idea-of-begumpura/.

Chatterjee, Anirvan. "Beyond Gandhi and King: The Secret History of South Asian and African American Solidarity." Black Desi Secret History, 2020. https://blackdesisecrethistory.org/.

Chew, Carissa. "Africans of India." Histories of Colour, December 10, 2020. https://historiesofcolour.com/africans-in-india#:~:text=The%20approximately%2025%2C000%20people%20of,Pradesh%2C%20Hyderabad%2C%20and%20Karnataka (accessed August 5, 2022).

Desai, Radhika. *Indian Migration and Empire: A Colonial Genealogy of the Modern State*. Duke University Press, 2018.

Equality Labs. "Caste in the United States: A Survey of Caste Among South Asian Americans." 2018. https://clerk.seattle.gov/~cfpics/cf_322573f.pdf.

Equality Labs. "South Asians for Black Lives." 2021. https://www.equalitylabs.org/south-asians-for-black-lives#challenging-anti-blackness (accessed December 15, 2021).

Getachew, Adom. *Worldmaking After Empire: The Rise and Fall of Self-Determination*. Princeton University Press, 2019.

Grewal, J.S. *Guru Gobind Singh (1666–1708): Master of the White Hawk*. Oxford University Press, 2020.

Henderson, Phil. "Federalism and Settler Imperialism: Racial Regimes, Whiteness and Conquest in Canadian Constitutionalism." *Canadian Journal of Political Science* 57, no. 2 (2024): 466–87. http://dx.doi.org/10.1017/S0008423924000155.

Jafri, Beenash. "Refusal/Film: Diasporic-Indigenous Relationalities." *Settler Colonial Studies* 10, no. 1 (2020): 110–25. https://doi.org/10.1080/2201473X.2019.1677133.

Judge, Rajbir Singh, and Jasdeep Singh Brar. "Guru Nanak Is Not at the White House: An Essay on the Idea of Sikh-American Redemption." *Sikh Formations: Religion, Culture, Theory* 13, no. 3 (2017): 147–61. https://doi.org/10.1080/17448727.2017.1305944.

Kaur, Harleen, and prabhdeep singh kehal. "Sikhs as Implicated Subjects in the United States: A Reflective Essay on Gurmat-Based Interventions in the Movement for Black Lives." *Sikh Research Journal* 5, no. 2 (2020).

Kenoyer, Jonathan Mark. "Trade and Technology of the Indus Valley: New Insights from Harappa Pakkistan." *World Archaeology* 29, no. 2 (1997): 262–80. https://doi.org/10.1080/00438243.1997.9980377.

Macklin, Audrey. "Historicizing Narratives of Arrival: The Other Indian Other." In *Storied Communities: Narratives of Contact and Arrival in Constituting Political Community*, edited by Hester Lessard, Rebecca Johnson, and Jeremy Webber. UBC Press, 2011.

Mandair, Arvind-Pal Singh. *Sikh Philosophy: Exploring Gurmat Concepts in a Decolonizing World*. Bloomsbury Publishing, 2022.

Mani, Braj Ranjan. *Debrahmanising History: Dominance and Resistance in Indian Society*. Manohar Publishers, 2005.

Manmit and Manu. "When Will Caste-Oppressed and Queer and Trans Folk Find Liberation in Sikh Spaces?" *Kaur Life*, January 22, 2021. https://kaurlife.org/2021/01/22/when-will-caste-oppressed-and-queer-and-trans-folks-find-liberation-in-sikh-spaces.

Mongia, Radhika. *Indian Migration and Empire: A Colonial Genealogy of the Modern State*. Duke University Press, 2018.

Pannu, Santbir Singh. "The Divine Light of Anarchy: A Socio-Political Analysis of Conflicting Sikh Historical Narratives." MA thesis, York University, 2021.

Pardesi, Upkar Singh. "Social Justice from a Sikh Perspective." LinkedIn post, July 16, 2014. https://www.linkedin.com/pulse/20140716213508-31210902-social-justice-from-a-sikh-perspective/.

Patel, Shaista. "Complicating the Take of 'Two Indians': Mapping 'South Asian' Complicity in White Settler Colonialism Along the Axis of Caste and Anti-Blackness." *Theory & Event* 19, no. 4 (2016). https://muse.jhu.edu/article/633278.

Patel, Shaista. "The 'Indian Queen' of the Four Continents: Tracing the 'Undifferentiated Indian' Through Europe's Encounters with Muslims, Anti-Blackness and Conquest of 'the New World.'" *Cultural Studies* 33, no. 3 (2019): 414–36. https://doi.org/10.1080/09502386.2019.1584906.

Sandhra, Sharanjit Kaur. "White Feminism or Feminisism Redefined? The Sikhī Perspective." Guru Nanak Institute International Sikh Research Summit, Surrey, BC, June 18, 2022.

Sehdev, Robinder Kaur. "People of Colour in Treaty." In *Cultivating Canada: Reconciliation Through the Lens of Cultural Diversity*, edited by Ashok Mathur, Jonathan Dewar, and Mike DeGagné. Aboriginal Healing Foundation, 2011.

Sian, Katy Pal, and Rita Kaur Dhamoon. "Decolonizing Sikh Studies: A Feminist Manifesto." *Journal of World Philosophies* 5, no. 2 (2022): 43–60.

Sikh Socialists. "Langar in Transition: A Sikh Socialists Reflection." *Interfere* 3 (2022): 99–100.

Singh, Harinder. "Who Is God to a Sikh?" Sikhri, Sikh Research Institute, October 18, 2021. https://sikhri.org/videos/who-is-god-to-a-sikh.

Singh, Harinder, and Jasleen Kaur. *Sikhi & Sexuality—State of the Panth, Report 6*. Sikhri, Sikh Research Institute, September 2020. https://sikhri.org/articles/sikhi-sexuality.

Singh, Harinder, and Jasleen Kaur. *Miri-Piri: The Spiritual-Political Sikh Doctrine—State of the Panth, Report 7*. Sikhri, Sikh Research Institute, July 2021. https://sikhri.org/articles/miri-piri.

Yengde, Suraj Milind. "Race and Caste in the making of US sociology," *Current Sociology* 72(7): 1212–32.

On the Merits of Being an Asshole

ayumi goto and peter morin

LET'S JUST START WITH THIS DISCLAIMER: THE FOLLOWING essay isn't meant to give you a free pass to be an unmitigated asshole. Instead, we are hoping that it will open up conversations about thinking through difficult relationships with senses of social complexity, creatively respectful (at times, self-)adversity, and hegemonic refusals. In a previous essay, we discussed reaching the limits of goodness,[1] so consider this essay as part of a literary diptych of a kind. Rather than summarizing "In Reaching the Limits of Goodness" here, we leave it up to you, dear lovely reader, to determine for yourselves whether these two essays should be paired, can stand alone in their own right, or both. Whereas in the first essay we were intentionally blending our voices, in this piece, we are aiming to be distinctively peter and ayu.

We are performance artists(!) who have been collaborating both closely and distally since 2013. You know, we often find that performance artists are the most untethered, underpaid, playful, exuberant weirdos of the art world. We'll try anything, truly. And as our joint bio states, we like to jump and clap a lot. Peter is one of the inheritors of Tahltan Art History. He also continues to be one of the contributors to future Tahltan Art History. His parents met in a small town called Cassiar, BC. This town was built by an asbestos mining company. His mom fell in love with his dad because of a mutual respect for hockey, and his "pretty good" slapshot. Peter has laboured over and through his addiction to colonization and is now focused on honouring and protecting his parents' love story. Peter is moving closer and closer to studying chaos theory and will continue building beautiful generative spaces that are more powerful than "institutions," spaces that acknowledge the deep skill and expertise of global ancestries. Ayu has a not-so-secret mission to reconceptualize immunology from an embodied, in vivo perspective, displacing colonization and war metaphors with love and care in order to understand microbial development and their relationships to humans. With no formal art training, ayu draws upon wareware[2] upbringing as a Japanese diasporic daughter in a multi-Asian, multilinguistic mushroom farm setting, as well as work experiences in HIV, primary care, and disability to explore human-nonhuman relations artistically. Ayu approaches performance as an investigative format to expand and dishevel closed and paradigmatic thinking in microbiological discourse.

Peter and i are best friends. In perceiving a best friendship to be a new subjectivity that exists in excess of the individuals involved, Peter and i might be predisposed to presenting ourselves in a continuous state of "we." This "we-ness" can become problematic in that one can easily fall into the habit of speaking for the other, presenting a homogenous front when, in fact, there exist differential histories, political stances, and interpretations of shared social engagements. The line between "speaking on behalf of us" and "speaking for the other" can blur quickly and without notice. Depending on the relational dynamics between best friends, one can consistently be too 陰 (in/yin), and the other too 陽 (yō/yang) in the public presentation of the relationship as well as in private interactions. Straightforwardly put, unequal power relations can build up in the best of friendships, even with the noblest of starts and intentions. Enter the 糞たれ (kusotare), for better and worse, challenging the steadfastness of relationships, which, left unchecked, can become weighed down by political and epistemic rigidities that arise from such symbioses.

I come from a family of assholes. In Japanese, 糞たれ loosely translates into a combination of *asshole* and *shithead*, and it is a term that was bandied around a lot in our household, especially by お父さん (otōsan/father). One might assume that no one wishes to be known as a 糞たれ, but i can safely say that, many times, in our family, being an asshole has been pronounced with a certain amount of pride. Behaving like a 糞たれ is not a defining characteristic only within our nuclear family but seems to have been passed down matrilineally, just like the 後藤 (Gotō) name, through

お父さん's bloodline. According to お父さん, his father, 定 (Sadamu), who was born 甲斐 (Kai), was not a 糞たれ, but a quiet, mild-mannered, and kind-hearted man even after he adopted しなえ's (Shinae's) surname as well as her relations. しなえ had a reputation for having a larger-than-life personality. The sombre 遺影 (iei/commemorative photo) of お婆さん (obāsan/grandmother) adorning the walls of her descendants' houses does a disservice to representing how people remember her: someone with a booming laugh, which created a slight whistle between her widely gapped teeth, who drank with hearty abandon, slapping those around her in inebriated anger or jubilation. The 後藤 property was frequently packed with extended family, farmhands, and casual workers, who were promised accommodation, food, and payment in exchange for their labours. While お爺さん (ojīsan/grandfather) quietly and persistently cooked delicious cuisine for everybody, お婆さん kept spirits up or down, depending upon her mood. In the household, she would have the final say on who belonged and who should be shunned. The 糞たれ quality undeniably has been carried over from Japanese into other socio-political contexts.

For example, it is because they were both 糞たれ, that お父さん and his older brother, Uncle Elephant, got into a heated argument about dividing the mushroom farm shares, which devolved into the two adult brothers chasing and hitting each other with 剣道 (kendō) sticks as our neighbours in a rural southern Alberta town looked on with fascinated horror. As a 糞たれ, following the fracas, Uncle Elephant immediately packed up his family and belongings and returned to Japan, with both brothers refusing to talk to one another for eight ridiculous years. (Elephant wasn't even actually my uncle's name, but in Japanese *elephant* is homonymous with some type of delicate flower after which Uncle was named. お父さん lied to us about this name just to annoy his older brother; i only found this out from お母さん [okāsan/mother] long after お父さん had died.)

This is an intergenerational thing. Because we children, too, were 糞たれ, on the rare occasions that the farm had produced a surplus of mushrooms to give away at the annual August long-weekend town parade, お父さん would drive slowly in the procession while my sister and i were tasked with handing out two-pound bags of mushrooms to the cheering crowds. The thing is, some of the audience members were greedy, egging their children to jump onto the back of the truck and knick more than their share, making our job of mushroom dispersal that much more complicated. We would switch up roles of being the runner, handing out bags of mushrooms, and guarding the back of the truck like an overturned dung beetle, vigorously kicking at any shithead who dared grab a little extra, all the while yelling "one bag per family, you assholes!" as they tumbled away while giving us the finger. We were ten and eleven at the time.

Of course, being a 糞たれ is not restricted to the realm of human-to-human relations. お父さん and お母さん lived in a farmhouse attached to the mushroom farm property. Due to age-related dementia and severe osteoporosis, and no longer able to navigate the stairs, お婆ちゃん (Grandmother) had been moved to the trailer home next door, approximately 150 metres away from the family house and also within the boundaries of the farm property. お母さん would cook meals, and my job was to walk over to Grandma's to ensure she ate properly. On one particular occasion, i was in a terribly foul mood. お父さん kept saying, "おまいの態度が悪い。カルマだよう、カルマ // you've got a poor attitude. It's called karma." I was cursing to myself, yelling at お父さん to leave me alone, yelling at お母さん to hurry up with the food, then i walked with much aggravation towards お婆ちゃん's place. About maybe fifty metres away, i saw a low rustling in the grass, and suddenly a skunk, which had taken up permanent residence underneath the family house months prior, seriously bolted towards me. I tried running with the tray at first, then i just threw the tray to the ground and yelled at the skunk, trying to break its relentless pursuit. The little 糞たれ just kept chasing me down until i was trapped, then it turned its butt and sprayed me squarely on my front side. Bad attitude ayu being schooled by a literal 糞たれ. I didn't know at the time that Mum and Dad had been watching the whole unexpected encounter from the kitchen window, laughing their asses off. Did i mention that お父さん, お母さん, and i had to attend a wedding later in the afternoon? Took the weirdest and hopefully a once-in-a-lifetime bath of spaghetti sauce, ketchup, and tomato purée. People kept coming up to me at the wedding, asking, "Hey, are they serving pasta for dinner?"

But right now i want to suggest that the asshole trait can be a powerful clonus, disrupting the status quo and polite relations that otherwise sustain systems of great inequity. Truth be told, i am an inveterate rule follower and collectively oriented to a fault. Raised in a multi-Asian environment, the concept of 孝行 (kōkō/filial piety) was deeply ingrained from early childhood. I live in fear of breaking the rules and in equal fear of not breaking them. In terms of transnational relations, it has been argued that the nationalized sense of the collective duty to abide contributed profoundly to the Japanese imperial and colonial armies committing gross human atrocities across Asia.[3] Members of my family, who were stationed in China, Burma (present-day Myanmar), and scattered throughout other parts of Asia both prior to and during WWII, participated in Japan's endeavours to colonize these countries. 孝行, which in abstraction is presented as a positive ethical precept, can be used as a justification to blindly adhere to familial and social protocols so as to lead to political disaster.

But the inherited 糞たれ can sabotage the presentation of goodness in restive political times. Without the 糞たれ spirit, it would be unimaginable to do performance art. As an introvert, prone to deep social anxiety, the thought of undertaking public interventions is not particularly enticing. In preparing for and doing a performance, as my body becomes racked with nerves and a cold sweat breaks out across my skin, i can hear お父さん's voice in my head: "負けないぞ！頑張れ！頑張れ！頑張れ!" He advises to challenge convention, and "反対しな," that is, to play a trick on myself, dare to overturn my earnest and obligatory intentions. The 糞たれ characteristic provides the guts to break out of emotional, cognitive, and cultural habits. It allows for facing criticism head-on, which can be especially acerbic when a performance has struck a nerve or suddenly unsettles onlookers. In those moments, ayu reverts to the mushroom farm girl, kicking those brats off the back of the truck. The 糞たれ spirit has become one of the apparatuses from which a performance moves from private imaginary to social materialization. Arguably, it is a skill that can be honed with practice to serve as an invaluable counterbalance to self-inscribed positionings of goodness.

Take for instance the current etiquette of self-introductions. We have become a society of oral 名刺 (meishi/business cards). Instead of listing what we do, however, we are politically prompted to present how we identify through a series of hyphenated adjectives that signal our preferred pronouns, our cultural and community affiliations. In these introductions, i have yet to come across anyone who describes themselves as an asshole, liar, or thief unless it is by way of a testimonial, a statement of how they are trying to change their errant behaviours. Not that i wish for people to boast about wayward actions that have caused harm to others, but at the same time representational declarations that eschew or deny one's less socially admirable qualities become suspect. In these short self-introductions, the complexity and scope of being human becomes radically constrained, and critical reflection, potentially truncated. Even as our oral 名刺 might inscribe our aspirations of who we wish to be and where we wish to belong, implicit in these hyphenated identities are demands to be taken at face value. These declarations can serve as incontrovertible and fixed self-truths. What happens at a larger relational scale when good characteristics pertain only to the self and bad characteristics become the preserve of others? When whole groups or cultures are self-designated as good, then badness becomes externalized. Fault falls squarely on those who do not or should not belong, because something shameful and usually hidden from view has reared itself to the detriment of others. Wars have been fought on the basis of collective senses of moral superiority, battle lines drawn to create ideological and impermeable borders between us and them.

But sometimes, are we not, each of us, just plain shitty? Do we not catch ourselves making terrible decisions and committing appalling acts based on a limited purview, on misreading the air, emotional upheaval, and states of biological instability such as hunger and fatigue? The 糞たれ can function as an internal corrective, be it personal, cultural, political, interspecious. Never to be taken as a moral high ground, one's inventory of 糞たれ behaviour gives pause to reflect on our own culpability in a situation gone askew.

• • •

I, too, am an asshole. I'm tired of having to "deal" with colonization. I want more than what that colonial cultural capital has to offer to me. That being said, I don't feel broken by having to live inside of this system. I feel tired at having to "address" the system's bullshit gifts. I have also come to realize that in digging-down-deep to understand what being an "asshole" can mean, beyond what we would understand as its societal meaning, I keep coming up against a piece about a learned fear. This unnamed fear sits in front of, or beside, what being an "asshole" can offer. In doing this thinking/dreaming work, I see that this "fear" has a shape. It has a feeling. This fear guides us to blindly trust, or rely, on a system (a.k.a. capitalism) that doesn't really care about it. It's important to note that Ayumi is not talking about being mean or just being purely disruptive to the "status quo." We spend all of this time pursuing "something." Work teaches us skills/tools. Life teaches us skills/tools. This asshole trait opens the unimagined possibility for truth and power to be experienced and expressed. This avenue of thinking/theorizing also opens up the possibility that all of those "skills" you've been working so hard to develop are also responsible for keeping you immersed within a system that doesn't care about you. This is different from learning that there are limits to goodness, and how when we achieve those "limits" we might performatively contribute to violence. Being an asshole can bring a truth and a power that rests in our bodies to the front of our shared experiences. In one of our last visits about this shared writing, Ayumi said: merit unknowability, merit the uncontrollable, and merit unreliability. This kind of action does affect a kind of transformation of the system, and, perhaps, it is a way to become free from this mess called colonization in Canada. Being an asshole opens up the possibility that ALL OF YOUR ACQUIRED SKILLS MIGHT BE LIES. This is also the fear, the fear that everything you worked so hard to make/become might also be a lie is overwhelming. When we think about it this way, then being an asshole could be a useful tool for building something new for all of us. THIS COULD MEAN A COMPLETE REDESIGN OF EVERYTHING YOU FIND COMFORT IN.

Our mom lives full-time in a memory care facility with a passenger called Alzheimer's. As you can imagine, this is a highly controlled and highly structured environment, one that is dependent on following the directional lines painted on the floor. There is a locked door with a code. There are mealtimes, snack times, medication times. In this environment, that there is something important about "structure" is very clear, and there is no debating whether "structure" is needed or not. These structures and routines are designed to keep residents and care workers and nurses safe. I don't want to disrespect that, even though I could. I would never disrespect that. There is also something here about implementing control, and the subtle/direct ways nurses/care workers can take aim at mom and our/her family because they are overworked, undersupported by a broken-ass system, tired. I remember, early on in this Alzheimer's journey, overhearing a care worker say, not quite under her breath, What the fuck do they expect? What more do they want? This space has become, and continues to be, a fluid living space for this intersection of folx whose first real connection is that they all have some version of dementia or Alzheimer's, and probably the majority of them are given antipsychotic drugs so that they don't hit the care workers. It is a very complex environment, one that requires care and being kind first. And then there is our mom, who swears a lot more now. Who moves her body with a wheelchair now. On good days, she laughs and smiles and makes incredible jokes. On the good days, and the bad days, she might scratch when you try to help her change into her bedtime clothes. She will tell you to *Fuck right off* because that is how she rolls now. One time she told my sister, I wouldn't even trust you with my piss. I never mind these "asshole" expressions. We laugh together. We cry together. Everything is on a full spectrum of living. This behaviour spills out into the common area on the daily, and I know that our mom's neighbours feel it. I hear about all the "f-bombs" our mom drops on the daily. Mom's behaviour is adding life to this environment that relies on control...I say *So what? It's just a word*. This is never the reaction that the system wants to hear, and that's okay. Like I said earlier, I'm not here to take care of the system. I (we) owe this system nothing. I'm adding this into the mix because now I openly hear Mom's neighbours swearing. I was walking by a conversation between two elderly women who have dementia, they were moving side-by-each down the hallway in matching wheelchairs, and one said to the other, Stop being such a fucking idiot. I was a little shocked by this type of calling out by nice little old white ladies. It's like this, life is continually happening, and we need to stop trying so fucking hard to control it.

My own brother and I have had some serious fights over the years. He's older, the oldest child of the sibling group. There is a lifetime of experience between our two ages. The fights include him walking across the room, putting his face a couple of inches from my face, yelling loudly, and threatening to punch me. In the recounting of these experience(s) among friends, I've always positioned myself as the weaker. Where did this "training" come from? The recounting of these experiences creates a fixed narrative, one that has no mobility for either of us as the main character, nor for the witnesses to the encounter, and the listeners often get stuck with a one-sided recounting. Fuck that static noise. We need to break free from these dynamics. I need to break free from these bad habits of positioning "myself" in the retelling. I am not more of an "Indian" than my older brother, and I am definitely not a better person than him either. This essay, these words, this idea, this practice of being an "asshole" is aimed towards what the asshole can do to shift the energy of the room. What if I felt like I didn't need to "defend" myself? Why be comfortable in the retelling? Who benefits from us being comfortable in the room?

It's also important/significant to consider what comfort/privilege is doing for you while you are reading these words. This feeling might be a "landed comfort," or a "settler comfort," that emerges from being in control of the narrative and believing in the lies that we tell ourselves. This idea of control returns us to an earlier idea in this essay concerning learned/acquired unnamed fear. This fear might be a lie that you tell yourself because, of course, you have never participated in the theft of Indigenous land. Being an "asshole" means that you understand that this word "theft" is covering up the actual word that has any value in this scenario, which is "absence." This absence is forced on top of Indigenous bodies and Indigenous histories that perform deep, and complicated, relationships to these territories. Absence in this regard is an outright denial of collective ancestral presence. Funny how easy the identification of "theft" as a past tense theoretical proposition becomes like a place of warmth and comfort for most of us. All of this, and I still feel troubled with how so many readers are comfortable in this "reading" of an interaction and comfortable with assigning "blame" to others. This muscle memory enforces an uncomfortable structure that makes someone into a "settler" so that they are not sitting alone in the room built by the disciplining of Settler Identities.

Today I drove the car from Smithers to Terrace, BC, in order to pick up a parcel. There is a deep connection between these two sites, a history that is actually quite beautiful. Terrace is a place in the North, and, like so many places in what is called Canada, there is a lot of history and a lot of scars on the land and on our bodies as a result of these systems that are embedded deeply within the colonial standards. First, an acknowledgement of all of the icons of Settler History. You can't just drive by these landmarks. In the middle of Terrace is this incredible chainsaw carving of a "logger man," for example. This sculpture is connected with an isolated roadside monument that is about thirty minutes away by car from downtown Terrace, that acknowledges the loggers of the past who lost their lives while harvesting resources for Canada.

I'm also thinking about bridges here as monuments to settler history, and you can't drive to Terrace without driving over a concrete bridge. There are also lots of unmentioned histories and presences here. The two local Indigenous reserves are on the outskirts of town, like you would have probably imagined. There is also an unacknowledged history of immigrants moving here, living here, growing generationally in these territories. Anyways, back to picking up the parcel. Racism can also be a Settler Monument. When I showed up and asked about my parcel, the worker behind the counter audibly sighed on seeing me. This sigh continued as several loud commands, sarcastic comments, then retorts, as I stood there in front of her asking what I thought were reasonable questions. Eventually, we both couldn't take it anymore. I left with her telling me that I should call DHL (the shipping company) and tell them my troubles, to which I responded, as I was walking out the door, Don't worry, I will be calling DHL about my impending delivery. The "asshole" in me wanted to say I would prefer to call DHL because at least the AI I'll talk to will know how to do their job. All of this. All of that. All of that troubling exchange. All of it in front of an older white guy who worked in the warehouse and who just stood there staring at me. And then, the following hours of puzzling through, asking myself Why did that exchange happen? What could I have done differently? Why did I need her to see me and know that I'm a nice person? And being fully present to that unending weight of naming her behaviour as racism towards me. The worst part of this is always imagining and moving through the fantasy scenarios where I feel "heard" at the end, or "seen" at the end, or I feel like I'm victorious over her efforts to make me disappear. Like imagining her saying to me as a response, Racist? Racist! Well, you don't even look like an Indian. And me responding, That's the point isn't it? If I looked like a full white man, you wouldn't have even *begun* treating me like this. Actually, both she and I were "assholes" to each other. We weren't being mean about it. And now, I'm grateful for this exchange. That asshole opened up an unimagined space for my body to feel "something." That asshole helped me to put these words onto the page: I never thought about my own whiteness in exchanges like this. And I've always felt like I needed to protect my Indigeneity in exchanges like this (there is more explanation probably required with that last sentence, but this essay isn't about my Indigeneity). Until I met this asshole, I never thought about how sad it felt to see other white people acting racist. My mom is Tahltan. My dad is a French Canadian who has lived with Tahltan people for the last fifty-five years of his life. That asshole (from the warehouse), and this asshole (me), this exchange, returned me towards my whole body, back towards all of the scars we carry and how we are trained to rely on those scars, scars like records of the racism that you've experienced. I also started thinking how these continued and repeated actions of attack and defence, because of things like racism, have created very strong muscle memories that we think we need. The opened-up possibilities here, because of this recent "asshole" exchange, is teaching me that it's time that we teach these muscles how to "forget" what isn't needed anymore. I'm not saying the experience of racism is just going to magically stop. I'm saying that she might just have been having a bad day while being white and it's the "asshole me" that was forcing all of those words/pathologies/histories on top of our skins. Sometimes, you just need to eat to calm down.

I live full-time in a body that exists on a spectrum. Indigenous/white. Tahltan/French Canadian. Mocha-coloured skin that often gets read as ethnic-ish, even though I'm never the "Indian" that you had in mind. Grey hair that was once black. History of being poor, and now I have one of those posh academic gigs. I get paid to read, and I get paid to write my thoughts about what I've read. In thinking about this chapter topic, I've realized that I am that posh "asshole." I have developed a practice of thinking I need to protect my Indigeneity, through a history of positioning myself as the weaker one in the story. This is supposed to be a gift for myself and the listener.

And even in that positioning, I struggle with ending my deep reliance on colonial structures that continue to influence my thinking/dreaming work. The asshole would throw that shit out. Who the fuck needs colonialism anyways? This awareness helps me to understand why the philosophical possibility of the asshole becomes so difficult. The asshole blows shit up because it needs to happen, not just because they want it to happen. THIS MEANS BEING AWARE OF HOW YOU ARE ALSO LYING TO YOURSELF. I'm speaking to you, now, Dear Lovely Reader. This is also something that is infected by capitalist competition. Someone needs to state the obvious, like an asshole would, within the proposed situation, by cutting through the capitalist bullshit. See, the thing is I owe the capitalist enterprise nothing because my Tahltan ancestors have already paid in full, and I hope my French-Canadian ancestors will catch up to the work of being accountable. I say this fully aware that these colonial structures continue to be tyrannical towards the spectrum of ancestries we bring into the room and live every day. This asshole understands who I am accountable to and what the practice of accountabilities means for the world(s) I want to contribute to.

• • •

Yeah, so, we, Peter and Ayu, had a major falling out during the writing of this essay, no joke. Seriously, no joke. We may no longer be friends. Sometimes things just fall apart. And sometimes, they fall apart because they are thrown from a great distance and shatter on contact with the unforgiving pavement. The asshole has an awesome shot put, has the flex to know when they have been had by a fellow asshole. Who's at fault here? Who takes responsibility and to what extent?

Our relational entanglements exceed our self-designated identities. We want to argue that when socio-political behaviours become overly scripted, the asshole serves as a counterbalance, exposing performances of goodness: the upright citizen, the established cultural producer, the dutiful family member, the paramount human. The 糞たれ/asshole throws a spanner in the works, shakes us out of our comfort zones, and boorishly creates a full circle back to one's sense of humanity. If one were to externalize blame—that is, to deny one's capacity to cause harm or associate with morally questionable characteristics—then that person is no longer consorting in human realms but attempting to run with the gods. This dependency on one's sense of only goodness is relationally problematic because when things fall apart, you have only the outside other to blame. Taking it further, at a collective level, if a whole group or culture unequivocally self-proclaims moral goodness, becomes untouchable except only in the praise of those who belong, then over time and practice, a sense of moral superiority seeps into every action, every movement, every thought. And this serves as the seed for colonizing others, educating those who would benefit from such culturo-political perfection.

But what do we know? We're just a couple of assholes.

Notes

1 Morin and Goto, "On Reaching the Limits of Goodness."

2 This is a Japanese gender-ish pronoun, at times translated as a collective honorific *we*. If you wish to read more about the linguistic decolonization of gender pronouns, you are welcome to read the essay Goto, "Studies in Shapeshifting."

3 Horiguchi, *Women Adrift*.

Sources

Goto, Ayumi. "Studies in Shapeshifting." Studio Project. https://www.studioproject.ca/ayumi-goto-residency/studies-in-shapeshifting.

Horiguchi, Noriko J. *Women Adrift: The Literature of Japan's Imperial Body*. University of Minnesota Press, 2011.

Morin, Peter, and Ayumi Goto. "On Reaching the Limits of Goodness." *Public* 32, no. 64 (2021): 172–79. https://doi.org/10.1386/public_00081_1.

Who Are We Here?

Settler Colonialism, Mobility, and Relationships Across Distance

Emma Battell Lowman and Adam J. Barker

SETTLER COLONIALISM IS "ALWAYS ALL ABOUT THE LAND"[1]—Indigenous lands are the focus of settler power and policies intended to dispossess, dehumanize, and displace Indigenous Peoples. These lands are in turn the foundation of new settler identities, rooted in the imagined geographies of a settler colonial "home," stretching across scales from the domestic to the national. Who settlers are and how they think of themselves derives in no small part from their relationships to these stolen lands and the disavowed relationships with the Indigenous Peoples from whom those lands were stolen. So, what happens when settler people leave their settler society? Do identities, relationships, and narratives endure when stretched across distances? Does settler colonialism dissipate in the absence of a settler society? Do we stop being settlers if we leave the settler state without a clear intent to return?

In this chapter, we use autoethnographic recordings over more than a decade and interrogate what it means to be settler people both distant from our "homelands," and situated in the heart of the former empire that exerted the most power over what became Canada. Considering Indigenous relational ontologies, it is clear that relationships of responsibility and respect change form when their spatial geometry is altered, but they endure and continue to call on settler people to address their own coloniality and the ongoing imperialism and colonialism that the creation of societies such as Canada has normalized around the globe.

Settler colonialism, for all that it has been extensively examined and analyzed, remains a slippery concept. The exact boundaries of settler colonial space have yet to be mapped, in part because they are simultaneously pervasive and ephemeral, structured by the shifting relationships of settlers to each other, to the lands they claim, and to the other non-settler populations alongside whom they exist. This is part of the reason why we have for some time used ourselves and our experiences as a—but not *the*—window into the internal logics and dynamics of settler colonialism. We identify as settlers and have engaged deeply with this as both identity and subjectivity for many years.[2] At the same time, we have not lived in a settler society as our primary residence for over a decade. We relocated to the United Kingdom in 2009 while pursuing our PhD studies, and while not choosing this course actively, we have largely resided in the United Kingdom—and in a particular city, Leicester—for the decade-plus since. We do not experience this place in exactly the same way, though our paths are similar. One of us (Emma) is a British citizen whose white English parents immigrated to Canada in the 1970s and whose extended family is still based in the United Kingdom; the other (Adam) has white English, Scottish, and Irish ancestry, and his ability to live in the United Kingdom required a series of visas (student, work, ancestry) and culminated in 2021 with achieving indefinite leave to remain.[3] But despite all of that, we know (and feel) after all this time that we are still Canadian, and very much still settler. So, what does that mean for settlers elsewhere (in this case, the colonial metropole, the centre of the empire that spawned the settler colony of Canada) or for our understanding of the social and political dynamics of settler polities and collectives?

The role of settler colonialism in *placemaking* is partly what we are examining in this chapter. In the words of Barry and Agyeman,

> placemaking can be seen to advocate for both belonging to place, and what that place can become. Many definitions of placemaking emphasize both the belonging aspects, such as sense of place, place-attachment, rootedness, etc., and the becoming aspects of collective reimagining/reinventing. However, in our opinion, too often practitioner literature and some academic writings tend toward uncritical boosterism about what places can become, by simply promoting case studies of purportedly "successful" projects.[4]

In the context of settler colonies, this "boosterism" compels us to define Canada and Canadians through stories of opportunity, freedom, and equality, both in comparison to the originating metropole and to the perceived *terra nullius* that existed before us. It is in this context that we examine settler colonial placemaking—the actions of living in and relating to a particular location through which that place is imbued with particular meaning, and through which we come to "belong" there, in the way that a house becomes a home when it is lived in—as a process in which we are bound up even when we are not in a settler society, a process that affects people very differently based on their personal, familial, and national histories and genealogies.

What it means to be a settler remains highly contested, as the many diverse settler collectives that make up what we think of as the nation of Canada, for example, debate the meaning, applicability, and content of the term. Veracini[5] has proposed a set of triangular relations to help explain, in part, how and why people experience settler colonialism differently. He argues that settler societies perceive three basic subjectivities: "settler" (like "us," however defined); "indigenous Other" (based not on actual Indigenous Peoples but on the colonial perception of what Indigeneity means); and "exogenous Other" (the not-settler and not-Indigenous category that includes chattel slaves and migrant labour, among others). Of course, what differentiates a settler from the others in the perception of the settler colonizer varies: race, class, religion, and many other factors are at play. And crucially, there is no agreement within a settler society about who sits where in the triangular relationship and no authority to enforce a singular perspective.

As we have outlined elsewhere,[6] there is no "centre" to settler colonial societies, but rather a diverse and shifting topography of power that changes as groups or communities of settlers form, dissolve, reform, contest with each other, create alliances, and so on. Who may be considered "us" within the settler subjectivity is not agreed; race and ethnicity, class and legal status, duration of time inhabiting in a settler society, allegiance to and performance of particular political ideologies, and so on are all lines of difference upon which communities and individuals are perceived as being "in" or "out" of the settler society in a varied, heterogeneous, and changeable way across that society. As the uncertain edges of settler colonial geography shift constantly, we choose to investigate the consistencies and inconsistencies of our own experiences as "settlers abroad," colonizers returning to the heart of empire, to try and think through some of the enduring, thorny questions posed by settler colonial analysis.

This examination is conducted against the backdrop of fierce and ongoing debates about how settler colonial systems and structures do or do not implicate people beyond white, property-owning Canadians. Are Black Canadians settlers? Are refugees or other newcomers? Scholars such as Jodi Byrd (Chickasaw) position folks whose presence in the settler colony came against their will, like enslaved people, as "arrivants" and have worked to carefully unpack the degree to which settler colonialism has impacted both groups, simultaneously but differently.[7] Justin Leroy has argued that settler colonialism and anti-Blackness have always relied upon the same logics, and that we should understand colonization and enslavement as entangled rather than separate histories.[8] As such, our examination of ourselves as settler people abroad also hinges on several key facts about ourselves: First, we are white, and that has and will directly impact our experiences. Second, our whiteness is read in particular ways where we are—the United Kingdom, and, more specifically, England, the heart of the empire that built our settler society. British people do not perceive our settler Canadian whiteness in the same way that they perceive, for example, the whiteness of Eastern Europeans. In times past, both British and Canadian whiteness has racialized nationalities, like Italians, who were dehumanized and rejected by settler Canada as "not white enough," but who have since become key and accepted members of settler society.[9]

So, who actually is a "settler"? Perhaps it is as difficult a question to answer as "What is authentically British?," a question that has seemed to obsess the British media during our entire tenure here. Yet the asking of the question tells more than the answer. The question in the United Kingdom is often asked in relation to the arrival of immigrants or migrants, usually from the Global South and often from places formerly colonized by Britain. The anxiety that the arrival of Black and Brown people from the Global South causes in powerful and populist sectors of the British population is evidence that these visibly non-white populations are still subjectivized according to their past construct as labour rather than people.[10]

As settlers abroad, then, we certainly benefit from our whiteness in a society that also relied on racial slavery, while being seen ourselves as exotic or interesting based on our experiences settling on Indigenous territories, and coming from North American (and specifically Canadian) contexts that to most British people are spaces of opportunity. And what we are observing here is not simply a shared prejudice but the persistence of political economies around which myths of white supremacy and European civilization were built, alongside the cities and war machines built from stolen resources by stolen labour. Our own connections to and ability to transit between metropole and settler colonies are simultaneously material and racial privileges.

We often hear—and have ourselves said—it's less useful and interesting to argue over *who* qualifies as settler, and more important to look at what settlers do and how they do it.[11] However, accepting that settler polities are dynamic (changing to incorporate or exclude variously identified "exogenous Others" over time) and internally inconsistent (there is no agreement among Canadians as to who is "like us" and therefore located in the settler subjectivity of the triangular relations of settler colonization), it is important to examine conditions of settlers in unusual circumstances to see how internal identities and perceptions of settler subjectivity are impacted, potentially revealing hidden dynamics within settler societies writ large.[12]

We have brought together memories and experiences over ten years that represent something about our settlerness in this place, and what our "common sense" actions and reactions in the context of the United Kingdom reveal about what we are taking for granted, and perhaps ways to intervene in the normal processes of settler colonization. We try here to think through settler colonial theory to understand in greater detail how settlers attach to places (the idea of "belonging"); how the mobility of individual settlers affects the larger structures and systems of settler colonization; and how settler people moving through the world affect the intersection between settler colonization and global systems of state and capital.

A Vignette—A Strange, Inverted Argument

Adam: It was 2012—I remember the London Olympics were on, which I did not want to discuss, and I was finishing my PhD thesis, which I *also* did not want to discuss. We—Emma and I—were at a writing retreat in rural Devon, in a two-hundred-person village called Sheepwash that attracted creatives, authors, and academics from all over and made them feel like family. One of our fellow guests was Shane, a man of South Asian (Indian) heritage, born and raised in London, who had family in India, Canada, and many other places around the world.

After dinner one evening, Shane and I got into a discussion of whether or not Canada was a "good" country. Shane's experience was through relatives who had escaped poverty and, later, racial and religious violence and made successful lives in Toronto. They had become Canadian citizens and were proud of their achievements—How could I critique this? he asked. I explained that the possibilities were only founded on the genocide of Indigenous Peoples. He fired back that this point must surely apply to my family, too; I said it did, that my family fled poverty conditions in postwar England, and that they simultaneously made the "right" decision for themselves *and* that the decision was only possible because of the historical and ongoing elimination of Indigenous nations. Shane appeared angry, but we agreed to let the conversation drop, unfinished.

Triangular Relations—Identity and Subjectivity

In the story above, we see the incoherence that can and does easily arise as a result of the different identities and subjectivities that are made and mobilized through different colonial and imperial projects. There were a wide variety of identities at play around the table: Adam as a settler Canadian with tenuous legal status in the United Kingdom; the white, English guests and hosts of the writing retreat; Emma as a dual citizen, both British and not; and Shane, the only person of colour present, who while proud of being British had his own complicated relationships to the fact that his family's homelands were brutally colonized by the British. Along these lines of difference, we all experienced places differently: perceptions of safety or security, the possibility of belonging legally and ethically, where opportunities for building wealth or a legacy truly lay, and so on.

Shane's family had experienced colonialism in their homelands, experienced racism and poverty there, as well as in England, and found Canadian society to be a safe haven. Neither of us, as white settlers, nor our families have experienced racism; rather, we benefit from it. Neither we nor our families have been colonized, as we are the ones who colonize. The ability to critique Canada as a place that is fundamentally flawed and should not exist, then, can be read as a privilege of whiteness and nationality when compared to the perceptions of people for whom Canada, as imperfect as their experience of it may have been, stands as a symbol of a better life and future. This has clear implications for how we discuss concepts like "responsibility" or "complicity" in settler colonialism because our own identities and histories dramatically affect how we are seen by other settlers and how we think of ourselves in relation.

We return here to the point above regarding who considers themselves part of the settler polity in Canada, and who others consider to be part of it, much of which breaks down along lines of race and ethnicity. It is an obvious but true point that settler people identify with those seen as "like us" as part of the settler subjectivity in the set of triangular relations, and that frequently "like us" means the same racial and cultural characteristics. However, this provides a shifting response to the questions of "who is a settler," and one that is not internally coherent. Neither social bias and racism nor government policies of inclusion and exclusion fully capture the racialization of the settler polity. The dynamics by which people are included or excluded from settler society are deeply structured by whiteness and capital, and despite the shifting and uneven nature of this structuring, it tends to produce a broadly agreed "ideal type" settler subject.

Complex negotiations have and continue to occur regarding the uncomfortable fusion of settler colonial eliminatory and discriminatory processes and broad understandings of liberalism and liberal inclusion. Relatives who identify as Canadian nationalists (and live in Alberta) have accused us on more than one occasion of being "traitors" or "unpatriotic" because we left Canada and because we once challenged their settler and white supremacist ideologies. Clearly most Canadians—and the laws of the state—still consider us to be part of the settler Canadian polity, but it is important to understand two points. First, unanimity or consensus is not required for the formation of a settler colonial polity. Second, not just race but also law and status and other labels that may be applied to people may for some disqualify those thus labelled from belonging in the polity. It is further worth noting that, while we have ourselves seen strident upholding of settler colonialism from right-wing positions (in pursuit of an exclusionary and "pure" settler polity), liberal positions of inclusion can be just as colonial as these conservative versions.

This includes Paulette Regan's concept of the peacemaker myth, by which Canadian settlers differentiate themselves from the perception of more violent settlement and settlers in the United States.[13] Canada has long cherished and jealously defended its reputation as a global peacemaker.[14] From Lester B. Pearson, through UN Peacekeeping missions in the 1950s onwards, to the people of Gander, Newfoundland, hosting stranded travellers after the 9/11 terrorist attacks (made famous in the last decade by the musical *Come From Away*, which ran for four years in London's West End and is now touring the United Kingdom), the idea of Canada as a fundamentally "good" place and the peacemaker myth of Canadian expansion are co-terminus. For us, we continually encounter British people who say how *nice* Canada is, how *good* Canadians are, how much they wished they lived in Canada and cannot understand why we moved. There is an element here of spillover from how settler Canadians discuss themselves, as Velednitsky and colleagues describe: "In addition to describing indigenous people as disappearing, settlers also narrate their histories and values in ways that promote a progressive image of the settler state. The resulting liberal narratives mask the foundational violence of settler colonialism, producing the present absence of settler colonial relations."[15]

Part of how we know we are still settlers here is that when British people project these Canadian mythistories (Regan's term) at us, it is very difficult to not reflect them back—even when we know they are wrong! This happened more than once in my discussion with Shane (above). His points were not difficult to engage factually, but the argument was extremely emotionally draining. Saying things confidently out loud to others is a very different exercise than understanding them quietly in our own heads. Partly this is because accepting that these narratives are true if they come to us externally is a move to comfort[16]—"at least I'm not the one saying it, but yeah, there's some truth there!" Partly this is because pushing back against these narratives can generate a different but very similar kind of pushback to confronting Canadians about their own settler colonialism—discomfort, disbelief, and frustration.

There is a habit of settlers thinking of something having gone "profoundly wrong" in the originary metropole,[17] while the settler societies are portrayed as simply "better," as "opposed to an overly congested, somewhat dystopian UK."[18] It is this persistent perception, one that seems to manifest regardless of whether someone was born in or moved to a settler state, and even when we settlers know better, that brings us to our next consideration: the nature of belonging.

A Vignette—I Will Never Belong Here

Adam: I remember the general if not specific date. It was April 2010—I remember because it was during the Icelandic volcanic eruptions that disrupted air travel, including delaying a transatlantic family visit. Though we had visited Emma's extended family outside London several times previously, we had been living in the United Kingdom for less than a year. I was standing in our kitchen, in a rented terrace (row)house so narrow we could hold hands in the middle of the living room and touch both outside walls, where you step from the sidewalk right into the living room, in a neighbourhood in Leicester. I was washing dishes, as the hot water surged then disappeared, a result of a strange combination of an antique hot water tank in the upstairs bathroom and a gas-fired boiler (a cheap one) in the kitchen. In the background, the radio was playing over an old AM/FM alarm clock. The news finished, and *The Archers*—a radio soap opera about rural life in England that has been running since 1950, with a ubiquitous theme tune known by seemingly everyone—began playing. It was at that exact moment that I remember looking around and being suddenly struck with the thought "I will never belong here." A decade and a half later, and I feel the same.

Relationships to Land, Near and Far

Settler colonialism is, as we have elsewhere argued, defined by relationships—primarily the ways that settler people relate to the land itself and the consequential eliminatory relationships to Indigenous Peoples. As we have previously argued, just because these relationships are abusive and destructive does not make them "non-relationships." There are many ways of relating to the land, but here we focus on relationships in two broad categories: relationships of property and ownership, and relationships of belonging on and with land.

Relating to Land as Property

As our friend and mentor Chaw-win-is taught us, settler colonialism is "always all about the land."[19] Settler people are said to be defined by a particular set of relationships to land as much as anything else, with the most common form being through property. The transformation of land into property through colonial processes has been well investigated, especially through the histories of legal and political challenge and change.[20] In so much as we relate to land as property, we imply ownership—including the double bind of the underlying title held by the settler state, and the fee simple ownership of private property by millions of settler Canadians. Both forms of ownership require wealth, necessitating a connection to global circuits of capitalism and reinforcing the perception of individual opportunity in frontier spaces. As Rifkin has articulated, the frontier can be understood as a mobile space of exception that settler colonizers can project onto a wide variety of spaces and landscapes.[21]

However, two important points must be raised here, derived from these works on property and frontier claims. First, while settler colonialism is intensely localized in some ways—for example, the domestic spaces of frontier settlers whose individual actions connect with but do not overdetermine the colonialism of other settlers—the dynamics of colonialism that happen at larger scales also manifest in our everyday experiences of land and placemaking. The system of property and ownership, the global circuits of capital, and changes to international patterns of migration and settlement all impact on individuals and families far more than most settler people would like to think. Second, while property and property ownership are clearly part of the settler colonial project in Canada, they are not necessarily so. As we have argued elsewhere, anarchist and communist settler people, who by definition are ideologically opposed to the creation and ownership of private property (and in some cases the authority of the state itself), are also able to participate in and benefit from settler colonialism, and a radical "Left" settler colony would be no better for Indigenous Peoples regardless of attempts to address class inequality if settler colonialism is not also challenged.[22]

Therefore, we do not need to necessarily *own* land appropriated from Indigenous nations or even to be *on* those lands to have benefited from the larger transformation of Indigenous territory into property—as people in the United Kingdom have done for generations, and as we continue to do despite our distance from those specific places. That which we both materially need and affectively cherish about the land can continue to come to us over distance and following personal displacements. The "disconnection" of mobility is illusory and obscures the lack of restoration and reparation towards the land and Indigenous Peoples. Connections to the settler society are not so easily severed, which turns us to the concept of "belonging."

Relationships of Belonging on the Land

As discussed in much of the literature regarding placemaking, we settler people also relate to land through our identities and sense of belonging, processes that continue across distance and as we change locations. Often, our investment in a settler society is premised on an equation between a place being "good" and therefore the people residing in that place being "good" by extension.

Settler collectives are often motivated to self-displace in the first instance due to an ongoing, shared dissatisfaction with the metropolitan core and a sense "something has gone wrong" in the "old country," as noted by Karen Ordahl Kupperman, among early American settlers, and which we have identified in many later articulations of the impetus for pursuing settler colonization among individuals and families.[23] There is a pervasive and ongoing perception of superior opportunity in the settler colony. This can be construed as economic freedom (entrepreneurship), social support (a "better" social safety net), and even the paradox of the promise of increased diversity *and* the promise of a frontier-derived white masculine purity. The perception of opportunity fits the person; we focus on what we want to see in the settler colony. The mythology of the frontier undergirds this.[24]

This has certainly been our experience and, oddly, also what British citizens and residents have reflected to us: it is not just a settler colonial self-delusion, but a trope, narrative, or discourse that has spread far beyond the settler polity. Connections of nationality and identity, including constant reinforcement from metropolitans as to how spacious, nice, clean, natural, and well-off Canada is and the demand to perform Canadian stereotypes that reinforce settler colonial tropes, drive a recuperation of settler colonial relations to land. British people need Canadians to be like their idea of Canadians, and, by extension, Canadians need to be seen as legitimate on the lands they claim so as not to undermine their own sense of self. It is a parallel to the assertion of the peacemaker myth of Canadian settler colonialism, which relies on the supposed extreme-by-comparison violence and militancy of American settlement to absolve Canadians of blame. However, these parallel narratives are in part reinforced through the assertion of common heritage and entangled histories, rather than national and geopolitical difference, as in the case of how the peacemaker myth positions Canadians and Americans. Another key part of the peacemaker myth is the story that Canada was created out of treaty-making and the gifts of civilization rather than conquest, and thus Britain is entangled in the myth because many of the treaties were made by British officials—for example, the Robinson Superior and Robinson Huron Treaties were negotiated in 1850, before the *British North America Act* that created the Dominion of Canada in 1867; the Haldimand Grant that still forms the basis of Haudenosaunee land claims along the Grand River stems from 1784. These and many other treaties are a legacy of British imperialism and attempts to secure the colonies that would become Canada, thus the peacemaker myth is also a myth that supports the benevolence of British imperialism and Canada as a place particularly shaped by that benevolence.

For settler Canadians, there is a clear motivation to accept British colonialism as benevolent (at least in Canada) and themselves as the righteous inheritors of what it produced. As such both British and Canadian identities rely on a perception of a relationship with the other that reinforces the other as virtuous, and we perform this in our social lives in both places—settler Canadians from many backgrounds conspicuously celebrated the crowning of a new monarch in 2023 just as they mourned the former monarch that same year. And British people with no personal knowledge or connection to Canada are quick, during casual conversations, to declare that they would not want to "insult" us by mistaking us for Americans (implied to be vulgar and violent). This becomes a fearful inversion of Holm, Pearson, and Chavis's Indigenous peoplehood matrix, which includes relationships to sacred places—including relationships across space and time through stories of "lost sacred spaces."[25] For settlers, our belonging is rooted in a "land" that is not and never was, so the relationship to other external societies and metropoles is constantly invoked to fill in the blanks and give substance by way of differentiation to our idea of where we belong. As such, the passage of time does not necessarily alter these relationships—constant "friction" with our host society and constant (unfavourable) comparisons to "home" happen all the time living in England, and even we ourselves often look around and think "something has gone wrong here" and "wouldn't it be so much better if we lived in Canada …" This affective pull to lands that are being transformed and reterritorialized to match our settler colonial expectations means that one literally can't "go back" to the originary metropole—we are literally different types of people than our parents, grandparents, and great-grandparents who originally settled in Canada.

Power, Intent, and Mobility

Settler collectives are differentiated from migrants on several grounds, but crucially with respect to the "intent to stay" versus "intent to return." However, *intent* needs to be balanced with the ability or capacity to *stay*/

return: the desire does not overdetermine the material and political nature of mobility. Veracini, in differentiating between settlers and migrants, argues that settlers "carry their sovereignty with them."[26] Today, settlers may carry sovereignty with them, but settler societies may or may not choose to recognize that sovereignty. This includes both settlers in settler states attempting to assert their own sovereignty contra state sovereignty, such as the Bundy Ranch occupiers who, while performing settler frontier occupation, ran afoul of American law.[27] While Bonds and Inwood note that the armed, white libertarian group, which occupied US federal land in the state of Oregon in 2014 after being fined for illegally grazing cattle there, were treated much better than other protest occupations such as the Standing Rock resistance to the Dakota Access Pipeline in 2016—a clear evidence of their privilege—they were still not able to assert sovereign control of this space contra the state.

In some situations, settlers are more privileged and powerful in their ability to "be sovereign" in different states due to ties with multiple state governments (i.e., dual nationals). This allows for some to transit back and forth across colonial lines, maintaining a foot in each camp. We are "migrants" by Veracini's definition in that we have in many respects an intent to return to Canada. We are more precisely economic migrants in the sense that our lives and livelihoods have been linked to the United Kingdom since we chose to emigrate for the purposes of PhD studies. Further, we—or at least one of us (Adam)—is legally a migrant according to the United Kingdom's rules on visas and status. Emma holds dual citizenship in Canada and the United Kingdom, claimed as a minor through her parents and grandparents' UK citizenship. Her maternal grandparents immigrated to Canada in the 1940s because her grandfather was recruited for the nuclear program at Chalk River, Ontario. They returned to England as a result of a chronic illness with their young family several years later. Emma's mother, born in Canada and raised in the United Kingdom, immigrated to Ontario with her England-born father in the 1970s. Her knowledge of the country, citizenship, and family connections facilitated the move, and his desire to escape the socially and economically declining United Kingdom drove it. Mirroring her mother, Emma did the same thing, but in reverse.

Adam, however, is only a citizen of Canada.[28] Adam's grandparents and great-grandparents, like Emma's, were born in the United Kingdom. However, Adam's ancestors did not have the mobility, spatially or socio-economically, that (some of) Emma's did. The result is that when Adam's Nana (from Ireland), Papa (from Scotland), and Grandma (Nancy, from England) crossed the Atlantic, they did so with neither the *intent* nor the *option* of return. Indeed, only Nancy ever even returned to visit, and then only in her sixties, over four decades after she left. Finally, Emma's connection to family who have always lived in England and never left has created levels of cultural understanding and awareness of social systems that Adam lacked and had to learn by experience, and almost certainly this impacted our different experiences of being settlers in England, making the transition more jarring for Adam, while saddling Emma with the role of acting as a cultural interpreter. Between us, we grew up with many of the same cultural touchstones, especially relating to comedy: our respective families both watched *Monty Python*, *Fawlty Towers*, and similar fare. However, it was not until moving to the United Kingdom that we began watching these comedies in the same way: Adam had always seen them as simply absurdist and slapstick; Emma knew as Adam does now that the impenetrable class consciousness, the rudeness and obstruction of people in public service jobs, and the resignation and acceptance of so much silliness as "just how things are" among most people are biting satire of actual, lived British culture.

Across these three different experiences of mobility between European state and settler colony, we view three different scenarios, all of which speak to something of the settler abroad:

1. The settler for whom the return to a non-settler polity is an option
2. The settler for whom mobility between metropole and settler colony is an enduring fact
3. The settler for whom the metropole is effectively alienated

Of these three, only the first promises any "escape" from the settler colonial condition that could be considered "transcendence" of an ethical sort. That is the first scenario, in which the once-settler renounces the settler colony and returns to a non-settler polity. This is, we would suggest, an unknown or little-known occurrence, but worth considering to the extent that the boundary between settler and migrant, while useful as concept, is more difficult to define in lived reality. The migrant may decide to settle, the settler may decide to uproot and migrate back. This indicates that settler subjectivities and identities are malleable to a certain extent but that plasticity is heavily influenced by differences in material and political power. Wealth and class, legal status, and the geopolitical relations between states on a global stage now all influence our idea of how sovereignty is "carried" by settlers. That many of these differences in material and political power are generated not within the settler society but within a different/distant society to which the settler subject is also connected. This points us towards the necessity of considering the relations of settler states to other states alongside individual intent and decision-making.

In so doing, we return to the concept of "belonging" and placemaking. Settler societies make places imbued with settler colonial power, but the systems and structures that they impose on places are globally interconnected. The attachments of settler people to particular lands and places can be stretched across distance, or even left dormant for long periods of time, only to be reinvigorated by a return, whether accompanied by the intent to return or forced by broader state powers. The reverse is also true: geopolitics beyond settler states still must be examined through a settler colonial lens because, as Veracini has argued, settler colonialism is very much now a global phenomenon.[29] On this point, our experiences and his analysis absolutely agree.

Conclusion: Being Here and There

As settlers abroad, we frequently find ourselves strategically invoking our "Canadianness" in social interactions. Especially when confronted by aspects of English society that we find objectionable—most especially the classist assumptions about accent, education, material possessions, and so on that are still very palpable in everyday life—we find ourselves "being Canadian at people." What we mean is, we self-consciously lean into our cultural differences and the stereotypes that English people have about Canadians. We smile at and make direct eye contact with strangers; we ignore class-based social cues with an "aw shucks" attitude; we ask about relatives who have moved to Canada and exclaim over how great this or that place is; we share travel tips and ideas for holidays. At the same time, we work to push back on the ubiquitous narratives of Canada as peacemaker and the "nostalgic" lens of the settler colony. We mix discussions of how much we love our hometowns with discussions of how the placemaking of settler colonialism inherently involves genocide. We speak with more admiration for Indigenous land defenders than for settler politicians.

We talk about how cool it is that canoe and kayak clubs across England are founded on and promote Indigenous technologies.

The reverse is also true. When we return to Canada, we slip back into our taken-for-granted practices in many ways, but not all. Practices that previously had seemed ordinary start to become uncomfortable, such as cheering for Team Canada; the seemingly enormous dwellings, vehicles, shops, and food portions; or the taken-for-granted desirability of a detached home in the suburbs. We can perceive in ourselves how many of these desires and doings are pervasive and entangled in our settler culture, and we begin to refuse to participate. We point out these practices to other settler people, even knowing it will create discomfort, as we do when pushing back on peacemaker narratives of Canada in the United Kingdom. In so doing, we are attempting to employ what Seawright calls an "epistemic practice" of transgression:

> An epistemic praxis (the operationalization of an alternative or critical epistemology) that goes against the grain and is counter to the tradition that defines the social environment. For conversations concerning the cultivation of criticality... this break in tradition is absolutely desirable and can inspire what José Medina (2013) calls epistemic friction. Epistemic friction is contained in those uncomfortable moments in which our taken-for-granted assumptions about the world begin to crack. These moments can be transformative and catalyze critical consciousness to imagine and hopefully actualize an alternative epistemology.[30]

This epistemic friction is enabled by the fact that we remain connected to multiple places. We are not just settler or just migrant; we are not only Canadian or only British; we do not live simply "here" or "there." Our connections, like our identities, are multiple and enduring across space and time. And for that reason, if no other, regardless of whether or not we ever do return to the settler state, we remain settler people and therefore obligated to pursue decolonization how we can, wherever we are.

Notes

1 Battell Lowman and Barker, *Settler*.

2 Barker, *Making and Breaking Settler Space*; Lowman and Barker, *Settler*.

3 Immigration to Britain was made increasingly difficult, expensive, and dehumanizing thanks to more than a decade of scapegoating of immigrants by the British Conservative Party (in power from 2010 through 2024). The "hostile environment" deliberately created by the Tories during their tenure to deter immigration and better exploit migrant workers impacted us directly in 2014–15 when Adam was forced to leave the United Kingdom and was not allowed to take up an academic post.

4 Barry and Agyeman, "On Belonging and Becoming," 24.

5 Veracini, *Settler Colonialism*.

6 Barker, *Making and Breaking Settler Space*.

7 Byrd, *The Transit of Empire*.

8 Leroy, "Black History in Occupied Territory."

9 For an examination of how various ethnicities, identities, and subjectivities have been subsumed into "multicultural" Canadian society and the changing understanding of whiteness that corresponded to these shifts, see Day, *Multiculturalism and the History of Canadian Diversity*.

10 Day, "Being or Nothingness," 113.

11 Lowman and Barker, *Settler*.

12 Seawright, "Settler Traditions of Place," 557.

13 Regan, *Unsettling the Settler Within*.

14 See Jefferess, "Responsibility, Nostalgia": Chalmers, "Settled Memories on Stolen Land."

15 Velednitsky, Hughes, and Machold, "Political Geographical Perspectives," 8.

16 For more on this term, see Lowman and Barker, *Settler*, 99–105.

17 This observation and terminology were first made about early American settlers by Karen Ordahl Kupperman, and we have since observed it to be a repeated trend. See Kupperman, *Indians and English*.

18 Higgins, "Lifestyle Migration and Settler Colonialism."

19 Lowman and Barker, *Settler*, 52.

20 See for example Nadasdy, "'Property' and Aboriginal Land Claims"; Pasternak, "How Capitalism Will Save Colonialism"; Egan and Place, "Minding the Gaps"; Schmidt, "Bureaucratic Territory."

21 Rifkin, "The Frontier."

22 Barker and Pickerill, "Radicalizing Relationships"; Barker, *Making and Breaking Settler Space*, 148–87.

23 Kupperman, *Settling with the Indians* (1980), 135, 141.

24 Higgins, "Lifestyle Migration and Settler Colonialism," 8.

25 Holm, Pearson, and Chavis, "Peoplehood."

26 Veracini, *Settler Colonialism*.

27 Bonds and Inwood, "Beyond White Privilege."

28 This was true at the time of the original writing of this chapter. As of August 2024, Adam applied for and was granted British citizenship.

29 Veracini, *The Settler Colonial Present*.

30 Seawright, "Settler Traditions of Place," 558.

Sources

Barker, Adam J. *Making and Breaking Settler Space: Five Centuries of Colonization in North America*. UBC Press, 2021.

Barker, Adam J., and Jenny Pickerill. "Radicalizing Relationships to and Through Shared Geographies: Why Anarchists Need to Understand Indigenous Connections to Land and Place." *Antipode* 44, no. 5 (2012): 1705–25. https://doi.org/10.1111/j.1467-8330.2012.01031.x.

Barry, Janice, and Julian Agyeman. "On Belonging and Becoming in the Settler-Colonial City: Co-Produced Futurities, Placemaking, and Urban Planning in the United States." *Journal of Race, Ethnicity and the City* 1, nos. 1–2 (2020): 22–41. https://doi.org/10.1080/26884674.2020.1793703.

Bonds, Anne, and Joshua Inwood. "Beyond White Privilege: Geographies of White Supremacy and Settler Colonialism." *Progress in Human Geography* 40, no. 6 (2016): 715–33. https://doi.org/10.1177/0309132515613.

Byrd, Jodi. *The Transit of Empire: Indigenous Critiques of Colonialism*. University of Minnesota Press, 2011.

Chalmers, Jason. "Settled Memories on Stolen Land: Settler Mythology at Canada's National Holocaust Monument." *American Indian Quarterly* 43, no. 4 (2019): 379–407. https://dx.doi.org/10.1353/aiq.2019.a736438.

Day, Iyko. "Being or Nothingness: Indigeneity, Antiblackness and Settler Colonial Critique." *Critical Ethnic Studies* 1, no. 2 (2015): 102–21, https://doi.org/10.5749/jcritethnstud.1.2.0102.

Day, Richard J.F. *Multiculturalism and the History of Canadian Diversity*. University of Toronto Press, 2000.

Egan, Brian, and Jessica Place. "Minding the Gaps: Property, Geography, and Indigenous Peoples in Canada." *Geoforum* 44 (2013): 129–38. https://doi.org/10.1016/j.geoforum.2012.10.003.

Higgins, Katie W. "Lifestyle Migration and Settler Colonialism: The Imaginative Geographies of British Migrants to Aotearoa New Zealand." *Population, Space and Place* 24, no. 3 (2018). https://doi.org/10.1002/psp.2112.

Holm, Tom, J. Diane Pearson, and Ben Chavis. "Peoplehood: A Model for the Extension of Sovereignty in American Indian Studies." *Wicazo Sa Review* 18, no. 1 (2003): 7–24. https://dx.doi.org/10.1353/wic.2003.0004.

Jefferess, David. "Responsibility, Nostalgia, and the Mythology of Canada as a Peacekeeper." *University of Toronto Quarterly* 78, no. 2 (2009): 709–27. https://doi.org/10.3138/utq.78.2.709.

Kupperman, Karen Ordahl. *Indians and English: Facing Off in Early America*. Cornell University Press, 2000.

Leroy, Justin. "Black History in Occupied Territory: On the Entanglements of Slavery and Settler Colonialism." *Theory & Event* 19, no. 4 (2016). https://muse.jhu.edu/article/633276.

Lowman, Emma Battell, and Adam J. Barker. *Settler: Identity and Colonialism in 21st Century Canada*. Fernwood Publishing, 2015.

Nadasdy, Paul. "'Property' and Aboriginal Land Claims in the Canadian Subarctic: Some Theoretical Considerations." *American Anthropologist* 104, no. 1 (2002): 247–61. https://doi.orgs/10.1525/aa.2002.104.1.247.
Pasternak, Shiri. "How Capitalism Will Save Colonialism: The Privatization of Reserve Lands in Canada." *Antipode* 47, no. 1 (2015): 179–96. https://doi.org/10.1111/anti.12094.
Regan, Paulette. *Unsettling the Settler Within: Indian Residential Schools, Truth Telling, and Reconciliation in Canada*. UBC Press, 2010.
Rifkin, Mark. "The Frontier as (Movable) Space of Exception." *Settler Colonial Studies* 4, no. 2 (2014): 176–80.
Schmidt, Jeremy J. "Bureaucratic Territory: First Nations, Private Property, and 'Turn-Key' Colonialism in Canada." *Annals of the American Association of Geographers* 108, no. 4 (2018): 901–16. https://doi.org/10.1080/24694452.2017.1403878.
Seawright, Gardner. "Settler Traditions of Place: Making Explicit the Epistemological Legacy of White Supremacy and Settler Colonialism for Place-Based Education." *Educational Studies* 50, no. 6 (2014): 554–72. https://doi.org/10.1080/00131946.2014.965938.
Velednitsky, Stepha, Sara N.S. Hughes, and Rhys Machold. "Political Geographical Perspectives on Settler Colonialism." *Geography Compass* 14, no. 6 (2020): 1–17. https://doi.org/10.1111/gec3.12490.
Veracini, Lorenzo. *Settler Colonialism: A Theoretical Overview*. Palgrave Macmillan, 2010.
Veracini, Lorenzo. *The Settler Colonial Present*. Palgrave, 2015.

A Settler Twice Over in a Changing Canadian Landscape

The Importance of Knowledge, Acknowledgement, and Respect to Indigenous-Settler Reconciliation

Huma Haider

THE CHURCH NEAR OUR HOUSE HAS 215 ORANGE RIBBONS tied on the fence. I first noticed them with my two young children. While they were aware of residential schools from class and books, they were shaken by what the ribbons represented. Soon after, we went on a tour at a settler museum, which told the Indigenous narrative alongside. My children enjoyed learning about the seven Anishinaabe teachings, carved onto plaques in the garden. Such experiences were absent when I moved to Toronto from Japan as a child in 1989. As a mixed-race minority settler, I grew up unaware of Indigenous cultures and of the devastating extent to which Canada sought to eliminate them. After twelve years overseas, I moved to Toronto again in 2017 with my British husband and British-born children.

I was struck by the greater exposure given to Indigenous cultures and to the history of atrocity, through educational initiatives, land acknowledgements, and a rise in Indigenous narratives in arts, literature, and media. This chapter explores the contributions that these developments can make to processes of reconciliation—through my perspective as a racialized settler, mother, and legal professional working in transitional justice. Researching transitional justice elsewhere, I have learned how youth armed with knowledge and openness can become agents of change. As a racialized settler, I recognize that we are still settlers, benefiting from settler colonialism, even if our own ancestral histories are marred by colonialism and our lived experience subject to racism. As a mother and settler, I seek to ensure that my children know of the harms committed, understand their privilege, and celebrate Indigenous Peoples and cultures. While wary of limitations, including our lack of everyday contact with Indigenous Peoples, such knowledge-seeking, acknowledgements, and respect can be important steps in reconciliation.

• • •

"O, Canada. Our home and native land." I had never heard the Canadian national anthem until that first day in grade 8, a few days after my family arrived in Toronto, Ontario. Upon hearing it every day, I learned the words, and, over time, I started to think of Canada as my home. I always felt uncomfortable singing the "native land" part though. Canada was not my native land. I was a "landed immigrant" (the term used back then), having come here from Japan, with a Pakistani father and a Chinese mother. At the time, I didn't give any thought to the fact that this applies not only to us racialized settlers, but also to white settlers. This was the early 1990s.

Fast-forward to 2024. My son, eleven, and my daughter, nine, are in primary school in Toronto. For years, they have also stood for the national anthem, just like I used to do every morning. I wonder how they feel about the term "native land" and what they view as "native." They were both born in England—part white, part racialized settlers in Canada. Notably, what first follows the anthem now is not the morning announcements, as when I was in school, but a land acknowledgement. My son can recite it.

I first heard a land acknowledgement at the Toronto International Film Festival (TIFF) in 2017, just after moving back to Toronto from England, where I had lived for twelve years. I was pleasantly surprised and intrigued. At the time, I thought it was just TIFF, but I realized later that these acknowledgements are widespread, including in schools. I have often wondered what effect hearing this land acknowledgement on a daily basis at school will have on children. Will they internalize that they live on Indigenous land, or will this become a routine exercise that fails to instill this truth?

As in many "transitional" contexts—whether transitioning from authoritarianism to democracy, from conflict to sustainable peace, or from neglect of mass human rights abuses to addressing this legacy in developed democracies[1]—it is impossible to rely on any one initiative. Rather, there need to be initiatives and changes in a multitude of sectors and on many levels to effectively drive processes of reconciliation. In Canada, this includes fundamental changes to the lens through which we as settlers view the world.

The Dominance of the Eurocentric Perspective

I used to feel jealous of my sister every time yearbooks were distributed in our school in Japan. We attended an international school, with expatriates from all around the world. The yearbook specified our nationality under our photo and name. I was born in Japan, but I had to claim my father's nationality—so under my name was "Pakistan." My sister was born in Hong Kong, then still a British colony—so under her name was "Great Britain." Even while growing up in Asia, attending a global school with countless multiracial students, I still wanted to be European and to be seen as European.

We moved to Canada from Japan during the first big wave of Chinese immigrants from Hong Kong and, subsequently, the first big backlash. The term *FOB* (fresh off the boat) was common—shouted at me at school in equal measure to the question posed of why I spoke such good English. This bothered me, similar to when I would travel in Europe and residents would stare at me, calling out, "Nihau" or "Konichiwa." They're just trying to be friendly, I was often told. To me, it felt more like unwelcome attention to my "otherness," a feeling I experienced through my teen years and early adult life. I remember the satisfaction I used to feel when asked if I was part white.

Fast-forward again to 2024. My nine-year-old is upset I hadn't told her it was Eid al-Adha and she missed sharing Eid greetings with her class. She has happily relayed to her classmates in the past that she celebrates Eid, explaining to them that she is part Pakistani. I felt elated. What I used to try to minimize, she publicizes with pride.

I often tell my children when we watch films like *Shang-Chi and the Legend of the Ten Rings* and *Turning Red*, and read stories with characters with different colour skin, that these portrayals weren't there when I was growing up. I rarely got to see myself represented—even less so in any kind of positive light or in the absence of stereotyping. Popular media has long represented white characters and Eurocentric portrayals as the norm and glorified their stories, at the expense of racialized minorities and Indigenous communities.[2] The same can be said for the teaching of history.

The Canadian Citizenship Test

As a teenager, I was exempt from taking the citizenship test, so I never read the study guide. I can't recall much of the specifics of the history of Canada that I learned at school, but I do know that the curriculum did not include the history of Indigenous-settler relations or lessons from an Indigenous perspective.

My husband recently applied for Canadian citizenship, and in preparation he read the *Discover Canada* study guide. The section on Canada's history begins with "When Europeans explored Canada," indicative of the Eurocentric perspective adopted throughout.[3] There is only passing and reductive reference to treaties, residential schools, and Indigenous culture. My husband is a white settler, already having learned this kind of history lesson in his school system in England. Racialized newcomers to Canada have now also been taught this partial and biased history as their introduction to the country.[4] Some may, similar to me, already have grown up idealizing the European standard, which increases the possibility of accepting these words and this version of history as legitimate.

What Happens When History Is Incomplete?

I attended a lecture when I was working at the University of Birmingham in England, sometime during the early 2010s. The woman beside me struck up a conversation and asked me about my background. Her expression changed as soon as I told her that my mother is Chinese. Seemingly flush with shame, she told me that she is Japanese, bowed her head, and said that she was very sorry for what happened during the war. I was taken aback. Being a scholar and practitioner of transitional justice, where apology can be considered an important form of reparation, I was also intrigued.

Transitional justice, as defined by the United Nations, is "the full range of processes and mechanisms associated with a society's attempts to come to terms with a legacy of large-scale past abuses, in order to ensure accountability, serve justice and achieve reconciliation."[5] Germany has often been upheld as a country that has successfully acknowledged its past and the destructive role it played in the world wars, including through apology, reparations, memorials, documentation of a shared narrative in German textbooks, and open teaching of the wars in classrooms.[6] This is in contrast to Japan, which has failed to fully acknowledge the country's harmful actions in World War II, to revise its history textbooks, or to educate its public about the atrocities committed.[7] This not only results in the persistence of tensions in the region but can also contribute to feelings of shame among Japanese people. They may either have not learned about their country's actions in the war and defended their country in the absence of this knowledge, or they are aware of the atrocities but also of the country's failure to properly account for them. The latter is what I perceived to be behind the unexpected apology I received.

In May 2021, Tk'emlúps te Secwépemc First Nation revealed the devastating discovery of what was suspected to be the remains of 215 children on the site of the former residential school near Kamloops, British Columbia, Canada. Sadness and horror ripped through the country, from coast to coast—along with the echo of "I didn't know" among settlers. Prior to the discovery of these remains, two-thirds of Canadians surveyed said they knew only a little or nothing about the residential school system.[8] This lack of knowledge, followed by a sudden awakening, can very quickly translate into feelings of shame.

I was aware that Canada had a history of mistreatment of Indigenous Peoples. But I had not been taught or exposed to the historical details, to Indigenous lived experiences, nor to the ongoing struggles of Indigenous communities stemming from the legacy of colonialism—during my time in school, university, or through the media. I had unfortunately also not yet chosen to educate myself. As racialized newcomers who have adopted Canada as their home, there can be a sense of idealization of the country. I regret that I bought into and immersed myself in the dominant Eurocentric narratives. I recalled all the Canada Days celebrated—all the red and white adorned. I recalled all the times while living overseas that people from all different countries spoke highly of Canada—and I just agreed and felt pride.

This has now been severely tempered with a shame I feel for Canada and as a Canadian. I also feel guilty for not having sought out this much-needed knowledge earlier and for having perpetuated the myth of Canada. I have also felt neglectful as someone working in transitional justice.

The Transitional Justice Process

I moved to England in 2005 to study international human rights law at the London School of Economics, with a focus on transitional justice and reconciliation. I have since researched and worked on various aspects of conflict, transitional justice, and reconciliation, particularly with regard to the wars and atrocities committed in the Western Balkans during the 1990s. This includes working at the War Crimes Chamber in Sarajevo and researching the effectiveness of coexistence initiatives throughout Bosnia and Herzegovina (BiH).[9] Ironically, I left Canada with the view that there was limited transitional justice work to be engaged in here. How wrong I was.

The concept of transitional justice has only in recent years been debated in scholarship as applicable to established democracies, such as Canada and Australia. Transitional justice first emerged as a separate field of research and action during the "third wave" of democracy in Latin America in the 1980s and in Eastern Europe after the fall of the Soviet Union in the 1990s. As such, it was primarily focused on addressing dictatorial or authoritarian regimes and the transition to democracy, evolving subsequently to become an essential aspect of post-conflict transitions and peace-building.[10]

In Canada, an established democracy, there has been no transition from one regime to another. In settler colonial contexts, transitional justice's traditional focus on state-building can instead be utilized by the state to legitimate itself.[11] Canada presents itself as a democratic human rights defender that can assist other states in their transitions from conflict and authoritarianism to long-term peace and stability, rather than requiring or engaging in transitional justice processes internally.[12] Yet, Canada has been implementing mechanisms internally that are core components of transitional justice. The International Centre for Transitional Justice, one of the key organizations operating in this field, now cites transitional contexts as also including "developed democracies dealing with unaddressed human rights violations associated with systemic racism and marginalisation."[13]

A key mechanism of transitional justice are truth commissions. Canada's Truth and Reconciliation Commission (TRC), which operated from 2009 to 2015, is such an institution. Truth commissions are official, non-judicial (or post-judicial) commissions of limited duration established to investigate human rights abuses, usually those perpetrated by government or other state institutions.[14] The Canadian TRC provided the space for residential school survivors, their families, and communities to tell their stories, many for the first time, and to be heard. These testimonies, in turn, have produced a historical record. The TRC also aimed to raise public awareness through national events and regional and local activities.

The participation of Indigenous survivors has required remarkable acts of bravery and strength—and, in turn, it requires much psychological, emotional, cultural, and financial support. Working with survivors at the War Crimes Chamber in Sarajevo, I have witnessed the understandable difficulty with which they recount the violations witnessed and/or committed against them. At the same time, for some, it seemed to create a pathway to some form of healing.

Trials in BiH—a large component of the post-war transitional justice strategy—have yet, however, to produce significant progress towards processes of reconciliation, particularly with regard to improved relationships between the conflict groups. The Dayton Agreement, which ended the war in 1995, divided the country into two autonomous ethnic entities (the Bosniak-Croat Federation and Republika Srpska); produced government institutions based on ethnic power sharing; and allowed nationalist politicians to cement their power. Such top-down politicization of ethnicity and ethnic discourse can have a divisive and polarizing effect within and among communities.[15]

My research on the effects of transitional justice in BiH on processes of reconciliation reveals that the creation of a historical record through trials has not produced a unifying narrative, but has instead, in some cases, exacerbated divisions and intensified ethnic identity politics. Prosecuted individuals are often touted as either war criminals or war heroes depending on identity group allegiances, and court decisions can reinforce divisive group narratives and contribute to ongoing tensions.[16]

Canada, too, seems to struggle with incomplete and countering narratives, despite the creation of a historical record and growing awareness of atrocities committed against Indigenous Peoples. While this awareness marks a significant and necessary development, it may fail to adequately reshape and improve Indigenous-settler relations if decoupled from acknowledgement of the connection of these atrocities to colonialism and settler-based structures and to ongoing violations of the rights of Indigenous Peoples.

Some scholars have argued that the Canadian government has compartmentalized residential schools, failing to place them within the larger project of colonialism.[17] Combined with indoctrination into Eurocentric narratives and the portrayal of Canada as a peaceful nation, this allows for settlers to view the mistreatment and deaths of Indigenous children as an extreme but individual tragedy from which they are far removed.[18] In the South African Truth and Reconciliation Commission, critics argued that the focus on individual victims and perpetrators obscured attention to apartheid's structure and systemic injustices, which continue to marginalize Black South Africans. It has also undermined recognition that all white people in the country benefited from apartheid.[19]

If countries and societies do not adequately address the past and the persistence of injustices, it is very difficult to find a way forward. Reconciliation in the context of Canada does not have to mean returning to prior relations, since there was never a positive relationship between Indigenous Peoples and settlers—but it can mean jointly addressing the past and its ongoing legacy in order to look to a shared future.

Racialized Settlers *Are* a Party to This Process

This is the first time in my career working in transitional justice and reconciliation that I am a party to the process in a direct way. I am not a facilitator, working in the courts, nor an external researcher, interviewing participants and examining processes and outcomes. I am a direct party as a settler and as a mother of settler children who has taken for granted that I am privileged to live on this land—on land that was taken unjustly from Indigenous Peoples. I am privileged to have my children with me and for them to be with us—not having had them ripped from my arms and dragged away to schools unknown or to non-Indigenous families (during the Sixties Scoop and with the ongoing over-representation of Indigenous children in foster care), an unimaginable horror that has been atrociously committed against many Indigenous families.

It has taken me far too long to recognize this. As racialized newcomers who have experienced racism and/or come from countries that have also suffered from colonialism, we may not immediately consider ourselves to be complicit in violations committed towards Indigenous Peoples. Rather, we may think of settlers as the early Europeans and perhaps their descendants. However, under settler colonialism, all non-Indigenous people benefit from the settler colonial system—even if we may benefit to a lesser extent than white settlers, due to systemic racism that also disadvantages non-Indigenous minority groups.

While recognizing that we are a party to the process, racialized settlers can also act as allies. Recent studies conducted in Canada find that non-Indigenous minority Canadians are more supportive of providing reparations to Indigenous Peoples compared to the white majority. This may be due in part to a sense of collective victimhood among minority ethnic groups (e.g., Japanese Canadians, who experienced forcible internment during World War II) and shared solidarity in victim consciousness, extending to political solidarity.[20]

Reconciliation in Canada requires a process in which non-Indigenous people, like myself, seek out the truth about this country's history (in media, literature, art, news stories, public events, etc.) and accept that we can feel grateful to live in Canada while insisting that it do better—that we all do better. It also involves reflecting on the truths revealed and engaging with the TRC's Calls to Action. These seek to address structural inequalities and the legacy of the atrocities committed, including through commemoration and education.

Seeking Knowledge and Filling in the Gaps

I have continually been seeking ways to correct for my lack of knowledge and to make it more likely that my children will grow up never having had these gaps in the first place. The process of education through literature and media has been made much easier in recent years with a notable rise in adult and children's books by Indigenous and non-Indigenous authors. These address the history and legacy of residential schools and the treatment of Indigenous populations, and they celebrate Indigenous voices. The announcement in 2023 by the Toronto District School Board, the largest school board in the country, that it will create a mandatory grade 11 course focused on Indigenous voices is an important step.[21] There has also been a rise in Indigenous programming in media and the arts in recent years, although much more is needed.

I have read powerful, insightful, informative, and beautifully written books on residential schools and on Indigenous life and challenges in Canada. As a parent of two young children, I found it extremely difficult to process the cruelty of the residential school system—and I was only experiencing it through storytelling. I have read children's books and watched films and short videos with my family on these same topics. Fortunately, my children also read these books with their teachers and classmates at school now—a benefit not afforded during my time at school.

We have also attended Indigenous theatre performances and cultural festivals, including festivals for National Truth and Reconciliation Day. After experiencing a spectacular hoop dance performance at one such event, my son told me it was one of the best things he had ever seen. We have participated in Indigenous-led tours, including visiting a settler's museum in Mississauga, Ontario, that showcased an Indigenous viewpoint and raised questions about how history is taught.

These little steps have yet to come anywhere close to tackling the scale of reforms and changes that are needed, but they are steps nonetheless—and if taken across communities and society, they can and will accumulate.

Commemoration

The day after the discovery of the 215 children was reported, I struggled with how to discuss this with my children. Then, I overheard one of my son's teachers discuss it with the class during their virtual school session with such grace. I was very grateful as it is essential that nothing be kept from this younger generation, even if it may be hard to process. My son said later that he would have rather not known, but he engaged with it, we discussed it—and both he and his sister later placed *Every Child Matters* posters and orange ribbons on our porch as our own simple form of commemoration.

The church near our house has 215 ribbons tied on the fence that leads to the child-care centre. I first noticed these with my children. While they had knowledge of residential schools and were aware that children's remains had been uncovered, it was difficult to see in visual representation the vast number of ribbons, knowing what each one represented—and knowing also that there were so many more.

Such sites of commemoration are important. Every time we go by the church, we are reminded. Every time we go by the church, we acknowledge.

Snowball Effect

While it is difficult for any single initiative to contribute effectively to real change and to processes of transitional justice and reconciliation, multiple initiatives engaging many people and institutions over time have the potential to accumulate and to produce a snowball effect, as indicated in the case of BiH, discussed below.[22] The ninety-four Calls to Action apply to multiple sectors, providing opportunities for many forms of advocacy by settlers and Indigenous communities alike. Similarly, a growing presence of Indigenous narratives and representations in arts and media has the potential over time to alter the popular consciousness of Canada and of settler Canadians.

It is these kinds of accumulation of steps and potential "spillover" effects that I have explored in different transitional contexts, primarily in relation to the Western Balkans, where youth are seen as agents of change.[23] While the transitions in the region represent the conventional authoritarian to democratic development and post-conflict peace-building contexts of transitional justice, rather than settler colonial contexts, the necessity and challenges of countering dominant, one-sided narratives and reframing the "other" resonate across the Western Balkans and Canada.

There is evidence that attitudinal and behavioural changes stemming from reconciliation-related initiatives in BiH have contributed to participants engaging in spin-off activities, which can have a wider impact on society beyond the direct participants. These spin-off activities were designed to bring about positive change to the political situation.[24] Youth in Mostar, for example, who participated in music-based reconciliation-related activities have subsequently collaborated to develop their own cultural and arts-based projects. These have sought to counter the pervasive political nationalist rhetoric in the country—creating alternative spaces and narratives (e.g., walking tours of the city through a different lens) that enable individuals to imagine alternative lives.[25] In Canada, there are now also various Indigenous walking tours, such as in Ottawa and Toronto, that explore these urban areas through an Indigenous lens.[26] A key way through which projects and programmes in the Western Balkans have been able to scale up and attain broader reach is to give participants the tools for activism, enabling them to become "multipliers of peace" within their own communities and societies.[27]

Youth in Canada also have the potential to be "multipliers of peace." My children and their peers are growing up with more awareness, knowledge, and understanding, all of which will increase with ongoing reforms and achievements in the Calls to Action. They can become a different, more empowered generation of white and racialized settler Canadians, with a broader understanding of settlers, Indigenous Peoples, the history of colonialism, Indigenous-settler relations, and Canada—and with a new relationship with Indigenous Peoples and with Canada. They must recognize their privilege and how they benefit from settler structures, their need to listen and learn, and their role to play in creating change.

Since 2022, my children's primary school has taken part in a Walk for Wenjack event.[28] As part of this, students wrote letters addressed to Chanie Wenjack. My daughter expressed a sadness, awareness of harms committed, and desire to act: "I really feel like Indigenous peoples should not have been treated how they were. I hope you find your family, I would do anything to make it right."

Limitations in a Lack of Contact

Despite this progress, and the potential for progress, I am wary of limitations due to the lack of meaningful and everyday contact between settlers and Indigenous populations, including in my own community in Toronto. Contact theory has long argued that interpersonal contact is one of the most effective ways to reduce prejudice between group members.[29] In other transitional contexts, such as in the Western Balkans, efforts at reconciliation have involved dialogue and coexistence initiatives that have sought to physically bring together groups divided along conflict lines. These interactions can occur through structured meetings and in unstructured ways through everyday shared spaces. The aim is to (re)humanize the "other" through personal contact and dialogue, to discover shared goals that bring to light identities alternative to those targeted during conflict, and to prompt empathy.[30]

In Canada, the dominance of Eurocentric viewpoints, the inadequate space given to Indigenous voices and narratives, and the gaps in history and storytelling have produced an environment in which many settlers have had little opportunity to know Indigenous Peoples—or worse, to only know them in a dehumanizing way. This is exacerbated by the lack of contact that we experience in our everyday lives. While beyond the scope of this chapter, this also draws attention to the requirement for reconciliation in Canada to be accompanied by the decolonization of these ongoing features of settler colonialism in Canadian society.

Recognizing Progress and Continuing to Move Forward

Despite such limitations, the visible changes in environment in the Canada that I left in 2005 and the Canada to which I returned in 2017 is cause to be optimistic. The greater exposure to and awareness of Indigenous cultures and lived experiences, and the history of atrocity, is significant progress.

My experience as a settler in Canada the second time around is different. My perception of Canada and my role has evolved. Only recently have I come to fully understand the feeling and impulse behind the apology I was given by the Japanese participant in that lecture in Birmingham—the shame and guilt for not having known for so long, the horror and tremendous sadness in knowing, and, in the case of being a settler in Canada, the difficult reality and remorse that we are implicated.

As a scholar and practitioner of transitional justice, I recognize that there is still a very long way to go in Canada's journey towards reconciliation, particularly at the political level. However, the many steps that have been taken by Indigenous persons and settlers, at micro, community, and societal levels, must be recognized and built upon. There should never be another moment where we, as settlers, say and hear "I didn't know." We must all hold this painful knowledge, acknowledge the devastating experiences of Indigenous Peoples, recognize and reflect on our role, advocate for systemic change, and, together with Indigenous communities, map out a shared future—one that propels us further along the path towards reconciliation.

Notes

1 See International Centre for Transitional Justice (ICTJ), "What Is Transitional Justice?"
2 See for example Ramasubramanian, Riewestahl, and Ramirez, "Race and Ethnic Stereotypes in the Media."
3 Government of Canada, "Study Guide—*Discover Canada*."
4 Call to Action 93 seeks to address the problems with the citizenship test. Yet in 2024, *Discover Canada* still remained the official study guide.
5 United Nations Secretary-General, *The Rule of Law and Transitional Justice*, 4.
6 See for example Berger, *War, Guilt, and World Politics*; Hanke et al., "When the Past Haunts the Present."
7 See for example Rienzi, "Other Nations Could Learn."
8 Abacus Data, "Canadians React."
9 Haider, "Social Repair in Divided Societies."
10 Haider, "Breaking the Cycle of Violence."
11 Barolsky, "Truth-Telling"; Stanton, "Reconciling Reconciliation."

12 This is based on a review of Canadian governmental documents. See Matsunaga, "Two Faces of Transitional Justice."
13 ICTJ, "What Is Transitional Justice?"
14 Haider, "Transitional Justice."
15 Haider, "(Re)Imagining Coexistence."
16 Haider, "Breaking the Cycle of Violence"; Haider, "Social Repair in Divided Societies."
17 James, "Changing the Subject"; Park, "Settler Colonialism and the Politics of Grief."
18 Rice et al., "Identifying and Working Through Settler Ignorance"; Park, "Settler Colonialism and the Politics of Grief."
19 Park, "Settler Colonialism and the South African TRC"; du Toit, "Justice Promised or Just a Promise," 85–120.
20 Starzyk et al., "The Case for and Causes of Intraminority Solidarity."
21 CBC News, "TDSB Makes Indigenous Authors Course Mandatory."
22 Haider, "Scalability of Transitional Justice"; Garson, "Defying Gravity"; Howell, "Post-War Life-Space."
23 See Haider, "Scalability of Transitional Justice."
24 Garson, "Defying Gravity."
25 Howell, "Post-War Life-Space."
26 See for example Destination Indigenous, "Indigenous Walks"; Sasaki, "Seeing Toronto Through a Lens of Indigenous Stories."
27 Fairey and Kerr, "What Works?"
28 Chanie Wenjack was an Anishinaabe boy from Marten Falls First Nation, Ontario, who died fleeing residential school to return to his family at the age of twelve. For more information, see Gord Downie & Chanie Wenjack Fund, "Walk for Wenjack."
29 See Haider, "Social Repair in Divided Societies"; Halpern and Weinstein, "Empathy and Rehumanization After Mass Violence."
30 Haider, "Scalability of Transitional Justice."

Sources

Abacus Data. "Canadians React to the Discovery of Remains at Residential Schools." Canadian Race Relations Foundation, June 14, 2021. https://crrf-fcrr.ca/2021/06/canadians-react-to-the-discovery-of-remains-at-residential-schools/.

Barolsky, Vanessa. "Truth-Telling About a Settler-Colonial Legacy: Decolonizing Possibilities?" *Postcolonial Studies* 26, no.4 (2023): 540–56. https://doi.org/10.1080/13688790.2022.2117872.

Berger, Thomas U. *War, Guilt, and World Politics After World War II*. Cambridge University Press, 2012.

CBC News. "TDSB Makes Indigenous Authors Course Mandatory for Grade 11 English Credit." Last updated February, 2, 2023. https://www.cbc.ca/news/canada/toronto/tdsb-indigenous-course-credit-1.6734437.

Destination Indigenous. "Indigenous Walks." https://destinationindigenous.ca/listings/indigenous-walks.
du Toit, Fanie. "Settling on a Fair Future." In *When Political Transitions Work: Reconciliation as Interdependence*. Oxford Academic, 2018. https://doi.org/10.1093/oso/9780190881856.003.0003.
Fairey, Tiffany, and Rachel Kerr. "What Works? Creative Approaches to Transitional Justice in Bosnia and Herzegovina." *International Journal of Transitional Justice* 14, no. 1 (2020): 142–64. https://doi.org/10.1093/ijtj/ijz031.
Garson, Melanie. "Defying Gravity: Evaluating the Trickle-Up Effects of Reconciliation Programmes." *Ethnopolitics* 19, no. 2 (2020): 188–208. https://doi.org/10.1080/17449057.2019.1653017.
Gord Downie & Chanie Wenjack Fund. "Walk for Wenjack." https://downiewenjack.ca/our-work/walk-for-wenjack.
Government of Canada. "Study Guide—*Discover Canada—The Rights and Responsibilities of Citizenship*." Last modified August, 8, 2024. https://www.canada.ca/en/immigration-refugees-citizenship/corporate/publications-manuals/discover-canada.html.
Haider, Huma. "Breaking the Cycle of Violence: Applying Conflict Sensitivity to Transitional Justice." *Conflict, Security & Development* 17, no. 4 (2017): 333–60. https://doi.org/10.1080/14678802.2017.1337420.
Haider, Huma. "(Re)Imagining Coexistence: Striving for Sustainable Return, Reintegration and Reconciliation in Bosnia and Herzegovina." *International Journal of Transitional Justice* 3, no. 1 (2009): 91–113. https://doi.org/10.1093/ijtj/ijn035.
Haider, Huma. "Scalability of Transitional Justice and Reconciliation Interventions: Moving Toward Wider Socio-Political Change." Institute of Development Studies, March 5, 2021. https://www.ids.ac.uk/publications/scalability-of-transitional-justice-and-reconciliation-interventions-moving-toward-wider-socio-political-change.
Haider, Huma. "Social Repair in Divided Societies: Integrating a Coexistence Lens into Transitional Justice." *Conflict, Security & Development* 11, no. 2 (2011): 175–203. https://doi.org/10.1080/14678802.2011.572458.
Haider, Huma. "Transitional Justice: Topic Guide." GSDRC, University of Birmingham. 2016. https://gsdrc.org/topic-guides/transitional-justice.
Halpern, Jodi, and Harvey M. Weinstein. "Empathy and Rehumanization After Mass Violence." In *My Neigbor, My Enemy: Justice and Community in the Aftermath of Mass Atrocity*, edited by Eric Stover and Harvey M. Weinstein. Cambridge University Press, 2004.
Hanke, Katja, James H. Liu, Denis J. Hilton, Michal Bilewicz, Ilya Garber, Li-Li Huang, Cecilia Gastardo-Conaco, and Feixue Wang. "When the Past Haunts the Present: Intergroup Forgiveness and Historical Closure in Post–World War II Societies in Asia and in Europe." *International Journal of Intercultural Relations* 37, no. 3 (2013): 287–301. https://doi.org/10.1016/j.ijintrel.2012.05.003.
Howell, Gillian. "Post-War Life-Space and Music in Bosnia-Herzegovina." *Risk, Protection, Provision, and Policy* 12 (2015). https://doi.org/10.1177/1321103X241242.

International Centre for Transitional Justice (ICTJ). "What Is Transitional Justice?" 2024. https://www.ictj.org/what-transitional-justice.

James, Matt. "Changing the Subject: The TRC, Its National Events, and the Displacement of Substantive Reconciliation in Canadian Media Representations." *Journal of Canadian Studies* 51, no. 2 (2018): 362–97. https://doi.org/10.3138/jcs.2016-0011.r1.

Matsunaga, Jennifer. "Two Faces of Transitional Justice: Theorizing the Incommensurability of Transitional Justice and Decolonization in Canada." *Decolonization: Indigeneity, Education & Society* 5, no. 1 (2016). https://jps.library.utoronto.ca/index.php/des/article/view/26530.

Park, Augustine S.J. "Settler Colonialism and the Politics of Grief: Theorising a Decolonising Transitional Justice for Indian Residential Schools." *Human Rights Review* 16, no. 3 (2015): 273–93. https://doi.org/10.1007/s12142-015-0372-4.

Park, Augustine S.J. "Settler Colonialism and the South African TRC: Ambivalent Denial and Democratisation without Decolonisation." *Social & Legal Studies* 31, no. 2 (2021): 216–37. https://doi.org/10.1177/09646639211022786.

Ramasubramanian, Srividya, Emily Riewestahl, and Anthony Ramirez. "Race and Ethnic Stereotypes in the Media." *Oxford Research Encyclopedia of Communication*. 2023. https://doi.org/10.1093/acrefore/9780190228613.013.1262.

Rice, Carla, Susan D. Dion, Hannah Fowlie, and Andrea Breen. "Identifying and Working Through Settler Ignorance." *Critical Studies in Education* 63, no. 1 (2022): 15–30. https://doi.org/10.1080/17508487.2020.1830818.

Rienzi, Greg. "Other Nations Could Learn from Germany's Efforts to Reconcile After WWII." *John Hopkins Magazine* (Summer 2015). https://hub.jhu.edu/magazine/2015/summer/germany-japan-reconciliation/.

Sasaki, Chris. "Seeing Toronto Through a Lens of Indigenous Stories: Jon Johnson Brings 13,000 Years of History to Life." U of T News, January 20, 2019. https://www.utoronto.ca/news/seeing-toronto-through-lens-indigenous-stories-jon-johnson-brings-13000-years-history-life.

Stanton, Kim. "Reconciling Reconciliation: Differing Conceptions of the Supreme Court of Canada and the Canadian Truth and Reconciliation Commission." *Journal of Law and Social Policy* 26 (2017): 21–42. https://doi.org/10.60082/0829-3929.1254.

Starzyk, Katherine B., Katelin H.S. Neufeld, Renée M. El-Gabalawy, and Gregory D.B. Boese. "The Case for and Causes of Intraminority Solidarity in Support for Reparations: Evidence from Community and Student Samples in Canada." *Journal of Social and Political Psychology*, 7, no. 1 (2019): 620–50. https://doi.org/10.5964/jspp.v7i1.673.

United Nations Secretary-General. *The Rule of Law and Transitional Justice in Conflict and Post-Conflict Societies*. UN Security Council, 2004.

PART FOUR

Indigenous Relational Knowledges in Settler Contexts

nikāwiy to ôtānisa Narratives—Cree Mother to Daughter Stories

Calendar of Life, miyo-pimātisiwin (Good Life)

Evelyn Poitras and Marie Alma Poitras

Methodology

kiskinaw-kīsikwan—Teachings from the Moon Guide

KISKINAW-KĪSIKWAN IS THE TERM THAT NIKĀWIY (MY mother) learned from her mother; the translation is "teachings from the moon guide." Nikāwiy calls this "from a language that is from the old people," the language from my grandmother's grandparents' time—the late 1800s. She mentions that the language was "pretty pure then." She has noticed that terms for these teachings may differ in regions. According to nikāwiy, this understanding is directly from her mother, ôkāwiya *pīwapiskok-kahwīkit,*[1] Marie Cecile Quinney, who was born in 1908. "She was raised by old people all the time," nikāwiy mentions of her mother. Nikāwiy credits ôkāwiya for this knowledge that was taught to nikāwiy based on the life's teachings of ôkāwiya. This was a way of life that was being practised by both of her parents, including ôhtāwiya, her father's way of life based on hunting and trapping.

In my doctoral dissertation (Trent University), I tell the basic life story of nikāwiy. Each chapter of the thesis represents one of the thirteen moons that nikāwiy uses in her "Calendar of Life—miyo pimātisiwin" circle model. The circle and moons are organized by four seasons of spring, summer, fall, winter, and in the four directions. Spring, starting in the east, is her childhood, including a genealogy and story of her Cree grandparents from Kehewin Cree Nation and her Cree ancestors from Frog Lake First Nation, Alberta, Treaty 6. This includes her memories from St. Anthony's Indian Residential School on Onion Lake Reserve, her Cree First Nation situated on the provincial border between Alberta and Saskatchewan. Summer is a time of her young womanhood, moving to Peepeekisis, Saskatchewan, Treaty 4, where she is married to her partner and my father, the late George Poitras, and where they raise their six children. Fall is the memories of her late partner and of her late siblings. It is her own journey as a Cree language and elementary school teacher for many years until her retirement at the age of seventy-two. Winter is a time of storytelling for nikāwiy and her earliest memories from the winter round dance and ceremony. She achieved a Master's of Education at the age of seventy-four, and her ongoing focus of this program is her legacy of a Cree curriculum. Finally, the Eagle Moon tells of the nêhiyaw highest law of love.

pimātisiwin/Circle, mâwmoscikēwin/Ceremony

When I first used the circle as my research methodology, I started with ceremony and my personal prayer. My parents, who both attended the Indian residential school, did not teach their children ceremony as they raised us. The circle methodology starts from personal ceremony. As I followed my parents down this path, I was able to experience my own personal journey and meaning. My parents "came back" to ceremony when they were older with their own adult children.

My late father took a stand for treaty.[2] Dad and my uncle did what some other First Nations people were also doing, obtaining and selling cigarettes on-reserve without paying taxes or charging taxes on them on the basis that our reserve was our jurisdiction. It was at this time that it was also necessary for him to go to ceremony as he would learn and come to know how treaties are our laws. As he made this stand, we would see how our laws could be drawn in the Canadian law system, that our laws might be declared "unlawful" by these standards. We witnessed what our late father, along with his younger brother, my late uncle Jimmy, were subjected to in a conflict over taxation on reserve land. In 1994, they would be put on trial in the Court of Queen's Bench in Melville, Saskatchewan. Here, they refused to swear on the Bible and requested to make their oath on the ôspwākan, the ceremonial pipe, instead (which they were granted and did).

At the end of the trial, the judge ruled that they were *guilty*. He went on to read his ruling and also declared that they would be fined, but that there was no penalty, such as a jail sentence, if they did not actually pay the fine. Interestingly, the provincial government had *won* this case but immediately launched an appeal that they would later drop.[3] I remember being in that courtroom and looking at Dad at times—I would see how his eyes were almost closed—only later did I realize that he was praying. They had already sought their judgment in our lodges—they had nothing left to fear. My dad's faith was always dear to him, deeply meaningful. I saw this clearly in him that day. *paskwaw mostos kahpimotēht*, Walking Buffalo, nohtāwiy (dad)...this is the way he faced the storm that day. The buffalo will face the winter storm to break a trail for others to follow. tapwē (truly), we follow him in our storms today. *hiyhiy*.

How ceremony "came back" to us was each in our own way and time. We each decide whether we will take the "red road" or not. I know in my family that it has made all the difference in our lives, though we will always struggle and encounter the challenges in life that we all do. I recall in the step programs that we would say "higher power" to acknowledge whatever people wanted to—some were atheist, and we could not have prejudice for this. In many First Nation communities today, there are strong denominations of different religions and Christianity. When it comes to Indigenous Knowledge, much of this is actually based in *ceremony*. It is these very real and personal experiences that teach the sanctity of Creator's laws.

kiskinohtahiwēwina

Teachings (Reminders, Guidance): Sovereignty

The circle is the foundational model for the methodology of nikāwiy. It is based in ceremony. It is how prayers are said, acknowledging the "circle of life." Four directions are acknowledged in prayers, beginning with the east, going to the south, west, north. Ceremony is also spiritual law and Creator's law. When nikāwiy uses the circle, she is grounding herself in this framework. She also makes a rejection of the "box" that she says Western knowledge is. This rejection is also a foundation of sovereignty in the circle. This is where she deliberately places herself in ceremony.

The thirteen moons are the knowledge passed on to her from her mother, ôkāwiya. This is from her life experience and personal teachings. These are the memories and knowledge that she draws on for her development of a curriculum to teach nēhiyawēwin, the Cree language. Language is from the land, she will also say. It is from this land, no other land in the world. This is how we are grounded when we speak nēhiyawēwin. Again, this is sovereignty.[4]

Calendar of Life, miyo pimātisiwin

After my father passed away in 2005, I lived in the small town of Ituna, Saskatchewan, north of Peepeekisis. I recall a visit from nikāwiy one day as she came by to request my assistance to develop a diagram for her. She had already drawn out this diagram—a circle with quadrants in each direction. There were hand-drawn illustrations of animals, trees, and people. nikāwiy was an artist and loved to draw. This is the template I used to develop another circle with the computer and some basic program. I used clip art for the pictures. This was my first introduction to the calendar of nikāwiy. Years later, we developed this and other related "circles" in a presentation to illustrate the curriculum of nikāwiy.

As I adopted this calendar for my research methodology, I learned more about the meaning for each part. I learned about the moons, and now I pay attention to each of them. I have seen nikāwiy always observant about the changes in nature and seasons. Now I find myself beginning this seasonal observation too. It is easy to look up some of this knowledge on the Internet now. We can see the online pictures of turtles with the thirteen sections on their back, the thirteen moons. But before the Internet, there were her memories of ôkāwiya, her mother, saying what the moons were as this "living calendar." This was their way to tell time: this was their "knowing."

I find this interesting now, too, when there is a question of how prevalent the turtle is in the land of where nikāwiy was raised. Does the concept of thirteen moons necessarily come from the turtle? nikāwiy recalls her mother telling time this way, according to the months by the cycles of moons. nohkom, my grandmother, might have attended the Indian residential school for a short time in her younger life, but she never lost her

Cree language, and this was really her primary communication all of her life. I know this from all of my experiences with her: she could barely say anything in English, and my knowledge of Cree was the same. nikāwiy credits her mother for what Cree we did come to understand. It is true that we also had familiarity with the language as we heard this being spoken whenever nikāwiy was with her sister and brother, our auntie and uncle, who have been constants in our lives.

Thirteen Moons, Four Seasons

According to the methodology of nikāwiy for a Calendar of Life, pimātisiwin is used as a framework to illustrate her life story in chapters that follow the thirteen moons that are part of this calendar. In her Calendar of Life, the thirteen moons are in a circle with the four seasons in the four directions: spring, summer, fall, winter. The life story of nikāwiy, including her genealogy, is examined in this model through narrative, observation, collective memory, and interview to derive inherent teachings. In my discussion with Dr. Paula Sherman of Trent University, my supervisor, she also calls this "story weaving,"[5] as I am going back and forth in time from present day to past times in the life of nikāwiy and as I also draw my personal narrative into her life story through my own experience and interpretation as her ôtānsa, her daughter.

For this chapter and for brevity, I am presenting one moon for each season.

sākastēnohk miyoskamin (Spring)

The moons of sakastenohk miyoskamin (spring) and the youth of nikāwiy (my mother) follow with the Goose, Frog, and Leaf Budding Moons. For this chapter, I choose niski-pīsim, the Goose Moon.

niski-pīsim (Goose Moon)

The Goose Moon, niski-pīsim, tells of collectivity as well as leadership. The moons of miyoskamin (spring) start with the Goose Moon. This moon is about family, pēyakoskan, "one unit," and collectivity. It is also about extended family in an introduction to the genealogy of nikāwiy and her cāpanak (ancestors). Even as a young girl, nikāwiy would profoundly know a relationship with the land and these laws. She had an awareness that she was already an integral part of the family circle.

Duck Eggs

There is a story I recall nikāwiy and nikāwiys[6] telling me of how they would hunt for duck eggs in the spring. One time, they went out and found a slough where they went to hunt for their duck eggs. Even as girls, they had this responsibility and knowledge to go by themselves. They knew where to go and what to do. On this trip, though, nikāwiy was making her way through the slough carrying her eggs when she walked into an unseen dip. nikāwiy did not know how to swim so this was treacherous. She hung on to her precious eggs and managed to come out of the slough. The reality of life on the land was this real for them. Laws of the land were meant to be respected, or the consequences could be very real. As girls, they were already depended on to help feed their family.

I see nikāwiy as a young girl delicately carrying the eggs she found even as she stepped into a dip under the water in the slough. As this young girl, she was empowered with responsibility to help her family...to survive. I see her as a young mother carrying each of us protectively as her children even as she faced unseen dips in life that threatened to overwhelm her—she never lost her footing...would return always to her balance. I see her as notikwēw (old woman) and nohkom (grandmother), cāpan (great-grandmother), holding each generation in turn as protectively. nikāwiy is my land; she is my nitisiy (my belly button).

kiskinohtâhiwēwina

Teachings (Reminders, Guidance): Collectivity and Leadership

The collectivity of pēyôkaskan (family) is a threat to the notion of individualism that was at the heart of the 1969 Liberal government's proposed White Paper and the policy of assimilation that would bring us under a foreign law to say then that we were only a minority under domestic legislation. This is an affront to our international treaty with the Crown as *nation to nation*.[7] nikāwiy as a nēhiyaw iskwēw is a further threat to colonialism that is based on white patriarchy. These ideas of colonialism and events of Indian policy are called "historical" today, but this is a testament to their longevity and their entrenchment.

pēyakôskan, family, is also revealed in genealogy. Extended kinship and relationship to ancestors becomes very meaningful when there is an opportunity to make this discovery. The knowledge of nikāwiy was only of her grandparents until later in life. The connection she makes to her cāpanak (ancestors) is personal and strong. It gives support and direction. This was the knowledge that she was cut off from in the residential schools when she was taken from her family.

The Goose Moon, niski-pīsim, is also a definition of leadership. It is not who is "boss," okimāhkan, but rather the "one who leads," ēnikānīt. An Indian chief under the *Indian Act* colonial system is called okimākahnak, "pretend chief." Imposed elected systems and elected leadership are defined as "not real."

This is what I see in the sky now. I see our law of collectivity. For me, this breathes new and ongoing, continuing life into our laws and into our treaty.

sāwânohk nīpin (Summer)

The moons of sāwânohk nīpin (summer) and the start of her own family as a young wife and mother follow with the Egg Laying Moon, the Moulting Moon, and the Flying Up Moon. The summer moons start with Egg Laying, the time of nikāwiy as a young mother. The Moulting Moon is the loss of feathers so that new ones may grow again. Finally, the Flying Up Moon is leaving the nest and the strength to find her own place in the world. For this chapter, I choose the Moulting Moon.

paskowi-pīsim (Moulting Moon)

Old feathers make way for new feathers. This has been the personal growth of nikāwiy and lifelong learning in miskāsowin, *the search for herself.* I also related this to Abraham Maslow's Hierarchy of Needs and self-actualization. I would learn that this was an example of colonial appropriation as Maslow never credited his work as inspired by the Blackfoot[8] concept and knowledge. In her lifelong learning, a finding is also how education is ongoing colonial violence.

kiskinohtâhiwēwina

Teachings (Reminders, Guidance): miskāsowin, Finding One's Self.

miskāsowin is a Cree concept that is identified by Harold Cardinal and Walter Hildebrandt in *Treaty Elders of Saskatchewan* (2000). It was identified by a group of Elders that they consulted in the development of this book as a term that was a guiding principle for Cree people.

I recall that this was one of several terms that we used from this text for a class on Teaching Treaties in the Classroom at the University of Regina.

I acknowledge Drs. Angelina Weenie and Audrey Amondt, of First Nations University of Canada and the University of Regina, respectively, who developed a course curriculum for this class.

In my own experience and observation, I have witnessed nikāwiy on her miskāsowin journey in her life. This has been in her education but also in all of her growth. This has been her lifelong learning and healing.

Personal leadership is about healing. Due to the event of colonization, and as this is an ongoing onslaught and experience, *healing* becomes a personal responsibility. Leadership starts at a personal level, and for Indigenous Peoples who have been subjected to colonization, healing is a fundamental requisite. Otherwise, the disruption and pain of colonization is carried in generations and in families, extended families, communities, nations. Part of healing is calling out the spectre of colonization that casts itself over our Indigenous generations and is evident in its carnage in personal lives. Leadership is standing up to this to rebuke and reclaim. As my lifelong teachers, these have been the personal examples that I have witnessed in my parents' lives.

nikapēhanohk takwākin (Fall)

The moons of nikapēhanohk takwākin (fall) and the maturity of nikāwiy (my mother) as a grandmother follow with the Autumn, Rutting, Migrating, and Frost Moons. For this chapter, I choose the Frost Moon.

iyīkopīwi-pīsim (Frost Moon)

I sit in the home of nikāwiy at her dining room table. There is a peace and comfort here like no other. This is the small home that she shared with my late father until he died. For the year following his death, nikāwiy could not bear to be here without him so she rented a house in a nearby village. In that year she also forgot to register her driver's licence and only realized this the following year when she went to renew it. These were two examples of the particular ways that nikāwiy experienced the grief of losing her partner. They had been married forty-three years when Dad passed away on November 7, 2005. We had celebrated the birthday of nikāwiy only the previous week. Dad ate Chinese food with us and had a piece of cake. nikāwiy and I spent the last night of his life with Dad in the Fort Qu'Appelle All Nations' Healing Hospital. Family were called early the next morning, and nohtāwiy, our father, left on his spirit journey in the first light of the morning. It was always his favourite time of day. As I sit at the dining room table, I am surrounded by the presence and memories of Dad.

As the seasons come full-circle, the Frost Moon is the time for the season of nikāwiy as grandmother and great-grandmother, capan. It was in the Frost Moon that nikāwiy lost her partner in 2005. It is also the month of her birth and the time she was born just as the war ended in 1945. Where were you born, nikāwiy? "… on the land," she answers. In 2025, nikāwiy turned eighty.

nohkom (my grandmother) had thirteen children and one adopted son who was actually her nephew, John Watchmaker of Kehewin, Alberta. She would give birth to all of her children at home with the exception of her last-born son, Jimmy, who would be born in a hospital. nikāwiy was born on November 1, 1945. It is possible she was born on the land at that time of year as they lived in tents as much as they could, but also possible that she was born at home in a log house.

The snow is on the ground where my father's grave was dug by hand by some of the men of the McNab family, who lived down the road from us. They were good friends of my brother, Brian, and helped out of respect for our family and for Dad. It would have been easier and is more common now just to use a backhoe to dig and cover graves. I know Dad would have been truly honoured by all of these last respects and homage. I try to remember if the snow was falling then. I see people moving by the grave while letting the dirt from their hands fall on Dad's coffin in the frozen ground. I sense movement in this memory. It is a time of transition and transformation for my mother from wife to widow. nohtāwiy, my father, paskwaw-mostos-kahpimohtēt, Walking Buffalo, goes on ahead to make the trail for us in winter. We follow his footsteps in the storms to come.

Legacy

The "Calendar of Life—miyo pimātisiwin" of nikāwiy is a circle illustration and model that she has developed to teach Cree. After so many years of teaching Cree without any curriculum, nikāwiy has always had to develop her own teaching materials. The Calendar of Life of nikāwiy becomes the curriculum and teachings that are her legacy now. She is mindful about this.

When I apply the "Calendar of Life—miyo pimātisiwin" to my methodology now, it becomes a very personal framework. As nikāwiy says of her teaching, "I put myself in the circle, we are all at the centre of the circle in our lives—I am not in a box." She, more or less, rejects the "box" as Western knowledge. The *boxes* were the classrooms in the residential schools. The *circle* is, in this way, an act of sovereignty.

kiskinohtâhiwēwina

Teachings (Reminders, Guidance):
nohkom (Grandmother), cāhpan (Great-Grandmother)

It is a time of coming full circle. nikāwiy becomes a kohkum (grandmother) and a cāhpan (great-grandmother). She enjoys the bounty of her growing family generations alone when she loses her partner. She becomes mindful of her own legacy now, and she continues her work in education. nikāwiy maintains a vital place at the centre of her family.

The full moon shines in a great circle of moonlight. They say it is very feminine, and they also say she is our grandmother. I remember when one of my nieces, who has another grandmother named Mona, would say, as a young girl, "there is kohkom Moona" when she saw the full moon and make us laugh. The moon controls the ocean tides. It pulls at the water of women. Now I think they are such sacred grandmothers. Each face tells their own time. Their narrative now is incredible to me.

pipon (Winter)

As a kētēh-aya, old one, memories of her childhood and family before the Indian residential schools are told in chapters that include the moons of pipon (winter)—Frost Exploding, Great, and Eagle. For this chapter, I choose the Frost Exploding Moon.

pahwācâkinâsīsis-pīsim (Frost Exploding Moon)

The winter moon of Frost Exploding is the time for the ceremony of the Round Dance and sacrosanct childhood memories of nikāwiy where she was lifted up in the arms of her father into the shelter of the hall or into the horse-drawn wagon to return home on starry winter nights with horse bells ringing. I smell the woodfire, I hear the drums and songs, and I see the dance. I hear the ladies' wrap-around moccasins sliding on the wooden floors in time to the drums. I see children quietly sitting on the floor along the wall with their parents watching and listening. I see the brilliant night skies, I hear the sound of the horse bells, the Cree language, nēhiyawēwin, and the laughter. I see children sleeping...always by the side of their parents, at the heart of their families and the centre of this circle.

In my experience, nikāwiy has generally related to me some of her first memories as part of her identity as a daughter and as a sister. To be truthful, in specific instances these were not easy memories for nikāwiy to recall. She was born into particular responsibility as both a younger and older sister. Childhood is both idyllic and also heavily laden with important responsibilities. There was much discipline and much demand. The child at the centre of the circle was integral but was also a great support and foundation for the family structure overall. This would become more evident in the later experience of the children leaving to attend the Indian residential schools. It was the labour of the children in these schools that would now be utilized to hold up these colonial institutions rather than contribute to their own families and kinship development.

kiskinohtâhiwēwina

Teachings (Reminders, Guidance):
ahkamēyimok (Persevere), ēsīspisīyan (to the Limit of Ability)
I think of despair when I think of a nēhiyaw-iskwēw or all the many Indigenous women who face challenges in their life. I feel I have not really known difficulty—as nikāwiy and nohkom, my mother and grandmother came to know. Though, I am sure I have faced my own particular challenges and that I continue to. I am here because they carried me here, each in their own ways and as I adopted what I was able to from their strength and knowing as my own. Every day of their lives, I believe they had faith and fortitude. They carried on.

I remember being a young girl by my granny's side and there were the times I would ask her to sing. I could feel the great power of her voice travelling through her body and almost vibrating next to my own body. There is a beautiful full moon in the winter night, and we are travelling through the valley in a car with others. I know nikāwiy is here too. nohkom honours me to oblige my request, and she sings her nēhiyaw (Cree) song. I am mesmerized: my young spirit is fed for all of my life.

kohkom-tipiskaw-pīsim (grandmother-moon)—it is the Frost Exploding Moon in December when I write this—shines bright in my memory. Years later, I would notice the age in my granny's voice, and it would surprise me that her breath had become weaker. I once knew how great and strong her voice could be: okīcitaw-iskwēw, she was my sacred woman leader.

The times I falter today remind me of my great weakness and especially how I pale in comparison to nikāwiy and to nohkom. These are the times I remember where I come from and I call on them, once again, to carry me through. I have been through nothing compared to what they survived. ēsīspisīyan, to the best of my ability, is also vital that I "let go" to maintain balance. It is self-love and self-respect. This was a great teaching from nohkom, my grandmother, for otānisa (her daughter), nikāwiy (my mother).

I have a memory of my granny lying in bed at night and praying. I can barely see that she is holding her hand up to the sky and saying her heartfelt words. When she would pray, she would speak from her heart, and I felt this though I could not understand her Cree words. In other ways, I understood her clearly. Sometimes she might cry. I knew she cried because she loved our Creator so much. I remind myself that I am still in her prayers. I know nikāwiy prays the same.

Even when unexpected things come as they do in life, and as disruptive as colonialism continues to be, I feel a responsibility to never give up. ēsīspisīyan, to the best of my human ability, is a balance with ahkâmēyimok, not to give up! Both of these are the teachings that are the gifts of nikāwiy ēkwa nohkom (my mother and grandmother), the nēhiyaw-iskwēwak (Cree women) who teach me to be a nēhiyaw-iskwēw (Cree woman).

ēkosi. It Is Finished.

I do not know what concept of treaty nohkom (my grandmother) had. I know that nikāwiy would speak of the treaties as "the sacred promises." Our nēhiyaw nistohtamōwin (understanding) is "spirit and intent," covenants that are spiritual and living. kētēh-ayak (Elders) warnings are not to go by the literal interpretation as "that is not to our favour." The patriarchal lens refused to see nēhiyaw-iskwēwak (Cree women) at the time of the treaty negotiations. What some say now is that the treaties were, therefore, negotiated without the true owners, the nēhiyaw-iskwēwak.

I know that some things in our history were silenced with the hanging of the eight Cree men in North Battleford, Saskatchewan. nēhiyaw-nāpēwak (Cree men), in particular, may have been silenced this way. The Indian residential school children who were purposely brought to witness this event and who were, no doubt, traumatized, would also likely be silenced this way. But there would be time when the sacred fires would be lit and the people would travel on the land and occupy all of their territories this way to sit with each other for these talks once again. They would affirm who they always were and who they continued to be.

Like nohkom, they might lift their hands to the sky and cry to the Creator. This was the love she knew for the Creator. This was the law of nohkom (my grandmother). This is Creator's law. This is the teaching of the Eagle Moon and nēhiyawak's (the Cree people's) highest law of love. This is treaty, our ancestors' words and promises.

nikāwiy waits faithfully for the north wind to end the winter. She waits faithfully to hear the frogs sing before she believes it is spring. She was born on the land. She is my land. ēkosi.

Notes

1 My grandmother's Cree name is deliberately not translated out of respect.

2 In this court case, *R. v. Poitras*, the resulting case law explains, "The accused argued that as a result of ancient treaties entered into by their ancestors with the British Crown, they were not subject to the jurisdiction of the court, nor to Canadian tax laws." Notably, the term *ancient* is not used by George Poitras in his own words from this case: "I guess I am of the same view as Jim, that as Indian people, we came up (inaudible word) honour and respect your courts. Now having done that, we now ask the Court to honour and respect the basis and the (inaudible word) that we have set up here as an Indian nation, therefore, we also have to exercise those things that come under nationhood status, one of exercising our sovereignty, exercising our jurisdiction within our own territory, and we must go back and start learning more about what has happened in the past and why were those Treaties made and what were the spirit and intent of those Treaties. Were they to be interpreted by the courts of Canada? That was not who we made Treaties with." *R. v. Poitras (J.L.)* (1993) 121 Sask.R. 95 (QB).

3 *R. v. Poitras (J.L.)* (1994), 121 Sask.R. 95 (QB), 6.

4 In our nation, we understand sovereignty as our own authority and nationhood. In the Numbered Treaties, the relationship was nation to nation with the Crown. The Crown recognized the authority and sovereignty of the Indian nations that were on this land and the need to acquire permission to enter and settle on these territories. Tidridge, *The Queen at the Council Fire.*

5 Hemispheric Institute, "Spiderwoman Theatre."

6 nikāwiy means "my mother." nikāwiys is a diminutive form of nikāwiy and means "my little mother." This is what I would call my aunt: my little mother.

7 "The Proclamation Line of 1763 was a British-produced boundary marked in the Appalachian Mountains at the Eastern Continental Divide. Decreed on October 7, 1763, the Proclamation Line prohibited Anglo-American colonists from settling on lands acquired from the French following the French and Indian War." George Washington Library at Mount Vernon, "The Proclamation Line of 1763."

"The Dominion of Canada is not a party to any treaties. The permissions that the nations granted in treaties are personally held by now King Charles III. Canada did not negotiate treaties. All negotiators were for the king/queen. The fact that they may have lived in the Dominion of Canada at the time of their appointments did not make that Canada negotiating. At all times, it was the king or queen negotiating through them. There wasn't even such a thing as Canadian citizenship back then.... As the result of self-government passing in stages to the Dominion of Canada, the federal government became responsible for the Crown's obligations to the nations. The King retains all power to enter into treaties. At first observers were allowed from the Dominion of Canada to today where officials of the Dominion of Canada do the negotiations but only the King can enter into treaties." Janice Switlo, email communication, August 18, 2023.

"Canadian citizenship, as a status separate from British nationality, was created by the Canadian Citizenship Act of 1946, which came into effect on 1 January 1947. (Although passed in 1946, it is often referred to as the '1947 Citizenship Act' because it came into force in 1947.)" Wikipedia, "Canadian Citizenship Act, 1946."

8 The traditional territory of the Blackfoot Confederacy has been described as roughly the southern half of Alberta and Saskatchewan and the northern portion of Montana. In the west, the confederacy was bounded by the Rocky Mountains, and its eastern limits stretched past the Great Sand Hills of eastern Saskatchewan. Their hunting area included the rich bison ranges of southern Alberta and northern Montana. In the 2016 census, 22,490 people identified as having Blackfoot ancestry. Dempsey, "Niitsitapi (Blackfoot)."

Resources

Dempsey, Hugh A. "Niitsitapi (Blackfoot)." *Canadian Encyclopedia*. Historica Canada. Article published December 6, 2010; last edited April 17, 2025. https://www.thecanadianencyclopedia.ca/en/article/blackfoot-nation.

George Washington Library at Mount Vernon. "The Proclamation Line of 1763." In *The Digital Encyclopedia of George Washington*, edited by Zoe Horecny and Alexandra Montgomery. https://www.mountvernon.org/library/digitalhistory/digital-encyclopedia/article/proclamation-line-of-1763/.

Hemispheric Institute. "Spiderwoman Theatre." https://hemisphericinstitute.org/en/hidvl-collections/itemlist/category/476-spiderwoman-theater.html.

R. v. Poitras (J.L.) (1994), 121 Sask.R. 95 (QB). https://ca.vlex.com/vid/r-v-poitras-j-681257817.

Tidridge, Nathan. *The Queen at the Council Fire: The Treaty of Niagara, Reconciliation, and the Dignified Crown in Canada*. Dundurn Press, 2015.
Wikipedia. "Canadian Citizenship Act, 1946." https://en.wikipedia.org/wiki/Canadian_Citizenship_Act,_1946.

tâpwîwin ikwa wâkôwîcihiwîwin—Truth and Reconciliation

Solomon Ratt

tâpwîwin:
    awâsisak kî-sipwîhtahâwak;
tâpwîwin:
    onîkihikomâwak kî-maskamâwak otawâsimisiwâwa;
tâpwîwin:
    âtiht awâsisak namwâc kî-ohci-kîwêwak;
tâpwîwin:
    awâsisak kî-nanôcihâwak ispî kâ-kî-pîkiskwîcik opîkiskwîwiniwâwa;
tâpwîwin:
    âtiht awâsisak kî-otihtinâwak;
tâpwîwin:
    âtiht awâsisak kî-nipahâwak;
tâpwîwin:
    awâsisak kî-wanihtâwak opîkiskwîwiniwâwa;
tâpwîwin:
    awâsisak kî-wanihtâwak otisîhcikîwiniwâwa;

tâpwîwin: namwâc wâkôwîcihiwîwin ta-kî-ispayin pâtimâ
    naskwîwasihtâtwâwi ayamihikimâwak mîna okimâwak
    okimânâhk ohci ôho tâpwîwina.

ᑖᐿᐏᐣ ᐃᒀ ᐙᑰᐑᒋᐦᐃᐑᐏᐣ—Truth and Reconciliation

ᑖᐿᐏᐣ:
ᐊᐙᓯᓴᐠ ᑮ ᓯᐿᐦᑕᐦᐙᐗᐠ;
ᑖᐿᐏᐣ:
ᐅᓃᑭᐦᐃᑯᒫᐗᐠ ᑮ ᒪᐢᑲᒫᐗᐠ ᐅᑕᐙᓯᒥᓯᐙᐗ;
ᑖᐿᐏᐣ:
ᐋᑎᐦᐟ ᐊᐙᓯᓴᐠ ᓇᒹᐨ ᑮ ᐅᐦᒋ ᑮᐍᐗᐠ;
ᑖᐿᐏᐣ:
ᐊᐙᓯᓴᐠ ᑮ ᓇᓅᒋᐦᐙᐗᐠ ᐃᐢᐲ ᑳ ᑮ ᐲᑭᐢᑺᒋᐠ ᐅᐲᑭᐢᑺᐏᓂᐙᐗ;
ᑖᐿᐏᐣ:
ᐋᑎᐦᐟ ᐊᐙᓯᓴᐠ ᑮ ᐅᑎᐦᑎᓈᐗᐠ;
ᑖᐿᐏᐣ:
ᐋᑎᐦᐟ ᐊᐙᓯᓴᐠ ᑮ ᓂᐸᐦᐙᐗᐠ;
ᑖᐿᐏᐣ:
ᐊᐙᓯᓴᐠ ᑮ ᐗᓂᐦᑖᐗᐠ ᐅᐲᑭᐢᑺᐏᓂᐙᐗ;
ᑖᐿᐏᐣ:
ᐊᐙᓯᓴᐠ ᑮ ᐗᓂᐦᑖᐗᐠ ᐅᑎᓲᐦᒋᑮᐏᓂᐙᐗ;

ᑖᐿᐏᐣ: ᓇᒹᐨ ᐙᑰᐑᒋᐦᐃᐑᐏᐣ ᑕ ᑮ ᐃᐢᐸᔮᐣ ᐹᑎᒫ ᓇᐢᑺᐗᓯᐦᑖᑢᐏ
ᐊᔭᒥᐦᐃᑭᒫᐗᐠ ᒦᓇ ᐅᑭᒫᐗᐠ ᐅᑭᒫᓈ᙮ ᐅᐦᒋ ᐆᐦᐅ ᑖᐿᐏᓇ᙮

Truth and Reconciliation

Truth:
    Children were taken away;
Truth:
    Parents had their children taken away from them;
Truth:
    Some children never went home;
Truth:
    Children were punished when they spoke their languages;
Truth:
    Some children were raped;
Truth:
    Some children were killed;
Truth:
    Children lost their languages;
Truth:
    Children lost their cultures;

Truth: reconciliation will not happen until the churches and
    government are accountable to these truths.

Where Is the Love?

Solomon Ratt

tâniwî sâkihiwîwin?
cîst! mâmitonîthihta ôho:

1) î-tipiskâk kîkiwâhk:
kipônînâwâw kotawânâpiskos;
kisaskahînâwâw wâsiskocînikanis;
kitanâskânâwâw ikwa kitakwanahonâwâw
opîwayakohp ohci;
mâci-âcathôhkîw kikâwiy.
ôhôw matwî-kitow wathawîtimihk;
kotawânâpisk matwîhkotîw;
wâsiskocînikanis cikâstîpathiw;
kikâwiy papiyahtak âcathôhkîw.
kitati-nipân.

2) ê-tipiskâk ayamihâwi-kiskinwahamâtowikamikohk:
kinîpikâpawinâwâw kita-otinamâsoyêk piskitis (dog biscuit);
kitayamihânâwâw;
kikawisimonâwâw;
âstawêhikâtêw.
kinwêsk kikanawâpahtên cikâstêsiniwina tahtwâw sêhkêpayîs
    kâ-pimakocihk wayawîtimihk.
piyisk kinipân.

ᑖᓂᐐ ᓵᑭᐦᐃᐐᐎᐣ?
ᒌᐢᐟ! ᒫᒥᑐᓃᔩᐦᑕ ᐆᐦᐅ:

1) ᐄ ᑎᐱᐢᑳᐠ ᑮᑭᐚᕽ:
ᑭᐴᓃᓈᐚᐤ ᑯᑕᐚᓈᐱᐢᑯᐢ;
ᑭᓴᐢᑲᐦᐄᓈᐚᐤ ᐚᓴᐢᑯᒌᓂᑲᓂᐢ;
ᑭᑕᓈᐢᑳᓈᐚᐤ ᐃᑿ ᑭᑕᑿᓇᐦᐅᓈᐚᐤ
ᐅᐲᐘᔭᑯ‴ ᐅᐦᒋ;
ᒫᒋ ᐋᒐᔩᐦᑮᐤ ᑭᑳᐎᐩ᙮
ᐆᐦᐆᐤ ᒪᑗ ᑭᑐᐤ ᐘᔭᐐᑎᒥᕽ;
ᑯᑕᐚᓈᐱᐢᐠ ᒪᑗᐦᑯᑏᐤ;
ᐚᓴᐢᑯᒌᓂᑲᓂᐢ ᒋᑳᐢᑏᐸᔩᐤ;
ᑭᑳᐎᐩ ᐸᐱᔭᐦᑕᐠ ᐋᒐᔩᐦᑮᐤ᙮
ᑭᑕᑎ ᓂᐹᐣ᙮

2) ᐁ ᑎᐱᐢᑳᐠ ᐊᔭᒥᐦᐋᐎ ᑭᐢᑭᓌᐦᐊᒫᑐᐎᑲᒥᑯᕽ:
ᑭᓃᐱᑳᐸᐎᓈᐚᐤ ᑭᑕ ᐅᑎᓇᒫᒋᔭᐠ ᐱᐢᑭᑎᐢ (dog biscuit);
ᑭᑕᔭᒥᐦᐋᓈᐚᐤ;
ᑭᑲᐎᓯᒧᓈᐚᐤ;
ᐋᐢᑕᐍᐦᐃᑳᑌᐤ᙮
ᑭᓀᐧᐢᐠ ᑭᑲᓇᐚᐸᐦᑌᐣ ᒋᑳᐢᑌᓯᓂᐎᓇ ᑕᐦᑤᐤ ᓴᐦᑫᐸᔩᐣ ᑳ ᐱᒪᑯᒋᕽ ᐘᔭᐐᑎᒥᕽ᙮
ᐱᔩᐢᐠ ᑭᓂᐹᐣ᙮

Where is the love?
Listen! Think on these:

1) it is night at your home:
you put wood into the stove;
you light the candle;
you lay out the blanket and cover yourselves with a down quilt;
your mother starts telling stories.
outside an owl hoots;
the fire in the stove crackles;
candle casts shadows;
softly your mother tells stories.
you begin to sleep.

2) it is night at the residential school:
you line up to choose a biscuit, dog biscuit, for yourself;
you say your prayers;
you lay down to sleep;
lights are turned off.
for a long time you watch the shadows every time a car drives by
 outside.
eventually you sleep.

Rights and Responsibilities

Indigenous Realities, Indigenous Priorities

Joyce Green

THIS CHAPTER IS CONCERNED WITH THE ONGOING political implications and consequences for Indigenous Peoples of the colonial encounter with Project Canada. I frame this within the colonial condition in Canada and my own territory, ʔamakʔis Ktunaxa. I do this relationally, to move our thinking beyond the echo chamber of Canadian political science, where the state and its fundamentally racist institutions and mythologies are definitive of what we study. I do this to foreground Indigenous resurgence, uncaptured by the conceptual frames of the settler state, such as federalism, constitutionalism, citizenship, the rule of settler law, reconciliation, democracy and diversity, self-government and treaty-making, and, above all, the primacy of capitalist economic relations. Instead, I speak to the ongoing political implications and consequences for Indigenous Peoples of the colonial encounter with Project Canada. I consider the conceptual frameworks of rights and of responsibilities and how they can be deployed to object to and reject contemporary colonial logics and priorities. Finally, I offer some thoughts on the current discourse of reconciliation.

Canadian constitutional rights frameworks and reconciliation impulses are still utterly contained by the logic of colonial triumphalism. To the extent that they engage Indigenous Peoples and their rights, they do so in order to define and contain them within the assumed uncontestable and pre-eminent sovereignty of the settler state. Constitutional rights are not identical to nor as robust as fundamental human rights and fundamental Indigenous rights that set the framework in international law for state behaviour and for Indigenous rights claims; moreover, their anemic formulation in the Constitution has not automatically led to state recognition and implementation of them. Where the state has recognized Indigenous rights, it fails to implement them completely, enthusiastically, or sometimes at all.

Indigenous rights are often not recognized or treated respectfully by the state or by its settler population, which frequently expresses resentment of Indigenous rights that constrain settler entitlements, privileges, or priorities (the resistance of white fishers to Mi'kmaq fishers subsequent to the Marshall decision is an example of this[1]).

Indigenous perspectives on rights are less absolutist, more contextual, and more relational and reciprocal than those of Canada's settler societies. Moreover, in addition to the oppressive history, cultures, and practices of colonialism, it is the maintenance of relationships that draws the attention of much Indigenous thinking. For these scholars, the conceptual framework of personal and collective responsibilities is more compelling than rights discourse. Relationships are accompanied by responsibilities, requiring we enact appropriate behaviour. Those relationships, responsibilities, and behaviours are frequently laid out in foundational myths. Our enactments of those responsibilities and behaviours recreate the practices that define our nations and their responsibilities. They express Indigenous laws.[2]

Indigenous insistence on being in relationship in culturally appropriate ways is itself a rejection of colonialism and an affirmation of our intentions to live authentically into the future. In order to exercise the responsibilities that reconstruct and animate Indigenous cultural, legal, and political orders, the preconditions for those responsibilities are a foundational requirement for Indigenous human rights. One cannot exercise relational responsibilities, land-based practices, cultural practices, and so on if the conditions for them have been erased, if the places and territories are circumscribed so as to eliminate or limit Indigenous jurisdictions and activities, and if the relevant animals and other creatures are extirpated or extinct. If the law of the settler state prohibits them. If there is no water to protect. If the land itself is captured as "Crown" land and "private" property, thus excluding Indigenous Peoples and our activities. Thus, Indigenous rights are dependent for their implementation on a political and social order that is largely hostile to them.

Indigenous rights, like all human rights, are abstract until they are violated.[3] Yet, Indigenous rights are invoked against the very state that must uphold them and require an anti-colonial rights theory in order to attain state political and legislative implementation. Such a theoretical framework must indicate how rights may be animated in ways that are liberatory rather than assimilative, in the context of relationships that are de facto oppressive, but which have potential to be transformed into something more positive. There can be no robust theory of Indigenous rights that fails to challenge the legitimacy of the state and to delve into resolutions of the contradictions created by the usurpation of Indigenous title and the de facto existence of settler society.

Colonialism

Colonization has been deployed around the world in the service of imperialism. Its various iterations contain certain common assumptions but deploy distinct methodologies shaped by politics, economics, religions, and cultural frameworks. Colonization on Turtle Island has a particular set of fingerprints, and liberation will have particular characteristics as well. After all, human beings struggle against oppression in specific contexts.

Given the Westphalian state order and the structure of the United Nations, colonialism is largely tolerated and ignored by the major players in the international community and in international law. Many states continue to be directly implicated in colonialism, its primary motivations of territorial and resource theft, and its geopolitical advantage. The international order itself amounts to a thieves' compact that assumes the sovereignty and integrity of states, not of peoples involuntarily supplanted by states. (The Palestine problematic is the most prominent example of this phenomenon at present.)

At its core, colonialism is about profit acquired by stealing someone else's land and resources while denying the sovereignty and humanity of those oppressed. It is legitimated by racism, and by belief in the inferiority of those who are being replaced, who "need" to be replaced. The process and the belief system are bureaucratized into public policy, enforced and administered in the name of all citizens, on behalf of governments that continue to deny our rights. The system is distilled into the dominant culture. It is reproduced in the canon of advanced education, where it produces a comfortable racism infused by invisible privileges held by settlers[4] at the expense of Indigenous Peoples. It also reproduces the structures and institutions in which racism is embedded, enacted, and transmitted, and in which we are all enmeshed.

The facts of Indigenous history and life are invisible to most, as is the privilege settler Canadians enjoy because of colonialism and racism. As chair of the Truth and Reconciliation Commission Murray Sinclair said, "the public school system is teaching white supremacy."[5] So, too, are universities, because universities sanction elite knowledge and train successive cohorts of experts who know little or nothing about colonialism.[6] Thus, generations of settler Canadians have been denied information, analysis, and opportunity to turn away from white and settler privilege and towards justice for Indigenous Peoples.

Colonialism is always oppressive, always motivated by the intention to take someone else's land, resources, and political capacity—their sovereignty. Indigenous sovereignty is a capacious sovereignty, not limited to the Westphalian notion of authority in international relations and with respect to governance within a boundary, but including a primary jurisdiction over and relationships to lands, waters, and other creatures; the political and cultural capacity to define and execute those relationships; and the resources of those lands. Where the colonial initiative is transformed into a settler state, the state's legal supremacy is constructed in law and mythology and dignified with recognition as "H"istory or political philosophy. These studies, these accounts, justify the emergence of the settler state and the righteousness of its practices and aspirations.

Canada is a settler state, intended to be a very white one.[7] It sanitizes its genocidal history and contemporary oppression of Indigenous Peoples with myths about creating something where there was nothing; about brave white male Mounties in red serge, and plucky white settlers breaking ground to bring agriculture and industrial activity for the benefit of white citizens; about rebellions put down, and national policies that led to "Confederation." Every stitch of this mythology is premised on Indigenous containment, dispossession, and political annihilation.[8]

Canadian politics, scholarship, and cultures seldom acknowledged Indigenous Peoples, except when the state unleashed army or police force on them, disciplined them with colonial laws through colonial courts, or, more recently, when it found itself under public censure for its human rights abuses and genocidal behaviour.[9]

The ongoing political implications and consequences for Indigenous Peoples of the colonial encounter with Project Canada are still utterly contained by the logic of colonial triumphalism. This includes many festivals across the country, as well as Canada Day—self-congratulatory celebrations of that which is mythologized, even when token stereotypical Indian inclusion exists.

These myths and untruths erase the reality of Indigenous encounters with colonial and settler state power; with the loss of land and resources; with the loss of languages and cultures; with the loss of children and Elders; with the loss of ourselves.[10] The stories Indigenous Peoples tell and the values we celebrate are resurgence, resistance, our histories, relationships, and territorial sovereignty. Indigenous reality is far more than only oppression and loss. And no amount of chatter about reconciliation can erase the reality of the losses colonialism in Canada has imposed on Indigenous Peoples, nor can it compensate for them.

Canada's political economy is underwritten by Indigenous dispossession, enforced by the state even when treaties were signed and negotiations held.[11] In the experience of my Ktunaxa ancestors, dispossession and occupation were enforced through processes not worthy of the term "negotiation," and which included the threat of military and police force for their execution.[12]

The oppression of Indigenous Peoples in all their diversity was conducted through the singular policy of dispossession and containment and by genocidal practices of cultural, linguistic, and political repression by the state and its agents.[13] All of this was sustained by racist assumptions viewing Indigenous Peoples as deficient and in need of close supervision until they assumed an assimilated form consistent with citizenship in the state. Thus, settlers could feel good about occupying Indigenous lands and never feel badly about Indigenous repression and genocide—which was, according to many, inevitable for progress and ultimately beneficial for the culturally eviscerated and landless Indigenous Peoples across Turtle Island (the name given by many Indigenous Peoples to North America).

The army and the police have been the strong arm of the Canadian state, supporting the political and bureaucratic classes that designed the genocidal policies. For those recruited as "settlers," the entire apparatus of the state is designed for them. They are the preferred citizens, those intended to populate and replicate the social, political, and economic institutions of the state (though not all in the same way). This is what we call "privilege."

The colonial state chose its citizens, preferring white northern European people, particularly from the British Isles, and rejecting racialized others.[14] It was an explicitly racist process intended to produce a white Canada, and the fingerprints of that racism can be read in the historical record and seen in contemporary political culture and in the everyday racism of many Canadians.[15]

Far from being a vestigial consequence of a historical event, colonialism is systemically embedded in the Canadian state and reproduces itself in emerging contemporary circumstances, such as state-enforced appropriation of Indigenous lands for ski hills and golf courses, logging, mining, and hydroelectric and petrochemical infrastructure, without the consent of Indigenous Peoples. Its continuous effects frame the political context of all of us on this part of Turtle Island. When I frame it thusly, I am inviting your attention onto our relational context and onto our specific locations of privilege, dominance, subordination, and responsibility. I am implicating political and scholarly discourse in the framing of colonialism as inevitable, as progress, as democratic, and as benevolent.

Thus, it is time for a new discourse, one that is rigorously critical of the colonial process and of the settler state that implements it while airbrushing its logics out of accounts of political decisions and history.[16] Colonialism operates via the policing, carceral, social-work and health-care systems, the corporate elite so well supported by Canadian public governments with Indigenous lands and resources, and the "whole of government" assault on Indigenous lands that continues today.

Some Canadians dismiss the claim that Canada has practised genocide. They are wrong. Genocide is defined in Article II of the 1948 Convention on the Prevention and Punishment of the Crime of Genocide,[17] a component of international law to which Canada is signatory.[18] Many Canadian policies directed at Indigenous Peoples fit its definition. Moreover, we have official recognition, through the unanimous consent of the House of Commons in October 2022, of Canadian genocide against Indigenous Peoples.[19] Genocide deniers have no ground left to stand on.

There was a time when I thought that the state could accommodate Indigenous liberation through self-government formulas, through democratic engagement, through land claims and treaties, "self-government," and a robust inclusive citizenship regime. I no longer think that. These things simply legitimate colonial occupation of our territories, the violation of our relationships with our territories and the beings on it, and the denial of the processes of genocide that have been enacted upon Indigenous Peoples since contact and into the present. Moreover, "negotiations" with the state and its corporate clients have been deeply problematic, fraught by the power imbalances and the coercion inherent in the will of the state and corporations to "get to yes" at all costs. Indigenous consent is a foregone conclusion by governments and corporations, despite the "free, prior and informed" nature of Indigenous consent required by the largely unimplemented United Nations Declaration on the Rights of Indigenous Peoples.

Canada wants Indigenous land and resources. It remains willing to annihilate Indigenous Peoples, cultures, and relationships to get these things. In a democratic order, that renders all citizens complicit with these objectives and methods.

I imagine liberation from this.

Rejection, Recovery, Reconstruction, Resurgence

Indigenous resurgence is both a movement and an objective, the theorization of which has moved into scholarly literature.[20] Resurgence arises from "political strategies and cultural practices that are grounded in Indigenous visions of freedom and autonomy";[21] it encompasses Indigenous self-determination apart from "state structures and paradigms" in the context of traditional Indigenous territories and political practices, including ecological relationships and the recovery of Indigenous languages.[22] It involves turning away from the settler state and towards Indigenous conceptions, aspirations, and other "prefigurative practices"—in short, by centring Indigenous considerations and ignoring political initiatives of the settler state.[23] It "calls on us to be attentive to how power structures and determines which narratives, modes of understanding our world and the web of relationships in operation, are given primacy."[24]

Resurgence is intended to produce radical transformation from the colonized condition of Indigenous nations. Its characteristics derive from Indigenous cosmologies and from both traditional and contemporary iterations of Indigenous legal and political orders, informed by other liberatory tools found in critical race, anti-colonial, Indigenous feminist, and anti-capitalist thinking. Resurgence draws on history and on ancient relationships, practices, and languages for its political torque. This knowledge survives in sometimes fragmented memories, stories, songs, and practices.

It is the knowledge found in the words of the past, resonating in the present, telling Indigenous Peoples how and why to be who we are.

Our pasts contain the instructions for how we are to be in the world, in relationships with specific territories and all the beings on them. Our cultural and political frameworks are territorially based. In other words, our fundamental identities, cultures, and political formations are, through resurgence politics and scholarship, taking us into the future as who we are, connected to our territories.

Indigenous Peoples turn to resurgence to survive the colonial practices and the racism that stripped people of their languages, making it harder to recount the stories that prove specific Indigenous title—the loss of language, stories, and practices that make us fully who we are and demonstrate our title to our territories. That title is to unceded stolen land and to sovereignty and jurisdiction over it. In the words of the late great Nisgaa leader Joe Gosnell, we own it "lock, stock and barrel,"[25] despite settlers being squatted on it and federal, provincial, and state governments claiming it.

Title is practised by the specific relationships we have with our land. For Ktunaxa, that is framed by the principle of ʔa·kxamis q̓api qapsin—our responsibility to all living things. This relationship is mandated by Nupik̓a, the Creator. This ancient order proves, in the Ktunaxa language, our pre-eminent claim on Ktunaxa traditional territory and our responsibilities to the relationships invoked by that claim. Nor are Ktunaxa alone in these radical relational conceptualizations.[26] Many—perhaps all—other Indigenous nations have similar frameworks. While each culture has its own iteration of these frameworks, all are centred on relationships that include and are responsible to the land and to all living things.

Any politics of transformation requires a coherent, theoretically and empirically informed political agenda for change. It also depends upon the mobilization of a critical mass of people committed to the agenda and its objectives. Both Indigenous and settler people must be convinced that their aspirations and their futures can be accommodated if political solidarity is to ensue. Hair shirts are ineffective for building political solidarities. Indigenous liberation must construct a politically potent movement that foregrounds Indigenous justice, including Land Back,[27] with the solidarity of those for whom this state is designed and who have benefited from the erasure, the genocide, and the dispossession of Indigenous Peoples. It is a big ask.

For many Indigenous Peoples, the change we seek is against generations of oppression by the settler states that have occupied our lands, stolen our resources, racialized and discriminated against our peoples, and misrepresented their history and ours. There are many cases continuing to the present day, and invariably they benefit the Canadian government in any of its political iterations; its citizens, some more than others; and the corporate players. They do not, however, benefit Indigenous Peoples as a people (even if they benefit a handful of employees or capitalists), and they do not appropriately address questions of jurisdiction, consultation, consent, benefit, and restitution. Nor could they be executed without some practical consideration of impact on and access to Indigenous lands, obtaining or avoiding Indigenous compliance, and so on. These and similar practices on the historical continuum to the present have led to policies and consequences that we understand to be genocidal.

State oppression of Indigenous Peoples, however, has been quite beneficial for settler peoples. Thus, Indigenous justice and liberation require some significant settler recognition of the injustices afflicting us, recognition manifest as political will for Indigenous-led transformations, and for return of at least some of our territories, along with the incidents of sovereignty over them, and recognition of the privileges Canadian citizens enjoy because of Indigenous oppression. Then, we must collectively find the political will for transformation, a set of shifts in power relations and in policy objectives that will destabilize the status quo in favour of measures of justice and relational possibility.

Indigenous Human Rights

For Ktunaxa and many other Indigenous Peoples, the notion of and the terrain of rights claims arise as a consequence of colonization and of extractive capitalism.[28] Without those factors, it is more likely that a foundational Ktunaxa principle, ʔa·kxamis q̓api qapsin (the principle of all living things) and similar principles in other Indigenous cultures, would frame our considerations rather than rights discourse. All things have a place—rights, if you will. In the mandate of ʔa·kxamis q̓api qapsin, the best way of life is achieved through carrying out the responsibilities to those relationships. In matters of rights and responsibilities, Indigenous Peoples hold title and related rights and have responsibilities to those lands, water, and all things on and in them. Rights are in relation to the occupying state and are claimed, ineffectively, on behalf of individuals and communities, as a shield against state oppression; the responsibilities are to the land, to the nation, and to all other beings. Those responsibilities predate the state. And if colonialism is the context for Indigenous rights claims, self-determination is the foundational Indigenous right.

Indigenous rights are, in my view, fundamental human rights essential for the ability to live as Indigenous persons, in the context of colonized Indigenous communities and nations.[29] These rights have been abrogated systematically, intentionally, around the world, wherever colonial adventurers have set up shop. Even where, over time, emerging settler states have constructed democratic orders that rely on a formula of state protection of human rights, Indigenous rights remain essentially abrogated. This is because the foundational motivation for colonial and settler states, that little land-theft matter, remains operative. It includes the historic and current practice of the removal or containment of Indigenous Peoples in order to make their territories and resources available to the state and its settler citizens and to its corporate allies, and for state legitimacy in the international community of states that are essentially allied on the proposition that Indigenous sovereignty is an existential threat to settler state sovereignty and corporate profitability.[30] This is also an indictment of the origins and contemporary practices of settler states and of major corporations resident or active in states.[31]

Because of this continuous history of occupation, dispossession, and oppression, Indigenous Peoples engaged the language of rights in relation to certain actions of the state and its client corporations. Some Indigenous thinkers have resisted rights discourse, insisting it is inherently a white colonial conception. But as Black American legal scholar Patricia Williams wrote, "In the law, rights are islands of empowerment."[32] This is a powerful insight: rights empower us when we are oppressed. They are shields against oppression. Colonialism and genocide are indeed oppressive. Claims to Aboriginal and Treaty Rights, for land and water rights, and for the rights at international law, particularly in the United Nations Declaration on the Rights of Indigenous Peoples (UNDRIP), are claims against the state and its oppressive destructive practices towards Indigenous Peoples, towards all living things, and towards Indigenous territories.

The Western theoretical frameworks that have established rights discourse have been animated by resistance to oppression and by the defence of the necessities of life and dignity for disempowered people. Those are valuable frameworks. It is not my intention to dispense with them, but to place them in the context in which we find ourselves: that of a predatory settler state, infused by colonialism's assumptions and the racism that legitimates them, and by the economic framework that is always invoked in favour of settler and corporate priorities rather than Indigenous ones. But for state practices of colonialism and genocide, of land theft and the state-supported economic practices of extractive capitalism, Indigenous Peoples would have no need to claim rights against the state. In this context, rights claims are contextualized by the history, law, and politics framing Indigenous oppression; these rights claims are liberatory. Rights claims offer us terrain on which to stand and resist, in a conceptual framework that others recognize. Indigenous rights are often not implemented or protected by Canada even when recognized at Canadian law. For example, Mi'kmaw fishing rights in Nova Scotia have been violated and constrained repeatedly since they were recognized by the Supreme Court of Canada in 1999,[33] and subsequently, the right has been constrained and regulated by federal governments pressured by non-Indigenous commercial fishers, a group of which has sought a role in defining Mi'kmaw rights.[34] Another example is found in Wet'suwet'en hereditary Chiefs' resistance to TC Energy's Coastal GasLink project,[35] recently rammed through Wet'suwet'en territory in British Columbia[36] without "free, prior and informed consent"[37] as required by the UNDRIP.[38]

As with Mi'kmaw fishers and traditional Wet'suwet'en leaders opposing the Coastal GasLink pipeline in BC, Indigenous rights are often not implemented or protected by Canada even when recognized at Canadian law. Indigenous rights-holders are often hauled back into negotiations or into court by the federal government rather than seeing their rights legislatively implemented. Think about the implications of having to negotiate one's rights, rights affirmed at law but denied in policy and practice. It suggests those rights are always secondary to other interests, which the political and legal apparatus is always able to inhabit and animate against Indigenous rights. And doesn't this suggest who the state was designed by and for?

Corporate interests have been a preoccupation of Canadian governments—especially important to the policies of land theft, and in support of extractivist capitalism. Furs and fish, bison meat and hides. Railways, highways, hydro dams. Clear-cut and old growth logging. Coal and mineral mining. Pipelines, ski hills, and golf courses. That's colonialism.

In ʔamakʔis Ktunaxa (Ktunaxa territory) and in the territories of other Indigenous nations, all of these things and more produce wealth from our lands for settler communities, corporations, and governments, while violating ʔa·kxamis q̓api qapsin—the Ktunaxa instruction for our relationships, our responsibilities to all living things. When challenged by Indigenous communities and nations, federal and provincial governments, political party representatives, media commentators, and "stakeholders" invoke the absolute primacy of the economy relative to Indigenous rights. Guess whose rights are always sacrificed on that capitalist altar.

The constitutional history of Canada has produced an emancipatory trajectory for many Canadians. With the adoption in 1982 of the Canadian Constitution and the Charter of Rights and Freedoms many were recognized and included in the national community of rights-holders, in relation to the governments we choose (albeit through a badly flawed undemocratic electoral system[39]) and thus to the agendas they pursue. Constitutional emancipation is not the experience of Indigenous Peoples in Canada, and inclusion in the settler state and societies is arguably the wrong goal for Indigenous Peoples. Inclusion has always been framed as either the liberal notion of bringing diversity into the putatively neutral settler mainstream, where it is tolerated or consumed, or as assimilation, which is inherently an erasure of Indigenous human rights, some of which are gestured at in the Canadian Constitution but most of which exist as political claims against the settler state, and in the growing recognition of Indigenous human rights and states' obligations to animate these rights at international law, particularly in the UNDRIP, adopted (although not implemented) by Canada.

The Charter, however, is silent on colonialism, on systemic forms of oppression such as racism and misogyny, on settler state land theft from Indigenous Peoples, and so on. Nor does it protect Indigenous rights—"Aboriginal and treaty rights," in constitutional parlance. It does not derogate from section 35 rights[40]—and section 35 is not part of the Charter—but neither does it secure them. Note, too, that section 35 is anemic in its framing of Indigenous rights and places them at perpetual legal jeopardy: they are to be "existing"—that is, recognized by the law of the settler state—and inure only to constitutionally recognized Aboriginal peoples: "Indian, Inuit and Metis," which ignores Indigenous Peoples who do not fit neatly into those categories. The rights are to be located in "pre-contact" practices integral to particular cultures.[41] In this way, Aboriginal rights are always conceived of as frozen in time, unable to progress; thus, Aboriginal cultures are framed as pre-contact practices incapable of contemporary expression and continuous evolution.[42] The Constitution itself restricts Indigenous rights to those recognized by the state and the rights-holders to only those Indigenous Peoples the state recognizes. In all of this, the Charter is Indigenous-blind and its provisions are Indigenous-deficient; it is silent on the past and continuing genocidal realities endured by Indigenous Peoples. The Constitution of which the Charter is a part privileges the settler state and limits Indigeneity and Indigenous rights utterly to state recognition and implementation. Theories of Indigenous resurgence reject this state-centred and state-dominant discourse.

And yet the concept of rights remains important for Indigenous liberation. Rights arise in contexts of oppression and abuse. While this is not an entirely satisfactory paradigm, it has produced terrain for public political struggle and for the achievement of some significant benefits for at least some oppressed people.

The Truth About Reconciliation

Reconciliation was framed by the *Final Report* of the Truth and Reconciliation Commission as a necessary relational objective to be pursued by the Canadian state in order to create a reparative context for Indigenous Peoples and settlers in a colonial state. It has been reduced to banality by its constant invocation by the political class, who conflate it with state provision of basic human rights, equality, and infrastructure for Indigenous Peoples, and by the utter failure of the state to recognize the fundamental structuring event of Indigenous oppression, that of land theft, which makes it all the more evident now that "reconciliation" will not return even a portion of Indigenous lands, sovereignty, economic capacity, and national autonomy.

Indeed, the popular framing of reconciliation seems to assume that those claims are irrelevant and off the political table, and that equality of services and recognition of "culture" will lubricate the perpetual objective of the Canadian state to assimilate Indigenous Peoples and politics within the state enterprise. This is evidently the objective embedded in federal and provincial approaches to Indigenous nationalism and resistance to colonialism. It is resonant of the assimilatory focus of the aptly named 1969 "White Paper" and the 1985 "Buffalo Jump of the 1980s."[43] Non-Indigenous support for meaningful restitution as part of reconciliation is challenged because of self-interested opposition from those who have benefited from white (and male) privilege personally and in institutional and structural design. As Truth and Reconciliation Commission chair Murray Sinclair said, "Reconciliation is going to be harder than getting to the truth because there's a population of people who will push back against Indigenous effort to reclaim rights, positions, lands or to re-assert ourselves...we're talking about changing a huge relationship here between Indigenous and non-Indigenous people."[44] This political opposition frustrates the reality that "reconciliation is going to eventually require a rebalancing of access to the levers of power."[45]

Reconciliation is a state of renewed relationship, a state of amity, that follows a relational rupture that is then mended. That does not describe the relationship between the Canadian state, government, and population with Indigenous Peoples. The conditions for reconciliation have not been met. The steps towards reconciliation have not been made. Nor can they be made in the context of a settler state, squatted on Indigenous lands, that marginalizes and tokenizes Indigenous Peoples.

Reconciliation results from the healing of a ruptured relationship. It is initiated because of remorse by the party that injured the relationship. It comes about by way of a process. Remorse moves the one who caused the injury to wish to remedy it: It leads to action. It is not achieved by insisting that the injured party is reconciled because the party who did the injury says they are. In fact, reconciliation may not happen, but remorse still can motivate one party to remedy their bad behaviour, take responsibility for it, and make amends for it. One cannot force reconciliation. Indigenous Peoples may or may not choose to trust a relationship with the state of Canada, its governments, or its settler populations.[46]

The first step in moving towards reconciliation must be made by the party that performed the injury. The first step is remorse, a recognition of the wrong done. The second step is the wish to make amends, and it is followed by the action to perform the amends without any expectation of the injured party. The third step is to be humble and empathetic, to accept the decision of the injured party with respect to relationship. In other words, one cannot demand a reconciled relationship.[47]

None of these steps require anything from Indigenous Peoples. Reconciliation is something for Canadian governments, citizens, and public and private organizations to pursue. It is not something that needs action or even responses by Indigenous Peoples.

The former Liberal federal government, led until early 2025 by Justin Trudeau, made much of its commitment to reconciliation.. Yet, it did not perform the necessary steps. Instead, it treated its partial provision to some Indigenous communities of basic services such as water, health care, and education as a reconciliatory act. It is not. It is what the Canadian government is expected to provide to all of us.

But reconciliation should not be the end goal. Rather, the objective should be right relationship, which constitutes the preconditions for reconciliation. Relationships are the prime directive in Indigenous conceptions of how to behave appropriately, and refocusing from reconciliation to relationship could be transformative of state-Indigenous politics. If one is remorseful, committed to making amends, and willing to live with the relational decisions of the one who is injured, the act of making amends meaningful to Indigenous Peoples should be the objective.

Indigenous Resistance; Indigenous Rights

In Canada, Indigenous Peoples ("Indian, Inuit and Metis," according to s. 35 of the 1982 Canadian Constitution—but there are other communities, and possibly other categories, who are arguably authentically Indigenous) seek measures of autonomy, resurgence, and restitution from the immense damage done to them by the state, in the interests of the objectives I have laid out above. These aspirations arise from histories that precede the formation of the state and of the constitutional instruments that now guide it.

The ruling political class, the media, intelligencia, and others speak of "reconciliation" with Indigenous Peoples. Much of this seems directed at assimilative inclusion, and not at right relationship. National Indigenous Day remains focused on drumming and dancing, not on a politic of solidarity on Indigenous aspirations. Not all media budgets are being enhanced in accordance with Call 84 of the Truth and Reconciliation Commission's *Final Report*, which affects what Canadians learn about the issues raised in this chapter. Elected officials of Canadian governments express little accountability and remorse for the genocidal practices of the state since its inception, and contemporarily. No meaningful amounts of land, jurisdiction, and tax room are being ceded back to Indigenous governments.

Many Indigenous Peoples seek transformations of the legacies of lifetimes of oppression by the settler states that have occupied lands; stolen resources; racialized, brutalized, and discriminated against Indigenous Peoples; and misrepresented history. Those years, however, have been beneficial for settler people, who have been the focus of political institutions, of policy, of citizenship; and settlers have been the participants in the superficially democratic state, which does not exist separately from its privileged population. Thus, Indigenous justice and liberation require some significant settler recognition of the injustices afflicting us and the privileges that Canadian citizens enjoy because of Indigenous oppression. Then, we must all find the political will for transformation, for shifts in power relations, and in policy objectives that will destabilize the status quo.

Indigenous Peoples need a good way to move into the future. We need to be authentically ourselves, on our territories, with the capacity to enact and transmit our ancient knowledges and responsibilities. Inclusion in the liberal democratic state's benevolent colonialism and seductive economic system will not permit our survivance, though it may appeal to some individuals. It is not because of choice but because of reality that I recognize that we are all in this together, although we are not situated or empowered similarly. How shall we frame our de facto togetherness, our futures, our shared and separate political and temporal spaces? The way in which we imagine this, how we conceptualize and animate it, will either propel us into new and better relationships or will consolidate the atrocious ones left to us by the colonial and settler state order. The options can only be mobilized by politics and education.

And that will take us to the conditions for reconciliation, a term rendered meaningless by over-usage, superficial understanding, and little execution. The conditions for reconciliation do not guarantee it as an outcome—but without those conditions being met, reconciliation is impossible. Liberation, reconciliation, and relational formation are future possibilities that require acts of informed, committed will by us all.

Notes

1 Decembrini, "The Marshall Decision and Mi'kmaq Commercial Fishing Rights."

2 See also Lindberg, "Nehiyaw Hunting Pedagogies," 114–15.

3 Green, "Self-Determination, Citizenship and Federalism," 23.

4 I and others use this term not as a pejorative but to distinguish those whose antecedents are from elsewhere from those whose antecedents have been here for a very long time, generally framed as from "time immemorial."
5 CBC Radio, *Unreserved.*
6 Kuokkanen, *Reshaping the University*; Smith, *Decolonizing Methodologies*; Kovach, *Indigenous Methodologies*; Wallace, "Beyond the 'Add and Stir' Approach."
7 Thobani, *Exalted Subjects*; Mawani, *Colonial Proximities*; Dhamoon et al., eds., *Unmooring the Komagata Maru.*
8 Green, "Self Determination, Citizenship and Federalism."
9 Green, ed., *Indivisible*; Green, ed., *Making Space*; TRC, *Honouring the Truth, Reconciling for the Future.*
10 Green, ed., *Making Space*, 51; Million, "Spirit as Matter," 51.
11 Coulthard, *Red Skin, White Mask*; Daschuk, *Clearing the Plains*; Thomas and Coburn, eds., *Capitalism & Dispossession.*
12 Green, "Being and Knowing Home."
13 To review the conditions for genocide, see the Canadian Political Science Association (CPSA) Reconciliation Committee's "Briefing Note on Genocide" online.
14 Thobani, *Exalted Subjects*; Dhamoon et al., eds., *Unmooring the Komagata Maru.*
15 Green, "Self-Determination, Citizenship and Federalism," 329–52; Green, ed., *Making Space.*
16 Blackstock, "Foreword," xv. See also Backhouse and Milton, "Introduction."
17 CPSA Reconciliation Committee, "Briefing Note on Genocide."
18 Under the Rome Statute of the International Criminal Court. See Government of Canada, "Crimes Against Humanity and War Crimes Act."
19 Canadian Press, "Motion to Call Residential Schools Genocide." See also Talaga, "Genocide Is Not."
20 Alfred, *Wasáse*; Coulthard, *Red Skin, White Masks*; Starblanket, "Being Indigenous Feminists"; Asch, Borrows, and Tully, eds., *Resurgence and Reconciliation.*
21 Starblanket, "Being Indigenous Feminists," 23.
22 Asch, Borrows, and Tully, eds., *Resurgence and Reconciliation*, 4.
23 Allard-Tremblay, "Braiding Liberation Discourses."
24 Stark, "Generating a Critical Resurgence Together," 36, 13. Emphasis added.
25 Cuthand, "First Nations Are Fighting."
26 Corntassel, "Truth-Telling Amidst Reconciliation Discourses," 145.
27 Yellowhead Institute, "Land Back."
28 For more on the relationship between colonization and capitalism, see Coulthard, *Red Skin, White Masks*; Kuokkanen, *Reshaping the University*; Thomas and Coburn, *Capitalism & Dispossession.*
29 Green, *Indivisible.*
30 Green, "Enacting Reconciliation," 237–51.
31 Coulthard, *Red Skin, White Masks*; Thomas and Coburn, *Capitalism & Dispossession.*

32 Williams, *The Alchemy of Race.*
33 Decembrini, "The Marshall Decision and Mi'kmaq Commercial Fishing Rights."
34 Withers, "N.S. Fishing Industry." See also Metallic and MacIntosh, "Canada's Actions."
35 Pasternak, "The State, the Company, and the Police."
36 Pasternak, "The State, the Company, and the Police."
37 See the explanation of FPIC by the Office of the High Commissioner for the United Nations Human Rights Committee at https://www.ohchr.org/en/indigenous-peoples/consultation-and-free-prior-and-informed-consent-fpic.
38 See also the Declaration on the Rights of Indigenous Peoples at https://www.un.org/development/desa/indigenouspeoples/wp-content/uploads/sites/19/2018/11/UNDRIP_E_web.pdf.
39 Consult Fair Vote Canada online (https://www.fairvote.ca/) for more information on this, as well as Pilon, *The Politics of Voting.*
40 "Canadian Charter of Rights and Freedoms," s. 35, Part 1, of the *Constitution Act, 1982.*
41 *R v. Van Der Peet,* [1996], 2 S.C.R. 507.
42 Stark, Craft, and Aikau, eds., *Indigenous Resurgence*; Borrows, "Frozen Rights in Canada."
43 Interested readers may consult Indigenous Foundations, "The White Paper," for a précis of the paper and its context. The Yellowhead Institute writes that "The 'Buffalo Jump of the 1980's' is the nickname for the shift that occurred when the Conservatives took power in 1984 and interpreted demands for Indigenous self-government as an opportunity to transfer federal obligations onto First Nations, provinces, and territories once and for all." Yellowhead Institute, "Glossary."
44 Waddell, "Former TRC Chair Murray."
45 Waddell, "Former TRC Chair Murray."
46 Green, "Enacting Reconciliation."
47 Green and Burton, "Twelve Steps to Post-Colonial Reconciliation."

Sources

Alfred, Taiaiake. *Wasáse: Indigenous Pathways of Action and Freedom.* University of Toronto Press, 2005.

Allard-Tremblay, Yann. "Braiding Liberation Discourses: Dialectical, Civic and Disjunctive Views About Resistance and Violence." *Canadian Journal of Political Science* 55, no. 2(2022): 259–78. https://doi.org/10.1017/S0008423922000191.

Asch, Michael, John Borrows, and James Tully, eds. *Resurgence and Reconciliation: Indigenous-Settler Relations and Earth Teachings.* University of Toronto Press, 2018.

Backhouse, Constance, and Cynthia E. Milton. "Introduction." In *Royally Wronged: The Royal Society of Canada and Indigenous Peoples,* edited by

Constance Backhouse, Cynthia E. Milton, Margaret Kovach, and Adele Perry. McGill-Queen's University Press, 2021.

Blackstock, Cindy. "Foreword." In *Royally Wronged: The Royal Society of Canada and Indigenous Peoples*, edited by Constance Backhouse, Cynthia E. Milton, Margaret Kovach, and Adele Perry. McGill-Queen's University Press, 2021.

Borrows, John. "Frozen Rights in Canada: Constitutional Interpretation and the Trickster." *American Indian Law Review* 22, no. 1 (1997). https://digitalcommons.law.ou.edu/ailr/vol22/iss1/2/.

CBC Radio. *Unreserved with Rosanna Deerchild*. 2021.

"Canadian Charter of Rights and Freedoms." Part 1, *Constitution Act, 1982*, being Schedule B to the *Canada Act 1982* (UK), 1982, c 11.

Canadian Political Science Association (CPSA) Reconciliation Committee. "CPSA Reconciliation Committee's Briefing Note on Genocide." https://cpsa-acsp.ca/cpsa-reconciliation-committee.

Canadian Press. "Motion to Call Residential Schools Genocide Backed Unanimously." *Globe and Mail*, October 28, 2022. https://www.theglobeandmail.com/politics/article-motion-to-call-residential-schools-genocide-backed-unanimously.

Corntassel, Jeff Ganohalidoh. "Truth-Telling Amidst Reconciliation Discourses: How Stories Reshape Our Relationships." In *Indigenous Resurgence in an Age of Reconciliation*, edited by Heidi Kiiwitinepinesiik Stark, Aimée Craft, and Hōkūlani K. Aikau. University of Toronto Press, 2023.

Coulthard, Glen S. *Red Skin, White Masks: Rejecting the Colonial Politics of Recognition*. University of Minnesota Press, 2014.

Cuthand, Doug. "First Nations Are Fighting the Sask. First Act." *Saskatoon StarPhoenix*, April 22, 2023. https://thestarphoenix.com/opinion/columnists/doug-cuthand-first-nations-are-fighting-the-sask-first-act.

Daschuk, James. *Clearing the Plains: Disease, Politics of Starvation, and the Loss of Indigenous Life*. University of Regina Press, 2013.

Decembrini, Angela D'Elia. "The Marshall Decision and Mi'kmaq Commercial Fishing Rights: An Explainer." First Peoples Law, October 8, 2020. https://www.firstpeopleslaw.com/public-education/blog/the-marshall-decision-and-mikmaq-commercial-fishing-rights-an-explainer.

Dhamoon, Rita, Davina Bhandar, Renisa Mawani, and Satwinder Kaur Bains, eds. *Unmooring the Komagata Maru: Charting Colonial Trajectories*. UBC Press, 2020.

Fair Vote Canada. https://www.fairvote.ca/.

Government of Canada. "Crimes Against Humanity and War Crimes Act." Justice Laws Website. https://laws-lois.justice.gc.ca/eng/acts/c-45.9/page-1.html.

Green, Joyce. "Being and Knowing Home." In *Indigenous Womxn Write and Orate the Land*, edited by Christine Sy. Wolsak & Wynn, forthcoming.

Green, Joyce. "Enacting Reconciliation." In *Visions of the Heart: Issues Involving Indigenous People in Canada*, 5th ed., edited by Gina Starblanket and David Long. Oxford University Press, 2019.

Green, Joyce, ed. *Indivisible: Indigenous Human Rights*. Fernwood Publishing, 2014.

Green, Joyce, ed., *Making Space for Indigenous Feminism*, 2nd ed. Fernwood Publishing, 2017.

Green, Joyce. "Self-Determination, Citizenship and Federalism: Indigenous and Canadian Palimpsest." In *Reconfiguring Aboriginal-State Relations*, edited by Michael Murphy. McGill-Queen's University Press, 2005.

Green, Joyce, and Mike Burton. "Twelve Steps to Post-Colonial Reconciliation." In *Wrongs to Rights: How Churches Can Engage the United Nations Declaration on the Rights of Indigenous People*, edited by Steve Heinrichs. Mennonite Church of Canada, 2016.

Indigenous Foundations. "The White Paper, 1969." https://indigenousfoundations.arts.ubc.ca/the_white_paper_1969/.

Jang, Brent. "Coastal GasLink Completes B.C. Pipeline Installation After Five Years." *Globe and Mail*, October 30, 2023. https://www.theglobeandmail.com/business/article-coastal-gaslink-completes-bc-pipeline-installation-after-five-years.

Kovach, Margaret. *Indigenous Methodologies: Characteristics, Conversations, and Contexts*, 2nd ed. University of Toronto Press, 2021.

Kuokkanen, Rauna. *Reshaping the University: Responsibility, Indigenous Epistemes, and the Logic of the Gift*. UBC Press, 2007.

Lindberg, Darcy. "Nehiyaw Hunting Pedagogies and Revitalizing Indigenous Laws." In *Indigenous Resurgence in an Age of Reconciliation*, edited by Heidi Kiiwitinepinesiik Stark, Aimée Craft, and Hōkūlani K. Aikau. University of Toronto Press. 2023.

Mawani, Renisa. *Colonial Proximities: Crossracial Encounters and Juridical Truths in British Columbia, 1871–1921*. UBC Press, 2010.

Metallic, Naomi, and Constance MacIntosh. "Canada's Actions Around the Mi'Kmaq Fisheries Rest on Shaky Legal Ground." *Policy Options*, November 9, 2020. https://policyoptions.irpp.org/magazines/november-2020/canadas-actions-around-the-mikmaq-fisheries-rest-on-shaky-legal-ground.

Million, Dian. "Spirit as Matter: Resurgence as Rising and (Re)Creation as Ethos." In *Indigenous Resurgence in an Age of Reconciliation*, edited by Heidi Kiiwitinepinesiik Stark, Aimée Craft, and Hōkūlani K. Aikau. University of Toronto Press, 2023.

Pasternak, Shiri. "The State, the Company, and the Police: Who Invaded Wet'suwet'en Lands?" Keynote address to the Canadian Political Science Association, Co-sponsored by the CPSA Reconciliation Committee and the Canadian Political Science Association, York University, May 31, 2023.

Pilon, Dennis. *The Politics of Voting: Reforming Canada's Electoral System*. Emond Montgomery, 2007.

R v. Van Der Peet, [1996], 2 S.C.R. 507. Supreme Court Judgments, Supreme Court of Canada. https://scc-csc.lexum.com/scc-csc/scc-csc/en/item/1407/index.do.

Smith, Linda Tuhiwai. *Decolonizing Methodologies: Research and Indigenous Peoples*, 3rd ed. Zed Books, 2021.

Starblanket, Gina. "Being Indigenous Feminists: Resurgences Against Contemporary Patriarchy." In *Making Space for Indigenous Feminism*, 2nd ed., edited by Joyce Green. Fernwood Publishing, 2017.

Stark, Heidi Kiiwetinepinesiik. "Generating a Critical Resurgence Together." In *Indigenous Resurgence in an Age of Reconciliation*, edited by Heidi Kiiwitinepinesiik Stark, Aimée Craft, and Hōkūlani K. Aikau. University of Toronto Press, 2023.

Stark, Heidi Kiiwetinepinesiik, Aimée Craft, and Hōkūlani K. Aikau, eds. *Indigenous Resurgence in an Age of Reconciliation*. University of Toronto Press, 2023.

Talaga, Tanya. "Genocide Is Not in Canada's Past. It Is Still Happening, to This Day." *Globe and Mail*, December 7, 2022. https://www.theglobeandmail.com/opinion/article-genocide-is-not-in-canadas-past-it-is-still-happening-to-this-day/.

Thobani, Sunera. *Exalted Subjects: Studies in the Making of Race and Nation in Canada*. University of Toronto Press, 2007.

Thomas, David P., and Veldon Coburn, eds. *Capitalism & Dispossession: Corporate Canada at Home and Abroad*. Fernwood Publishing, 2022.

Truth and Reconciliation Commission of Canada (TRC). *Honouring the Truth, Reconciling for the Future: Summary of the Final Report of the Truth and Reconciliation Commission of Canada*. Truth and Reconciliation Commission of Canada, 2015. https://ehprnh2mwo3.exactdn.com/wp-content/uploads/2021/01/Executive_Summary_English_Web.pdf.

Waddell, Dave. "Former TRC Chair Murray Sinclair Talks About the Pathway to Reconciliation." *Windsor Star*, December 10, 2021. https://windsorstar.com/news/local-news/former-trc-chair-murray-sinclair-talks-about-the-pathway-to-reconciliaton.

Wallace, Rebecca Audrey. "Beyond the 'Add and Stir' Approach: Indigenizing Comprehensive Exam Reading Lists in Canadian Political Science." *Canadian Journal of Political Science* 55, no. 3 (2022): 687–708. https://doi.org/10.1017/S0008423922000506.

Williams, Patricia J. *The Alchemy of Race and Rights*. Harvard University Press, 1991.

Withers, Paul. "N.S. Fishing Industry Wants Say in Mi'kmaw Treaty Rights Case." *CBC News*, September 22, 2021. https://www.cbc.ca/news/canada/nova-scotia/nova-scotia-mikmaw-fishing-rights-court-case-1.6186106.

Yellowhead Institute. "Glossary: Key Terms and Definitions from Cash Back." https://cashback.yellowheadinstitute.org/glossary/.

Yellowhead Institute. "Land Back: A Yellowhead Institute Red Paper." October 2019. https://yellowheadinstitute.org/resources/land-back-a-yellowhead-institute-red-paper.

Indigenous Women, Settler Colonial State–Sanctioned Gendered Violence, and Reconciliation in Canada

Emily Grafton

FORMER FEDERAL MINISTER OF JUSTICE AND ATTORNEY General Jody Wilson-Raybould (Kwakwaka'wakw Nation) has argued that in light of the pervasive violence against Indigenous women, the state/societal response to this violence must serve as a litmus test (or the measurement of change) for the progress of reconciliation in Canada.[1] The current political environment of truth and reconciliation among Indigenous and non-Indigenous/settler Canadians is fraught with the centuries-long legacies of colonialism, and reconciliation is one approach to address these impacts. Wilson-Raybould's assertion is a crucial intervention into the present state of Indigenous and settler relations in Canada.

This chapter reflects on the ideas behind Wilson-Raybould's litmus test. I explore the extent to which Indigenous women, girls, and two-Spirit, lesbian, gay, bi-sexual, transgender, queer, questioning, inter-sex, or asexual (2SLGBTQQIA+) individuals are able to access safety and well-being in an environment where the dominant structures continue to uphold gendered and racialized violence. I am of Métis ancestry, and I teach a course on Indigenous women and politics in Canada; the discussion put forward in this chapter is based on how I observe the many fractured, competing, and overlapping pieces of colonial dispossession, gender, and liberation coalescing. Through a review of the evolution of historical and contemporary gendered and racialized violence targeted at Indigenous women, this chapter argues that settler colonial Canada is deeply rooted in this violence. Specifically, it explores how gendered and racialized violence[2] was conceived, generated, and weaponized against Indigenous communities to enable the project of settler colonial Canada to be implemented and operationalized. The chapter concludes by questioning the nature of reconciliation given these realities.

Settler Colonial Constructs and Reconciliation: In Brief

This chapter will explore the biopolitics that constitute a settler colonial construct, which contributes to contemporary violence against Indigenous women and girls. This brief provides a broad overview of the settler colonial construct of biopolitics as it relates to the litmus test for reconciliation. Subsequent sections will provide more detail on this construct as enacted in settler Canada, highlighting the effects of colonization and resulting impacts to be considered through reconciliation.

The settler colonial construct of biopolitics was used to target the ancestral/traditional social relations of Indigenous communities, or those social relations that existed before colonial assimilation efforts. These pre-colonial social relations were altered to varied extents as a result of settler colonialism. This transformation involved the establishment of hetero-patriarchal oppression as it relates to biopolitics, which is the use of ideologies of sex and race to enforce the colonial project.[3] In settler colonial Canada, as explained by settler scholar Julia Emberley, biopolitics can be understood as political interference through hetero-patriarchy, implemented by manipulating gender norms and practising sex discrimination. Emberley explains that the patriarchal family (with a husband as head and wife and children as subordinate) and gender binaries (male and female) are biopolitical constructs that were deliberately imposed on Indigenous Peoples to disrupt their kin relations, aiming to subordinate and assimilate Indigenous women.

The impact of biopolitics results in colonial constructs that create harmful stereotypes of Indigenous women, contributing to the ongoing crisis of murdered and missing Indigenous women and girls (MMIWG).[4] These stereotypes not only perpetuate the devaluation of Indigenous women but also serve as tools of settler oppression, normalizing this devaluation. Scholars argue that the devaluation of Indigenous women parallels that which occurs in the context of land through resource extraction, use, and environmental degradation. From these stereotypes, the settler Canadian state developed legislative mechanisms that both stem from and reinforce this devaluation. Specifically, the *Indian Act* is rooted in systems of existing oppression in settler colonial society—colonization, racism, and hetero-patriarchy—and informed by the stereotypes that have resulted in and perpetuated gender-based violence against Indigenous women.

The resulting violence stemming from this structural devaluation is evident in the over-representation of Indigenous women, girls, and gender-confirming peoples, or 2SLGBTQQIA+, who are victims of gender-based and sexual violence in Canada. This crisis has been well documented by the National Inquiry into Murdered and Missing Indigenous Women and Girls (NIMMIWG), which took place from 2016 to 2019 and outlined 231 Calls for Justice aimed at ending the epidemic of gender-based colonial violence against Indigenous women. Statistics Canada (SC) data demonstrates the ongoing crisis. As of 2018, the data shows that 56 percent of Indigenous women have experienced physical assault and 46 percent of Indigenous women have experienced sexual assault in their lifetime, compared to 34 percent and 33 percent, respectively, of non-Indigenous women.[5] In addition to SC data, in 2021, the RCMP released a report that indicated that 1,017 Indigenous women and girls were murdered between 1980 and 2012—a homicide rate roughly 4.5 times higher than that of all other women in Canada. The NIMMIWG has pointed out that these numbers do not adequately capture the scope of the crisis. SC data evidences that over the course of 2009 to 2021, Indigenous women and girls were homicide victims at a rate six times higher than their non-Indigenous counterparts.[6] The NIMMIWG and others have named these murders—and the structures that enable and support them—a genocide: "The truths shared in these National Inquiry hearings tell the story—or, more accurately, thousands of stories—of acts of genocide against First Nations, Inuit and Métis women, girls, and 2SLGBTQQIA people."[7]

Despite the NIMMIWG's mandate, facilitation of a public inquiry, and reports, the development of a framework for addressing these statistics related to gendered violence within the context of Indigenous and non-Indigenous/settler reconciliation remains incomplete. In Wegner and Lawless's comprehensive assessment of the impact of the NIMMIWG, the authors note the ongoing public criticism towards the government because of a perceived lack of meaningful change.[8] These criticisms shed light on the challenges faced by reconciliation actions, which Wegner and Lawless characterize as "thin reconciliation," or a form of reconciliation that does not change the settler colonial construct and its resulting violence targeting Indigenous women, girls, and 2SLGBTQQIA+ peoples.[9]

Despite the government rhetoric of reconciliation, tangible progress is nearly non-existent. The federal government's initiative, written into their 2021 "Federal Pathway to Address Missing and Murdered Indigenous Women, Girls and 2SLGBTQQIA+ People," was intended to combat colonial gender-based violence by promoting Indigenous rights, Indigenous collective guidance and decision-making, and government action.[10] Yet, in 2023, the Canadian Broadcasting Corporation's evaluation of the government response to the NIMMIWG's *Final Report* found that only two of their 231 Calls for Justice had been completed at that time.[11] This chapter argues that the deeply ingrained stereotypes that underpin the gender-based colonial violence against Indigenous women, perpetuated by social norms and legislation, remain largely undone by any related government programs. With only two calls completed, settler colonial domination persists unabated from reconciliatory change. The intersection of gender that has resulted in gender-based violence does not dissipate; it is ongoing and entrenched in settler colonial Canada.

Early European Contact and Hetero-Patriarchal Underpinnings

The settler colonial power structure, specifically the biopolitics of hetero-patriarchy, demonstrates the ways in which Indigenous women are the litmus test for the reconciliation movement in Canada. For example, ancestral/traditional roles of Indigenous women in community was—and for many, continue to be—defined through socio-political influence and importance. Indigenous social relations are often described as egalitarian or matriarchal, with women exercising key leadership roles.[12] Canada's 1996 Royal Commission on Aboriginal Peoples (RCAP), a historic Royal Commission on colonial legacies in Canada, documents, "Women were highly respected in many traditional Aboriginal societies; their thoughts and views were sought before decisions affecting the community were made."[13] These roles would undoubtedly vary across the diverse and differing Indigenous nations throughout Canada and have also been impacted to varying degrees by the colonial project. That said, we might summarize these ancestral/traditional social relations as comprised of a variation of roles and responsibilities surrounding the well-being and functional organization of the community.[14] As Verna St. Denis (Cree and Métis) writes, "In this belief, Aboriginal women are valorized both as mothers and as caretakers of the nation."[15] Kim Anderson (Métis Nation) illustrates that these ancestral/traditional roles in society reinforced women's prominence as leaders and sustainers: they provided resources, advice, and direction, and held significant responsibilities that evolved throughout their lifetimes.[16]

The status of Indigenous women, in particular their socio-political prominence and authority, was reduced—though never in totality—through colonization. RCAP writes, "With the onset of colonization, the position and role of Aboriginal women were undermined by imported ideas and values that displaced and devalued them."[17] These ancestral/traditional roles were drastically altered after the introduction of European hetero-patriarchal social norms. These social roles were introduced in early colonialism through economic exchanges, political diplomacy, and social interactions. This contact and engagement occurred at differing times because imperial colonial contact and settlement were not uniform processes and structures in what became Canada. As these early colonial encounters matured into lasting imperial presence, hetero-patriarchal social norms reinforced and entrenched the evolution of settler colonial presence. How these systems of oppression function in settler colonial spaces contribute to our understanding of Wilson-Raybould's suggested litmus test for reconciliation.

Settler scholar Emily Snyder has argued that colonialism and hetero-patriarchy are co-occurring forms of oppression.[18] Colonialism is understood to be established on patriarchy, a system of social organization founded on male dominance and female subordination.[19] Patriarchy, as a system of oppression, supports heteronormativity,[20] or a form of social organization that prescribes heterosexuality and a gender binary of male/female as a normalized social construct: we can call these co-occurring oppressive systems *hetero-patriarchy*. Hetero-patriarchy was wielded in part by the biopolitics of the patriarchal family. Emberley has argued that biopolitical socialization, the process by which biopolitics are accepted, embedded, and perpetuated through social normativity, played a crucial role in the enforcement of hetero-patriarchy as a tool of settler colonial state and society. Hetero-patriarchy and the patriarchal family became a form of colonial conformity and social surveillance,[21] partially through the enforcement of gender binaries, which establish a dichotomy based on the adherence and enforced conformity to two genders: male and female. One of the results of this binary is the prescribing of normative gender roles situating "men as active public agents and women as private subjects."[22] These social constraints (gender binaries) were imposed on Indigenous-centred social relations that often understood gender as a spectrum, where masculine and feminine traits do not translate into social roles, but individuals' natural inclinations and interests shape their social contributions.[23]

Settler colonial actors, including government and society, weaponized hetero-patriarchy as a system aimed to dismantle women's power, particularly Indigenous women, who were seen as obstacles to the success of colonial power and profit through land expropriation. Indigenous women were further perceived an "obstacle" to the success of Christian religious orders through church-based expansion and control, which supported and profited from imperial expansion.[24] The churches and state operated together in the building of Canada: churches promote these hetero-patriarchal norms that are also ingrained in the state. These ideas were imported by "explorers" and missionaries and were implemented into legislation and politics in Canada, primarily through the *Indian Act*, as will be discussed. The Indigenous ancestral/traditional gender roles within Indigenous societies were significantly impacted by these colonial attitudes of patriarchy and social norms. One example of the imposition of hetero-patriarchy was through Christian-based marriage, which contributed to dismantling women's established leadership and political standing.[25] While marriage was an existing social practice among Indigenous Peoples, it was, in many communities and nations, understood differently, whereby women had a higher degree of autonomy than within the Christian institution of marriage.[26] For instance, one distinction from European understandings of marriage was that in Indigenous communities, women were not considered chattel or property through marriage, but, instead, they held autonomy and had the support of community to dissolve marriage unions.[27] This agency and autonomy held by Indigenous women provides insight into what is suppressed by colonial hetero-patriarchy. The application of hetero-patriarchy, through the Western Christian patriarchal institution of marriage and gender binaries, served to diminish the autonomy of Indigenous women and separate them from the safety provided by their kinship systems, subjecting them to control.[28]

The devaluing and dismantling of women's roles as central figures in Indigenous society and politics were essential for the success of the colonial project: "In order to fully execute the goal of assimilation, colonization required that Indigenous women's roles be devalued."[29] In Canada, this assimilationist approach required the suppression of autonomy and leadership and has resulted in racial and gendered violence wielded against Indigenous women, girls, and 2SLGBTQQIA+ communities.[30] The devaluation and suppression that Indigenous women have experienced in settler Canada, as will be discussed, is supported by stereotypes and legislative/state mechanisms that must be countered in reconciliation efforts.

Stereotypes: Tools of Colonial Oppression

When Europeans came to North America on behalf of imperial powers in the sixteenth century, long before Canada was an imagined state, in many ways they encountered Indigenous nations with egalitarian social models that did not oppress women. The imposition of a hetero-patriarchal system was a deliberate strategy to subjugate these nations to the expanding European empires. This involved mirroring European patriarchal society onto Indigenous social relations, which necessarily targeted Indigenous women.[31] The strategy was centred on those biopolitical mechanisms of hetero-patriarchy, and stereotypes were used to justify colonial oppression through demeaning portrayals of Indigenous women. Scholars have argued that these stereotypes, such as portraying Indigenous women as hypersexualized and sexually disposable, and resulting violence are linked to settler entitlement to lands.[32]

These early colonial encounters among Indigenous Peoples and Europeans led to the development of specific stereotypes about Indigenous women that continue to influence Canadian society. The settler colonial encroachment on Indigenous lands and the degradation and devaluation of these lands have been perpetuated through social constructs concerning Indigenous women's bodies.[33] The expropriation of land should be seen as a fundamental aspect of colonialism, and it cannot be separated from the biopolitics of settler colonialism.[34] For example, settler colonial constructs tied land to Indigenous women's bodies: "These two dimensions are indivisible and mutually constitutive. The encroachment on Indigenous lands is always connected to the assault on Indigenous bodies, especially those of women."[35] Over time, Indigenous women were made expendable, as were the lands,[36] leading to the normalization of the devaluation of Indigenous women, as occurred with lands, waters, and more-than-human beings. The takeover of lands by colonial force also led to the exploitation of Indigenous women, such as their use as sex slaves in the fur trade.[37] This exploitation fostered dehumanizing stereotypes of Indigenous women as hypersexualized and sexually disposable,[38] which in turn perpetuated power imbalances between colonizers and the colonized.[39] Settler colonial projects rely on this devaluation of women to support and justify colonizer/colonized power differentials.[40] These historically entrenched stereotypes continue to influence the devaluation of Indigenous women in settler Canada.[41]

These colonial-enforced stereotypes have deeply affected settler society. Robyn Bourgeois, a mixed-race Cree scholar, explains that colonial violence and the legislated sex discrimination in the *Indian Act* have become normalized in society due to these stereotypes that devalue Indigenous women.[42] According to Bourgeois, these stereotypes also serve to deflect criticism from the state to the victim, which is why we see comparatively little or inconsistent moral outrage at the MMIWG crisis. These devaluing stereotypes effectively silence, marginalize, and make Indigenous women invisible. The stereotypes of amorality and promiscuousness are encoded in Canadian society, leading to a lack of understanding and indifference towards the suffering of Indigenous women.[43] This normalized sex discrimination is evident in contemporary Canada through the *Indian Act* or other policies that target Indigenous women, including Métis and Inuit women.[44] As a result of this discrimination, many women and their children have lost their Indian status, leading to reduced access to rights, increased vulnerability to violence, and assimilation tactics.

Structures of Control: Legislation and the Courts

The biopolitics of hetero-patriarchy that are facilitated through the structures of the Canadian government perpetuate colonial violence against Indigenous women, girls, and 2SLGBTQQIA+ peoples. According to Joyce Green (Ktunaxa Nation and Cree-Scots Métis), "For indigenous women there is a constant tension between protections guaranteed in the constitution and the limitations of law and policy."[45] One of the most integral components of this structural state violence is the *Indian Act*: it normalizes the stereotypes that devalue and diminish the rights of Indigenous women, girls, and 2SLGBTQQIA+ peoples.[46] In Canadian society, this oppression tied to the *Indian Act* is maintained through parliamentary and judicial mechanisms. These stereotypes are justified by the marginal or low socio-economic conditions that can be common among Indigenous women's lived experiences.[47] These state structural mechanisms are also a root cause of violence against Indigenous women and 2SLGBTQQIA+ communities.[48]

The *Indian Act* has a significant impact on the rights of Indigenous women, specifically those who hold status or are denied status under the act. According to the RCAP, "The colonial and post-Confederation legislation applied to Aboriginal people finds its conceptual origins in Victorian ideas of race and patriarchy."[49] One of the *Indian Act*'s rules, known as the "marrying out" rule, results in the disenfranchisement of those Status First Nations women who married men without status, and the descendants of these unions. The *Indian Act* simultaneously gave Indian status to non-status or non-Indigenous women who married Status First Nations men, as well as their children. This effectively reinforces patriarchal control,[50] privileging First Nations men and their children while discriminating against First Nations women and their children.[51] In these ways, the *Indian Act* has "maligned and devalued" Indigenous women while male privilege has been "normalized and legitimized."[52] Accordingly, there is little disagreement that Indigenous women are disproportionally impacted by settler colonialism in Canada through the state's infrastructure.[53]

Shelagh Day summarizes the legal resistance enacted by Indigenous women against the state-sanctioned sex discrimination within the *Indian Act*, leading to incremental changes in the legislation. Beginning with *R. v. Bedard* (1971), which later merged in 1973 with *Canada [AG] v. Lavell* (1974), two Indigenous women, Yvonne Bédard (Haudenosaunee Nation) and Jeannette Corbiere Lavell (Anishinaabe), brought a case against the Canadian government that argued the marrying out rule was discriminatory under the sex equality provision of the *Canadian Bill of Rights* (1960). The case was unsuccessful as five of the nine Supreme Court justices ruled against it; however, those four dissenting opinions were viewed as a success. It is generally understood that this case in part inspired Sandra Lovelace Nicholas's (Tobique Nation) appeal to the United Nations (UN) Human

Rights Committee in *Lovelace v. Canada* in 1981, arguing that the *Indian Act* discriminated against Indigenous women through its marrying out rule. This UN committee found that Canada breached the *International Covenant on Civil and Political Rights*. The federal government responded to the Lovelace decisions through Bill C-31 or *An Act to Amend the Indian Act* (1985). Bill C-31 (as its commonly referred) intended to bring the *Indian Act* in line with gender equality in the Canadian Charter of Rights and Freedoms and restore lost Indian status due to the marrying out rule. Bill C-31, however, brought in a clause that maintained gender-based discrimination through a tiered approach to Indian status (the 6(1) and 6(2) mechanism) that ultimately continues to implement sex discrimination by enforcing limits to Indian status.[54]

Due to the ongoing nature of gender-based discrimination of the *Indian Act*, Day describes the continued legal and political efforts of redress. The *Report of the Aboriginal Justice Inquiry* (issued in 1991 by a group established by the Manitoba government in 1988) and RCAP (1996) both recommended that this discrimination be eliminated, and between 2003 and 2009 various UN bodies looked at this issue. In 1994, Sharon McIvor (Lower Nicola Indian Band) launched a legal case against the Registrar of Indian and Northern Affairs, who has sole jurisdiction over the determination of who is and is not an Indian under the *Indian Act*. It took more than one decade of litigation before the Government of Canada passed Bill C-3, the *Gender Equity in Indian Registration Act* (2010). This restored status entitlement to more than 45,000 individuals, but it is still piecemeal. Three subsequent cases have arisen concerning this ongoing gender-based discrimination: *Matson v. Canada (Indian Affairs and Northern Development)* (2015), *Descheneaux c. Canada (Procureur général)* (2015), and *Gehl v. Canada (Attorney General)* (2017). *Descheneaux c. Canada* ruled that the *Indian Act* discriminated against and violated section 15 of the Canadian Charter of Rights and Freedoms, which states that individuals are equal with equal protection under Canadian law.[55] At the time of writing, gender-based discrimination still exists, and the federal government is currently responding to these decisions, notably through Bill S-3 (2017 and 2019).

This overview does not provide the detail sufficient to demonstrate the toll this legislation has had on Indigenous women and their children, nor the advancements it allows for the maintenance of settler colonial biopolitics or the subordination of Indigenous political orders. Instead, the summary demonstrates the significance of Green's assertion that, "particularly in Canada, Indigenous women have been socially and legislatively deprived of their connections to their territories through colonial practices."[56] These legal deprivations have broad-based impacts on Indigenous women's identity as well as their access to culture, language, and community. Furthermore, the legislation is legally unfounded as much as it is morally unjust.[57] Day's overview supports settler legal scholar Mary Eberts's claim that the *Indian Act* makes Indigenous women "legal nullities" by continuing to place them outside of the rule of law and the protection and benefit of the law.[58] The Canadian state has resisted the efforts by Indigenous women to effectively remove sex discrimination from the legislation, and this demonstrates a steadfast commitment to the continued suppression of Indigenous women's fundamental rights. The state has done so through the ideologies of biopolitics and legislated mechanics informed by hetero-patriarchy and stereotypes. Indigenous women must argue for equity by using the very structures of Canadian laws that have implemented this historic and ongoing colonial legacy: they are caught playing within settler-controlled arenas using settler instruments.

The Biopolitics of Resurgence in Settler Colonial Spaces

In contemporary settler colonial Canada, there are movements across Indigenous nations to restore many ancestral/traditional social relations, including those roles specific to women. This process, often known as re-matriarchy, aims to centre Indigenous women in their pre-contact roles.[59] In Canada, Indigenous thought leaders and Indigenous resurgence scholars have clarified mechanisms for the authentic practices of ancestral/traditional Indigenous social relations.[60] These include language, cultural, and political practices and laws that ensure the sharing, understanding, and application of Indigenous social relations from pre-colonial contexts can flourish in contemporary Indigenous communities.

The identification and determination of authentic pre-colonial contexts is a challenging task. The efforts to restore traditional or ancestral social relations of colonized peoples are often hindered by the enduring impacts of colonialism.[61] Post-colonial theorists from various global colonial contexts have identified several obstacles to decolonization, which can impede attempts to revive traditional cultural social practices, such as resurgence movements.[62] For instance, it can be argued that re-establishing pre-colonial social relations is unattainable due to the ongoing colonial assimilative influence over language, culture, and government bureaucratic and legal structures.

Although reclamation of language and culturally specific practices can inform contemporary Indigenous social relations, these are not necessarily devoid of colonial influence. Striving to revive authentic social relations can, instead, lead to inauthentic representations or fabrications of past cultures and social relations. One result of the influence of such inauthentic representations is essentialism, which poses a challenge for movements aiming to revive authentic ancestral/traditional social relations in contemporary settler colonial Canada. Essentialism involves defining a group based on a few characteristics; it is reductive and leads to simplified or essentialized assumptions.

An essentialist understanding of gender and ancestral/traditional Indigenous social relations might associate women primarily with motherhood due to the biological ability to have children. According to scholar Gina Starblanket (Star Blanket Cree Nation), essentialist notions of traditional social relations linked to biological reproduction can have various consequences. Some individuals might find empowerment with motherhood, and it can contribute to the well-being of the community.[63] For others, the complexities of the gender binary in association with social relations are dismissive of lived experiences. For example, some female-identifying individuals may be unable or choose not to have children. When motherhood is understood as an essentialist role, a reductionist understanding of female-identifying people to rhetorical figures based on biology (or reproductive capabilities) limits their agency.[64]

Starblanket also points out that Indigenous women may encounter limitations based on essentialist ideations of gendered norms in, for example, ceremonies (this could include restrictions on participation or expected dress codes) or spaces influenced by the politics of masculinity (such as Indigenous sovereignty movements).[65] In these ways, Starblanket explains that cultural memory can perpetuate biased practices that reinforce essentialist views of Indigenous women.[66] In some ways, contemporary understandings of gender reflect and uphold colonial ideations that continue to marginalize Indigenous women, girls, sexually diverse, and gender-nonconforming individuals. This is often understood as a result of settler colonial–based hetero-patriarchy, and these inauthentic representations can hinder reconciliation movements.

While Indigenous resurgence movements face challenges related to the misrepresentation and inauthentic representation through practices of undoing colonial constructs, effective reclamation and resurgence do occur. Many Knowledge Keepers I have worked with emphasize the strength of ancestral/Traditional Knowledge preserved within language and cultural expression. They argue that colonial assimilation and other impacts of conformity have not changed the core of ancestral/traditional ways of being, which are protected in language, expressed in culture, and enacted on the land.

As post-colonial theorists articulate, decolonization is a complex process revealing the challenges of preserving authentic ancestral/traditional cultural expressions in decolonial environments. Just as Canada's colonization processes were not uniform, Indigenous Peoples engage in and undertake decolonial work in diverse ways that are at differing stages, yielding varied outcomes. The biopolitical settler constructs, perpetuated by stereotypes, legislation, and gendered norms, continue to marginalize Indigenous women and, as such, serve as a litmus test for reconciliation. The specific and unique challenges resulting from settler colonial biopolitics, including those encountered by decolonial attempts through resurgence, impede broader reconciliation efforts in Canada.

Conclusion: Ongoing Gendered and Racialized Violence as Continued Barriers to Reconciliation

Contemporary Canada is currently facing a crisis of gender-based violence, as highlighted by the NIMMIWG (2019) due to the disproportionate rates of murdered and missing Indigenous women, girls, and 2SLGBTQQIA+ communities. The Canadian state has established structures that are influenced by systems of biopolitical oppression—colonialism and heteropatriarchy—that shaped the settlement of this country and continue to exert influence today. Violence and oppression are integral to the workings of settler colonialism,[67] and it is not accidental, but rather intentional, that Indigenous women, girls, and 2SLGBTQQIA+ individuals are targeted with gendered and racialized violence in settler colonial Canada. This violence is often overlooked, disregarded, and rationalized, resulting in a lack of meaningful action and reconciliatory change, with only minimal efforts being made. These forms of oppression lead to a devaluation of the lives of Indigenous women, girls, and gender-nonconforming individuals, as is evidenced by the NIMMIWG findings of disproportionate rates of violence against these demographics.

The NIMMIWG concluded that the structures that support this violence amount to a calculated genocide against Indigenous women, girls, and 2SLGBTQQIA+ communities. They outlined 231 Calls for Justice to address this ongoing genocide. And yet, we see that at a time of truth and reconciliation in Canada, only two calls are completed. The litmus test for reconciliation of settler colonial harms does indeed hinge on the safety and well-being of Indigenous women. Founded in the very fabric of settler Canada is the marginalization and erasure of Indigenous women; without addressing this thread, truth and reconciliation will not gain political traction.

Notes

1 Wilson-Raybould, *From Where I Stand*, 181–84.

2 Racialized and gender-based violence does not only target Indigenous communities; many racialized minority groups experience racism and violence in Canada.

3 Emberley, *Defamiliarizing the Aboriginal*, 47.

4 See NIMMIWG, *Reclaiming Power and Place: The Final Report*.

5 Heidinger, "Violent Victimization and Perceptions of Safety."

6 Burczycka and Cotter, "Court Outcomes in Homicides."

7 Amnesty International, "Missing and Murdered."

8 Wegner and Lawless, "The Missing and Murdered Indigenous Women and Girls National Inquiry."

9 Wegner and Lawless, "The Missing and Murdered Indigenous Women and Girls National Inquiry," 27.

10 Government of Canada, "Federal Pathway."

11 Taylor and Schneider, eds., "A Report Card."

12 St. Denis, "Feminism Is for Everybody," 46.

13 Royal Commission on Aboriginal Peoples, "Women's Perspectives," 7.

14 Anderson, *Life Stages and Native Women*, 98–101; NIMMIWG, *Reclaiming Power and Place: The Final Report*, 40.

15 St. Denis, "Feminism Is for Everybody," 38.

16 Anderson, *Life Stages and Native Women*, 98–99.

17 Royal Commission on Aboriginal Peoples, "Women's Perspectives," 8.

18 As Emily Snyder has carefully evidenced, heteronormativity, patriarchy, and colonization are forms of oppression that all sustain one another. Snyder, *Gender, Power, and Representations of Cree Law*, 16.

19 Green, "Taking More Account of Indigenous Feminisms," 7.

20 Snyder, *Gender, Power, and Representations of Cree Law*, 16.

21 Emberley, *Defamiliarizing the Aboriginal*, 25.

22 Snyder, *Gender, Power, and Representations of Cree Law*, 108.

23 Starblanket, "Being Indigenous Feminists," 29.
24 NIMMIWG, *Reclaiming Power and Place: The Final Report*, 238.
25 Emberley, *Defamiliarizing the Aboriginal*, 14; NIMMIWG, *Reclaiming Power and Place: The Final Report*, 236–38.
26 Historian Sarah Carter, referenced in NIMMIWG, *Reclaiming Power and Place: The Final Report*, 242–43.
27 Emberley, *Defamiliarizing the Aboriginal*; Snyder, *Gender, Power, and Representations of Cree Law*.
28 Emberley, *Defamiliarizing the Aboriginal*, 28; NIMMIWG, *Reclaiming Power and Place: The Final Report*, 243; Carter, *The Importance of Being Monogamous*.
29 NIMMIWG, *Reclaiming Power and Place: The Final Report*, 238.
30 Bourgeois, "A Perpetual State of Violence"; NIMMIWG, *Reclaiming Power and Place: The Final Report*; Snyder, *Gender, Power, and Representations of Cree Law*, 16.
31 Emberley, *Defamiliarizing the Aboriginal*.
32 Razack, "Gendered Racial Violence and Spatialized Justice," 128–30.
33 Kuokkanen, *Restructuring Relations*, 17.
34 NIMMIWG, *Reclaiming Power and Place: The Final Report*, 247.
35 Kuokkanen, *Restructuring Relations*, 17.
36 Kauanui, "Native Hawaiian Decolonization," 285.
37 NIMMIWG, *Reclaiming Power and Place: The Final Report*, 242.
38 Green, "Taking More Account of Indigenous Feminisms," 10; Eberts, "Being an Indigenous Woman," 82.
39 Wilson, "Confronting Canada's Indigenous Female Disposability"; Carter, "Categories and Terrains of Exclusion," 148.
40 Baskin, "Contemporary Indigenous Women's Roles," 2088.
41 Carter, "Categories and Terrains of Exclusion"; Razack, "Gendered Racial Violence and Spatialized Justice"; Snyder, *Gender, Power, and Representations of Cree Law*, 21.
42 Bourgeois, "A Perpetual State of Violence."
43 Green, "Taking More Account of Indigenous Feminisms," 10.
44 Eberts, "Being an Indigenous Woman," 70 and 93.
45 Green, "ReBalancing Strategies," 173.
46 Bourgeois, "A Perpetual State of Violence."
47 Royal Commission on Aboriginal Peoples, "Women's Perspectives," 7–20.
48 NIMMIWG, *Reclaiming Power and Place: The Final Report*.
49 Royal Commission on Aboriginal Peoples, "Women's Perspectives," 34.
50 Emberley, *Defamiliarizing the Aboriginal*, 61.
51 Day, "Equal Status for Indigenous Women—Sometime, Not Now," 175.
52 Ladner, "Gendering Decolonisation," 66.
53 Ladner, "Gendering Decolonisation," 65.
54 Vowel, *Indigenous Writes*, 28–30.
55 Section 15 of the Canadian Charter of Rights and Freedoms states, "15. (1) Every individual is equal before and under the law and has the right to the equal protection and equal benefit of the law without discrimination and, in particular, without discrimination based on race, national or ethnic

origin, colour, religion, sex, age or mental or physical disability. (2) Section (1) does not preclude any law, program or activity that has as its object the amelioration of conditions of disadvantaged individuals or groups including those that are disadvantaged because of race, national or ethnic origin, colour, religion, sex, age or mental or physical disability." Government of Canada, "Section 15."

56 Green, "Taking More Account of Indigenous Feminisms," 4.

57 Day writes, "There is no domestic or international law which permits ongoing gender discrimination against Indian women and their descendants." Day, "Equal Status for Indigenous Women—Sometime, Not Now," 179. Various sources have argued this much: for example, section 15 of the Charter says females cannot be discriminated against because they are female, and Article 44 of the United Nations Declaration on the Rights of Indigenous Peoples confirms Indigenous males and females have the same rights. For more on these violations of rights, consider the following rights-sources that protect against gender, sex, and race discrimination: The International Convention on the Prevention and Punishment of the Crime of Genocide (PPCG); the International Convention on the Elimination of All Forms of Racial Discrimination (ICERD); the International Covenant on Civil and Political Rights (ICCPR); the International Convention on Economic, Social, and Cultural Rights (ICESCR); the Convention on the Elimination of All Forms of Discrimination Against Women (CEDAW); the Convention on the Rights of the Child (UNCRC); and the United Nations Declaration on the Rights of Indigenous Peoples (UNDRIP). NIMMIWG, *Reclaiming Power and Place: The Final Report*, 221.

58 Eberts, "Being an Indigenous Woman," 69.

59 Defriend and Cook, "Reawakening of Indigenous Matriarchal Systems."

60 Simpson, *As We Have Always Done*.

61 Bhabha, *The Location of Culture*; Memmi, *The Colonizer* .

62 See Said, *Orientalism*; Memmi, *The Colonizer*; Fanon, *The Wretched of the Earth*.

63 Starblanket, "Being Indigenous Feminists," 31–32.

64 Snyder, *Gender, Power, and Representations of Cree Law*, 9.

65 See Kuokkanen, *Restructuring Relations*; Ladner, "Gendering Decolonisation."

66 Starblanket, "Being Indigenous Feminists," 25–28.

67 Veracini, "Colonialism, Frontiers, Genocide."

Sources

Amnesty International. "Missing and Murdered Indigenous Women and Girls: The Facts." January 29, 2021. https://www.amnesty.ca/blog/missing-and-murdered-indigenous-women-and-girls-understanding-the-numbers/.

Anderson, Kim. *Life Stages and Native Women: Memory, Teachings, and Story Medicine*. University of Manitoba Press, 2011.

Baskin, Cyndy. "Contemporary Indigenous Women's Roles: Traditional Teachings or Internalized Colonialism?" *Violence Against Women* 26, nos. 15–16 (2020): 2083–101. https://doi.org/10.1177/1077801219888024.

Bhabha, Homi K. *The Location of Culture*. Routledge, 1994.

Bourgeois, Robyn. "A Perpetual State of Violence: An Indigenous Feminist Anti-Oppression Inquiry into Missing and Murdered Indigenous Women and Girls." In *Making Space for Indigenous Feminism*, edited by Joyce Green. Fernwood Publishing, 2017.

Burczycka, Marta, and Adam Cotter. "Court Outcomes in Homicides of Indigenous Women and Girls, 2009 to 2021." Statistics Canada, October 4, 2023. https://www150.statcan.gc.ca/n1/pub/85-002-x/2023001/article/00006-eng.htm.

Carter, Sarah. "Categories and Terrains of Exclusion: Constructing the 'Indian Woman' in the Early Settlement Era in Western Canada." *Great Plains Quarterly* 13, no. 3 (1993): 147–61. http://www.jstor.org/stable/23531720.

Carter, Sarah. *The Importance of Being Monogamous: Marriage and Nation Building in Western Canada to 1915*. Athabasca University Press, 2008.

Day, Shelagh. "Equal Status for Indigenous Women—Sometime, Not Now: The Indian Act and Bill S-3." *Canadian Woman Studies / Les cahiers de la femme* 33, nos. 1–2 (2019). https://cws.journals.yorku.ca/index.php/cws/article/view/37770.

Defriend, Courtney, and Celeta M. Cook. "Reawakening of Indigenous Matriarchal Systems: A Feminist Approach to Organizational Leadership." *Healthcare Management Forum* 37, no. 3 (2023): 160–63. https://doi.org/10.1177/08404704231210255.

Eberts, Mary. "Being an Indigenous Woman Is 'a High Risk Lifestyle.'" In *Making Space for Indigenous Feminism*, edited by Joyce Green. Fernwood Publishing, 2017.

Emberley, Julia V. *Defamiliarizing the Aboriginal: Cultural Practices and Decolonization in Canada*. University of Toronto Press, 2009.

Fanon, Frantz. *The Wretched of the Earth*. Grove Books, 1963.

Government of Canada. "Federal Pathway to Address Missing and Murdered Indigenous Women, Girls and 2SLGBTQQIA+ People." June 3, 2021. https://www.rcaanc-cirnac.gc.ca/eng/1622233286270/1622233321912.

Government of Canada. "Section 15—Equality Rights." https://www.justice.gc.ca/eng/csj-sjc/rfc-dlc/ccrf-ccdl/check/art15.html.

Green, Joyce. "ReBalancing Strategies: Aboriginal Women and Constitutional Rights in Canada." In *Making Space for Indigenous Feminism*, edited by Joyce Green. Fernwood Publishing, 2017.

Green, Joyce. "Taking More Account of Indigenous Feminisms: An Introduction." In *Making Space for Indigenous Feminism*, edited by Joyce Green. Fernwood Publishing, 2017.

Heidinger, Loanna. "Violent Victimization and Perceptions of Safety: Experiences of First Nations, Métis and Inuit Women in Canada." Statistics Canada, April 26, 2022. https://www150.statcan.gc.ca/n1/pub/85-002-x/2022001/article/00004-eng.htm.

Kauanui, J. Kēhaulani. "Native Hawaiian Decolonization and the Politics of Gender." *American Quarterly* 60, no. 2 (2008): 281–87. https://dx.doi.org/10.1353/aq.0.0000.

Kuokkanen, Rauna. *Restructuring Relations: Indigenous Self-Determination, Governance, and Gender*. Oxford University Press, 2019.

Ladner, Kiera L. "Gendering Decolonisation, Decolonising Gender." *Australian Indigenous Law Review* 13, no. 1 (2009): 62–77. http://www.jstor.org/stable/26423117.

Memmi, Albert. *The Colonizer and the Colonized*. Beacon Press, 1965.

National Inquiry into Missing and Murdered Indigenous Women and Girls (NIMMWG). *Reclaiming Power and Place: The Final Report of the National Inquiry into Missing and Murdered Indigenous Women and Girls*. National Inquiry into Missing and Murdered Indigenous Women and Girls, 2019. https://www.mmiwg-ffada.ca/final-report/.

Razack, Sherene H. "Gendered Racial Violence and Spatialized Justice: The Murder of Pamela George." *Canadian Journal of Law and Society* 15, no. 2 (2000): 91–130. https://doi.org/10.1017/S0829320100006384.

Royal Commission on Aboriginal Peoples. "Women's Perspectives." In *Report of the Royal Commission on Aboriginal Peoples*. Vol. 4, *Perspectives and Realities*. Royal Commission on Aboriginal Peoples, 1996.

Said, Edward W. *Orientalism*. Penguin, 1977.

Simpson, Audra. "The Sovereignty of Critique." *South Atlantic Quarterly* 119, no. 4 (2020): 685–99. https://doi.org/10.1215/00382876-8663591.

Simpson, Leanne Betasamosake. *As We Have Always Done: Indigenous Freedom through Radical Resistance*. University of Minnesota Press, 2017.

Snyder, Emily A. *Gender, Power, and Representations of Cree Law*. UBC Press, 2018.

St. Denis, Verna. "Feminism Is for Everybody: Aboriginal Women, Feminism and Diversity." In *Making Space for Indigenous Feminism*, edited by Joyce Green. Fernwood Publishing, 2017.

Starblanket, Gina. "Being Indigenous Feminists: Resurgences Against Contemporary Patriarchy." In *Making Space for Indigenous Feminism*, edited by Joyce Green. Fernwood Publishing, 2017.

Taylor, Jillian, and Bertram Schneider, eds. "A Report Card on the MMIWG Inquiry's Calls for Justice." *CBC News*, June 5, 2023. https://www.cbc.ca/newsinteractives/features/cfj-report-cards/cfj1.

Vowel, Chelsea. *Indigenous Writes: A Guide to First Nations, Métis & Inuit Issues in Canada*. Highwater Press, 2016.

Wegner, Diana L., and Stephanie Lawless. "The Missing and Murdered Indigenous Women and Girls National Inquiry: Meta-Genre, Genre Hybridity, and Social Change." *Discourse and Writing / Rédactologie* 31 (2021): 1–37. https://doi.org/10.31468/dw/r.835.

Wilson, Kara Jo. "Confronting Canada's Indigenous Female Disposability." *Canadian Journal of Native Studies* 38, no. 1 (2018): 153–63.

Wilson-Raybould, Jody. *From Where I Stand: Rebuilding Indigenous Nations for a Stronger Canada*. Purich Books, 2019.

Afterword

Gina Starblanket

Like many settler states, the story of Canada's treatment of Indigenous Peoples is not a tale to be proud of but warrants reflection if for no other reason than to ensure comprehensive, informed, and critical accounts of Indigenous-settler relations today. For now what is centuries, Indigenous Peoples have faced an ongoing yet evolving problematic: how to manage the presence of newcomers while resisting imperial and settler colonial forces designed to eliminate our ways of life, dispossess us of lands and territories, and restrict our ability to relate to one another on our own terms.

Popular representations of Indigenous interactions and entanglements with settler Canada portray consensual and non-violent processes of settlement and development, advancing understandings of nation building that have scrubbed the subjugation of Indigenous Peoples from the record. These depictions overlook many aspects of the colonial encounter, including the comprehensive state regulation of Indigenous lives, violent forms of racialization and gendering, impoverishment, criminalization, and other processes of marginalization that configure Indigenous Peoples' experiences with settler institutions. Such representations have long been resisted and complicated by Indigenous Peoples, who have repeatedly steered conversations back to key issues of land and decolonization while also emphasizing the need for greater public awareness around the violences of colonialism, including the implications of the residential school system, land and resource theft, and the persistent matter of Indigenous legal and political subordination.

The real and material impacts of the stories we share, and how they are conveyed, are profound. In the context of settler colonial Canada, imagined political formations have narrated themselves into being through constructed notions of sovereignty, jurisdiction, and community or national interest. Settler governments and societies have manifested and sustained themselves through the negation and containment of Indigenous voices, including our knowledge of treaties, ongoing appeals for Crown honour and integrity, and expressions of our agency and self-determination relative to the natural world.

Indigenous Peoples engage with matters relating to decolonization and land in varied ways across geographies and contexts, but all point to the need to reconfigure the Indigenous-settler relationship, be it through treaty implementation, resurgence movements, or other efforts geared towards transformation. In response, settler governments too often divert questions about their relations with Indigenous Peoples to the courts or to narrow policy sectors. They interpret and engage with Indigenous positions in ways disconnected from our knowledges and epistemologies, suggesting solutions that are often partial and seldom on terms that Indigenous Peoples have authored or agreed to. In the process, Indigenous understandings of and responses to colonialism become obscured, along with the on-the-ground priorities and needs of our communities today. Misapprehension and misrepresentation of our intellectual, grassroots, and activist movements serve to minimize, delegitimize, and suppress them, justifying the surveillance and criminalization of efforts geared towards transformation or liberation, historically and in the present.

Anyone living in lands presently claimed by Canada has a responsibility to acquaint themselves with transparent and critical accounts of Indigenous encounters with settler colonialism. This is a history marked by Indigenous efforts to bring forward relations of coexistence, mutuality, and respect, sometimes within the frameworks advanced by settler governments and, at other times, through means that exceed Western conceptions of rights, citizenship, culture, identity, and liberal theories of recognition and accommodation of difference. The politics of telling this story are complex; the history of Indigenous-settler relations should not be overdetermined by the violence we have suffered nor our resistance and struggles against it. Throughout Canada's legacy of colonial occupation and settlement, Indigenous Peoples have maintained and adapted our world views and ways of being, formed new kin and community, modelled expansive forms of care and reciprocity with other human beings and with the living earth, maintained relational economies and modes of law and governance, and enacted forms of joy and fulfillment despite the conditions that have been imposed on us. Indigenous political life should be contemplated through the diversity of ways that Indigenous Peoples across generations are imagining and embodying forms of self-determination, love, creativity, and resurgence within our homes, our families, our communities, and our commitments to future generations. Yet we also require honest accounts of our losses, for they have not been minimal, nor are they immaterial for many Indigenous Peoples today. While we must be cautious not to gratuitously reproduce notions of deficit within our accounts, we also require space for open and transparent dialogue around the intergenerational impacts of settler colonialism to appreciate the ways in which our practices of relationality and governance as Indigenous Peoples have changed from their pre-contact form.

Western legal, political, and economic orders have deeply limited Indigenous Peoples' ability to live freely in relation to the land and Creation and, in turn, to attend to the obligations and responsibilities that flow from these relationships. They have had long-term impacts on Indigenous Peoples' relationships with ourselves, our families, our communities, and all living beings that we share our lives with. They have had enduring effects on how we receive, interpret, and respond to difference within our communities, including identity-related differences and differences in political ideas, conceptions, and opinions. As colonial, capitalist, and hetero-patriarchal logics have been internalized across cultures, Indigenous Peoples' own understandings of how to live well in relation have been harmed. Contemporary conversations around decolonial transformation or liberation, then, necessitate space for contestation and debate to ensure that all subjects of our interrelations can exercise agency within them. Indigenous feminist, decolonial, antiracist, intersectional, and queer theories and analytics have a great deal to contribute here, as they offer important tools to help enable critical dialogue and inquiry within and across sites of community.

Contributors in this volume model the application of a variety of important critical theories and approaches, offering thorough, nuanced, and careful insights in their accounts of the colonial condition. Many explain how they are working towards transformation by embodying the forms of relational accountability they want to bring forward, implicating themselves in structures of power and privilege, and critically reflecting on their own positionality and responsibilities. These include honest examples of lessons learned and reflections on decolonial initiatives of varying scales and levels of success. They speak of work being undertaken within relationships of many forms: friendships, family, kin, and diverse sites of community. Together, they point to convergences across our political movements and map out a beautiful constellation of liberatory goals held by Indigenous Peoples and our allies.

As a collection, this volume enables a broad, expansive view of Indigenous-settler relations from diverse lived and intellectual traditions, drawing attention to the on-the-ground ways that Indigenous communities, allies, and activists are working around and against settler colonial structures in Canada. Importantly, authors circumvent the academic tendency to adopt expert mentalities or to absent themselves from the conversation under the guise of objectivity or neutrality. They also take up inquiries that are grounded in time and place, rather than abstracting and universalizing the problematics underlying Indigenous-settler relations. This allows for historically informed and contextual inquiries that are shaped by the diversity of ways that Indigenous communities are working towards decolonization and resurgence from interpersonal to structural scales, from everyday to long-term horizons of transformation.

The conflicts that reside at the heart of Indigenous-settler relations require close and critical inquiry; attending to them can involve reading between the lines available in the settler archives. Important details can be revealed not by looking at visible imprints directly but by examining the traces that much of Canada would prefer to remain out of sight. Markings that have been scrubbed from formal accounts can be difficult to see and decipher in tidy, clinical terms. Sometimes, only the application of a dirty, messy layer to the page can make these traces visible. Perhaps we all could benefit from getting a bit messy sometimes, in order to gain an in-depth, granular understanding of the conditions we are working to transform.

As scholars, our approaches and analyses can function to conceal and sustain violence, but they can also serve to identify and challenge it. They can be used to deconstruct and problematize different angles in how we encounter and live with one another, so that together we have a fuller or more comprehensive view of the relations we inhabit. We know that settler colonialism is racialized, hetero-patriarchal, and configured by many actors and forces both domestic and international, and so we need strategies attuned to the inner workings of systems of power and their interactions at multiple scales. We need contextual approaches and analyses with adequate understandings of localized knowledge and experience to help illuminate the nuances and distinctions that our disciplinary frames can eclipse.

One of the central contributions of this volume is its attention to the rich multiplicity of ways that Indigenous Peoples and communities are undertaking acts of relationality across sites and scales. It offers accounts of scholarly and activist work undertaken with evident thoughtfulness and care, as authors generously share important reflections from their own locations and lived experiences. Authors in this volume point to the significant relationship between the personal and political; several engage matters that are often considered to reside in an interpersonal or individual domain, demonstrating how these relate to the broader political terrain and collapsing binary approaches to Indigenous social and political life. This provides important insight into the ways that Indigenous Peoples and allies are enacting our political visions and intentions outside of Western processes and structures. Such interventions will resonate for anyone interested in learning more about and/or supporting the transformation of Indigenous-settler relations.

We should all be invested in the possibilities of relational worlds, of renewing our respective resources for relationship and bringing forward non-violent and generative ways of talking to each other, trusting one another, laughing, and living together across our differences. Settler colonialism is a long-term, complex, and enduring problem that requires a variety of ideas, tools, and contributions to transform. While scholars have theorized the nature of encounters between dominant and subordinate groups in many imperial and colonial contexts, this volume offers an important account of the multiplicity of ways in which the colonial condition in Canada is being actively disrupted and circumvented in real-world contexts. Volumes such as this make a crucial contribution to the scholarship on decolonization and resurgence, both in modelling relational ways of being and doing and in calling others into our respective and shared movements towards more just and free relations.

Index

B

J

K

L

T